Theatre of Operations, 1588

- –·–→ Spanish military corridor
- ·····→ Track of the Armada, 28 May – 9 August 1588.
- ——→ 'North-about' sailing instructions.
- – – –→ Track of the SAN JUAN, vice-flagship of Castile, c. 20 August – 14 October 1588. From the Journal of Marcos de Aramburu.
- • Location of Armada ship loss
- ▨ Possessions of Philip II of Spain

```
0        100       200       300 miles
0   100   200   300   400   500 km
```

5°E

20°E

NORWAY

The Naze

SWEDEN

DENMARK

The Sound

Baltic Sea

Danzig

North

Sea

English Fleet breaks off

POLAND

Rostock
Lübeck
Hamburg

DUTCH REPUBLIC

Calais
Antwerp
SPANISH
NETHERLANDS
ppe
St Quentin
uen
Paris
Joinville
Nemours

THE

EMPIRE

Metz

Augsburg

AUSTRIAN

HABSBURGS

45°N

NCE

SWISS
CONFEDERATION
Geneva

Milan
Pavia
SAVOY
GENOA
Genoa

VENICE
Venice
Parma

OTTOMAN

EMPIRE

TUSCANY
Florence
PAPAL
STATES
Rome
Naples

NAPLES

Adriatic Sea

Ragusa

Lepanto

SARDINIA

Palermo

SICILY

Mediter

Tunis

MALTA

Algiers

35°N

n   Sea

a

15°E

20°E

THE
SPANISH ARMADA

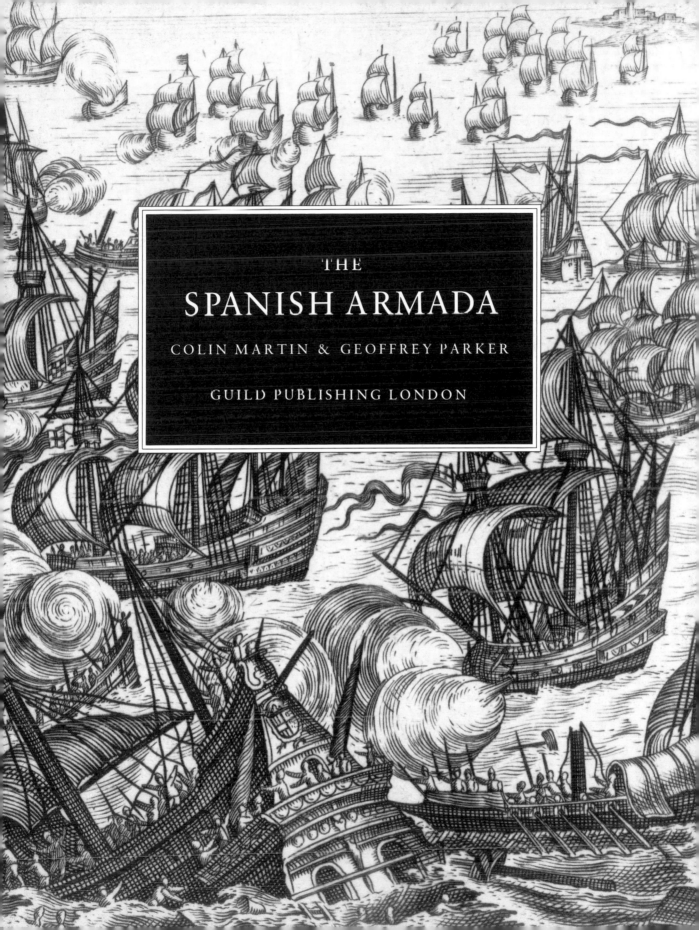

THE
SPANISH ARMADA

COLIN MARTIN & GEOFFREY PARKER

GUILD PUBLISHING LONDON

This edition published 1988 by
Guild Publishing
By arrangement with Hamish Hamilton Ltd
Copyright © 1988 by Colin Martin and Geoffrey Parker

Designed by Cinamon and Kitzinger
Maps drawn by Reginald and Marjorie Piggott
Typeset by Goodfellow & Egan Phototypesetting Ltd, Cambridge
Printed in Great Britain by
Butler & Tanner Ltd, Frome and London

For Paula and Jane

Contents

Acknowledgements

This book saw its genesis, gestation and birth in the thirteen years from 1973 to 1986, during which we were colleagues at the University of St Andrews. We are deeply grateful to that institution for encouraging our research, and for the generosity of its Research and Travel Fund in sponsoring so many of our rewarding quests. Other grants have helped us to conduct further research in archives and libraries, and to excavate wrecks lying off the coasts of Scotland and Ireland. We are indebted to the British Academy, the Carnegie Trust, the Leverhulme Trust, the Mac-Robert Trusts, and the Russell Trust, all of which have given generous support over the years.

The archaeological work which has yielded so much new information about the Armada would not have been possible without the far-sighted encouragement of the Ulster Museum, Belfast, and the Shetland County Museum, Lerwick. This has resulted in financial support, conservation services, and – most important of all – the safe housing of the recovered material as intact collections which have been, and remain, rich sources for study. We warmly thank these institutions, and the staff members with whom we have had the pleasure of working, for the trust they have placed in us.

Our primary debt is to the phalanx of friends and colleagues who have so unstintingly supported us along the way. We can only name the leading few, but we also remember and acknowledge our debt to the remaining many. Mr Sydney Wignall must top the list for demonstrating, in 1968, that the discovery of Armada wrecks could lead to exciting new historical conclusions: he also put the first-named writer through the stern apprenticeship of diving in Blasket Sound, where the wreck of the Guipúzcoan vice flagship *Santa María de la Rosa* was discovered. We salute him, and all the other divers with whom we have been associated – most especially the members of the City of Derry Sub-Aqua Club, whose unselfish forethought has safeguarded the remains of *La Trinidad Valencera* for posterity. We have also received valuable assistance from the Streedagh Armada Group and the Moville Sub-Aqua Group. Here, too, we must acknowledge the contributions made by the professional diving archaeologists who have helped with the work on the wrecks: Dr Nick Dixon; Mr Andrew Fielding; Mr Jeremy Green; Mr Tony Long; the late Mr Keith Muckelroy; and Ms Celie O'Rahilly.

Help in a variety of forms has freely been given by the following scholars, and we gratefully record our debt to them: Dr Simon Adams, University of Strathclyde; Professor José Alcalá Zamora, University of Madrid; Dr Richard Boulind; Professor J.R. Bruijn, University of Leiden; Dr Trevor Dadson, Queen's University Belfast; Mr Alan Ereira, BBC; Mr Laurence Flanagan, Keeper of Antiquities, Ulster Museum; Mr Tom Glasgow Jnr; the late Mr Tom Henderson, Shetland Museum; Dr John de Courcy Ireland, Maritime Institute of Ireland; the late Mr Paul Johnstone, BBC; Dr Piet van der Merwe, National Maritime Museum; Dr Marco Morin; Ms Jane Ohlmeyer; Professor Peter Pierson, University of Santa Clara; Mr Ray Sutcliffe, BBC; Dr I.A.A. Thompson, University of Keele; Dr Brian Scott, Queen's University Belfast; Dr Robert Sténuit; and Mr Andrew Williamson, Curator, Shetland Museum. We are also grateful to the following for research assistance: Nico Broens; Lucy Byatt; Louis Haas; Jill Hawthorne; James Reid; and Bill van de Veen.

Officials and staff of the many libraries and archives in which we have had the privilege of working have been – as always – unfailingly helpful and friendly. The institutions concerned are listed in the sources, and no discourtesy is intended by omitting to name them individually here. We must also thank Ms Penelope Hoare of Hamish Hamilton for her sympathetic editing of a work which grew in scale and scope far beyond the limits originally set for it.

Our final debt is to Mrs Paula Martin, who has been associated with the project almost from its inception. As a diving archaeologist she has worked on two of the wreck sites; as a scholar she has generously laid at our disposal the fruits of her own researches and made many helpful comments on the text; as a secretary she has provided us with a meticulous typescript; and as this book's picture researcher she has imparted her own stamp of originality.

Note

Dates throughout have been adjusted to conform with the New (Gregorian) Calendar which the Spaniards, but not the English, were using in 1588. Contemporary English dates, which were still based on the Old (Julian) Calendar, would otherwise appear to fall ten days earlier than their Spanish equivalents.

Four Spanish ducats were roughly equal to an English pound. The latter, prefixed '£', has been used as a common standard, and conversions to it from currencies other than Spanish have been made where appropriate. The results are necessarily approximate. With regard to weight units, equivalency has been assumed between the Castilian *libra* of 460 grams and the English pound of 454 grams. The Spanish *quintal*, like the English hundredweight, represents units of 100 pounds (the modern 112 pound hundredweight includes an allowance for the container).

In some important respects Spanish names for gun-types do not equate with their apparent English translations, and so the Spanish names have been retained in the text, expressed in italics. A discussion of these differences is contained in Chapter 11.

Spellings from contemporary English sources have been modernised. With proper names, too, the modern spellings have been preferred.

ÆTATIS SVÆ LVIII
Anno Dni 1591

Introduction

It was 10 August 1588 in the North Sea, and the summer weather was unseasonably bad. Before a brisk south-westerly gale, with storm-canvas set, ran the 600-ton English royal galleon *Victory*, scarred by recent action. Her gaudily-painted upperworks were stained with gunsmoke; the royal standard at the mainmast and the flags of St George which flapped at the fore and mizzen tops were in tatters. Some of the rigging showed signs of makeshift repair, the bowsprit and main mizzen were shot-splintered, and the ship's longboat was missing. And, although still seaworthy, the 34-gun *Victory* was in no condition to engage an enemy. Her shot lockers, upon which her whole capacity to fight depended, were completely empty.

Less than a week earlier the ship had been in the thick of the longest and fiercest artillery action which had ever taken place at sea. Somewhere to leeward the huge Armada from Spain against which she had fought, severely battered but with its formidable order and discipline still largely intact, was loose in the northern seas. Its ammunition stocks, though depleted, were not exhausted, while its massed companies of shipboard infantry would still be irresistible in any boarding action. Worst of all, the English did not know where this fleet was, nor what it might yet do.

In *Victory's* great cabin her captain, Sir John Hawkins, scrawled a postscript to the urgent report he had just completed, apologising for his poor handwriting: it was done, he explained, 'in haste and bad weather'. His dispatch, addressed to Sir Francis Walsingham, Secretary of State to Queen Elizabeth, shows Hawkins to have been an extremely worried man. The Spanish fleet, he warned, was still

'here, and very forcible, and must be waited upon with all our force, which is little enough. There should be an infinite quantity of powder and shot provided, and continually sent abroad; without the which great hazard may grow to our country; for this is the greatest and strongest combination, to my understanding,

13

that ever was gathered in Christendom; therefore I wish it, of all hands, to be mightily and diligently looked unto and cared for.'

A full week later the English Lord Admiral, Charles Lord Howard of Effingham, 'in haste and much occupied' aboard his flagship *Ark Royal*, was still anxious and uncertain about the Armada's movements and intentions, and in no doubt about its formidable strength. 'Some made little account of the Spanish force by sea', he confided to Walsingham on 18 August; 'but I do warrant you, all the world never saw such a force as theirs was.' Even by the month's end, the redoubtable Sir Francis Drake was by no means confident that the threat had passed. Although the Armada might have been driven back to Spain, a powerful army of invasion troops headed by one of the most determined and capable military commanders of the age still lay on the Flemish coast, poised to embark for England. From his flagship *Revenge* Drake warned on 20 August that the queen's ministers should not doubt that the general of the Army of Flanders, Alexander Farnese, duke of Parma, 'being so great a soldier as he is, . . . will presently, if he may, undertake some great matter . . . my poor opinion is that we should have a great eye unto him.'

English commemorative medal issued after the dispersal of the Armada: 'Flavit et dissipati sunt' ('God breathed and they were scattered').

England's best-informed opinion in 1588 was thus not disposed to underestimate the enormity of the threat which Philip II's great Armada had posed. But, as quickly as it had come, that threat evaporated. The Armada had no further tricks up its sleeve: it struggled on past the Northern Isles and into the Atlantic in an effort to gain sea room for a safe run southwards to the ports of Galicia and Biscay. But fortune did not favour the Spaniards. The autumnal gales of that portentous year – the winds of God, as their Protestant enemies would have it – blew early and with unusual violence, driving the returning ships towards the Atlantic coasts of Scotland and Ireland. Many were wrecked. For the Spaniards it was an unmitigated disaster, but one brought about as much by the forces of nature as by the hand of man. In English and Dutch eyes, however, it was both an overwhelming naval victory and a clear demonstration of where divine sympathies lay. The anxious realities expressed by the English commanders in the campaign's immediate aftermath were thus soon swamped, in the euphoria of deliverance, by a tide of patriotic fervour which saw the events as an affirmation of England's inevitable superiority over her Catholic foes.

That fervour, and the misconceptions which it generated, have tended to dominate perceptions of the campaign ever since.

The Armada in popular legend: a 19th century view of Drake continuing his game of bowls on Plymouth Hoe as the Spanish fleet is sighted.

During the four centuries which have passed since the event, accounts of the Armada have proliferated. The story has a perennial appeal as the heroic climax of a long maritime, military, economic and ideological struggle between England and Spain, and in many respects it is exceptionally well documented. It is a good yarn, and it has provided generations of historians with an abundance of fine material with which to spin it.

On the Spanish side, the three years of planning and preparation which culminated in the sailing of the Armada generated – literally – several tons of meticulous documentation. The Dutch and English records are less comprehensive, since the defensive effort of 1588 was an *ad hoc* response to a sudden crisis, and much less was committed to paper. But even so, the sources still available are considerable.

Serious study of this material began in the late nineteenth century, with the calendaring and editing of a selection of the documents contained in both Spanish and English archives. These great works of transcription and condensation, together with their excellent commentaries, have formed the basis of most subsequent accounts of the Armada campaign. But although their value remains undiminished they are, as their editors were at pains to point out, no more than personal selections of those documents which were considered to be, in the light of late nineteenth century historical perceptions, the most relevant.

For almost a century, in consequence, Armada studies have tended to stagnate in the rich but unreplenished pond provided by their late Victorian progenitors. The calendared documents have come to be regarded by most historians as the primary source, while the archives from which they sprang have been almost totally forgotten. In the case of the less comprehensive English and Dutch sources this confidence has largely (though not entirely) been justified. It has manifestly not been so with the Spanish ones.

Four distinct classes of first-hand evidence have survived. First comes the mass of reports, memoranda and letters concerning the formation of Spanish foreign policy and the minutiae of putting that policy into effect. Most of these are preserved among the state papers housed in the imposing castle of Simancas, outside Valladolid, where Philip II created Europe's first public record office, and are relatively well-known though greatly under-exploited. Some of the most intimate and important documents in this category, however, are to be found among the so-called 'Altamira papers' – the private archive of Philip II, now scattered among half-a-dozen European collections. They reveal his direct concern for every detail of the Armada campaign, his deteriorating health as he pored over his papers, and his profound spiritual crisis when he first discovered the magnitude of the failure.

Few of these papers have previously been consulted for the crucial information they contain on the Armada story.

A second category of Spanish material relates to the formation and the execution of policy from the standpoint of the officers most directly concerned. This is contained in the archives of the two commanders designated to lead the amphibious attack on England in 1588. Unfortunately the papers of the duke of Parma, the army commander, have been seriously damaged – those at Naples by Italian partisans in 1943; those at Parma by termites and rodents; those at Brussels by theft – but there is still enough to piece together, for the first time, the crucial importance of the Army of Flanders in the Armada plan.

Simancas Castle, outside Valladolid, where Philip II's administrative archives are housed.

The archive of the ducal house of Medina Sidonia, by contrast, still exists in excellent condition at San Lúcar de Barrameda, though for many years the key papers relating to the seventh duke's role in leading Philip II's fleet against England have been missing. A few were acquired by the National Maritime Museum in England, and in 1986 some more re-emerged in a private library in Madrid. They shed new light on a number of important issues concerning the conduct of the Spanish campaign.

To these unconscious 'memoirs' of the principal commanders can be added the personal accounts of lesser men: commentaries and narratives contained in diaries, reports, or interrogations. By combining their disparate impressions of events it is often possible to perceive the whole with greater clarity, particularly during the confusion of battle, where each man's viewpoint and experiences are different, and later recollection is clouded by the noise, activity, emotion and pressing urgency of the moment.

And then, thirdly, there is the mountain of administrative papers which survive concerning the ships themselves, and the men and munitions on board. These extensive and painstakingly detailed records – the daily output of numerous quartermasters, accountants, paymasters and filing clerks – have lain in Simancas and Seville, accumulating dust, for almost four centuries. They have apparently never before been consulted by historians of the Armada. Through them we can reconstruct, often in extraordinary detail, exactly how individual ships were armed, equipped, and manned; how they performed in combat; and what finally became of them. Every time a gun was loaded and fired, the fact was noted in the records; and if a ship was wrecked, the accountants had to determine the full circumstances of its loss – not for posterity, but simply to justify a final closing of the account.

All of these documentary sources, together with many others throughout Europe, have been examined and analysed to provide a narrative framework for our account. But this mass of documentary evidence, new and old, is complemented by a fourth and previously quite unconsidered source which has allowed us, in effect, actually to go on board the ships themselves and examine their contents as they were in 1588.

In the terrible aftermath of the Armada more than thirty Spanish ships were lost off the western coasts of Scotland and Ireland. Underwater archaeological evidence from the Armada wrecks has, in many important respects, revolutionised our understanding of the events of 1588, particularly when viewed in concert with the full documentary material. The sites of eight wrecks are now precisely known, providing between them examples of most of the many types and varieties of ship which sailed with the Armada. In 1968–9 the remains of *La Santa María de la Rosa*, the Basque-built vice-flagship of Miguel de Oquendo's Guipúzcoan squadron, were found and excavated at the eye of a tide-race in Blasket Sound, County Kerry. Between 1970 and 1983 the wrecks of the Rostock hulk *El Gran Grifón* off Fair Isle, and the Venetian troop-carrier *La Trinidad Valencera* in Kinnagoe Bay, County Donegal, were investigated in an extended series of excavation campaigns. Off the coast of County Antrim, during 1967–8, the remains of the Neapolitan galleass *Girona* were carefully excavated by Dr Robert Sténuit, and it is to be hoped that the same approach will be adopted towards three further wrecks located in 1985 off the Sligo coast – the *Santa María de Visón*, the *Juliana* and the *Lavia*, all from the Levant squadron. Another member of that ill-fated squadron, the Ragusan *San Juan de Sicilia*, was wrecked in Tobermory Bay in the Isle of Mull, though her remains – together with most of the information they once contained – have unfortunately been destroyed by more than three centuries of determined hunting for her elusive (because illusory) treasure.

All this new material does not, of course, alter the broad outline of the Armada story. Philip II attempted to invade England and failed disas-

A diving archaeologist at work on the wreck of *El Gran Grifón* off Fair Isle. Exactly the same painstaking techniques are used in archaeology under water as on land.

trously because the defensive effort of England and her Dutch allies prevailed. But there is much more to history than broad outlines. With the new evidence at our disposal we can now chronicle every stage in these processes with greater accuracy than ever before, and, perhaps more importantly, explain *why* events turned out as they did. Instead of the pseudo-patriotic jingoism and speculative theorising which has dominated so many studies to date, our account rests firmly upon a wide range of objective information from documents and from the physical remains of the ships. And all this evidence tends to confirm the views of Hawkins, Howard and Drake quoted above: that Philip II's 'Grand Design' against England in 1588 came within an ace of success.

At the time no one could have predicted the outcome, and Spain should no more be denigrated for losing than England's deliverance should be regarded as a manifestation of her inevitable superiority. Each nation possessed formidable strengths and fatal weaknesses, and we do not ourselves feel, four hundred years after the event, any predilection for one side or the other. The story stands on its own terms, and the only bygones to be forgotten are the myths.

1988 is surely an appropriate year in which to lay them to rest.

COLIN MARTIN / GEOFFREY PARKER

St Andrews and Urbana, New Year's Day, 1988

Chronology

1580
25 August
Philip II's forces capture Lisbon

1581
January
Duke of Parma begins reconquest of South Netherlands

1582
June
Battle of São Miguel

1583
July
Conquest of Terceira: Santa Cruz suggests follow-up attack on England

1584
23 June
Santa Cruz appointed Captain General of the Ocean Sea
31 December
Spain signs treaty of Joinville with duke of Guise and French Catholic League

1585
19 May
Philip II embargoes all English goods in Spain
August
Anglo-Dutch treaty of Nonsuch; fall of Antwerp to Spain
7 October
Francis Drake occupies ports in Galicia (to 17th), and goes on to sack Canaries and Caribbean islands
24 October
Philip declares readiness to invade England
December
Philip II invites Parma to prepare invasion plan (reply sent April 1586); earl of Leicester arrives to govern northern Netherlands

1586
January
Santa Cruz invited by Philip II to prepare invasion plan (reply sent March)
8 June
Recalde appointed to command new Squadron of Biscay

20 June
Parma's plan arrives at court
26 July
G. B. Piatti takes Masterplan to Parma
17 November
Philip II orders Naples and Sicily to send ships, munitions and troops to Spain

1587
February
Execution of Mary Queen of Scots; English garrison betrays Deventer to Parma
March
Hulks embargoed in Andalusian ports
12 April
Drake leaves Plymouth to singe the king of Spain's beard
29 April
Cádiz raid (to 1 May)
2 May
Recalde and Biscayan ships arrive in Lisbon
26 May
Philip II too ill to work (until early July)
18 June
Drake captures *São Felipe* off Azores and returns to England
12 July
Santa Cruz leads Armada to meet treasure fleets
29 July
Papal-Spanish accord on future government of Catholic England; one million ducats paid by Pope
4 August
Ships gathered in Andalusia arrive at Lisbon under command of Don Alonso de Leiva
4 August
Parma captures Sluys
14 September
Instructions issued for invasion of England
25 September
Santa Cruz brings Indies treasure fleet safely to Seville
29 September
Santa Cruz arrives at Lisbon; Armada begins to refit
16 November
Storm damage to ships in Lisbon

1588

January
Division of ships in Lisbon into 7 squadrons: Andalusia, Biscay, Guipúzcoa, galleasses, Levant, hulks and Portugal
9 February
Santa Cruz dies
26 February
Medina Sidonia reluctantly accepts appointment to command Armada
8 March
Anglo-Spanish peace talks begin in Netherlands
end March
Squadron of Castile arrives in Lisbon
1 April
Instructions for Medina Sidonia and Parma
29 April
Duke of Guise agrees to engineer Catholic rebellion in France
9 May
Lisbon muster
12 May
'Day of the barricades': Guise takes Paris
23 May
Anglo-Spanish peace talks moved to Bourbourg
28/30 May
Armada sails from Lisbon
3 June
English fleet concentrates at Plymouth
19 June
Armada puts into Corunna after 5 days' wait for victuals; storm scatters fleet
27 June
Council at Corunna advises Philip II to abandon Enterprise
4 July
English navy sails for Spain (returns after 2 weeks)
5 July
Parma inspects his fleet at Dunkirk; Dutch blockade squadron takes up station
19 July
Council at Corunna decides to try again
21 July
Armada sets sail against England
25 July
Medina Sidonia sends first warning to Parma of his approach
29 July
English sight the Armada and fleet puts to sea
30 July
Armada sights Lizard; Council of war aboard *San Martín*
31 July
First blood: loss of *Rosario* and *San Salvador*
1 August
Armada reforms into 'roundel'

2 August
Second fight: off Portland Bill. First letters from Armada reach Flanders
3 August
English council of war; division into squadrons
4 August
Third fight: off Isle of Wight. Duke of Guise named 'lieutenant general of the kingdom' in France
6 August
Armada reaches Calais; talks at Bourbourg broken off
7/8 August
Fireships attack
8 August
Fourth fight: off Gravelines
10 August
Army of Flanders completes embarkation; Seymour's squadron returns to Channel
13 August
Armada off Firth of Forth
18 August
Elizabeth's 'Tilbury speech'
20 August
Armada passes into Atlantic
21 August
Medina Sidonia sends Don Balthasar de Zúñiga to Court
31 August
Parma stands down fleet
12 September
Parma besieges Bergen-op-Zoom (to 30 October)
14/16 September
Wrecking of *Trinidad Valencera*
21 September
Gran Grin, *Santa María de la Rosa* and *Rata Encoronada* wrecked; Medina Sidonia arrives at Santander
24 September
Zúñiga arrives at court
25 September
Lavia, *Juliana* and *Santa María de Visón* wrecked on Streedagh Strand
28 September
Gran Grifón wrecked off Fair Isle
28 October
Girona wrecked off county Antrim
5 November
'Tobermory galleon' destroyed
10 November
Philip II prays for death
12 November
Spanish council in Madrid votes to continue war with England
24 November
Thanksgiving service at St Paul's in London

PART I
The Fleets Approach

CHAPTER I
'The greatest and strongest combination'

The duke of Medina Sidonia.

Shortly after dawn the watchers on the cliff saw the first Spanish ships: fleeting shapes glimpsed far offshore through banks of mist and squally showers. The tar-soaked brushwood of the beacon burst urgently into flame, and within minutes a replying pin-prick of light to the east confirmed that the alarm was passing along the chain to Plymouth and the waiting English fleet: from there the signal would be relayed to all parts of the kingdom.

It was Saturday, 30 July 1588, and Philip II's long-expected Armada had arrived off the English coast.

The day before, within distant sight of the Lizard, the Spanish flagship *San Martín de Portugal* had taken in sail and hoisted a flag near the great poop lantern to signal a council of war. As the fleet hove-to, senior officers in their pinnaces began to converge on the flagship. On the *San Martín's* high after-deck a short heavily-built bearded man of 38, simply dressed, stood awaiting them. Around his neck hung the insignia of the Golden Fleece, Spain's most exclusive order of chivalry, of which Philip II himself was Grand Master. Don Alonso Pérez de Guzmán el Bueno, twelfth señor and fifth marquis of San Lúcar de Barrameda, ninth count of Niebla and seventh duke of Medina Sidonia, was the king's Captain-General of the Ocean Sea, and the 125 ships and 30,000 men of the Armada were under his direct command. Yet Medina Sidonia was a landsman, without previous experience of war afloat.

Now, with due ceremony, his officers were coming aboard. Beneath their protective boat-cloaks flashed glimpses of sartorial splendour: garments of satin or silk laid with velvet and embroidery, gold buttons and lace, silk tassels, and the varied insignia of their knightly orders. Juan Martínez de Recalde had some difficulty in negotiating the *San Martín's* towering side, for he was 62 years old, and suffered from severe sciatica.

But Recalde was the most experienced naval officer in the Armada, with a lifetime of sea service behind him. Loyal, steadfast, resourceful, and immensely brave, he commanded the vice-flagship *San Juan de Portugal*, had administrative charge of the Biscayan squadron, and was second-in-command of the whole fleet. He would not, however, take it over in the event of Medina Sidonia's death. On the secret orders of the king, which Recalde carried in a locked chest, that honour would fall to another member of the council: the younger and more nobly-born Don Alonso Martínez de Leiva (like Recalde, a knight of the Order of Santiago), commander of the Genoese carrack *La Rata Santa María Encoronada*, in which the cream of Spain's young nobility sailed. A member of his crew later described Don Alonso as 'tall and slender, of a whitely complexion, of a flaxen and smooth hair, of behaviour mild and temperate, of speech good and deliberate, greatly reverenced not only by his own men but generally of all the company'. With his neatly-trimmed beard and the simple cross of Santiago about his neck, he was the very epitome of a Spanish warrior-aristocrat.

Juan Martínez de Recalde.

Miguel de Oquendo, in charge of the Guipúzcoan squadron, was less nobly-born but no less spirited; he was said later to have handled his flagship 'like a lancer' – an extravagant simile, perhaps, for his lumbering 1,200-ton Basque merchantman *Santa Ana*, though not for Oquendo's personal panache. Of sterling calibre too was Martín de Bertendona from Bilbao, commander of the Levant squadron, whose family had served in the Spanish navy for generations. Medina Sidonia could also rely on the experienced commanders of his two non-combatant units – Juan Gómez de Medina of the supply hulks, and Agustín de Ojeda of the communications squadron (successor to Don Antonio Hurtado de Mendoza, who had died three days earlier): both were solid, dependable men chosen for their reliability and administrative competence.

As the members of council came aboard the flagship they paid formal respects to the duke and his two principal staff-officers: Diego Flores de Valdés, chief adviser on naval matters, and Don Francisco de Bobadilla, the general in charge of the fleet's strong military contingent. These two men were aboard the *San Martín* on the direct instructions of the king – perhaps, as some had speculated, to make sure that his reluctant Captain-General of the Ocean Sea obeyed orders to the letter.

Personal relationships within this select group of senior officers were not, however, altogether harmonious. There was much envy of Bobadilla

Portrait by El Greco of a Spanish nobleman, thought possibly to be Don Alonso de Leiva.

Title page of Cardinal William Allen's admonition to the people of England and Ireland, exhorting them to rise in support of the Spanish invasion.

and Diego Flores, on the grounds that they had permanent access to Medina Sidonia's ear and used their advantageous position to discredit the other commanders. And Diego Flores, despite his extensive naval experience, was of a touchy and quarrelsome disposition: in particular, he nurtured an implacable hatred for his arrogant cousin Don Pedro de Valdés, commander of the Andalusian squadron. Bad feelings also existed between Medina Sidonia and the fiery Don Hugo de Moncada, who commanded a squadron of four heavily armed Neapolitan galleasses. Don Hugo considered himself, with some justification, an expert on oar-powered warfare – now something of an anachronism – and he seems to have resented serving under Medina Sidonia on professional if not on social grounds. These tensions were to erupt in a bitter clash later in the campaign.

These, then, were the councillors and commanders who filed into the *San Martín's* great cabin and took their seats, surrounded by a bevy of staff officers and aides. Most of them were, by sixteenth-century standards, old men. Only Leiva, Moncada and the duke were under 40; Recalde was certainly the oldest but Diego Flores was almost 60 and most of the rest were around 50. Their collective experience was enormous. Both the Valdés cousins had played a leading part in the reconquest of Florida in 1565–6, under the overall command of their uncle, Pedro Menéndez de Avilés; and in 1575, together with Recalde, Don Pedro had led a seaborne expedition from Spain to Flanders. They, like almost all members of the council, had taken part in the Spanish conquest of Portugal and the Azores in 1580–3 (Don Pedro having led an unsuccessful invasion of Terceira in 1581). Diego Flores had sailed from Spain to England in 1554, when Philip II married Mary Tudor. He had commanded an expeditionary force sent to the South Atlantic in 1581 and, like Recalde, had taken charge of several of the large fleets that sailed annually between Seville and America, bringing to Europe, among other goods, the silver bullion upon which both the king and Spain's merchant community depended. But Recalde had the greater experience of the North Atlantic: in 1572, and again in 1575, he had commanded expeditionary forces sailing from Spain to Flanders, while in 1580 he took charge of another sent to the west coast of Ireland. Finally, Bertendona and Oquendo had also commanded flotillas sailing from Spain into the North Sea and back. As they entered the Channel in 1588 these hard-bitten men were sailing into waters which many of them knew well.

The soldiers were no less experienced. Don Francisco de Bobadilla had marched with the duke of Alba to suppress the Dutch Revolt in 1567, and served in the Netherlands for the next ten years; thereafter he held commands in Portugal, Italy and again Flanders. Don Alonso de Leiva had also served in the Low Countries and Portugal, and his most recent experience was in Italy, where he had distinguished himself in galley warfare against the Muslim raiders who constantly disputed control of the western Mediterranean with their Christian adversaries.

It was Leiva who, at the council of war now in session aboard the *San Martín*, pressed for an immediate attack on the English port of Plymouth, below the north-eastern horizon and only some 45 miles to leeward. There, with luck, it might prove possible to destroy the English fleet at anchor. Medina Sidonia listened carefully to Leiva's arguments and then, in the courteous but firm tone his officers had come to know well, proceeded to demolish them, pointing out that the entrance to Plymouth's estuarine harbour was narrow and difficult, and well defended by shore batteries. In any event, continued the duke, Plymouth was not their objective; nor, for that matter, was the destruction of the English fleet. The stakes for which the Armada was playing were much higher than that.

King Philip II, creator and absolute director of the scheme in which the Armada was an integral part, had repeatedly laid down the goals for his fleet in unequivocal terms, and Medina Sidonia took this opportunity to remind his officers of them. The Armada was to sail up the English Channel and rendezvous in the straits of Dover with the Spanish forces stationed in the Netherlands, known as the 'Army of Flanders'. It would then escort a substantial part of that army, aboard specially prepared landing craft, to a beach-head in Kent. From this point the whole operation would come under the supreme command of the most successful general of the age, Philip II's nephew Alexander Farnese, duke of Parma. Parma's 18,000-odd men would land and secure a beach-head in the vicinity of Sandwich, upon which the Armada would off-load supplies, munitions, reserve troops and a heavy artillery train. This hard-hitting mobile army, well equipped to deal quickly either with opposing field forces or static defences, would then launch a fast-moving assault on London, its flank supported by the fleet in the Thames estuary. Whenever necessary the Armada would defend itself and, if the opportunity arose, it might even attempt to defeat the English fleet in a sea battle, but in no circumstances was this to be undertaken at the expense of progress towards the principal objective. In short, Medina Sidonia reminded his subordinates, the Armada was a component part of a co-ordinated plan which the king himself had devised – a plan which, if successful, would strike a mortal blow to the heart of Tudor England. To adopt an alternative strategy on the spur of the moment would be tantamount to treason. Pedro de Valdés spoke strongly in the duke's support, and Leiva's suggestion was dropped. When a vote was taken the council decided unanimously to proceed towards the rendezvous with Parma.

But Medina Sidonia was less confident of Philip II's plan than his public assertion might have suggested. On the following day, when he communicated the council's resolution by fast dispatch boat to the king, he felt constrained to add in a coded postscript his deep anxiety that he had so far received no news from the Netherlands. The duke had good cause for concern. There he was at the entrance to the Channel, with a force of 125 ships and nearly 30,000 men, 'and it amazes me [he wrote] that we have had no message from the duke of Parma for so many days, nor have we come across in our entire voyage any person or ship who has news of him'.

Mutual communication between the two forces was essential. Lack of it would not only set the whole complex operation at risk, but would also threaten the fragile security of the huge fleet for which he was responsible. The duke continued: 'in the whole coast of Flanders there is no port or place of shelter for great ships', so once the Armada reached its intended destination, 'the first storm that comes along' would either scatter the fleet or else drive it aground on the numerous offshore sandbanks. Sidonia was counting on a swift and effortless junction with Parma, to minimise the awesome risks (which ran against all military prudence) of effecting a rendezvous in uncertain weather and in the presence of an enemy.

'According to my instructions,' Medina Sidonia reminded the king with thinly-disguised anxiety, 'at the very moment when I arrive [in the straits], Parma's forces are to put out in their ships, without my having to wait for them a single moment.' But how could he be sure, as the Armada sailed on up the Channel, that Parma was indeed ready? Until confirmation of this vital fact was received, the duke emphasised, 'to a large extent we are navigating in the dark'. Accordingly, he concluded, 'it seems best not to sail further than the Isle of Wight, until I have heard from the duke of Parma'. Events were to show that Medina Sidonia's strategic grasp of the problem was faultless: circumstances beyond his control, however, would deny him a successful solution.[1]

As yet moreover, the duke was no better informed about the movements of the English fleet than he was of Parma's state of readiness, and the need for detailed information about the former was, at that moment, even more pressing than the latter. So on 30 July, as the Armada coasted eastwards and the beacon fires flickered along the Cornish skyline, Juan Gil, an ensign aboard the flagship, was sent away in its red-painted tender with 20 picked men to check on some unidentified sails which had been seen earlier, and to gather intelligence, if he could, on the whereabouts and intentions of the English fleet. At night he returned with a captured Falmouth fishing boat in tow. Its four terrified occupants were bundled up the side of the *San Martín* and their resistance to interrogation, if they made any, was short-lived.

The English fleet, they said, had left Plymouth in full strength that afternoon under Lord Admiral Howard and Sir Francis Drake.

At this point the Armada was arrayed, in the military terms still used by the Spaniards at sea, in line-of-march. Ahead sailed the vanguard under Don Alonso de Leiva, followed first by Medina Sidonia's main battle, and then by Recalde's rearguard.

As dawn broke on 31 July, with the wind blowing from west-north-west, a large group of English ships was sighted to windward. This was Lord Admiral Howard's main body, which had successfully cleared Plymouth the night before.

With action imminent, the *San Martín* hoisted the royal standard as a signal for the Armada to take up its prearranged battle formation. The fleet manoeuvres which followed echoed the precision drill of an army in the field: on a single word of command it transformed its line of march into line of battle. Leiva's vanguard fell back in an extended line on the left of Medina Sidonia's main battle, while Recalde's rearguard moved up to adopt a similar position on the right flank. The Armada was now arrayed along a broad front, facing up-Channel for an advance towards the rendezvous with Parma.

Previous interpretations of the Armada's formation have made the assumption that its various squadrons were discrete tactical units which sailed together in regular sub-formations under their respective commanders. But in fact the territorial fleets – those of Portugal, Biscay, Castile, Andalusia, Guipúzcoa, and Levant – were no more than administrative groupings and, once at sea, their individual members were randomly

dispersed throughout the Armada, and their nominal squadron commanders no longer exercised control over them. This arrangement explains a
number of apparent anomalies in the fleet's command structure. Diego
Flores de Valdés, for example, was technically the commander of the
Castilian squadron, yet he never set foot on board his flagship *San
Crístobal* during the whole campaign because his tactical function as
chief-of-staff to Medina Sidona demanded his constant presence aboard
the duke's flagship, the *San Martín*. Similarly Juan Martínez de Recalde,
who on paper commanded the Biscayan squadron, actually hoisted his
flag on the Portuguese vice-flagship *San Juan* as Medina Sidonia's
immediate subordinate within the senior squadron.

No detailed representation of the actual formation adopted by the
Armada appears to have survived. Such plans existed, and were issued to
each ship so that its captain would be in no doubt as to his allocated
station. The battle order can, however, be deduced from other sources. It
owed much to the precepts of galley warfare, in which precision drills and
rigid formation-keeping were paramount. The central core of the fleet,
Medina Sidonia's main 'battle', accounted for rather more than a third of
its strength, and included the flagship, a strong contingent of fighting
galleons, and the four galleasses, as well as the non-combatant transports.
The remaining ships were allocated to the extended flanks or 'horns'
(*cuernos*) of the formation under Leiva (left horn or vanguard) and
Recalde (right horn or rearguard). The strength of this tactical disposition
lay in the Armada's ability to defend itself without halting its advance. A
force attacking from the rear could be flanked and ultimately surrounded
by the horns, while any attempt to impede the Armada's progress from the
front might be countered by swinging the horns forward.

Most of the responsibility for defending the formation, however, was
vested in a relatively small group of powerful vessels – no more than 20 in
all – disposed at strategic locations throughout the fleet. These ships, all of
which belonged to senior or notably dashing commanders, were authorised to break station on their own initiatives in response to any attack
on the formation as a whole. In this way Medina Sidonia could control the
Armada's defence without setting its overall order at risk, simply by
moving powerful and well-officered ships to any position he felt appropriate, and by giving them whatever freedom to act he judged fit. Thus, for
example, when Don Alonso de Leiva was put in charge of an augmented
rearguard, on 1 August, we do not later hear of him actually controlling

Fleet dispositions of the Turks (*right*) and the Christians (*left*) before the battle of Lepanto, at the entrance to the Gulf of Corinth, on 7 October 1571. The formation of both fleets, with their powerful centres and extended 'horns', presages that of the Armada in 1588. Note the 4 Christian galleasses in line abreast ahead of the main battle, and the 2 others supporting the right flank.

A copy of the Armada's intended formation, obtained before the fleet sailed by the Tuscan ambassador at Madrid and forwarded to his government. The similarity to the Lepanto formation is clear. The letters in the key denote the different categories of ships, while the numbers indicate the locations of the fleet's powerful 'trouble-shooters'.

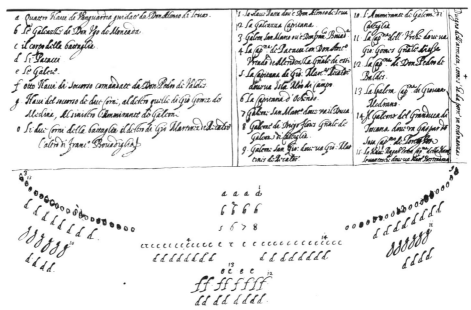

the rearguard as a coherent force under his personal command. Most of the ships simply plodded on as before. But thereafter Don Alonso's great carrack *La Rata Encoronada* was to be found wherever the fighting around the rearguard was hottest, blasting away in concert with, but not

31

commanding or commanded by, half-a-dozen or more of his fellow free-lance troubleshooters who had evidently moved from elsewhere in the fleet to support him, as Spanish gentlemen were honour-bound to do.

Such movements normally took place within the formation and not outside it, and the spacing between the ships was kept wide enough to allow free movement amongst them. As a group, the troubleshooters were vessels with a superior margin of performance over the progress of the fleet as a whole, which was naturally restricted to the speed of its slowest member. They could therefore fall back through the Armada, fight an action, and then regain station from a rearward position without slowing down the general advance.

This flexible and self-regulating tactical system neatly solved a less obvious but no less crucial problem of command. Medina Sidonia owed his unsought appointment, in part at least, to his elevated social position. He far outranked, in terms of nobility, every other officer in the fleet, so no one could object, on social grounds, to serving under him. But to have placed subordinates in positions of authority over their brother officers in a hierarchical command structure would have created insuperable difficulties of precedence. There were therefore, in effect, no subordinate commands.[2]

While the ships were taking up formation, those on board were preparing for action. From the high poop of the *San Martín* Medina Sidonia, resplendent in half-armour and surrounded by his staff, watched as the battle drills he had personally laid down for the flagship were put into effect. Around them the ship's contingent of 202 arquebusiers and 100 musketeers, encouraged by shouting officers, doubled to their stations along the aftercastle bulwarks, in the waist and forecastle, on the two gundecks, and up on the fighting tops. A dozen were even arrayed along the duke's private gallery at the stern. They presented a colourful sight. A list of the clothing taken from some prisoners who later fell into English hands includes several pairs of breeches made of cloth of gold, coloured cloaks with gold lace around the edges, 'a jerkin, embroidered with flowers, and laid over with gold lace', and, from the wardrobe of Lieutenant Bermudo, 'a blue stitched taffety hat, with a silver band and a plume of feathers'. The troops aboard the Armada were arrayed like dandies – no two soldiers were dressed exactly alike, and each strove to outshine his comrades in fashionable attire. In the words of a Spanish military expert, writing slightly later:

Spanish musketeers on shipboard. This reconstruction by Ian Lowe is based on the discovery of weapons, clothing, and accoutrements from the wreck of *La Trinidad Valencera*.

The men were dressed in high fashion, with no attempt at uniformity. Their distinctive feathered hats had a practical function: at the moment of firing the brim could be pulled down to protect the soldier's face and eyes from the violent blowback of burning debris. The heavy muskets, which weighed up to 20 pounds apiece and had to be fired from a forked rest, had straight stocks like modern rifles so that the recoil could be absorbed by the fleshy pad of the shoulder. When the long trigger lever underneath the stock was squeezed, a curved arm, or serpentine, brought a length of smouldering slow match down into the priming pan: this ignited with a flash and, after an appreciable delay, set off the main charge.

Each man carried 2 hopper-shaped powder flasks, covered with embroidered cloth and hung with ornate tassels. The larger flask, which held up to 2 pounds of fine-grained black gunpowder, was fitted with a steel spout which delivered a measured charge when the nozzle was inverted into the gun barrel. The smaller flask was used to prime the weapon. A leather pouch at the musketeer's belt held 20 or so 2-ounce lead balls. Looped over his belt was a further supply of slow match.

Side arms included a narrow-bladed sword and a long dagger. The musketeer's

battle equipment was completed by a welt-seamed goatskin bag lined with pitch, with a turned wooden filling funnel. This held his ration of 2 pints of wine or water: fighting was thirsty work.

'There has never been a regulation for dress and weapons in the Spanish infantry because that would remove the spirit and fire which is necessary in a soldier. It is the finery, the plumes and the bright colours which give spirit and strength to a soldier so that he can with furious resolution overcome any difficulty or accomplish any valorous exploit.'[3]

According to a general muster taken just before the Armada left Lisbon in May 1588, the 18,937 soldiers aboard the fleet were organised into 162 separate companies – 130 of them regular Spanish infantry, divided into five regiments or *tercios* each 26 companies strong, together with an *ad hoc* contingent of Portuguese levies and pioneers. There were no cavalry units. Rather less than half the troops carried firearms – either muskets,

MILITARY ACCOUTREMENTS

Items of equipment and dress which belonged to soldiers of Don Alonso de Luzón's Neapolitan tercio *aboard* La Trinidad Valencera. *(Top left) Brass fitting for hanging a sword; (top centre) brass holder for fixing a feathered plume to the back of the helmet on ceremonial occasions; (right) yellow braided silk buttons and button-holes from a soldier's tunic; (lower left) brass belt-buckle; (lower centre) decorated brass rivet plates for fixing the inner band which held the helmet padding in place; (lower right) rolled brass lace-ends (see Martin Frobisher's jerkin, colour plate 42).*

which delivered a one and a half ounce lead ball, or the lighter arquebuses, of half ounce calibre. The musketeers, with weapons so heavy they had to be fired from a forked rest, were something of an elite, distinguished by their elaborately feathered broad-brimmed hats. There were only about 1,000 of them. The Armada carried seven times as many arquebusiers – almost double the normal proportion – which perhaps reflects the suitability of lightly armed troops for the kind of close-quarter naval action anticipated by the Spaniards. Individual weapons, though their calibres were for the most part standardised, were fashioned and decorated to suit a wide variety of personal preferences. The remaining soldiers were normally armed with 18-foot pikes of Spanish ash, though such weapons were too cumbersome to handle afloat, and were bundled up in the hold: while at sea these men fought with arquebuses or short boarding pikes. Officers sported ceremonial halberds, their shafts cased in studded velvet, as marks of rank.

This preponderance of close-combat weaponry reflects the central fact that the Armada's main offensive potential lay in the troops it carried. 'The aim of our men,' Philip II had instructed Medina Sidonia shortly before the fleet sailed, 'must be to bring the enemy to close quarters and grapple with him.' It was held that the fleet's most effective way of defeating an adversary was to close with him, cripple and confuse him, and finally board him. All other weapons were subordinate to, and supportive of, this underlying tactical aim.

These weapons included fearsome incendiary devices which, in unskilled hands, could be as dangerous to friend as to foe, and only properly qualified personnel were allowed to use them. There were two kinds. One consisted of a ceramic pot filled with a mixture of gunpowder, spirits, and resin. It could be thrown, with lighted fuses tied round it, onto an enemy's deck, where it would burst and scatter its fiercely-burning, napalm-like contents. The other was a wooden tube mounted at the end of a long pole: this contained a series of gunpowder- and shrapnel-filled charges which, when ignited, would discharge in quick succession. It was designed to be thrust into the midst of an enemy ship's defenders by the leading men of a boarding-party.

The main pre-boarding weapon carried by each ship, however, was her complement of artillery. Some of the *San Martín's* 48 guns were light swivel pieces mounted on her upper works for anti-personnel use, either against the crew of an enemy vessel or, should she herself be boarded, to bring down enfilading fire across her own decks. But the bulk of her artillery was ranged along the ship's two continuous gundecks. On the main deck, close to the waterline, were 17 or so bronze muzzle-loaders firing iron shot of up to 30 pounds. A similar number, but of generally lighter calibre, were placed on the upper deck; these included several stone-throwing *pedreros* which, though only useful at short-range, could inflict formidable damage when they shattered on impact.

The 1,000-ton *San Martín* was one of the nine purpose-built warships acquired by Philip II when he annexed Portugal in 1580. Most of them were heavily armed two-deckers, built by the Portuguese crown to protect the maritime trade on which depended its subjects' prosperity and the tax-revenue thereby derived. These powerful oceanic battleships immediately became the core of the king's Atlantic fleet. With them sailed the flagship of the Tuscan navy, the *San Francesco* (sometimes called the *Florencia*, after her owner's principal city) bringing the combined fire-power of the squadron up to 360 guns.

Ten escort galleons detached from their normal duty of protecting the trans-Atlantic treasure fleets provided the Armada with a second squad-

(*Opposite*) Ian Lowe's reconstruction of a Spanish pikeman. These were elite troops: the Spaniards, according to the contemporary Englishman Thomas Digges, held the pike in 'so great esteem that they seldom commit them but to gentlemen'. This massive weapon was some 18 feet long and made of Spanish ash with a reinforced steel tip. It weighed more than 10 pounds.

The pikeman was equipped with steel corslet and morion, of which examples have been recovered from the wreck of *La Trinidad Valencera*. In this representation the soldier is shown 'on parade': in the field his feathered plume would be removed and his finely etched helmet encased in a protective cloth cover.

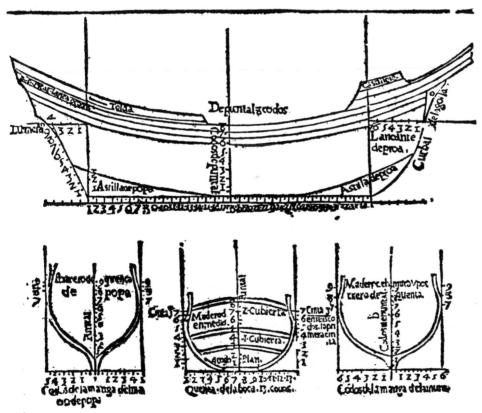

Profile and sections of an Atlantic galleon, from Diego García de Palacio's *Instrucción Nautica* of 1587. The squadron of Castile was equipped with vessels of this type.

ron of royal warships, that of Castile. Their 750-ton vice-flagship *San Juan Bautista*, though slightly larger than her seven sister galleons (all built in the early 1580s), was typical of them all. Low-hulled and weatherly, she was designed to out-sail and out-gun Caribbean pirates or Protestant privateers (the Spaniards drew no distinction between the two), and to stay at sea for six months on end. But when it came to the test, she was to prove no match for the English royal galleons. During the fighting of 4 August Pedro Calderón, an officer aboard one of the hulks, singled out 'the galleon *San Juan*' as the speediest vessel in the Armada. But unfortunately for the Spaniards the point of his story was that, in comparison with the English warship she was chasing, the *San Juan* 'appeared to be standing still'.

This was due to no inherent weakness in her design, but stemmed from the purpose for which she was built. The need to provide generous hold space to accommodate provisioning for long voyages affected the Indies galleons' sailing performance, and also required their single gun-deck to be placed well above the waterline. Stability considerations in turn severely restricted the weight of artillery they could carry. The *San Juan* herself boasted nothing larger than 7-pounder *pedreros*, of which she carried three, together with a hotch-potch of 20 light iron-throwing pieces ranging from 5-pound down to half-pound calibres. Though excellent for the specialised task for which they had been designed, these Castilian galleons could not be regarded as front-line warships in a full-blown naval battle.[4]

In contrast, Hugo de Moncada's squadron of four galleasses from Philip II's kingdom of Naples was extremely heavily armed. These hybrid 600-tonners, with their three-masted square rig and 28 rowing banks on each side, had been built some 10 years before to combine the oar-given mobility of a galley with the firepower of a fighting galleon. With a displacement roughly four times that of a comparable galley, however, they were exceedingly slow under oars, while their length and high windage made them clumsy under sail. The galleasses suffered another chronic weakness which, in the weeks ahead, would prove fatal to two of them: their broad rudders, hanging awkwardly on curved sternposts, were particularly susceptible to damage.

Nevertheless they presented an awesome sight. One English observer was particularly impressed by their vivid colour: 'The oars all red, the sails had upon them the bloody sword; the upper part of the galleass was also red – signs [he continued self-righteously] and manifest tokens of the bloody mind' that had sent them. Even the oarsmen – four convicts or prisoners to each oar – were dressed alike: in February 1588 they all received a red jacket from the fleet's storekeepers. It was as near to a 'uniform' as the sixteenth century ever came. The lot of these red-coated figures, sitting on their straw-filled cushions and chained to their benches, was scarcely enviable; but it could have been worse. For reasons of propulsive efficiency (rather than humanity) the rowers were provided with high-energy rations and special medical teams.[5]

The role of the galleasses was to bring devastating firepower to bear at points which a conventional sailing warship might not reach, and they were armed accordingly. Moncada's flag galleass, the *San Lorenzo*, mounted six great pieces in her bow, ranged directly forwards, and four firing aft from the stern. The smallest of these were 15-pounders, the largest 50-pounders. A further 20 pieces were crammed into the restricted space of her castleworks (because of the rowing banks she had no continuous gundeck), and these included two 10-pounder *medias culebrinas*, eight 5-pounder *sacres*, four 4-pounder *medios sacres*, and six 12-pounder *pedreros*. The vunerable rowing banks were shielded by raised catwalks running above the gunwales. These were fitted with eleven protective screens, each gaudily painted with heraldic devices. Between each pair of screens protruded the octagonal bronze barrel of a light breech-loading *esmeril*, ten on each side. Beyond the bow of the galleass extended a massive ram, shod with iron. The *San Lorenzo's* sister galleasses *Zúñiga, Girona,* and *Napolitana* were virtually identical to the flagship; together they constituted an apparently formidable battle-group. Great things were expected of them.

Great things had also been expected of the small squadron of four galleys which had sailed from Lisbon under Diego de Medrano, but these were no longer with the fleet: bad weather in the Bay of Biscay had forced them to run for the nearest port. These craft had not been intended for open-water fighting, for which they were known to be unsuited, but for close-support during the landings. Their loss was yet another of Medina Sidonia's growing catalogue of worries.

Nineteen big vessels of Spain's Atlantic-based merchant marine made up the squadrons of Biscay and Guipúzcoa (a twentieth ship, the Biscayan flagship *Santa Ana*, had become separated from the fleet along with the galleys, and never returned). These ships had been built in the Basque

A large 16th century merchant ship, from an engraving after Bruegel. Note the swivel guns at the stern and forecastle pointing downwards, and the large gun evidently mounted on a 2-wheeled carriage in the waist.

shipyards of San Sebastián, Bilbao, and Pasaje: stout, ocean-going work-horses intended for the trade routes of north-west Europe and the Newfoundland whaling run. Typical of their number was Guipúzcoa's vice-flagship, the 945-ton *Santa María de la Rosa*. She had been built the year before at San Sebastián, but before she could depart on her maiden voyage she was embargoed by Miguel de Oquendo, who was on the point

39

of taking his squadron to Lisbon. In October 1587, at Lisbon, her own light armament of twelve iron pieces was inventoried: most were antiquated wrought-iron guns of which the largest was a 7-pounder. To these, however, had been added four 18-pounder bronze *medios cañones* (cast some forty years before by the German master-founder Gregorio Lefer), six bronze *medias culebrinas* (manufactured in the 1550s at Mechelen in the Netherlands by Remigy de Halut) and three swivel guns, all belonging to the king. By the following March these had been augmented by the issue of a *pedrero* and a *media culebrina* from the Lisbon foundry. Even so, Oquendo had indented for a further 17 pieces to bring the *Santa María's* armament up to strength, for he still considered that his squadron as a whole was seriously under-gunned. It was a complaint current throughout the Armada.[6]

Unlike most of his colleagues, who regarded artillery as a secondary and somewhat ignoble arm, the commander of the Andalusian squadron, Don Pedro de Valdés, took a close technical interest in his guns. Don Pedro, like Oquendo, wanted more and heavier guns for his squadron, and had lobbied the king directly to get them. He appears to have met with some success, particularly with respect to his big flagship *Nuestra Señora del Rosario*. In April 1588 he obtained a *culebrina* in exchange for a *medio sacre*, and the following month, just before the Armada set sail, 10 more guns (including 4 *medios cañones* and 2 *cañones pedreros*) were issued to his ship. At some point, too, he managed to swap 6 *sacres* for 6 heavy stone-throwing *pedreros*. By the time she set sail for England, the 1,150-ton *Rosario* carried 46 guns, overwhelmingly of heavy-shotted, short-barrelled types. Don Pedro clearly subscribed to the 'close and board' school of tactical thought, and in this respect at least he was in accord with his less artillery-conscious brother officers.[7]

The ships of the other three squadrons were essentially support rather than combat vessels. Thus the ten big merchant vessels commandeered from Mediterranean ports which made up Martín de Bertendona's Levant squadron had mostly been grain carriers, with vast holds suited to bulk cargoes. But they were still expected to fight. Their overbearing magnificence, combined with the heavy armament and massed bodies of troops each of them carried, would give them, thought Bertendona, an overwhelming tactical advantage in close-quarter battle. Some optimists even claimed that each could 'give battle to ten or twelve Englishmen'. One of the largest, the 1,100-ton *La Trinidad Valencera*, from Venice, boasted –

Ian Lowe's reconstruction, based on finds from *La Trinidad Valencera*, of one of Remigy de Halut's *cañones de batir* mounted on its limbered-up campaign carriage. Pioneers from the artillery train ponder the problems of extricating this five-ton combination from a muddy pothole.

One of the siege gun wheels lying on the wreck of *La Trinidad Valencera*.

or so it seemed – a particularly heavy armament. In addition to the complement of 28 bronze guns she had carried as a Mediterranean merchantman – Venetian pieces ranging from light breech-loading swivels to long 18-pounders – the ship mounted four great battery cannons. One of them was a Turkish gun, perhaps captured at Lepanto seventeen years before. The other three were matching full *cañones de batir* – siege cannons – cast (like the *medias culebrinas* aboard the *Santa María*) in the 1550s by Remigy de Halut at Mechelen. These 2½-ton monsters hurled a

solid iron shot weighing more than 40 pounds, and they carried Philip II's royal arms combined with the English ones of Mary Tudor: their effect against an adversary at close range, it might be supposed, would be devastating.

But Master Remigy's *cañones de batir* were not intended for use at sea, though for the voyage they had been mounted on improvised ship carriages. They had been shipped, as the Spanish inventories of the fleet make clear, as part of a 12-strong battery of similar pieces of which eight were carried by the Levantine ships, together with their field carriages and other accoutrements. Packed into the *Valencera's* hold were the dismantled components of six such carriages and their limbers – two full sets for each gun. This was part of the siege train which would support Parma's march on London, and with it the *Valencera* carried a multiplicity of associated stores and munitions. Each gun was provided with a hundred rounds of ammunition, and an appropriate amount of powder. A tripod gun-hoist was supplied for mounting the heavy barrels on their assembled carriages, and spare spokes, felloes, and naves were provided for the massive iron-shod wooden wheels, each 5 feet in diameter. There were planks and baulks for the construction of gun platforms; gabions (basketwork cylinders which could be filled like sandbags) and esparto matting for consolidating protective earthworks; young fir trees with their branches trimmed to short spikes for making defensive entanglements; palisade stakes and woodchopper's axes; rollers and sledgehammers; wedges and handspikes, and screw-jacks for wheel changing in case of breakdown. Specialist tools were provided for the farriers, blacksmiths, carpenters, wheelwrights and pioneers attached to the train. So too were tents (for the munitions, not the men), buckets, lanterns, handcarts, rope-soled sandals, baskets, and wooden shovels.

In short, *La Trinidad Valencera*, in spite of her size and apparent strength, was not a true front-line warship. She was an armed invasion transport.[8]

El Gran Grifón, the 650-ton flagship of Juan Gómez de Medina's squadron of hulks was, like most of the other 22 vessels in her group, also a commandeered merchantman. But whereas most of Bertendona's squadron came from Mediterranean ports such as Venice, Genoa and Ragusa, Gómez de Medina's came from the Netherlands and the Baltic. The *Grifón* herself had been built at Rostock, and with her bluff bows and broad beam she was typical of the slow but capacious cargo ships that

A piece of esparto matting recovered from *La Trinidad Valencera*.

Trimmed fir sapling (*above*) from *La Trinidad Valencera*; (*right*) a detail from Erhard Schoen's *Siege of Munster* (1530) shows how these would have been used to construct defensive obstacles.

formed the staple of northern Europe's seaborne trade. She was embargoed at San Lúcar early in 1587, when she arrived with a cargo of timber, and to bolster her light merchantship armament of 27 iron guns, none of which was larger than a 6-pounder, eight newly-cast bronze pieces were issued to her at Lisbon. Four were light 3-pounders, but the others were *medias culebrinas*, long 10-pounders which ought to have given the *Grifón* a capability to inflict serious damage on an enemy's hull.

The rest of the hulks, however, were more lightly armed and sailed with the Armada simply as fleet auxiliaries, carrying additional troops, the field hospital, some 300 horses and mules for essential transport and traction upon landing in England, and general cargo and supplies.[9]

Agustín de Ojeda's 22 vessels of the communications squadron – *zabras* and *pataches* – made up the final unit of the fleet. There were three large

43

ships – the flagship, *Nuestra Señora del Pilar de Zaragoza*, and two embargoed British merchantmen (the *Charity* from England and the *St Andrew* from Scotland) – but the rest were pinnaces and caravels. Most of them were lateen rigged and could use auxiliary oar-power when needed. It was in ships such as these that Columbus discovered America, and their speed and seakeeping qualities were outstanding. A *patache* which had been sent by Medina Sidonia from Corunna to seek out units dispersed by the storm of 19 June was off the Devon coast within three days, and made the return journey in even better time. The inter-fleet communications support provided by these small vessels, and by the other pinnaces attached to individual squadrons, was one of the few unqualified successes of the campaign.

Such, then, was the Grand Fleet which on 31 July 1588 swung into line-of-battle within sight of the English coast. It numbered, according to the full muster held some weeks before, 125 ships (five of the original 130

Baltic hulks, from an engraving after Bruegel.

had dropped out since departure); 2,431 guns (with 123,790 rounds of ammunition), almost 19,000 soldiers and 8,000 sailors. There were, in addition, almost a thousand unattached personnel: gentlemen-adventurers, their servants, and junior officers without commands. Room had also been found for over 200 embittered English and Irish Catholic exiles, and 180 eager Spanish clerics.[10] Religion underpinned the fleet's morale, and regulated much of its daily life. Throughout the Armada the brooding presence of both the Catholic church and its self-appointed champion, Philip II, could never be forgotten:

'. . . The principal reason which has moved his Majesty to undertake this enterprise [wrote Medina Sidonia in a preamble to his General Orders] is his desire to serve God, and to convert to His Church many peoples and souls who are now oppressed by the heretical enemies of our holy Catholic faith, and are subjected to their sects and errors. In order that this aim should be kept constantly before the eyes of all I enjoin you to see that before embarking, all ranks be confessed and absolved, with due contrition for their sins.'

A banner showing Christ crucified, captured from the Portuguese galleon *San Mateo* after the battle of Gravelines. It is now preserved at Leiden.

The orders went on to prohibit blasphemy, swearing, gambling, feuding, and the illegal embarkation of women – the latter being regarded an 'evident inconvenience' as well as an offence to God. Each ship's company was expected to attend full service at least once a week, while at daybreak and dusk the ship's boys sang the *Salve* and *Ave Maria* at the foot of the mainmast. Daily watchwords were chosen for their religious significance, and the Armada's standard was blazoned with the royal arms between a Virgin and a Crucifixion, crossed with the blood-red diagonals of holy war. Beneath was embroidered the battle-cry: 'Arise O Lord and vindicate Thy Cause!' To those who participated in it, at any rate, the Armada was unquestionably a crusade. Medina Sidonia's chaplain carried a letter of authority from the General of the Dominicans to repossess all the houses of that Order in England secularised at the Reformation. And in Flanders, Cardinal William Allen, a Lancashire-born Oxford academic who had fled abroad at the beginning of Elizabeth's reign, awaited Philip II's word to cross over to England. He had received priest's orders at Mechelen, moved to Rome, and rose swiftly in the Church, being created a cardinal in 1587. Now, with the Armada expected, he returned to the Netherlands and published an *Admonition to the People of England* in July 1588, declaring Elizabeth to be deposed, promising the swift arrival of Parma and his army, and urging English Catholics to rise in arms to support them. After the Spanish conquest, Allen had been designated by both the Pope and

Philip II to take charge of the administration of the new Catholic state.[11]

The commanders of 'the greatest and strongest combination in Christendom' thus knew exactly what they had been sent to achieve, and why they had been chosen by the king as God's principal instrument against Protestant heresy and English wickedness. But there was somewhat less certainty as to how, precisely, Philip's clear purpose was to be carried out. Quite apart from the prevailing ignorance about Parma's state of preparation, there was the uncomfortable fact that Elizabeth's navy was already at sea, watching and waiting. The duke of Medina Sidonia cannot have been the only man aboard the fleet to find himself wondering, when he caught sight of the queen's distant sails, what was going to happen next.

CHAPTER 2

'A fleet to impeach it'

The fleet that had so laboriously warped out of Plymouth Sound during the night of 29/30 July was all that stood between England and defeat. To be sure, there were a few hundred regular soldiers scattered in garrisons along the coasts, and there were militia forces on stand-by – the beacon fires had been lit to alert men as well as ships. But they were far from ready. Many were not even familiar with the terrain upon which they might have to fight. Although military surveys of the defences and geography of most coastal regions had been prepared in 1587–8, some were highly inaccurate. One map of Norfolk in May 1588 was completed in such haste that the harassed cartographer was obliged to omit a vital finishing touch, explaining in a note to his map that 'Reason would a scale, but time permits not'.[1]

Much the same last-minute haste characterised the mobilisation of the queen's soldiers. Even in the capital, orders to arm 10,000 Londoners had only been issued in mid-March, and there was not enough modern equipment to go round. Many were given bows and arrows, although they had received no instruction in their use and a lifetime's experience was necessary to produce an effective archer. No further military steps were taken until 6 July, long after the Armada had left Lisbon, when the Privy Council decided to create a reserve army near London. This, however, could only be done by depleting the forces elsewhere. In every shire of southern England, officials were instructed to divide the county militia into three parts:

'Some to repair to the sea coast, as occasion may serve, to impeach the landing . . . of the enemy upon his first descent; some other part of the said forces to join with such numbers as shall be convenient to make head to the enemy after he shall be landed (if it shall so fall out); and another principal part of the said trained numbers to repair hither to join with the Army that shall be appointed for the defence of Her Majesty's person.'

An Elizabethan army on the march in Ireland, from Derrick's *Images of Ireland*, published in 1580.

For the moment, the troops designated for service near the queen were simply to stand ready to go wherever they were told 'upon an hour's warning'. But on 2 August full mobilisation was called: 'Her Majesty's pleasure is that you should forthwith send [them] into Essex, unto the town of Brentwood'. From there, England's heroes were directed to Tilbury, where a small fortress was under construction to provide a secure headquarters for Robert Dudley, earl of Leicester, 'General of Her Majesty's forces in the South'. Yet it was all in vain. The Armada's proposed beach-head lay not in Essex at all, but in eastern Kent, just south of Ramsgate, where in the past Roman legions, Saxons, and Danes had all stormed successfully ashore. The Spaniards might have done the same, and without effective opposition, for despite urgent and often ingenious improvisation by Elizabeth's commanders there was no integrated defensive system in the south-east of England able to withstand a sustained assault by a professional army equipped with heavy artillery.

Some, indeed, regarded all these preparations by land as a wasteful farce. As Sir Walter Raleigh wrote some years later:

'an army to be transported over sea . . . and the [landing] place left to the choice of the invader . . . cannot be resisted on the coast of England without a fleet to

Robert Dudley, earl of Leicester. Miniature by Nicholas Hilliard dated 1576, when Leicester was 44.

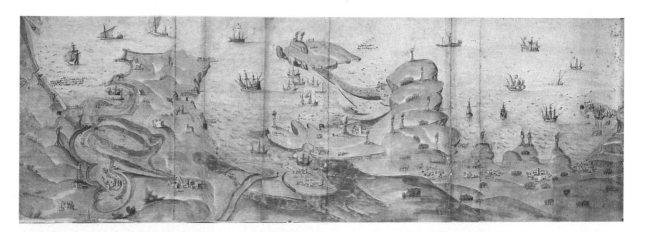

1. Part of the beacon system on the Dorset coast.

2. The port of Plymouth in the 16th century. Its principal anchorage was the final reach of the River Plym, known as the Cattewater. A 17th century Coasting Pilot describes the Cattewater as 'a good place, where ships ride that are bound to the Westward'. Most of Howard's ships were anchored here when the Armada was sighted off the Lizard.

3. A Portuguese galleon, probably the *San Martín*, in action off Calais after the fireship attack. This was painted by Hendrik Corneliz Vroom about 1600, and is probably based on reliable sources: note the soldiers on the decks and in the fighting tops, Philip II's arms on the main topsail, and the crusading symbols on the lower foresail.

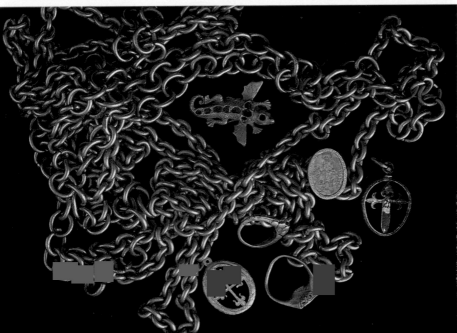

4. Gold chain and other jewellery from the wreck of the galleass *Girona*. Symbols of knightly orders include (*right*) a cross of Santiago and (*bottom centre*) a cross of Alcántara. The salamander pendant is set with rubies.

5. Cross of a knight of St John of Jerusalem – probably belonging to Fabricio Spinola, captain of the *Girona*.

6. Cloak collar of silk and wool from the wreck of *La Trinidad Valencera*.

7. Gold buttons from the *Girona*.

8. A musketeer's silk tassel from *La Trinidad Valencera*.

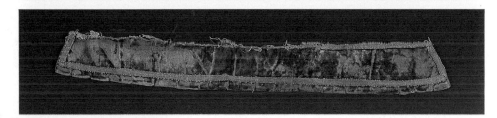

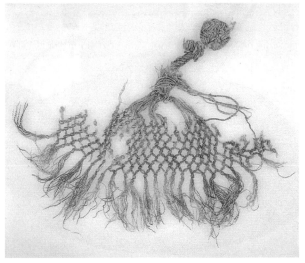

9. An Armada galleass, depicted in the anonymous Greenwich Cartoon. On her foremast the ship displays a standard incorporating the arms of Portugal, Leon, Castile, and Naples; at the mainmast, the crossed keys of the Papacy; on the mizzenmast, Spain's national ensign; and at the stern, an enormous banner showing Philip II's royal arms. This English painting includes subtle allegorical details: note the priest, the fools and the knave on the galleass's deck, and in the rowing boat the solitary figure overcome by the fury of the battle raging around him.

10. Golden box in the form of a book with compartments for 5 wax pellets or *Agnus Dei* (of which the remains of 2 were found). These were made in the Vatican from the drippings of Easter candles mixed with consecrated oil, and blessed by the Pope. They were considered to have miraculous powers against natural disasters, including shipwreck. To own 5 would be the mark of an important or pious man, perhaps a bishop. From the *Girona*.

11. Gold ring with IHS (an abbreviation from the Greek for Jesus) monogram from the wreck of the *Girona*. It probably belonged to one of the clerics aboard the galleass.

impeach it . . . except every creek, port, and sandy bay had a powerful army in each of them to make opposition . . .'

England's only defence lay, concluded Raleigh, in her 'many movable forts' – the galleons of the royal navy – and her wisest strategy was therefore to 'employ . . . good ships on the sea, and not trust to any intrenchment upon the shore.'

In truth Elizabeth possessed few enough of these vital 'movable forts', but the ones she had were unquestionably the best in the world. The roots of a standing navy lay in the reign of her father, Henry VIII, who had created a permanent defence establishment against the threat of Catholic attack following his excommunication by the Pope in 1535. By 1546 a full-time Admiralty was in being, and procedures for building, arming, and victualling the royal ships on a permanent basis had been established. Anthony Anthony's illustrated Roll allows us to glimpse Henry's navy in frozen review, while the remains of one of these very ships, the 600-ton *Mary Rose*, is on display and under study at Portsmouth, close to the dock in which she was built in 1510 and not far from the place where she sank during an action with the French in 1545.

The *Mary Rose* had been extensively rebuilt and re-equipped in 1536, and her wreck throws sharp light on the technologies and tactical thinking of Henry's professional navy at the close of his reign. For most of the time such ships were laid up on a care-and-maintenance basis to minimise cost to the crown, but in an emergency they could rapidly be mobilised for service in home waters. They were not designed for long periods at sea, or for extended voyages, and so the problems of victualling were minimal. All that was needed to make them operational was a full contingent of seamen and troops which, in the *Mary Rose's* case, amounted to some 100 and 600 men respectively. Virtually the full capacity of the ship was given over to weapons and men, who were expected to remain on board only long enough for a foray across the Channel, an expedition northwards to Scotland, or (as was the case in 1545) to repulse an enemy invasion. The type of fighting for which such ships were designed was short, sharp, and – it was hoped – decisive.

Tactics were very similar to those of the Spanish Armada a generation later. Soldiers were the primary weapon – in the *Mary Rose's* case they were predominantly archers, men trained from boyhood in the use of the yew longbow, who could cast a high-velocity barrage of armour-piercing missiles at a range of over 200 yards, and at a rate of up to six per minute.

For the final stage of a successful engagement – the physical boarding and capture of an adversary – 300 pikes and bills were provided. But, unlike the capital ships of the Armada in 1588, the *Mary Rose* seems to have carried few incendiary weapons (a single fire-arrow has been found in her wreck). Both for the preparatory bombardment intended to immobilise an enemy, and for the short-range salvo designed to create maximum confusion in the vital seconds just before a boarding assault, she relied almost entirely on her guns.

Throughout his reign Henry had taken a direct personal interest in the highly skilled and almost mystical art of gunnery, and with the help of foreign experts the gunfounders of England had become renowned throughout Europe. Even at the beginning of his reign, as a contemporary put it, the king already possessed 'cannon enough to conquer hell'; by its close his store of ordnance was truly formidable. And many of the guns, including some of the biggest, were to be found on the continuous gundecks of his big battleships.

The armament carried by the *Mary Rose*, attested both by contemporary documents and by archaeological discovery, was certainly impressive. In addition to a large number of iron guns, mostly quite small, she mounted fifteen bronze pieces, including two cannons royal, two demicannons, two culverins, six demi-culverins, two sakers, and a falcon. By the standards of their day these weapons were powerful and up-to-date, and the design of their carriages – of which a number of examples have been recovered from the wreck – shows that the English had already come to grips with the principal operational problems posed by repeated firing of heavy artillery at sea: namely, how to reload under battle conditions and how to elevate and traverse a gun firing through a gunport. The solution to both problems was to abandon the heavy field-carriage with a trail and two large spoked wheels (or cheaper solid-wheeled derivatives of it) originally designed to be hauled by teams of horses, upon which early shipboard artillery was frequently mounted. In its place a compact box-shaped carriage with stepped sides and four small solid wheels – or trucks – was developed. Mounted on such a carriage a gun could be handled and adjusted with relative ease, while the whole combination occupied far less deck space, so making it easier to run the gun back after firing and reload it inboard.

In spite of its widespread use aboard English ships as early as 1545, this simple device was still apparently eschewed by the Spaniards in 1588, who had not yet abandoned the 'close and board' mode of fighting rooted in medieval tradition. The navy that Henry left to his successors, however – while still exclusively composed of troop-carrying battleships designed for his 'narrow seas' policy – thus carried within it the seeds of a revolutionary concept which would flower under Elizabeth: the idea of a warship as a mobile weapons platform whose offensive capacity lay not in her soldiers but in her guns. The presence, or absence, of the truck carriage may be regarded as a clear indicator of the kind of artillery tactics a ship intended to use.

By 1547, the year of Henry's death, the navy royal consisted of 53 well-armed warships with a total displacement of some 10,000 tons. But it was a navy that England could not afford to maintain indefinitely. In a cost-cutting exercise of a kind all too familiar with modern peace-time navies, ships were sold off or scrapped, until in 1555 there were only 30 left. But then came one of history's great ironies. In September of that year Philip of Spain, who had just married Queen Mary Tudor (Henry VIII's daughter and Elizabeth's older half-sister) and was thus England's king-consort, appeared before the Privy Council to persuade its members that

'England's chief defence depends upon the navy being always ready to defend the realm against invasion, so that it is right that the ships should not only be fit for sea, but instantly available.'

Three capital ships of 500 tons and upwards were promptly laid down. All three, rebuilt and updated, were destined to serve in 1588 against the man who had assisted at their birth (one was even called the *Philip and Mary*, though in 1584 Elizabeth changed its name to *Nonpareil*). So, thanks to Henry VIII and (to a lesser extent) Philip II, the English navy, when Elizabeth Tudor came to the throne in 1558, was very much a force to be reckoned with.

By 1588 that fleet had 34 ships in commission. This might seem only a modest advance on the 30 inherited by Elizabeth at her accession, but while several were quite old – six dated from the reign of Henry VIII – eleven had been constructed since 1584 and twelve of the rest had been rebuilt to the same standards as the newer ones. Elizabeth's programme of naval development began under the charge of William Winter, Surveyor of the Navy, who started re-equipping the queen's fleet with new ships of medium tonnage, although the idea that they should be troop carriers as well as gun platforms was not immediately discarded: the 'Fighting

The Black Pynnes.

Many of the smaller vessels on both sides were small low-hulled pinnaces. This is the pinnace that brought Sir Philip Sidney's body back to England after he had been killed at Zutphen in 1586 – called the *Black Pinnace* on account of its sombre awnings.

Instructions' drawn up by Winter in March 1558 clearly envisage bombardment as a prelude, not an alternative, to boarding. But by 1588 this tactical approach had been entirely abandoned in favour of prolonged broadside firing at close range. This critical change seems to date from 1578 when the innovative (and, for his time, scrupulously honest) John Hawkins became Treasurer of the Navy.[2] Henceforth all the queen's new warships were 'race-built' galleons distinguished by four novel characteristics which Hawkins and his associates, from their privateering experiences on the Spanish Main, had identified as essential for the deployment of mobile artillery tactics. Such ships were longer in relation to their beam, and possessed finer underwater lines; their wind-catching castleworks at stem and stern were much reduced; they adopted a more efficient sail plan; and they mounted more heavy guns (and fewer anti-personnel weapons) along their continuous decks. The sailing performance and hitting power of such ships, in comparison with those that had gone before, was truly phenomenal.

Charles Howard of Effingham, Elizabeth's Lord Admiral, was unstinting in his praise for them: 'I protest it before God . . .,' he enthused after an inspection early in 1588 '. . . if it were not for her Majesty's presence I had rather live in the company of these noble ships than in any place.' Of his own flagship, the 800-ton *Ark* (built in 1587), he had this to say of her outstanding sailing performance: 'I think her the odd ship in the world for all conditions . . . We can see no sail, great nor small, but how far soever they be off, we fetch them and speak with them.' A few days earlier he reported to Burghley: 'I have been aboard of every ship that goeth out with me, and in every place where any may creep . . . and there is never a one of them that knows what a leak means . . . There is none that goeth out now but I durst go to the Rio de la Plata in her.'

Of these glowing statements we may accept at face value all but the last: Elizabeth's galleons, like the *Mary Rose* before them, were not designed to undertake long oceanic voyages. But this was a strength rather than a weakness. The shape and performance of a ship is conditioned by compromise: if one quality is to dominate, a penalty must be paid by the others. Carrying capacity – whether of provisions for long voyages, of troops, or of armament – cannot be achieved except at the expense of speed and sailing ability. It was the requirement to carry all of these, in bulk, that so disadvantaged the Spanish ships which sailed against England in 1588. But the English fleet was geared, by long tradition and the defensive requirements of an island nation, to speedy mobilisation in home waters: it was not a high seas fleet which had to carry provisions for sustained voyages far from base, and so its ships were not encumbered by the need for heavy and bulky loads below decks.

So the shipwrights of Elizabethan England were left with only one major problem of design: how to combine a fast hull with a heavy armament. And they balanced this fine equation with a precision bordering on genius. The sleek lines of the new English galleons are graphically seen in Matthew Baker's technical drawings of the 1580s, and all contemporary observers – on both sides – agreed that the performance of these vessels was greatly superior to the best of Spain's fighting ships. And yet they were still able to mount a formidable armament.

Information about the guns aboard individual English ships during the campaign is sketchy, but the armament carried by two of the queen's galleons three years earlier is probably typical. The 600-ton *Elizabeth Bonaventure* mounted, in all, 51.5 tons of ordnance (excluding carriages, ammunition, and equipment), amounting to more than 8 per cent of her rated tonnage, while the smaller *Aid*, of 250 tons, had 27 tons of artillery aboard – nearly 11 per cent of her total. And when, in 1591, the queen's galleon *Revenge* of 500 tons (Drake's flagship during the Armada campaign) was captured after an epic battle off the Azores, the Spaniards estimated that her 43 guns had a total weight of around 70 tons (14 per cent). The ability to carry loads of this magnitude on the decks well above the waterline indicates that the ships were especially strong and stable. That these characteristics were combined with a sailing performance far superior to that of the best of their rivals further emphasises the successful design of the late sixteenth century English warship.

By contrast the 1,050-ton Portuguese galleon *San Juan*, one of the most heavily gunned ships on the Spanish side, carried only 4 per cent of her tonnage in armament, and the 700-ton Castilian flagship *San Crístobal* could account for only 3 per cent of her rating in the weight of her guns. In exchange for their provision-filled holds and massed companies of troops, the Spaniards suffered heavy penalties both in firepower and in performance.[3]

But what of the men who manned these splendid English galleons? In Henry VIII's day, as with the Spanish Armada of 1588, most of a warship's crew were soldiers, and the command structure was based on separate military and naval hierarchies. But the naval reorganisations of Elizabeth's reign, and especially the highly individual genius of Francis Drake, had given rise to the more practical if socially revolutionary system of unified command under a single sea captain: a ship's complement, said Drake, must 'all be of a company'. His celebrated dictum that the gentlemen should 'haul and draw' with the mariners had evidently become normal practice aboard English warships by 1588, and even so illustrious an officer as Lord Henry Seymour, commander of the eastern squadron and a cousin of the Lord Admiral, was not above lending a hand on deck when it was needed. In June 1588 he dispatched a report to Walsingham from his blockading station aboard the *Rainbow* off Dunkirk, with a postscripted apology that it was not written in his own hand, which he had strained 'with hauling on a rope'. No Spaniard with pretensions to gentility, however modest, could have countenanced the task that Lord Henry lustily performed as a matter of routine.

Thus manned, and in a spirit of comradely teamwork under a single commander (who was first and foremost a seaman), the new ships could exploit their technical advantages to the full. Their sailing superiority allowed them to gain the most advantageous position during a fight and, having gained it, to concentrate sustained gunfire on the enemy. Moreover, in doing these things the English had a further inestimable advantage over the Spaniards. Their ships were manned exclusively by sailors: even though the men detailed to work the guns were still officially described as 'soldiers', they were no longer soldiers in the Spanish sense, but specialist naval ratings. On average, the fleet had a seaman for every two tons of shipping. Each Armada sailor, on the other hand, had to work seven tons. To some extent the Spaniards made good this deficiency by employing soldiers to carry out general duties about the ships, and to serve the guns in action. But the English system, where each seaman could turn his hand to working the ship or the guns as occasion demanded, was clearly much better. All in all, according to the English artillery theorist William Bourne, his sea-going compatriots were 'handsome about their ordnance in ships, on the sea'.

No such unity was to be found among Spaniards afloat. William Monson, a veteran of the Armada campaign, later provided a graphic critique of the shortcomings of his erstwhile opponents' command structure. They had, he wrote,

'more officers in their ships than we: they have a captain for their ship, a captain for their gunners, and as many captains as there are companies of soldiers; and, above all, they have a commander in the nature of a colonel above the rest. This breeds a great confusion, and is many times the cause of mutiny among them. They brawl and fight, commonly, aboard their ships as if they were ashore'.

Medina Sidonia, it is true, had anticipated such troubles, for in his General Instructions to the Armada he sternly enjoined that

'there should exist perfect good feeling and friendship between soldiers and sailors . . . there should be no possibility of quarrels amongst them, or other causes of scandal. I therefore order that no man shall carry a dagger, and that on no account shall offence be given on either side . . .'

But despite these precautions the underlying tensions remained. During the *Santa María de la Rosa's* final desperate moments off Ireland a bitter altercation broke out between the seamen and soldiers (of which she had carried 64 and 225 respectively), in which one of the military captains precipitately slew the ship's unfortunate pilot, Francisco de Manona, 'saying he did it [i.e. that the pilot had caused the wrecking] by treason'. It was a far cry from the 'haul and draw' philosophy of Francis Drake.

The English system offered numerous advantages in combat, especially in stand-off combat involving heavy artillery. First, there was the matter of experience and familiarity: the men who worked the Spanish guns were regular infantrymen, many of whom had never fought at sea before and virtually none of whom, except those attached to the squadrons of Portugal and Castile, had fought aboard the ship in which they sailed.

Their English counterparts, on the other hand, were familiar both with the weapons carried by their particular vessels and with the problems of handling them on shipboard. And then the Spanish gun-crews, as noted above, expected to fire only one salvo before boarding and so, having loaded their pieces, they dispersed to battle-stations that might be far distant from their guns. The English gunners, free of the cumbrous military weapons and accoutrements (to say nothing of the refulgent dress) of the Spaniards, merely stayed where they were and worked the guns continuously. They needed no soldiers, for they had no intention of boarding or being boarded. When, during the Channel battles, the governor of the Isle of Wight tried to send some musketeers to the fleet, Admiral Howard sent them straight back with a curt message saying 'that he had as many men as he desired or could well use'.

There was a third important social contrast in the organisation of the two fleets, once again expressed with brutal frankness by Sir William Monson, in a essay uncompromisingly entitled *The ill-management of the Spanish ships*: 'Their ships are kept foul and beastly,' he wrote, 'like hog-sties and sheep-cots in comparison with ours. And no marvel,' he continued, for no one on board was in charge of swabbing down the decks, and there was no galley to feed the entire company. Instead, according to Monson, in the Spanish navy 'every man is his own cook, and he that is not able to dress his meat may fast.' This was an exaggeration: although it is true that there was no communal cooking

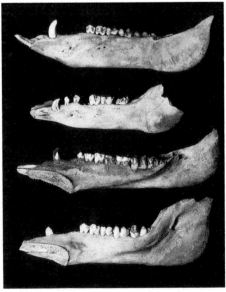

(*Far left*) An earthenware jar from *La Trinidad Valencera* which once contained half an *arroba* (about 11 pints) of olive oil. These distinctive containers were made under contract to India House in Seville, and were cased in woven straw for easy stowage.

(*Left*) Butchered pig jaw-bones from *La Trinidad Valencera*. Bacon was supplied in longitudinally-cleft half carcasses, including the head, as the cleaver marks on the lower pair testify.

WEEKLY RATION ALLOCATIONS

SPANISH

Daily: 1 ½ lb of biscuit, or 2 lb fresh bread
  1 ⅓ pints of wine, or 1 pint of Candia wine which was stronger
  3 pints of water, for all purposes
Sunday and Thursday: 6 oz bacon and 2 oz rice
Monday and Wednesday: 6 oz cheese and 3 oz beans or chick peas
Wednesday, Friday and Saturday: 6 oz fish (tunny or cod, failing which, 6 oz squid or 5 sardines), 3 oz beans or chick peas, 1 ½ oz oil and ¼ pint of vinegar

ENGLISH

Sunday, Tuesday and Thursday: 1 lb biscuit, 1 gallon beer, 2 lb beef, 4 oz cheese and 2 oz butter
Wednesday, Friday and Saturday: 1 lb biscuit, 1 gallon beer, one quarter of a stockfish or the eighth part of a ling, 4 oz cheese and 2 oz butter
Monday: 1 lb bacon, 1 pint peas, 4 oz cheese and 2 oz butter

An intact pine cone from *La Trinidad Valencera*. The kernels were regarded as a delicacy.

The skull of a grey rat which perished in the hold of *La Trinidad Valencera*

facility of the kind provided on every English ship, the Spaniards aboard the Armada were grouped into squads of eight or ten soldiers called *camaradas* (comradeships). Each group drew its rations individually under the watchful eye of the ship's notary (whose main concern was to balance his books), and prepared them in rotation in the main galley using its own cooking utensils and serving dishes. But this was bad enough. The risk to general health posed by (on a large ship) up to 50 separate food stores can easily be imagined. And general hygiene, even by the lax standards of the day, seems to have been exceptionally poor. The English mariners (whose own shipboard habits were by no means exemplary) who came aboard Spanish vessels during 1588 campaign all commented on the squalor and stench they encountered.[4]

The defence of England in 1588 did not rest solely upon the ships of the queen's navy: there was, in addition, a strong 'Volunteer Reserve'. Thirty of the private vessels that fought under Howard's command displaced between 200 and 400 tons and carried up to 40 guns. They were warships in all but name. Several, indeed, had considerably more battle experience against Spanish ships than the carefully husbanded royal fleet. Only two of the queen's ships had sailed under Drake to the Caribbean in 1585, with twelve large merchantmen (all of which served against the Armada); and only four sailed under him to Cadiz in 1587, with thirteen armed merchantmen (which, again, all served in 1588). This should not surprise us, for many of these private ships actually belonged to prominent figures in the queen's navy: Howard himself owned seven vessels, which he normally used for privateering but in 1588 threw into the campaign against Spain; Hawkins owned three; and Drake two. They were commanded by relatives or partners, creating a remarkably unified command structure among the fighting ships, whether royal or private.[5]

But it is misleading to dwell only upon the strengths of the English fleet. There were also serious defects. To begin with, the number of large fighting ships was not great. Ten of the 34 vessels of the navy royal were rated at 100 tons or less, and many of the 163 private ships involved at some stage in the campaign were small and of dubious value. According to Sir William Winter, they were about as useful to Howard as the hulks were to Medina Sidonia, 'I dare assure Your Honour' he wrote later to Secretary Walsingham, 'if you had seen what I have seen of the simple service that hath been done by the merchant and coast ships, you would have said that we had been little helped by them, otherwise than that they did make a show.'

Nor was the past record of some of the privateers inspiring. Two of the strongest galleons on the English side, the *Galleon Leicester* and the *Edward Bonaventure* (both of 40 guns) had departed in 1582 on an expedition to sail to 'China and Cathay'. The whole enterprise was a blackly humorous catalogue of incompetence and disaster. Off the coast of West Africa the fleet got lost. Its pilot, Mr Thomas Hood, deprecated the use of books on navigation, saying '[I] will not give a fart for all their cosmography, for [I] can tell more than all the cosmographers in the world'. His confidence was misplaced: having inadvertently returned in a circle to where it had started, the expedition was obliged to sell one of its supporting ships in exchange for better directions and new provisions. The ramshackle fleet next went to South America, where it ran into a Spanish flotilla under Diego Flores de Valdés (on board was another future Armada captain, Francisco de Cuellár). Although they managed to sink one of the Spaniards, the action had to be terminated because the crew of the *Leicester* became too drunk to fight and the galleon itself was so damaged that she had to return to England. Another ship (belonging to Sir Francis Drake and commanded by his nephew) was wrecked on the coast of South America, where John Drake and his men were either captured by the Spaniards, enslaved, or eaten by cannibals.

Such catastrophes, however, were common to all nations during the 'age of discoveries', and too much should not be made of them. A more serious disadvantage under which the English navy laboured in 1588 was the lack of commanders experienced in controlling large fleets. Drake had led only 22 ships (and perhaps 8 pinnaces) to the West Indies in 1585, and scarcely more against Cadiz two years later, yet these were the largest expeditions to leave England's shores before the Armada came. Winter, Hawkins and Frobisher all had experience of independent command, but with still smaller squadrons.

Moreover, the service record of their commander-in-chief, Lord Howard of Effingham, was extremely limited: during his long career (he was 52 in 1588) he had only commanded at sea on a handful of occasions, and had been appointed Lord Admiral of England as recently as 1585. On the other hand, he came from a family of shipowners and seamen – he was the fourth Howard to hold the office of Admiral under the Tudors – and he enjoyed excellent connections at Court. He was a cousin of the queen, and was related by either blood or marriage to most of the Privy Council. As with Medina Sidonia, no one questioned his right to command, and few criticised his skill in doing so. Again like Medina Sidonia, he possessed exceptionally gifted and supportive subordinates, whom he cultivated with sensitivity and tact: where the duke could turn to Recalde and Bertendona, Howard could count on men like Hawkins, Frobisher and, most especially, Drake.

And it was Drake who, after long argument, convinced Howard and the rest that their proper place in the summer of 1588 was at Plymouth. Drake had divined, as others had not, the grand strategy of Philip II: that the Armada was coming from Spain to join up with Parma and the Army of Flanders because Parma could not cross the Channel without the protection of a major fleet. Since that fleet could only reach Flanders via the Channel, Drake reasoned, it was folly to concentrate the bulk of England's naval strength in the Narrow Seas, covering the Flemish ports. Rather, the main force should be gathered in a secure base as far west as possible, whence it might use the prevailing westerly winds to gain the weather gauge of an enemy coming in from the Atlantic and then harry it from this advantageous position along the entire length of the Channel.

Drake's argument prevailed. In February he brought a detachment of the main fleet to Plymouth, under his own command. Then on 3 June most of the remaining ships arrived, led by Lord Admiral Howard and accompanied by Hawkins and Frobisher, leaving only 15 galleons and their supporting auxiliaries under Lord Henry Seymour to guard the Narrows. The western squadron was now 105 strong, including 19 of the queen's ships and 46 large auxiliary vessels.

They were still at Plymouth on 29 July, despite several unsuccessful attempts to launch another raid on Spain. Indeed, the main fleet was in the process of loading stores and munitions in the inner harbour when Captain Thomas Fleming of the 50-ton pinnace *Golden Hind*, one of the Lord Admiral's screen of pickets watching the Channel approaches, arrived with the momentous news that the Spanish Armada, in formidable strength and good order, had been sighted off the Lizard. Immediately the leading English ships began the tricky and laborious business of warping out of harbour with the ebb tide. But, once the vital order had been given, the English commanders ashore could do nothing until their ships had cleared port with the tide and were formed up, ready to sail, in Plymouth Sound. These few hours would have given Francis Drake, if the famous story is not apocryphal, ample opportunity to finish his game of bowls on Plymouth Hoe.

But not even Drake could be sure how England's ships would fare in the battle which was now inevitable. Each side had, as we have seen, very different aims, equipment and tactical doctrines; neither knew the intentions, strengths and weaknesses of the other, or how best to respond to them. No one – least of all those involved – could predict the outcome.

General summary of the fleet muster carried out at Lisbon on 9 May 1588, and published shortly afterwards. The document was supposed to be top secret, and Philip II was appalled when he learned that it was appearing in print even before the fleet sailed. This first Spanish edition of the document, published at Lisbon within a few days of the muster, belonged to Lord Burghley, Queen Elizabeth's chief minister of state. He may well have obtained it from one of the captured Armada ships.

SVMARIO
GENERAL DE TODA
EL ARMADA.

	Numero d Nauios	Toneladas	Géte d guerra	Géte d mar	Numero de todos	Pieças de artilleria.	Peloteria.	Poluora	Plomo quintales.	Cuerda quintales.
¶ Armada de Galeones de Portugal.	12.	7.737.	3.330.	1.293.	4.623.	347.	18450.	789.	186.	150
¶ Armada de Vizcaya de que es General Iuan Martinez de Ricalde.	14	6.567.	1.937.	863.	2.800	238.	11.900.	477.	140.	87
¶ Galeones de la Armada de Castilla.	16	8.714.	2.458.	1.719.	4171.	384.	23.049.	710.	290.	309
¶ Armada de naues del Andaluzia.	11.	8.762.	2.325.	780.	3.105.	240.	10.200.	415.	63.	119
¶ Armada de naos de la Prouincia de Guipuscua.	14	6.991.	1992.	616.	2.608.	247.	12.150.	518.	139.	109
¶ Armada de naos leuantiscas.	10.	7.705.	2.780.	767.	3523.	280.	14000.	584.	177.	141
¶ Armada de Vrcas.	23.	10271.	3.121.	608.	3729.	384.	19.200.	258.	142.	215
¶ Pataches y zabras.	22.	1.221.	479.	574.	1.093.	91.	4550.	66.	20.	13
¶ Galeaças de Napoles.	4.		873.	468.	1.341.	200.	10.000.	498.	61.	88
¶ Galeras.	4.			362.	362.	20.	1.200.	60.	20.	20.
	130.	57.868.	19295.	8050.	27365.	2.431.	123790.	4.575.	1.232.	1.155

Gente de remo.

En las Galeaças.	1.200.
En las Galeras.	888.
	2.088.

De mas de la dicha poluora se lleuá de respecto para si se ofreciere alguna bateria 600. qs.   600.

POr manera que ay en la dicha armada, segun parece por este sumario, ciento y treynta nauios, que tienen cincuenta y siete mil ochocientas y sessenta y ocho toneladas, y dezinueue mil dozientos y nouenta y cinco soldados de Infanteria, y ocho mil y cincuenta y dos hombres de mar, que todos hazen, veyntisiete mil trezientas y setenta y cinco personas, y dos mil y ochenta y ocho remeros, y dos mil y quatrocientas y treynta y vna pieças de artilleria, las mil quatrocientas y nouenta y siete de bronze, de todas suertes en que ay muchos cañones, y medios cañones, culebrinas, y medias culebrinas, y cañones pedreros, y las noueçientas y treynta y quatro restantes de hierro colado de todos caliuos, y ciento y veyntitres mil ciento y nouenta balas para ellas, y cinco mil ciento y setenta y cinco quintales de poluora, y mil y dozientos y treynta y ocho de plomo, y mil ciento y cincuenta y vn quintales de cuerda: y los generos de los nauios son en esta manera.

A 2

THE SPANISH FLEET

		TONS	GUNS
SQUADRON OF PORTUGAL	*San Martín* (flagship)	1,000	48
Duke of Medina Sidonia	*San Juan* (vice-flagship)	1,050	50
Total seamen 1,293	*San Marcos*	790	33
Total soldiers 3,330	*San Felipe*	800	40
	San Luis	830	38
	San Mateo	750	34
	Santiago	520	24
	Galeon de Florencia	961	52
	San Crístobal	352	20
	San Bernardo	352	21
	Zabra Augusta	166	13
	Zabra Julia	166	14
SQUADRON OF BISCAY	*Santa Ana* (flagship)	768	30
Juan Martínez de Recalde	*El Gran Grin* (vice-flagship)	1,160	28
Total seamen 863	*Santiago*	666	25
Total soldiers 1,937	*La Concepcion de Zubelzu*	468	16
	La Concepcion de Juan del Cano	418	18
	La Magdalena	530	18
	San Juan	350	21
	La María Juan	665	24
	La Manuela	520	12
	Santa María de Montemayor	707	18
	Patache *María de Aguirre*	70	6
	Patache *Isabela*	71	10
	Patache de Miguel de Suso	96	6
	Patache *San Esteban*	78	6
SQUADRON OF CASTILE	*San Crístobal* (flagship)	700	36
Diego Flores de Valdés	*San Juan Bautista* (vice-flagship)	750	24
Total seamen 1,719	*San Pedro*	530	24
Total soldiers 2,458	*San Juan*	530	24
	Santiago el Mayor	530	24
	San Felipe y Santiago	530	24
	La Asuncion	530	24
	Nuestra Señora del Barrio	530	24
	San Medel y Celedon	530	24
	Santa Ana	250	24
	Nuestra Señora de Begoña	750	24
	La Trinidad	872	24
	Santa Catalina	882	24
	San Juan Bautista	652	24
	Patache *Nuestra Señora del Rosario*		24
	Patache *San Antonio de Padua*		12
SQUADRON OF ANDALUSIA	*Nuestra Señora del Rosario* (flagship)	1,150	46
Don Pedro de Valdés	*San Francisco* (vice-flagship)	915	21
Total seamen 780	*San Juan Bautista*	810	31
Total soldiers 2,325	*San Juan de Gargarin*	569	16
	La Concepcion	862	20
	Urca *Duquesa Santa Ana*	900	23
	Santa Catalina	730	23
	La Trinidad	650	13
	Santa María de Juncal	730	20
	San Bartolome	976	27
	Patache *Espiritu Santo*		

Squadron	Ship	Tonnage	Guns
SQUADRON OF GUIPÚZCOA Miguel de Oquendo Total seamen 616 Total soldiers 1,992	*Santa Ana* (flagship)	1,200	47
	Santa María de la Rosa (vice-flagship)	945	26
	San Salvador	958	25
	San Esteban	936	26
	Santa Marta	548	20
	Santa Bárbara	525	12
	San Buenaventura	379	21
	La María San Juan	291	12
	Santa Cruz	680	18
	Urca *Doncella*	500	16
	Patache *Asuncion*	60	9
	Patache *San Bernabe*		9
	Pinaza *Nuestra Señora de Guadalupe*		1
	Pinaza *La Madalena*		1
LEVANT SQUADRON Martín de Bertendona Total seamen 767 Total soldiers 2,780	*La Regazona* (flagship)	1,294	30
	La Lavia (vice-flagship)	728	25
	La Rata Santa María Encoronada	820	35
	San Juan de Sicilia	800	26
	La Trinidad Valencera	1,100	42
	La Anunciada	703	24
	San Nicolas Prodaneli	834	26
	La Juliana	860	32
	Santa María de Vison	666	18
	La Trinidad de Scala	900	22
SQUADRON OF HULKS Juan Gómez de Medina Total seamen 608 Total soldiers 3,121	*El Gran Grifón* (flagship)	650	38
	San Salvador (vice-flagship)	650	24
	Perro Marino	200	7
	Falcon Blanco Mayor	500	16
	Castillo Negro	750	27
	Barca de Amburg	600	23
	Casa de Paz Grande	600	26
	San Pedro Mayor	581	29
	El Sanson	500	18
	San Pedro Menor	500	18
	Barca de Danzig	450	26
	Falcon Blanco Mediano	300	16
	San Andres	400	14
	Casa de Paz Chica	350	15
	Ciervo Volante	400	18
	Paloma Blanca	250	12
	La Ventura	160	4
	Santa Bárbara	370	10
	Santiago	600	19
	David	450	7
	El Gato	400	9
	San Gabriel	280	4
	Esayas	280	4
GALLEASSES FROM NAPLES Don Hugo de Moncada	*San Lorenzo* (flagship)		50
	Zúñiga		50
	Girona		50
	Napolitana		50
	Total seamen 468, total rowers 1,200, total soldiers 875		

PATACHES AND ZABRAS
Don Antonio Hurtado de Mendoza
22 ships, total seamen 574, total soldiers 479

GALLEYS
Diego de Medrano
4 galleys, each with 5 guns
total seamen 362, total rowers 888, no soldiers

Grand total: 130 ships / 29,453 men

Her Ma:^{ties} whole Armye at the sene against
the Spanish forces in Ao 1588

The Arke ———————— 425 ——— Lo: Admirall.
The Bonadventure ———— 250: ——— Earle of Cumberland
The Raynebowe ———— 250: ——— Lo: Henry Seymor
The Leyone ———————— 250: ——— Lo: Tho: Howarde
The White Beare ———— 500: ——— L: Edmond Sheffeld
The Saintgeorge ———— 250: ——— Sr Will: Wynter
The Revenge ———————— 250: ——— Sr Fra: Drake.
The Eliz: Jonas ———— 500:
The Victory ———————— 400: ——— Sr John Hawkins
The Antelope ———————— 160: ——— Sr Henry Palmer.
Tryomphe ———————— 500: ——— Sr Martin Frobisher
The Dreadnaughte ———— 200: ——— Sr Geo: Beston
The Marye Rose ———————— 250: ——— Edward Fenton.
The Nonpereily ———— 250: ——— Tho: Fenner.
The Hope ———————————— 250: ——— Roberte Crosse.
The Gally Bonavolia ——— 250: ——— Wr: Brough.
The Swyfteshure ———— 180: ——— Edward Fenner.
The Swallowe ———————— 160: ——— Rich: Hawkins.
The Foresight ———————— 160: ——— Chr: Baker.

204

91

THE ENGLISH FLEET

HER MAJESTY'S SHIPS, GREAT AND SMALL	TONS	MARINERS	GUNNERS	SOLDIERS
Ark (The Lord Admiral)	800	270	34	126
Elizabeth Bonaventure (Earl of Cumberland)	600	150	24	76
Rainbow (Lord Henry Seymour)	500	150	24	76
Golden Lion (Lord Thomas Howard)	500	150	24	76
White Bear (Lord Sheffield)	1,000	300	40	150
Vanguard (Sir William Winter)	500	150	24	76
Revenge (Sir Francis Drake)	500	150	24	76
Elizabeth Jonas (Sir Robert Southwell)	900	300	40	150
Victory (Sir John Hawkins)	800	270	34	126
Antelope (Sir Henry Palmer)	400	120	20	30
Triumph (Sir Martin Frobisher)	1,100	300	40	160
Dreadnought (Sir George Beeston)	400	130	20	40
Mary Rose (Edward Fenton)	600	150	24	76
Nonpareil (Thomas Fenner)	500	150	24	76
Hope (Robert Crosse)	600	160	25	85
Galley Bonavolia (William Borough)				
Swiftsure (Edward Fenner)	400	120	20	40
Swallow (Richard Hawkins)	360	110	20	30
Foresight (Christopher Baker)	300	110	20	20
Aid (William Fenner)	250	90	16	14
Bull (Jeremy Turner)	200	80	12	8
Tiger (John Bostocke)	200	80	12	8
Tramontana (Luke Ward)	150	55	8	7
Scout (Henry Ashley)	120	55	8	7
Achates (Gregory Riggs)	100	45	8	7
Charles (John Roberts)	70	36	4	
Moon (Alexander Clifford)	60	34	4	
Advice (John Harris)	50	31	4	
Merlin (Walter Gower)	50	20	4	
Spy (Ambrose Ward)	50	31	4	
Sun (Richard Buckley)	40	26	4	
Cygnet (John Sheriff)	30			
Brigandine (Thomas Scott)	90			
George hoy (Richard Hodges)	100	16	4	

34 ships / average tonnage 373 / total men 6,705

34 merchants' ships with Sir Francis Drake, westward
average tonnage 157 / total men 2,294

30 ships and barks paid by the city of London
average tonnage 151 / total men 2,130

33 ships and barks (including 15 victuallers), under the Lord Admiral and paid by Her Majesty
total men 1,561

20 coasters, great and small, under the Lord Admiral, paid by the Queen
average tonnage 97 / total men 993

23 coasters under the Lord Henry Seymour, whereof some were paid by Her Majesty,
but the greatest part by the port towns
average tonnage 98 / total men 1,093

23 voluntary ships, great and small, paid by the queen
average tonnage 95 / total men 1,059

Grand total: 197 ships / 15,925 men

South-east England and the Netherlands, 1588

Territories held by Dutch Republic

0   50   100 miles
0   50   100   150 km

North Sea

TEXEL

ENGLAND

Alkmaar

Haarlem   •Amsterdam
            •Naarden   •Deventer
                             Zutphen·
Leiden   •Utrecht
        Gouda
Brill

Grave

Brentwood
Tilbury   Flushing   •Bergen-op-Zoom
    Thames   North Foreland
    Estuary   ('Cape Margate')
Rochester   Ostend
Canterbury   Banks of   •Sluys   Antwerp
Sandwich   Flanders   Bruges   •Lier
    Dover   The Downs   Nieuwpoort   Ghent   •Mechelen
KENT   Goodwin   Dunkirk
Rye   Sands   Calais Gravelines   Aalst   •Brussels
                Boulogne   Bourbourg •Douai
                        FLANDERS
                        R. Scheldt

English
Channel

SPANISH   NETHERLANDS   R. Maas

R. Waal

R. Rhine

R. Maas

P I C A R D Y

Cateau
Cambrésis

FRANCE

N

PART II

God's Obvious Design

CHAPTER 3

'The great bog of Europe'

Justin of Nassau, son of William of Orange and commander of the Dutch inshore squadron.

As the Spanish and English fleets manoeuvred off the Lizard, another confrontation was taking place 300 miles to the east. Along the coast of Flanders an expeditionary force of almost 20,000 men commanded by Philip II's nephew, the duke of Parma, lay encamped close to its invasion transports, awaiting the approach of the Armada so that, under its protection, they might slip across the Channel to their assigned landing zone in eastern Kent. But without that protection they were helpless. In the shoal waters beyond the low coastline they could glimpse the sails of Justin of Nassau's 30 shallow-draught Dutch cromsters – well-armed, deadly, and pledged to destroy any of Parma's forces that put to sea. Just over the horizon, they knew, stood Queen Elizabeth's Narrow Seas fleet under Lord Henry Seymour, ready to intercept and annihilate the flotilla of open craft should it somehow evade the Dutch and make a sudden dash for England.

Most accounts of the Armada campaign concentrate upon the naval battles of the main fleets and pay scant attention to the vigil maintained by the forces in the straits. But their role in the defensive effort was just as important. And the Dutch had everything to play for too, for although the Armada was directed principally against England, it was also a bold attempt to counter a long-standing and deeply-seated challenge to Spanish power in the Netherlands.

The seventeen provinces of the Netherlands, which had been united under Habsburg rule by Philip II's father Charles V during the first half of the sixteenth century, formed the newest state in Europe. Some – including the prosperous western areas of Brabant, Flanders, Holland and Hainaut – had been familiar with firm government from Brussels for more than a century; but others – such as Friesland, Utrecht and Groningen – had not been absorbed until the earlier part of the sixteenth century.

Gelderland, the largest province, was not annexed by the Habsburgs until 1543. And even when all these provinces were given a single administrative structure in 1548 they all nevertheless retained a lively spirit of independence which was accentuated by their different histories and traditions and by their different languages (French in the south; German and East Dutch in the east; West Dutch and Fries in the north and west).

Into this patchwork of jurisdictions, customs, and languages the new Protestant faith, also born in the first half of the sixteenth century, found it easy to penetrate. Before long Calvinism, Anabaptism and Lutheranism all had their devotees in different parts of the Low Countries; and it was to counter the spread of these heresies that Philip II, who began to govern the seventeen provinces in 1556, decided to increase the number of Catholic bishops in the Netherlands, to sharpen up the laws against Protestantism, and to extend the scope of the Inquisition.

All these measures, however, required money; and money was in short supply. In 1564 the creation of new bishoprics was frozen, and two years later the enforcement of heresy laws and the activities of the Inquisition were suspended. These concessions only prompted further agitation and more demands. In the spring of 1566 Protestants in the Netherlands began to organise open-air prayer meetings defended by armed guards; then, in the summer and autumn, they began a campaign of iconoclasm, smashing Catholic religious images in wayside shrines and in churches, and demanding the right to worship indoors as well as in the fields. By August

Dutch Protestants tear down Catholic images in the iconoclasm of 1566.

1566, according to the king's representative in Brussels, one half of the local population had gone over to Protestantism and 200,000 people were in arms against the government.

These events threatened Philip II's authority to an intolerable degree; they were a challenge to which he felt obliged to respond, whatever the cost. In Spain, the king and his advisers took the highly alarmist – and, as it turned out, grossly exaggerated – estimates of Protestant strength at face value and determined to meet force with force. It was resolved that Spain's most experienced general, the duke of Alba, should be sent to the Netherlands at the head of 10,000 Spanish veterans, with orders to raise whatever additional forces were needed to restore order and extinguish heresy. But the kings's opponents fled first, and the Low Countries were effectively pacified before Alba's Spaniards arrived in August 1567.

However, the presence in the Spanish Netherlands of a professional standing army, commanded by perhaps the best general of his day, immediately transformed the international situation in northern Europe. The duke and his troops represented a standing challenge to the security of the neighbouring states: France, England, and the semi-autonomous princes of Germany. All now felt sufficiently threatened by Philip II to offer support to his enemies, the Protestant exiles and rebels led by William of Nassau, prince of Orange, when they invaded the Netherlands in 1568 and again in 1572. And although the first attempt proved a miserable and costly failure, the second achieved partial success, for the invaders managed to gain firm control over the heavily fortified coastal provinces of Holland and Zealand.

For four years the outcome lay in the balance. It was not only the impressive modern fortifications of the rebellious Dutch towns that complicated Spain's reconquest: there were geographical considerations too. The provinces in revolt, surrounded either by the sea or by broad rivers, were all islands or peninsulas, and communications within them were further complicated by lakes, marshes and waterways. In the words of an English traveller, Holland and Zealand constituted:

'The great bog of Europe. There is not such another marsh in the world, that's flat. They are an universal quagmire . . . Indeed it is the buttock of the world: full of veins and blood, but no bones in't.'[1]

And this 'buttock' was defended by a fleet of small ships, able to operate close inshore, and capable of both blockading enemy ports and preventing

William, prince of Orange. His curiously twisted expression was the result of a facial wound received during the abortive assassination attempt of 1582.

vessels sent from Spain from landing troops on Dutch territory. After the wrecking of one Spanish fleet on the Flemish coast in 1572, and the failure of another to reach the Netherlands at all two years later, no further naval attack on the rebels was attempted until 1588.

But Spain did not give up the struggle. Instead, the duke of Alba assembled a vast force of some 60,000 men, known to its contemporaries and to posterity as the 'Army of Flanders', and hurled it against one rebellious town after another: Mechelen, Zutphen and Naarden in 1572, Haarlem and Alkmaar in 1573. Those that they captured were sacked and a large part of their populations – irrespective of sex or age, and despite promises of clemency made beforehand – were massacred. It was all to no avail. Alba's draconian policy only intensified the resistance of the towns still in rebellion, and the duke was recalled in semi-disgrace at the end of 1573. But this, too, failed to end the revolt. 'There would not be time or money enough in the world to reduce by force the 24 towns which have rebelled in Holland [and Zealand], if we are to spend as long in reducing each one of them as we have taken over similar ones so far,' wrote Alba's dispirited successor in October 1574. 'No treasury in the world would be equal to the cost of this war,' he repeated more ominously in November.[2]

His prediction came true within the year. In September 1575, crippled by the cost of supporting 60,000 men for more than three years in the Netherlands, the Spanish treasury declared itself bankrupt and the flow of money to the Army of Flanders abruptly ceased. Within a few months Philip II's unpaid troops in the Netherlands either deserted or mutinied, while the Catholic political leaders of the provinces formerly under Spanish control made common cause with the Protestant rebels, still led by William of Orange. By May 1577 the prince of Orange was, in effect, the chief executive of a new 'government of national unity' established in Brussels and responsible to a States-General (Parliament) representing all the provinces, languages and religions of the Netherlands.

This was the high-point of the Dutch Revolt. The States-General demanded that Philip II accept them as his lawful government, and that crown officials be appointed only with their approval. Even more provocatively they insisted on freedom of worship for Protestants throughout the Low Countries. These were ultimata that no early modern monarch could accept with honour. As the king's advisers pointed out, concessions in the Netherlands would almost inevitably lead to a stream of similar demands from his other dominions. So, instead, Philip II

A Dutch cromster, from an early 17th century engraving. Ships of this kind were used by the Dutch to blockade the Flemish ports. The English soldier of fortune Sir Roger Williams, who had seen active service in the Low Countries from 1574, described cromsters as 'the best ships to fight in these waters by reason the most of them draw but little water and carry for the most part principal good artillery, some demi-cannons, and many whole culverins'. Such was their success in 1588 that, immediately after the Armada, 4 vessels of this type were built for the English navy; they were 200-tonners, with crews 100-strong, and each mounted 8 18-pounder culverins, 6 9-pounder demi-culverins, and 2 5-pounder sakers.

determined on a systematic reconquest of his defiant provinces, and began to build up loyal forces in the far south-east of the Netherlands, closest to his possessions in Italy. A 700-mile military corridor, known to contemporaries as 'the Spanish Road', conveyed troops and treasure from Lombardy to the Low Countries at regular intervals to encompass, by sheer attrition and weight of numbers, the defeat of the Dutch. From the autumn of 1578 these formidable troops were moulded into a doggedly professional fighting force of supreme quality and morale by the tough and energetic Alexander Farnese, prince (and later duke) of Parma.

Parma was an ideal choice for the command. In the first place, he was Philip II's nephew: his royal blood entitled him to deal directly with sovereign rulers, and gave him an effortless social status among the prickly Netherlands aristocracy. Second, he had grown up at the court of Spain, where he had developed valuable contacts among the king's ministers; at the same time, he had come to understand the complex processes by which policies were made (and unmade) at the highest levels. Third, through his wide travels he had acquired a penetrating appreciation of Europe's geography, and had come to know a large number of influential people. In 1557 he visited England, and was even spoken of as a possible bridegroom for the young and attractive Princess Elizabeth: thirty years later, on the eve of his planned invasion, he could still reminisce about the excellence of the hunting around London.[3] In the 1560s he was introduced to the geography and history of the Netherlands as well as to its leading political figures, while his mother (Philip II's illegitimate elder sister) served there as regent. By the early 1570s he was a staff officer in the Spanish Mediterranean fleet, taking part in the great Christian victory of Lepanto in 1571.

Parma, although still only 32 when he took charge of the Army of Flanders in 1578, had thus already acquired extensive political and military experience. He also possessed huge personal resources. As the heir (and after 1586 as the ruler) of a major Italian state, Parma maintained his own diplomatic service, used his own credit where necessary to achieve his ends, and maintained a glittering court of around 1,500 people. In most years, 50,000 ducats were sent from his Italian estates to Flanders to support the duke's household, and he was able to raise far more – by 1592 almost one million ducats – in loans secured on his extensive properies.

Through these formidable sources of power and influence, Alexander Farnese was able to offer a wide range of rewards, bribes and promises at many opportune moments to advance his cause. In 1578–9 his subtle diplomacy drew the Catholics of the southern Netherlands back into the royalist camp, and throughout the 1580s his bribes secured the surrender of numerous fortified centres without a siege. As a Dutch commander bitterly remarked after one such reverse: 'Everyone knows that Spain's golden bullets made a greater breach in the heart of the traitor who commanded [the town] than their battery [did in the walls].'⁴ But Parma was equally dexterous in the use of force. On the one hand, he was prepared to arrange the murder of those who refused his bribes: at Philip II's instigation he placed a price on the head of William of Orange, and an unsuccessful assassination attempt was made in 1582, followed by a successful one in 1584. On the other, thanks to the efforts of his 60,000 soldiers – Spaniards, Italians, Burgundians and Germans as well as native levies – Parma was able to starve one Dutch town after another into submission.

In January 1581 Parma's forces embarked upon a grand strategy that within four years would double the size of the Spanish Netherlands. Observing that Flanders and Brabant, the richest provinces involved in the revolt, depended for their prosperity upon waterborne trade, the prince realised that if his troops could occupy the Flemish coast and block the Scheldt below Antwerp the entire inland network of rivers and canals would be paralysed; and that without access to the sea and the major rivers all the major towns caught within his net would be forced to surrender.

A complete Spanish reconquest, however, was a prospect that Parma's neighbours in north-western Europe viewed with grave dismay. The 'great bog' occupied a position of permanent strategic importance, since an army stationed there could with ease intervene in France and the Rhineland or even, given a fleet, in England and Scotland. The creation of the powerful Army of Flanders, first under Alba and then again under Parma, therefore caused a diplomatic revolution in northern Europe.

Looking back in 1589, England's chief minister of state, Lord Burghley, mused that 'The state of the world is marvellously changed, when we true Englishmen have cause for our own quietness to wish good success to a king of France and a King of Scots.' For the previous five hundred years Englishmen had generally been opposed to – and often at war with – the rulers of France and Scotland, and had usually found themselves allied with the rulers of the Netherlands. But now England's 'natural enemy', like France's, was Spain. The continuance of a rebellion which committed a large part of Spain's army to an enduring and expensive war in the Low Countries was therefore something that suited both England and France, not to mention the Protestant states of the Rhineland, very well. Their political advantage clearly lay in lending support to the Dutch rebels whenever they seemed to be in danger of succumbing. Thus in 1572 virtually all the Netherlands' neighbours had sent support to William of Orange's invasion; in 1574, when the rebel cause seemed to be faltering, France began to send subsidies; and in 1578, after a Spanish military success, France and England took the overtly hostile step of sending troops to fight for the Dutch.

In 1581, as Parma launched his master strategy, the Dutch revolt once again seemed on the point of failing. Partly it was the religious divide, which made the Catholic and Calvinist rebels uneasy bedfellows; partly it was the petty provincialism of the Netherlands, which made Hollanders reluctant to assist Flemings. But above all, it was the absence of a firm and universally accepted government. According to an English observer in the Low Countries, writing in October 1581, the rebellion was about to collapse 'for want of a good government; for there is a number that commands in the country, and few will obey.' In January 1582 he repeated: 'Every man will command, and few . . . will be commanded, so there is no order nor good government among them.'[5]

Deliverance, however, was at hand. The prince of Orange contrived to persuade François de Valois, duke of Anjou and heir apparent to the French throne, to become 'prince and lord of the Netherlands'. In 1581 the States-General declared Philip II deposed from all his Netherlands titles, and Anjou arrived at the head of 10,000 troops to take over. Furthermore, he declared that the queen of England had announced her intention to marry him, and to place her resources alongside his in the defence of Dutch liberty. 'Froggy' therefore (as the contemporary English song had it) 'went a wooing' and spent the autumn of 1581 in England. The following February he returned, claiming that he was engaged to Elizabeth and bringing with him as a token of this new attachment her favourite, Robert Dudley, earl of Leicester, her cousin, Lord Hunsdon, Secretary Walsingham, and numerous other English courtiers. On 19 February, at Antwerp, they were all present when William of Orange, in the name of the States-General, invested Anjou with the regalia and dignities of the dukes of Brabant. Representatives of the other provinces soon followed suit and the duke, now in receipt of funds and recognition from France and England, became in effect sovereign ruler of the provinces in revolt against Philip II.

But it did not last. First, in March 1582, William of Orange was severely wounded in an assassination attempt arranged by Parma and, while he was out of action, Anjou and the States-General fell to disagreement. Early in 1583, indeed, the duke's French troops attempted to take control of eight leading Low Countries towns, including Antwerp. Anjou was disgraced, and left the Netherlands in June. He died a year later. Meanwhile, amid the confusion, Parma's stolid veterans advanced rapidly and captured most of the ports along the Flemish coast. In the summer of 1584 they struck inland and captured the key towns of Flanders – Bruges and Ghent – and in September the troops began a huge engineering project some thirty miles below Antwerp which would close the Scheldt and so cut off the metropolis from its vital access to the sea. It consisted of a great timber bridge 800 yards long, its central section floating on anchored pontoons, defended by a complex of emplacements containing almost 200 guns and booms moored up- and down-stream. Parma's blockade was completed at the end of February 1585. It was one of the wonders of the age, and the duke staked everything upon its success: it would be either 'his sepulchre or his pathway into Antwerp'.

Many contemporaries considered Antwerp, the great city on the Scheldt with a population of 80,000 and a five-mile circuit of powerful modern fortifications, to be impregnable. Certainly the States-General did very little to succour it (although this was due less to complacency than to the confusion and lack of leadership which followed a second, successful, assassination attempt against William of Orange in July 1584). Not until April 1585 was a major effort made to relieve Antwerp, when a fleet from Holland, commanded by Orange's son Justin of Nassau, waited at the mouth of the Scheldt while, at Antwerp, a small flotilla of ships filled with explosives was released on the ebb tide down the river towards Parma's bridge. These floating bombs had been designed by an Italian, Federico Giambelli, with considerable ingenuity. Some were constructed to explode on impact, others were given a delayed fuse to ignite the charge as the ship neared the bridge, and others still were simple fireships filled with powder and shot that exploded when the heat reached them.

As Giambelli had intended, the subtle variety of his 'infernal machines' caused confusion and carelessness among the Spaniards. The whole idea

Giambelli's 'Hellburners' are unleashed on Parma's bridge over the Scheldt during the Dutch attempt to relieve Antwerp on 5 April 1585.

of explosive ships was new, and the cataclysmic danger they presented was not fully appreciated. When the largest 'hellburner', which had been set to blow up almost harmlessly in the middle of the river just short of its target, spewed out its colourful pyrotechnics, the defenders of the bridge gathered by the water to watch the display. Even Parma came for a while. He had only just started back for his headquarters when one of the other vessels, primed to explode on impact, hit the bridge. At least 800 Spaniards were killed, many more were injured, and Parma himself was blasted by the shock wave. But the stolid troops of the Army of Flanders soon recovered their discipline and their wits: they temporarily made good the damage, stood to their battle stations, and prevented Justin and his fleet from exploiting their advantage. Counter-attack was swift. The beleaguered cities of Brabant, including Antwerp, all now fell; but the terrible experience of the exploding ships was not easily forgotten. The 'hellburners of Antwerp' entered the vocabulary, and the irrational fears, of every Spanish soldier.

Parma and the Army of Flanders had achieved a great deal against heavy odds in a short time. Within four years they had driven those in revolt against Philip II's power into an enclave scarcely larger than they had held in 1572. After the capitulation of Antwerp, which was signed in August 1585, Parma was at last free to consider how best to complete the reconquest. He had no doubt of the ability of the troops under his command to achieve anything that was humanly possible. Some of his soldiers had been on active service for thirty years, and they were commanded by officers who had spent many years in action before rising to senior rank. In the words of one of Parma's staff officers, the Army of Flanders contained 'few soldiers who were raw recruits. They were powerful men, well-armed and of martial aspect, highly trained and always ready to obey and to fight'; and Parma himself once boasted that his men were 'tough, disciplined, and born to fight with the people of the Netherlands'.

Those who had encountered Parma's troops in action could only agree. Sir Roger Williams, third-in-command of the army which awaited the Armada at Tilbury, held up the Army of Flanders as a shining example to others: 'To speak truth,' he wrote, 'no army that ever I saw, passes that of the duke of Parma for discipline and good order.' And Sir Roger had good reason to know, since he had fought with the Spaniards in the Netherlands from 1574 until 1578, and thereafter against them. The earl of Leicester, commander-in-chief of Elizabeth's forces, was likewise filled with apprehension: the Army of Flanders contained, he noted with regret, 'the best soldiers at this day in Christendom'.[6]

In them, Parma held the tool to complete the recovery of the Netherlands. The Dutch were losing their nerve. They had failed to save any of the towns of Flanders and Brabant from capture, and now they were bankrupt. In 1583 interest payments on the state debt had to be suspended for lack of funds, and even the tomb of the prince of Orange was, according to an English visitor, 'the poorest that ever I saw for such a person, being only of rough stones and mortar, with posts of wood coloured over with black'. And the Dutch lacked not only money; now they had no leaders. Following the deaths of Anjou and Orange in the summer of 1584, no one in the young Republic seemed capable of

Ian Lowe's reconstruction of an Army of Flanders arquebusier in field service order is based on contemporary pictorial evidence and on items recovered from the Armada wrecks.

His helmet of etched Milan steel, protected by a hessian cover, was padded inside with compressed pine needles. The 0.5 inch calibre arquebus he carried had a droop-curved stock, showing that it was fired French-fashion from the chest – a technique unsuited to the massive recoil of the much heavier musket. His combination front- and back-pack contained rations, cooking utensils and spare clothes, while his equipment included powder flasks and bullet pouch, sword and dagger, and goatskin canteen. The shoes hanging at his waist were leather *zapatos*, worn only on special occasions; on active service, particularly in the Flanders mud, open-fronted esparto-soled *alpargatas* with ankle gaiters were much more suitable.

Ian Lowe '87

exercising effective authority. If the problem in 1581–2 had been too many commanders, in 1584–5 it was too few. The provincial assemblies, and even the States-General, lacked statesmen accustomed to command in war or experienced in the conduct of diplomacy. Orange's son Maurice, although accepted as governor by Holland and Zealand, was only 17, and many years would pass before he gained the skill and sagacity required to reconcile the differing interest groups within the Dutch state. Indeed, in the wake of Parma's victories, a vociferous peace party grew up within the rebels' ranks, anxious to make a deal with their former master whilst they still had something to bargain with. In July 1585, when the States of Holland proposed to levy another tax for the defence of Brabant, the town council of Gouda (in Holland) refused to consent and argued instead that the surest way to relieve beleaguered Antwerp was to start immediate negotiations with Spain for 'a good peace'. Only the dispatch of a large body of loyal troops brought Gouda to heel.

And yet, as he contemplated his next move following the fall of Antwerp, Parma noted with frustration that the rebels did not offer to surrender. Perhaps, he argued in a letter to the king at this time, he should simply continue his offensive and invade Holland and Zealand. The experiences of 1572–6, however, had already shown the dangers and difficulties of that course. After all, it had been difficult enough in Flanders and Brabant: time and again, in the bitter fighting around the besieged towns, victory had hung upon a thread. On every occasion, it is true, the thread had held but, as Parma warned the king, one day 'God will grow tired of working miracles for us'.

And now, despite the miraculous fall of Antwerp, the Dutch 'show no sign of anything except renewed obstinacy'. Why? Parma was in no doubt about the reason. On 30 September 1585 he assured the king: 'English troops are arriving [in Flushing] every day, and already number four or five thousand men. And it seems that the queen of England wishes openly to take up their cause . . . for one can clearly see from the letter she has written to the rebels how much she is prepared to assist and encourage them'. It might be easier and more effective, he reasoned, to divert his forces from fighting the Dutch – who were certainly in no position to mount a counter-attack – to attacking their foreign supporters. Convincing evidence was to hand that, at several important junctions, the assistance of France and England had saved the rebel cause from collapse just when, militarily speaking, it seemed doomed. Now, with the death of Anjou and the outbreak of new civil dissension in France, further support from that quarter seemed unlikely; and, for the same reason, no French reprisals would be possible should Spain decide to deal with the Dutch rebels' persistent supporter on the other side of the English Channel.[7] But at precisely this moment, just as Parma was reaching the conclusion that war with England was the only way to break out of his impasse, Elizabeth of England declared war upon him.

CHAPTER 4

Armed neutrality, 1558–80

For the first decade of her reign, which began in 1558, Elizabeth made no change in traditional Tudor foreign policy. For ten years she remained a fairly loyal friend of Spain, and like her father before her seems to have done everything in her power to destabilise the governments of France and Scotland. To begin with, it is true, she had little choice, for she inherited a war with France and Scotland as Spain's ally by virtue of the fact that her elder half-sister Mary had married Philip II. This alliance soon became unpopular however, for although an English contingent took part in the great Spanish victory over France at St Quentin in August 1557, five months later the French retaliated by taking England's only continental possession, Calais. Then, in April, the heir to the French throne married young Mary Stuart, queen of Scots. It soon became clear that this manifestation of the 'auld alliance' between France and Scotland had serious implications: the following year, by which time Mary's husband had become king of France, the two sovereigns began to quarter the arms of England with their own, and to style themselves 'rulers of France, Scotland, England and Ireland'. According to Elizabeth's appalled ambassador in France, the couple even had these insignia emblazoned on their dinner service.

These events were to affect Elizabeth's foreign policy for decades, but to understand the reason for their significance it is necessary to consider some earlier developments.

Perhaps the story – and hence the story of the Armada – began in the 1530s with the decision of Henry VIII of England to divorce his wife Catherine of Aragon and then to marry one of his court ladies, Anne Boleyn. It was easier said than done: the divorce led to a major breach with the Papacy culminating in the separation of the church in England from its mother church of Rome, with Henry proclaiming himself its

The seal of Mary Queen of Scots and Francis II of France, proclaiming sovereignty over France, Scotland, England and Ireland.

(*Left*) Mary Stuart, Queen of Scots, by an unknown artist after Hilliard.

supreme head. These developments were internationally significant, both because Catherine was the aunt of Charles V, ruler of Spain and the Netherlands and Holy Roman Emperor, and because the breach with Rome opened England to the influence of the continental Reformation, which had already ended papal authority in much of northern Europe.

The Catholics soon struck back. They refused to acknowledge the validity of Henry's marriage to Anne Boleyn, and regarded the couple's only surviving child, Elizabeth, as a bastard; they rejected his claim to be supreme head of the church of England; and, on these grounds, they planned his deposition. In 1542 the Catholic James V of Scotland launched an invasion of northern England, and three years later the French sent an invasion fleet which entered the Solent and temporarily

12. An English shipwright and his apprentice at work in the drawing office, c. 1586.

13. A race-built galleon and its sail plan, probably drawn by the master-shipwright Matthew Baker in 1586. 4 of the guns in its waist are shown mounted on truck carriages.

14. The hull of Henry VIII's battleship *Mary Rose* undergoing conservation treatment at Portsmouth.

15. Charles Lord Howard of Effingham, Lord Admiral of England, at the age of 69. A miniature by Nicholas Hilliard.

16. Sir Francis Drake, by an unknown artist (post 1580).

THE MARINERS MIRROVR
Wherin may playnly be seen the courses, heights, distances, depths, soundings, flouds and ebs, risings of lands, rocks, sands and shoalds, with the marks for thentrings of the Harbouroughs, Havens and Ports of the greatest part of Europe: their seueral traficks and commodities: Together with the Rules and instruments of NAVIGATION.
First made & set fourth in diuers exact Sea-Charts, by that famous Navigator Lvke Wagenar of Enchuisen And now fitted with necessarie additions for the use of Englishmen by
ANTHONY ASHLEY.
Herein also may be understood the exploits latelye atchieved by the right Honorable the L. Admiral of England with her Mates Nauie and some former seruices don by that worthy Knight
Sr Fran. Drake,

17. Title page of the *Mariners Mirrour*, an English edition of Waghenaer's charts published in 1588. A wide range of contemporary navigational instruments is shown. The sailors' dress is probably typical, although it is doubtful whether they wore fancy ruffs at sea.

occupied the Isle of Wight. But Henry overcame both challenges. The Scots invasion was soundly trounced at Solway Moss and James V, who was already ill, died on hearing the news. His week-old daughter, Mary Stuart, succeeded him. In the south, Henry himself was present (though ashore, at Southsea castle) when his fleet engaged a French invasion force in the Solent: the affair was inconclusive, although one of the king's great ships, the *Mary Rose*, overset and sank during the action.

In 1547 Henry Tudor died peacefully in his bed. The crown of England passed to his 10-year-old son, Edward VI, whose regents introduced a fully Protestant church order in England and continued the war with France and Scotland. But Edward was a sickly youth, and six years later he died. In spite of attempts by the regents to continue the breach with Rome and secure a Protestant ruler, Henry's unilateral decisions of the 1530s were soon overturned, for the succession passed in 1553 to his daughter by Catherine of Aragon: Mary Tudor. In spite of prolonged harassment Mary had remained a determined Catholic, and she was now resolved to enforce her faith upon her new subjects. She was also determined to ally England firmly with Spain. Within a month of her accession she was in direct negotiation with her uncle, Charles V, offering herself as the bride of his sole son and heir, Philip II. The couple were married at Winchester in July 1554, and a formal reconciliation of England with the church of Rome was made in November. Three months later the first English Protestant heretics were burnt.

But Mary's 'Spanish Match' was not a success. Philip and his Spanish courtiers were unpopular, while the condemnation and execution of Protestants caused disquiet and unrest throughout the country. Most seriously, the queen – despite some false alarms – failed to conceive an heir. The fault may partly have been that of Philip II, who was physically absent from England between August 1555 and March 1557, and again after July 1557; but more probably Mary, 38 when she married, was already sterile through the cancer that was to kill her in November 1558.

Once again the question of succession was complicated by religion. Mary was survived by her half-sister Elizabeth who (although she had felt it politic to attend Mass after 1555) was clearly Protestant in her sympathies. She was, moreover, the daughter of Henry VIII's (to Catholics) adulterous and illegal liaison with Anne Boleyn. Mary had regarded her as illegitimate. So too did Mary Stuart, queen of Scotland, the legitimate Catholic grand-daughter of Henry VIII's sister, who conse-

PHILIPPVS
·REX·

...ICVNAS·MARICVS·A·LARA·FIERI·CVRAVIT
OPVS·REMIGY·DE·HALVT
ANNO·1·5·5·6·

The escutcheon on a bronze *cañón de batir* from the wreck of *La Trinidad Valencera*, cast by Remigy de Halut in 1556, carries the full arms of Philip II of Spain impaling those of Mary Tudor, Queen of England.

English silver shilling of Philip of Spain and Mary Tudor – the so-called 'kissing' coin.

quently regarded herself as the rightful heir to the English throne. Many Catholics agreed with her.

But Philip II was not one of them. Even though his authority in England ceased automatically with his wife's death, he still had hopes of keeping his late kingdom within the Habsburg orbit. Although several plots to

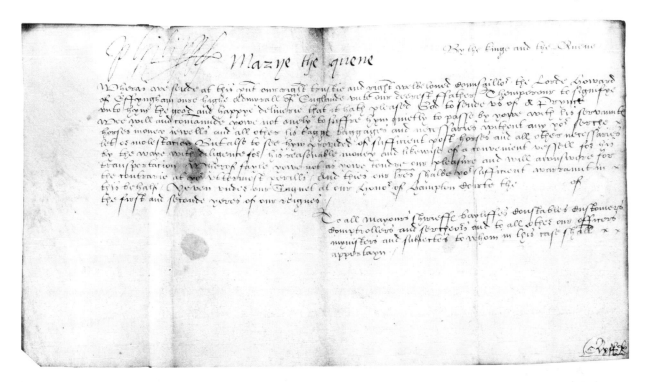

The signatures of Mary Tudor and her king-consort, Philip of Spain, validate a passport issued to Lord Howard of Effingham (father of the 1588 Lord Admiral) in May 1555.

overthrow Elizabeth in favour of Mary were submitted to him for approval, he always found reasons for rejecting them: the last thing he wanted was a French princess on the English throne.[1] So, instead, Philip afforded Elizabeth every assistance, even offering at one point to marry her. But he did so with great reluctance. In a confidential letter of 10 January 1559 to his ambassador at London, the count of Feria, the king explained that he had only made the offer 'to serve God and to stop that lady making the changes in religion that she has in mind.' He felt no personal enthusiasm for the match, and begged Feria to let him know as soon as possible Elizabeth's reaction to his proposal: 'Believe me', he explained to his ambassador, 'I shall be as happy with the one outcome as with the other!' Elizabeth Tudor rejected her lukewarm Habsburg suitor in February, and within a month the king of Spain had announced his engagement to the 13-year-old French princess Elizabeth de Valois.[2]

83

However Philip did nothing to prevent the queen of England from re-introducing Protestantism in 1559, or invading Scotland to support the Protestant faction there in 1560. In a sense he had no choice. Although he managed to make an advantageous peace with the French in April 1559, he failed to reach an agreement with the Ottoman Turks whose fleets continued to threaten Spain's Mediterranean possessions. By autumn 1559 the situation seemed so bad that, despite his growing anxiety about affairs in England and Scotland he left the Netherlands and returned to Spain, there to devote most of his energies and resources to organising the defence of the Mediterranean. England, so to speak, had been placed on the back burner.

But the king was under no illusion about the probable future of relations between himself and his former sister-in-law. 'It grieves me to see what is happening over there [in England],' he wrote in a secret dispatch to his ambassador at London shortly before leaving for Spain; 'and to be unable to take the steps to stop it that I want, while the steps I *can* take seem far milder than such a great evil deserves . . . But at the moment I lack the resources to do anything.' Later in this rather rambling letter Philip returned to the point in a more forceful and calculating way: 'The evil that is taking place in that kingdom has caused me the anger and confusion I have mentioned . . . but we must try to remedy it without involving me or any of my vassals in a declaration of war until we have enjoyed the benefits of peace [for a while].'[3] Philip II had thus decided upon confrontation with Elizabeth from an early point in his reign, however long that confrontation might, on the grounds of practical expediency, have to be delayed.

In the event, the 'benefits of peace' with England were enjoyed for ten years, but they did not long survive the arrival of the duke of Alba in Brussels in 1567. The amicable if distant relationship between Elizabeth and her former brother-in-law came to an end in 1569 as the result of two separate developments. The first concerned Spain's claim to a monopoly of all trade with, and colonisation in, the American continent. This stemmed from a decision of the Papacy in 1494, set out in the Treaty of Tordesillas, which in the aftermath of Columbus's voyage divided all lands discovered (and yet to be discovered) beyond Europe between the crowns of Castile and Portugal. Despite challenges by several French merchants this monopoly remained largely intact at the time of Philip II's accession. But in 1562 John Hawkins, a Plymouth merchant and shipowner who had been trading with the Canary islands (a Spanish possession off the Atlantic coast of Africa, and the staging post for all ships sailing from Spain to America), decided to set up a venture to take cloth and African slaves to the Indies, whence he would return to England with a cargo of hides and sugar. Although he made no application to the Spanish crown for a licence, Hawkins was careful to pay all the taxes due to Spain and to behave throughout, as he saw it, entirely within the law.

The voyage was a commercial success, and arrangements were made to repeat it on a larger scale in 1564–5. This time the queen invested in the venture, providing Hawkins with the 600-ton *Jesus of Lübeck*, an old warship from Henry VIII's navy which had been written off as unfit for front-line service. The second enterprise was as profitable as the first, but the Spanish colonists were now less open in their welcome of English merchants, for the officials in Madrid and Seville were anxious to exclude all interlopers and expressly forbade any trade with them. Hawkins was obliged to underpin his trade with the threat of force, though the threat was (he asserted) simply a charade which allowed the colonists to claim, in their own defence, that they had dealt with the English under duress.

On his third trans-Atlantic voyage, which began in 1567, Hawkins had ten ships, again including the *Jesus*, and another vessel belonging to the queen, the 300-ton *Minion*. At first things went well, and once more the Spanish colonists seemed glad to connive at the trade. As the fleet was preparing for its homeward passage, however, it was caught in a sudden storm in the Gulf of Mexico, and the crank and elderly *Jesus*, Hawkins' flagship, was severely damaged. Seeking temporary shelter, the battered ships limped to the small Spanish harbour of San Juan de Ulúa on the coast of Mexico. The sole function of this remote haven was to expedite the safe dispatch to Spain of the huge annual consignment of Mexican silver, and at other times it was virtually deserted. It was so on this occasion. No resistance was offered to the English fleet; after his customary courtesies Hawkins took the place over and set about repairing his ships and refreshing his men.

As fate would have it, however, two days later a fleet from Spain arrived off the port, under the command of Don Martín Enríquez, the newly appointed viceroy of Mexico. Hawkins protested his friendly mercantile intentions and, backed up by physical possession of the harbour and its defences, he obtained Don Martín's grudging agreement to complete his repairs and depart. But, as the Spanish fleet entered San Juan and moored alongside the English ships, each side covertly prepared for action.

To the viceroy, no agreement with a pirate, as (with some justification) he regarded Hawkins, was binding on a Spanish gentleman, and when he judged the moment right he launched a surprise attack on the English ships. A furious struggle ensued within the close confines of the harbour. The *Jesus*, after destroying two Spanish warships with her guns, was overwhelmed and captured, although Hawkins was able to transfer to the *Minion* with some of his men and escape, together with a 50-ton barque, the *Judith*, commanded by his young kinsman Francis Drake. Both ships eventually returned home, although only 15 men remained alive on board the *Minion* when she entered Plymouth Sound in January 1569. Elizabeth had thus lost to Spain one of her royal warships, with another damaged; while a good part of the proceeds of the voyage (from which the queen looked to receive a return on her investment) had been confiscated. Many of her subjects, too, had been killed, and others were in captivity.

News of this signal defeat arrived at a moment when relations with Spain were already strained for an entirely different reason. Philip II's determination to exclude 'interlopers' from the Americas extended to the French as well as the English and when, in 1564, news reached him that a party of French Huguenots had settled in Florida, he licensed a consortium of seafarers from northern Spain (including, as we have seen, Don Pedro de Valdés and Diego Flores de Valdés) to destroy them. In 1565 it was done: the French surrendered on the promise that their lives would be spared, and were promptly slaughtered.

The Huguenots, understandably incensed at this treachery, intensified their attacks on Spanish shipping in Atlantic waters. In November 1568 their privateers came upon five ships carrying some £40,000 in cash from Spain to the Netherlands. The French attacked, and the treasure-ships ran for shelter to England. It was explained to government officials that the money belonged to Philip II's bankers, and was being sent to Antwerp as part of a loan to pay the duke of Alba's army; nonetheless, the queen ordered the money to be taken to the Tower of London and the ships to be placed under arrest.

Elizabeth's intentions at this point are unclear, but it is unlikely that she expected her actions to be construed as more than tweaking the Spanish lion's tail. But the lion did not roar. He sprang. All English property in Spain and the Netherlands was seized; all trade was frozen. Elizabeth had failed to realise that her value to Philip II had suddenly diminished. The

Netherlands, following the defeat of Orange's invasion in 1568, were once again pacified, giving Philip a powerful but under-employed army with secure bases close to England. And reasons had now emerged which made the prospect of deposing Elizabeth in favour of her cousin Mary Stuart no longer seem so terrible.

The young queen of Scots had been brought up at the French court since the age of six; but when her husband, King Francis II, died at the end of 1560 – to the profound relief of both Elizabeth I and Philip II – Mary was encouraged to sail back to the land of her birth. But it was a land she scarcely knew, and a society in which she had no close kin or established power-base to sustain her. Even by 1566, after five years of not unsuccessful personal rule, her failure to build up a following in Scotland is reflected in the will she made on the eve of the birth of her son, the future James VI and I. Fewer than 60 beneficiaries were named – a small number for a monarch – and few of them were Scots: all the first seven, and ten of the first twelve, were her Guise relatives. Mary Stuart had remained, in essence, a French princess in exile.

But although the queen could not forget France, France soon forgot her. When, in 1567, a group of Scottish nobles rebelled against her, imprisoned her, and finally declared her deposed, she received support neither from the Scots, whom she had failed to cultivate, nor from the French, who were too busy fighting their religious wars to spare any help. So when, in May 1568, she escaped from her Scottish captors, she rode into England and threw herself upon the mercy of her only apparently friendly neighbour, Elizabeth. It was the biggest mistake of her life. In the eyes of many Catholics Mary was still the legitimate queen of England: Elizabeth simply could not afford to allow her either to take sanctuary with a sympathetic prince abroad, or to remain at large among the numerous and restless Catholic population of northern England. Her only course, irrespective of its morality or legality, was to imprison the queen of Scots.

The Catholic world was outraged. From the summer of 1568 onwards the Pope began to urge Philip II to invade England and depose Elizabeth in Mary's favour. When his overtures were rejected he turned in 1569 to the duke of Alba, going so far as to send him a golden sword, the symbol of a warrior of the faith, with its clear implication that Elizabeth should be struck down by force. But here too the Pope was courteously but firmly rebuffed; and so in February 1570 a new strategy was adopted. A bull excommunicating Elizabeth and absolving her subjects from obedience to her was promulgated, and Rome waited for some true-hearted Catholic, whoever he might be, to bring this decree into effect by violent action.

The first plot, known as the 'Ridolfi conspiracy', was hatched in the spring of 1571. It originated with the Spanish ambassador in England, and involved a group of Catholic peers led by the duke of Norfolk. Their plan was to instigate a Catholic rebellion, assassinate Elizabeth, and proclaim Mary. The coup was to be supported by a simultaneous invasion by Philip II's forces under Martín de Bertendona, who would lead a small fleet of warships from Spain into the North Sea and gain control of the seaway between England and the Netherlands. Across these safe waters the duke of Alba would then send a strike-force of 10,000 picked men from the Army of Flanders to land in England and secure Mary's throne.[4]

It was not a bad plan, and it clearly influenced the strategy finally adopted in 1588. By August 1571 everything was in place. But then a courier from the main conspirator, the Florentine banker Roberto Ridolfi, fell into Elizabeth's hands. Under torture he revealed all: the complicity of Norfolk, of the Spanish ambassador, and of Mary. Next, the servants of those implicated were brought in for rigorous interrogation. Faced with the full apparatus – legal and physical – of enquiry by torment Mary's confidant, the bishop of Ross, was particularly eloquent, and asserted that not only had Mary helped to murder her second husband, Lord Henry Darnley, but she had also poisoned her first, Francis II, and was not a fit wife for any man. 'Lord!' exclaimed his interrogator, 'What a people! What a queen!'.

Philip II, however, remained undeterred. Even after the confessions of the English conspirators had become public knowledge, he continued to urge the reluctant Alba to send his army to England. All the duke's objections that it was doomed, or that it was too late, were overborne by a sort of spiritual blackmail: the king now claimed to possess a divine mandate with respect to England. It was a belief he clung to for the rest of his life.

'I am so keen to achieve the consummation of this enterprise [he wrote to Alba in September 1571], I am so attached to it in my heart, and I am so convinced that God our saviour must embrace it as his own cause, that I cannot be dissuaded from putting it into operation'.

Philip only cancelled the project in November.[5]

In a way, the king's dogged insistence – so similar to his conduct in 1588 – was justified. The international situation in 1571 was uniquely favourable to an invasion of England. The Netherlands, from which the assault force was to sail, remained obedient and free of dissidents; France, although again at peace, was severely weakened by her recent civil wars; the Turks seemed fully occupied in the conquest of Cyprus. In October 1571 their fleet was resoundingly defeated by the combined forces of Spain, Venice, and the Papacy at Lepanto. But the opportunity was short-lived. With the Dutch revolt and the Turkish counter-offensive, both of which began in earnest in 1572, Philip II was once more deprived of the resources with which to assault Elizabeth.

It was now too late, however, to return to the harmony of the 1560s. The Ridolfi conspiracy – far more than Alba's pay-ships or the 'perfidy' of San Juan de Ulúa – had created a fatal rift between Elizabeth and her erstwhile suitor. She may not have been able to read (as we can) the minutes of the Spanish Council of State, or the ciphered letters of the king ordering his forces in the Netherlands to invade; but the intelligence reports she received left her in no doubt that Philip II had tried to encompass her death and destroy her kingdom. As far as she was concerned, Spain could never again be trusted, and her policy towards Philip was now transformed. She henceforth openly welcomed and protected refugees from his 'tyranny' – especially if they came from the Netherlands, for she was anxious to ensure that the Spanish regime in Brussels would never again be strong enough to launch an invasion against her. From time to time after 1572, therefore, military and financial aid was sent to keep the rebel cause alive.

At the same time the queen now tolerated – and sometimes even directly supported – privateering expeditions against Spanish interests. Hawkins and Drake, still smarting from their humiliation at San Juan de Ulúa, needed little encouragement. Between 1572 and 1577 there were eleven important English expeditions to Spanish America, starting with a daring joint exploit by Francis Drake and his Devon men, some French Huguenots from Le Havre, and a group of black slaves from Panama who had rebelled against their Spanish masters. Between them they seized a major treasure convoy near Nombre de Dios and raised the terrifying spectre for the Spaniards of white piracy allied with black rebellion. The series of raids culminated in the remarkable voyage of Drake through the straits of Magellan and into the Pacific, there to harry Spanish colonies and shipping at will. The voyage, which turned into the first English circumnavigation of the globe, came to its triumphant end in September 1580:

Drake brought back 100 tons of Spanish silver, and 100 pounds of gold, and was knighted by the queen for his labours. His flagship, the *Golden Hind*, was put on public display at Deptford as a national monument to England's achievements.

Philip II was incensed by the stream of reports that reached him concerning Drake's audacity; but for the moment England was left unpunished because, even though a temporary truce was arranged with the Turks in 1577, the situation in the Netherlands continued to tie down his resources. Moreover, a successful effort against England would demand extensive maritime forces. Such forces were notoriously difficult to raise, and even harder to maintain. Although in 1574 a fleet of 223 vessels (including 33 fighting ships and 34 Baltic hulks) had mustered at Santander, under the command of the redoubtable Pedro Menéndez, the conqueror of Florida, it never sailed because plague struck down the crews, delay decimated both the provisions and the ships, and no replacements could be found. And the Menéndez fleet had never been designed to attack England; its target was the Dutch rebel citadel of Flushing. But here, too, it failed. In September its commander died and eventually only 38 vessels (many of them small) were fit to set sail for Dunkirk. Even then, five of the ships were wrecked on the sandbanks off the Flemish coast, and three more were driven back to Spain by storms. Perhaps Philip then recalled, as he brooded over this costly reverse, the advice of his father, Charles V, concerning naval operations: 'Fleets at sea,' the old emperor had reminded his son as he groomed him for kingship, 'are as uncertain as the waves that bear them.'

But in spite of this, in 1580 Philip II did send another fleet against Elizabeth, albeit clandestinely. A year earlier Irish exiles, with papal support, had returned home to instigate a general rebellion. The activists landed at Smerwick, a wide and remote natural harbour close to the westernmost tip of Ireland, and spent the winter in a temporary fortification (of which the remains can still be seen) known as the *Castello del Oro*, the Golden Fort. From there they launched an appeal to the Catholic powers of Europe for reinforcement. In September 1580 some 800 volunteers raised in Italy and Spain under papal aegis were landed at Smerwick by a flotilla commanded by Juan Martínez de Recalde, who went on to survey the coasts of south-west Ireland before returning to Spain. Meanwhile the expeditionary force improved the defences at *Castello del Oro* and continued to await the general uprising. But it never came. Instead, a small but powerful English naval squadron under Sir William Winter sailed into the bay and attacked the Hispano-Papal position which was vulnerably perched, like a stranded warship, on a small peninsula jutting into the bay.

A contemporary map, sketched on the spot by one of the English participants, graphically shows Winter's ships in action. They include some of the vessels which, eight years later, would encounter the Armada: *Revenge*, *Swiftsure*, *Aid*, *Tiger*, and *Achates*. And already there is evidence of the mobile gunnery tactics which the English would employ to such good effect in 1588. The big ships are standing off in deep water, unanchored but with sails furled, bombarding the fort with their bow chasers. The three smaller vessels, however, are taking advantage of their shallow draught to run under full sail towards the enemy, firing as they go, and then coming about at the last possible moment to present first their broadsides and then their stern guns at close range. And the simple device which made these quick-firing tactics possible is also visible, with unequivocal clarity, in a detail on the map: guns from the fleet are being landed to invest the fort from the landward side and their carriages, tiny but unmistakable, are all naval-issue mountings of the efficient four-truck design.[6]

A few days later Winter's force was joined by troops under the queen's lieutenant in Ireland, Lord Deputy Grey, assisted by Sir Walter Raleigh and others. The *Castello del Oro* was doomed: after three days' bombardment its defenders surrendered on being promised fair terms. All but fifteen of them were massacred in cold blood.

But if Philip II and his lieutenants had failed in the Netherlands and in Ireland, in compensation they triumphantly conquered Portugal and gained her extensive overseas possessions, so creating an empire upon which the sun never set. The last legitimate male in the direct line of the Portuguese royal house died in January 1580, leaving the king of Spain, whose mother had been a Portuguese princess, as next-of-kin. There were other claimants, but none could match Philip II's power. The first phase of the conquest was the invasion of the Algarve in July by a small army commanded by the duke of Medina Sidonia, the most powerful Spanish grandee in neighbouring Andalusia. It was supported by a fleet of 87 galleys and 30 ships commanded by the marquis of Santa Cruz, a veteran of Lepanto and many other galley encounters, who worked his way along the coast from Cadiz to the Tagus. There Santa Cruz joined up with Philip

Lisbon and its harbour during the successful Spanish assault in 1580.

II's main invasion army, which had marched through the heart of Portugal to meet him, led (for the last time) by the ageing duke of Alba. In a brilliant combined operation the two commanders captured Lisbon on 25 August. Within two months the entire country was under Spanish control.

But there was also a new empire in Africa, Asia, and Brazil to secure. In 1581 the king (now resident in Lisbon) decided, for the first time since the Florida expedition in 1565, to reassert his control over the Atlantic. And it was a Floridan veteran, Diego Flores de Valdés, who was dispatched with a fleet of 20 vessels to clear the Atlantic coasts of South America of all intruders and to establish a fortress at the Straits of Magellan to prevent any repetition of Drake's progress into the Pacific. But long before its ill-fated garrison arrived, another challenge to Philip II's power had developed much closer to home.

CHAPTER 5

Cold war, 1581–85

Amid all the excitement of the Portuguese conquest an important enemy of Philip II had been allowed to escape: Dom António, prior of Crato, an illegitimate scion of the ancient Portuguese royal family. Before the Spanish annexation Dom António had been one of the principal ornaments of the court at Lisbon. One of the richest men in the kingdom (his priory of Crato alone yielded 120,000 ducats a year), and fluent in Latin and several other languages, the 50-year-old prior was a charismatic figure who found many supporters for his claim to be the next lawful king of Portugal. In 1580 he had organised the defence of Lisbon and the opposition of Oporto to the Spaniards; in 1581 he remained in northern Portugal, directing a resistance movement until a large manhunt (coordinated by the duke of Medina Sidonia) forced him to flee abroad. But he still had friends. Above all, his supporters had secured control of eight of the nine main islands of the Azores archipelago, lying 1,000 miles west of Lisbon. Only the largest , São Miguel, recognised the authority of Philip II and when, in the summer of 1581, a small expeditionary force under Don Pedro de Valdés was sent to attack Terceira island, the main opposition stronghold, it failed ignominiously – largely through the impetuous carelessness of Valdés. Dom António, who was in France, now set about gaining foreign assistance for a full-scale invasion of the Azores, which would then serve him as a springboard for the reconquest of Portugal. To Elizabeth of England he promised a fort in west Africa in return for support; to Henry III of France he offered Madeira, Guinea, and Brazil.

In the event, Elizabeth was persuaded to remain neutral by the threats of Philip II's ambassador, Don Bernadino de Mendoza, who indicated that open English aid for Dom António would be regarded by Spain as a declaration of war. Although the queen threatened that 'if he spoke to her again like that, she would put him in a place from which he could not speak at all', and although she allowed Dom António (known in most diplomatic sources as 'the Pretender'), to issue letters of marque to several of her privateering merchants, she felt obliged to banish him from her court. So he went to France, where 11 English privateeers (including 2 ships owned by Drake) joined him and sailed under his flag to the Azores in the summer of 1582. But most of the Pretender's fleet of 58 vessels and 6,000 men came from France, collected and commanded by a former colonel of the French guards, Filippo Strozzi.

In order to dislodge Dom António's forces from the Azores it was now clearly necessary for Philip II to mount a major amphibious operation. There was nothing intrinsically novel about this. His armed forces, and those of his father, had done it many times before – against Tunis in 1535 and 1573, against Algiers (a spectacular failure) in 1541, to relieve Malta in 1565, and to capture Lisbon in 1580. Such operations were extremely specialised: they were complex affairs involving large fleets of galleys, often working in conjunction with land forces. Efficient logistics, precision fleet drills, and the fine balancing of complex and subtle variables were the essential preliminaries to a successful outcome. In these matters Spanish galley commanders, of whom the most outstanding in the 1580s was Don Álvaro de Bazán, marquis of Santa Cruz, held a formidable and well-deserved reputation.

But such specialised techniques of maritime warfare were not often applied beyond the Pillars of Hercules, where galleys seldom ventured and where, by the late sixteenth century, the artillery-carrying sailing warship reigned virtually supreme. Until 1580 Spain did not possess an effective sailing navy in the Atlantic. Her only warships under sail were the relatively lightly armed escort galleons attached to the convoys of merchantmen that sailed annually between Spain and America and these, although extremely effective in their assigned role, were no match for heavy battleships of the type now developing in Northern Europe, especially England. The 12 galleons maintained by the Portuguese crown, however, were very different. They were powerfully built and powerfully gunned and, except for one which sank, they were captured intact by Santa Cruz and his galleys at the fall of Lisbon.

With them Santa Cruz had captured a superb naval base. The narrow approach at the mouth of the Tagus, already defended with forts, was strengthened with heavy artillery to create, in the wide roadstead beyond, a safe and sheltered haven for the largest fleet. No other port on the

Atlantic seaboard of the Iberian peninsula could offer this combination of almost unlimited capacity with total security both from enemies and from the weather. Lisbon would provide an ideal springboard should it ever prove necessary or desirable to mount an invasion of France, the Netherlands, or England, and in 1582 it offered the perfect base from which to intercept Dom António's fleet and mount an operation to recover the Azores.

Late in July Santa Cruz's fleet of 60 ships and 8,000 men made contact with Strozzi's ships off the island of São Miguel. After several days of sparring for position the two sides clashed in a close-range contest of attrition. Spanish tactics were simple: individual captains, having singled out an enemy ship, delivered a short-range broadside before grappling and boarding. Santa Cruz in his flagship *San Martín* sought out Strozzi's ship amid the smoke and chaos and, having found her, pounded her with gunfire until she was close to sinking. At the close, the Pretender's fleet had lost 10 ships sunk or captured, and well over 1,000 men – including Strozzi, who died of his wounds shortly after his ship was captured, and was peremptorily thrown over the side by Santa Cruz. Five days later most of the remaining prisoners were summarily executed.

But some thought that Strozzi had been unlucky to lose. His ships had been nimbler than those of Santa Cruz, and, like Hawkins at San Juan de Ulúa, they had used their artillery well, operating in mutually supporting groups of four 'to charge, and assail each of them one of the great vessels of the enemy'. This they did with considerable effect. When the galleon *San Mateo* dropped out of formation Strozzi's ships surrounded it, battered it with their artillery, and finally boarded it. Several other vessels in Santa Cruz's fleet, including his own flagship, were also severely damaged – even Philip II's commemorative mural in the Escorial's Hall of Battles depicts extensive shot damage on the Spanish side. The *San Martín* was barely able to tow the captured enemy flagship back to port.

All the same, Santa Cruz had won a great victory, and jubilation at his triumphant return seems to have gripped the whole of Spain. The French ambassador at Philip II's court sourly reported that some Spaniards went so far as to claim that 'even Christ was no longer safe in Paradise, for the marquis might go there to bring him back and crucify him all over again.' Later some of this pride and passion was turned against the vanquished: according to the same ambassador, in October 1582, the Spaniards had taken to spitting in the faces of any Frenchmen they happened to meet in the street.[1] And yet, for all that, Terceira remained in the Pretender's hands, and in the spring of 1583 800 fresh French troops arrived to reinforce the island.

But Santa Cruz now had total command of the sea, and knew what was needed to dislodge them. Secure within his Lisbon base he prepared an amphibious invasion of overwhelming force: 15,372 men and 98 ships, including 31 big merchantmen converted as troop transports, small vessels and landing craft, five fighting galleons, 12 galleys, and 2 galleasses. This time the aim was not to fight a fleet but to land an army: the task force could defend itself if necessary, but its primary role was to put troops, together with their supporting equipment and supplies, on a selected beach-head, and then to back them up until the military objectives had been gained.

An important element in the plan was surprise. The Terceirans expected the Spaniards to land at the harbours of Angra and Peggia, and had disposed their forces accordingly. On the basis of local information and personal reconnaissance, however, Santa Cruz decided to deliver his main thrust at Mole, a beach ten miles from Angra defended only by light earthworks occupied by infantry with some artillery support. Santa Cruz's own report of the landings has a strikingly modern ring:

'The flag galley began to batter and dismount the enemy artillery and the rest of the galleys did likewise . . . the landing craft ran aground and placed soldiers on the flanks of the fortifications, and along the trenches, although with much difficulty and working under the pressure of the furious artillery, arquebus, and musket fire of the enemy. The soldiers mounting the trenches in several places came under heavy small-arms fire, but finally won the forts and trenches'.

Dom António and a handful of supporters were lucky to escape with their lives.

The Atlantic, it now appeared, was no longer a barrier to Spain's military machine. She was now a truly oceanic power; her armies, carried by sea, could strike with surgical precision at any point on her enemies' coasts. All that was needed was money, and a fleet. A bowl commemorating the Terceira landings (found among the wreckage of one of the 1588 Armada's ships, and almost certainly belonging to an officer who had taken part in the 1583 operation) shows Spain's warrior patron saint, Santiago, with new attributes. He is depicted, as before, mounted on a charger, his cloak flowing in the wind and his sword-arm raised to strike down his foes. But these foes are no longer cowering infidels. They are the swirling waves of the Ocean Sea itself, waves now conquered along with the human enemies who sought refuge among them.

Beyond the swirling waves, and behind the defeated enemies, lay England. And, there, the rising tide of Spanish victory in 1583, with the conquest of Terceira in the south and of the Flemish coast in the north, made grim news; and the events of 1584, with the deaths of Anjou and Orange, and the fall of Ghent and Bruges, foreshadowed worse prospects. The likelihood of a full Spanish reconquest of the Netherlands, restoring the situation of 1570 and 1571 (and thus the chance of repeating the Ridolfi strategy) had to be faced. Yet England now possessed few allies. Dom António was a spent force, and his cause in Portugal (at least temporarily) was lost. The Netherlands, leaderless, seemed likely to go the same way.

Worse still, France clearly stood on the brink of civil wars even more terrible than those she had already endured. Until 1584, the conflict had pitted a Protestant minority, anxious to gain some official guarantees of toleration, against the Catholic government and its supporters. But the death of the duke of Anjou, heir apparent to the French throne as well as elected ruler of the Netherlands, changed all that. King Henry III was the last of his line. His heir presumptive was Henry of Navarre, leader of the Protestant party. As such he was totally unacceptable to the Catholic faction led by Henry duke of Guise, Mary Stuart's cousin. Rather than see Navarre succeed to the throne the Catholics formed a paramilitary organisation, known as 'the League' and dominated by Guise. Guise then entered into an alliance with the king of Spain. After three months of talks, the treaty of Joinville was signed on 31 December 1584, pledging mutual assistance for the Catholic cause in France and the Netherlands, recognising the Cardinal de Bourbon (an ally of Guise) as heir to Henry III, and promising a Spanish subsidy to the League of £125,000 a year.

Even before news of the treaty of Joinville leaked out in March 1585, it was clear that the authority of the French government was in rapid decline, and that the prospect of Spanish success in the Netherlands was thereby increased. Many in England believed that unless the queen acted at once to halt the rising tide of Catholic success it would be too late. In the words of Secretary Walsingham: 'the peril would be so great in case Spain should possess the said countries as, whether France concurs in the action or not, yet doth it behove her Majesty to enter into some course for their defence.'[2]

97

But how could this be done without precipitating full-scale Spanish retaliation? In October 1584 Elizabeth's leading councillors held a series of extended discussions on what England should do to stem the tide of Spanish victory. Everyone present seems to have accepted as inevitable that Spain would try, sooner or later, to make another attempt to topple the Tudor regime. But here unanimity ended. One group of councillors argued that the best response to this threat was to concentrate on domestic defence: strengthening the fleet, fortifying the coasts, organising supporters of the regime to fight more effectively in their own defence – but offering no offence to Spain abroad. 'So would England become impregnable,' they concluded, 'and she on every side be secure at home and a terror to her enemies.' The other councillors, however, who formed the clear majority, argued that this was not enough. If Philip II were to reconquer the whole Netherlands, they stressed, his power would be 'so formidable to all the rest of Christendom as that Her Majesty shall no wise be able with her own power nor with the aid of any other, neither by sea nor land, to withstand his attempts'.

In such an eventuality Elizabeth would become a prey to Philip's 'insatiable malice, which is most terrible to be thought of, but most miserable to suffer'. If 'Little England' was to survive, action to halt Spain's reconquest of the Netherlands had to be taken sooner, while at least one committed continental ally – the Dutch Republic – remained, rather than later, when England would have to stand and fight alone.[3]

It was a dilemma curiously similar to that which faced the British government in the later 1930s. But while it is possible to trace the steps from the Munich agreement of September 1938 to the Ultimatum of September 1939 through surviving Cabinet and Foreign Office papers there are few documents to illuminate the process whereby Elizabeth Tudor and her ministers led their country into open war against Spain in the autumn of 1584.

The central difficulty lies in the quixotic personality of the queen herself: vain, secretive and able, Elizabeth believed that she was her own best mentor, and over the years she had learned how to play off her various advisers in order to leave herself the greatest freedom of manoeuvre. Her councillors were a formidable body of men, almost entirely united in outlook and closely linked by a network of intermarriage and family connection (they were practically all cousins): even so they usually failed to impose their policies upon an unwilling queen. She rarely attended council meetings, and instead tended to seek the opinions of each councillor individually and then to 'leak' them to the rest (a practice surprisingly similar to Philip II's style of government). And, if the council nevertheless persisted in pushing a policy of which she disapproved, Elizabeth would stage a series of tantrums until the matter was dropped.

But there was one chink in the queen's armour, one path around her formidable temper: her highly emotional reaction to the discovery of plots aimed against her. Evidence of any attempt (especially one conceived abroad) to murder her and destroy her regime could make the queen throw caution to the winds. And it was the discovery of a series of international conspiracies, coinciding with the attempts on William of Orange's life, which appears to have secured Elizabeth's support for those of her councillors who favoured an open war with Spain.

A highly efficient secret service was operating in England during the 1580s, and in 1582 a bizarre stroke of fortune gave its chief, Secretary Walsingham, the breakthrough he needed. Early that summer a stranger in 'an old gray cloak' was apprehended on the Northumbrian fells close to the Scottish border by an English patrol: he refused to give his name (it was later suggested that he might have been a Jesuit), and eventually bribed his way clear, but not before he had been relieved of a bag containing his few possessions. It was forwarded to the Warden of the Marches, Sir John Forster, at Alnwick, who found in it a breviary, dental instruments, and a mirror. Hidden in a secret compartment in the back of the mirror was a coded message, which Forster duly dispatched to Walsingham. Walsingham's cryptographers got to work and, from the information they found, they eventually penetrated Mary Stuart's secret pipe-line to France. From then on, Elizabeth was privy to most of her captive rival's plots.

Sir Francis Walsingham, secretary of state and head of Elizabeth's secret service. Probably by John de Critz the Elder, c. 1585.

The first, late in 1583, was a conspiracy involving the Spanish Ambassador in London, Don Bernadino de Mendoza. Men were arrested and tortured, and some confessed. There were executions. Mary was placed under closer guard, and in January 1584 Ambassador Mendoza was ignominiously expelled. The following September a Jesuit priest travelling from Flanders to Scotland was found to possess a paper which revealed the existence of yet another plot to overthrow Elizabeth and replace her with Mary. Again, the conspirators were rounded up, tortured until they admitted the complicity of Mary and Philip II, and then executed. If their barbarous fate was meant to deter others, it failed. In February 1585 yet another scheme to assassinate Elizabeth was discovered, this time sponsored by the Pope. It was the third foiled plot against the queen's life in two years.

Events abroad were also getting out of hand. In March 1585 the Catholic League in France at last mobilised an army and demanded that Henry III join them in extirpating Protestantism from France. In July he reluctantly did so: by the treaty of Nemours, Henry ceded a number of important towns to the League's control and agreed to join them in making war on Henry of Navarre. The king of France had become, at least for the time being, the catspaw of the king of Spain's allies. Meanwhile, in the Low Countries, Parma tightened his blockade of Antwerp.

Elizabeth and her council continued to wonder what they should do next. In March 1585, in the light of recent developments, it was again argued by many councillors that England's security required a preemptive strike against Spain before Spain was in a position to overwhelm England. Underhand aid to the Dutch and a little Caribbean piracy were clearly no longer enough: full-scale military and naval action would be required if Spain was to be stopped. Already Dutch envoys were in London, offering to accept Elizabeth as their sovereign in return for military support in their struggle against Spain. The Privy Council fully recognised that outright assistance to the Dutch would be regarded by Philip as a *casus belli*, and would inevitably result in a Spanish attack on either England or Ireland. Therefore they hesitated. Nevertheless, a number of less controversial actions could be taken. First, Scotland, through its pliable and ambitious young king, was more tightly bound to Elizabeth's side: a draft alliance treaty was agreed in June 1585 and signed the following July. Second, Dom António was invited to return to England and reside at court. Finally, Sir Richard Grenville was given permission to sail with a small flotilla to found an English colony at Roanoke in North America. But the queen's advisers as yet dared not do more. Burghley believed that open aid for the Netherlands would lead England inexorably to an unnecessary war, condemned abroad and unwelcome at home.[4]

But then, out of the blue, Philip II himself offered the justification that Elizabeth's councillors had sought in vain. On 19 May 1585 he issued a decree confiscating all English goods and shipping in Iberian harbours which, he hoped, would frighten Elizabeth into breaking off her negotiations with the Dutch and ending her support for privateering at Iberian expense. It provoked exactly the reverse.

William Cecil, Lord Burghley – Elizabeth's chief minister of state. Attributed to Marcus Gheeraerts the Younger, after 1585.

Almost immediately a small squadron under Sir Walter Raleigh's brother attacked the Iberian fishing fleet off Newfoundland, capturing many boats and bringing 600 mariners back to imprisonment in England. The queen herself authorised the issue of letters of marque to any of her subjects who could claim to have suffered loss through the embargo, and licensed them to recover those losses by plundering Spanish shipping. But this was only a beginning: shortly afterwards she decided upon two major acts of aggression that could only lead to open war with Spain.

On 20 August Elizabeth concluded a formal treaty of alliance with Philip II's Dutch rebels: by the treaty of Nonsuch (named after the now lost Tudor palace) England agreed to provide 1,000 cavalry and 6,350 infantry to fight against Spain in the Netherlands and, in addition, to provide subsidies worth £126,000 per year (an estimated one-quarter of the war's total cost). England would also provide a governor-general, to be advised by a new council of state made up of English and Netherlanders, who would co-ordinate government and direct the war. In return, the Netherlanders promised to surrender the ports of Flushing, Brill, and Ostend to England, as sureties until the queen's expenses were repaid after the war. The treaty came too late to save Antwerp, which surrendered to the Army of Flanders on 17 August. But within a month (as the prince of Parma was quick to notice) 4,100 English troops were at Flushing, and by December the figure had risen to 8,000. Finally, just before Christmas 1585, the new governor-general appointed by Elizabeth arrived: her favourite and confidant, Robert Dudley, earl of Leicester.

While these events had been taking place the queen issued an even more direct challenge to Philip II. Since August 1584 Sir Francis Drake had been preparing another small expedition to sail once more into the Pacific in search of Portuguese spices and Spanish silver. Now it was increased to 25 ships, with eight pinnaces and 1,900 men – 1,200 of them soldiers. The commanders included veterans of Drake's circumnavigation and of the Azores battles, as well as several men prominent at court – Christopher Carleill (Walsingham's step-son), Francis Knollys (Leicester's brother-in-law) and, for a time, Sir Philip Sydney. But the main connection between the fleet and the Court lay in the ships: two of them were from the queen's navy, while four others belonged to John Hawkins, two to Leicester, and one each to Lord Shrewsbury, Lord Admiral Howard, and Sir William Winter. They all sailed from Plymouth on 24 September. Early in October they attacked Vigo and Bayona; in mid-November they took and sacked

Santiago in the Cape Verde Isles; and in late December they captured and burnt Santo Domingo, the capital of Spain's oldest Caribbean possession, Hispaniola.

At much the same time Sir Walter Raleigh, England's leading advocate of colonising North America, argued that:

'the way to humble the Spanish greatness is not by pinching and pricking him in the Low Countries, which only emptied his veins of such blood as was quickly refilled; but the way to make it a cripple for ever is by cutting off the Spanish sinews of war – his money from the West Indies.'

Sending Drake with royal warships to harry the Caribbean, and dispatching Leicester with an army to rule the Netherlands, however, was no 'pinching and pricking': as even Burghley admitted, it meant that England was about 'to sustain a greater war than ever in any memory of man it hath done.' Although Elizabeth issued a justification for her actions in several languages, claiming that she was merely retaliating against Philip's support for plots directed against her, and against his embargo on English shipping, few observers were convinced.[5] Everyone could see that England had challenged Spain to unconditional war. The question was no longer whether Spain would attack, but when and how that attack would take place.

CHAPTER 6

The Grand Design and its architect

> Why, man, he doth bestride the narrow world
> Like a Colossus, and we petty men
> Walk under his huge legs . . .

Shakespeare's lines on Julius Caesar could well have applied to the king of Spain, for after 1580 he governed one fifth of the land of western Europe and one quarter of its population. His dominions around the globe from the Philippines, Mexico and Peru, through the Iberian and Italian peninsulas, to the Portuguese outposts in Mozambique, Ceylon, Malacca and Macao, dwarfed those of the Roman empire at its apogee. Beneath his sceptre lay the bustling cities of Antwerp, Naples, Seville and Mexico, and subjects as diverse as the learned Benito Arias Montano, the painter El Greco, and the saint and mystic Teresa of Ávila. And that sceptre was charged with absolute power: King Philip, as one of his courtiers irreverently observed, was like Christ, for he could make and break men as if they were clay.

But who was the man at the hub of such immense power? Although the surviving collection of Philip II's writings is greater by far than that of any other early modern statesman, his personality remains elusive. As Robert Watson, Principal of St Andrews University, wrote in his *History of the reign of Philip II* in 1777: 'No character was ever drawn by different historians in more opposite colours than that of Philip.' But if we turn to the opinions of those living in the years before the Armada there is more unanimity. The famous portrait of the king by Alonso Sánchez Coello, painted in 1583, shows an austere face, with thin hair and neat beard almost entirely white, but steel-grey eyes that are clear and stern. He is dressed simply in black, his only decoration the Order of the Golden Fleece. In his hands he holds a rosary: it is as if the painter has surprised the king in a private moment, at prayer.

The king almost always dressed in plain black: he felt uncomfortable in anything else. He hated wearing coronation robes when he went to Portugal to be crowned (or so he wrote to his teenage daughters): and, although his household accounts show that he purchased a new suit of clothes every month, it was always made in the same simple style and the same plain colour. Even when he attended the wedding of his daughter Catalina to the duke of Savoy in 1585, everyone was richly attired 'except the king, who looked very ordinary, dressed in black just like the citizens'. Philip ate the same food as his subjects and relished the same enjoyments. He often liked to show it. In Valencia some fishermen offered him their day's catch, as an act of homage, and the royal party went out onto the balcony of the house in which they were staying and ate their supper in public, so everyone could see how much they enjoyed the local fish. In Zaragoza, the king happened to be walking through the streets when he met a religious procession coming the other way. At once he stepped back into the crowd and fell to his knees, bareheaded, and remained there in the midst of his subjects in prayer and reverence.

The Escorial under construction in 1576.

Perhaps this desire to blend with the rest of humanity, to avoid being identified as the man with supreme power and supreme responsibility, is significant. It certainly contrasts sharply with the pomp and ostentation with which Elizabeth Tudor sought to project herself as different from other humans. But the contrast is not surprising. Elizabeth had been brought up in the unstable household of Henry VIII and his wives (of whom no less than four came and went after Elizabeth's mother had been executed). As a young girl she had been proclaimed a bastard, and she spent part of her half-sister's reign under house arrest. Philip, by contrast, had from birth been groomed for government with meticulous care. In 1543, at the age of 16, he became regent for his father in Spain, an office he discharged intermittently over the next decade, with considerable success. In 1554 he was created king of Naples, shortly before becoming king consort of England; and gradually most of his father's lands fell under his sway. But Charles V set no ordinary standards for his son to emulate. A successful statesman and soldier, an experienced traveller fluent in five languages, a master of the regal gesture and apposite phrase, a natural leader of men: it was a hard act to follow, and Philip's long years of apprenticeship in the art of government only served to heighten his awareness of the elusiveness of success and the disgrace of failure.

The king had few other mentors within his family on whom he could rely absolutely for advice. His two surviving aunts, his second wife (Mary Tudor) and his father all died in 1558; of his siblings, one sister lived in Vienna and the other was something of a recluse; his half-brother, Don John of Austria, the fruit of a brief affair between the ageing Charles V and a young girl in Regensburg, was only 11 when his father died; and his elder half-sister (also illegitimate) lived all her life in the Netherlands and Italy, never visiting Spain. It is true that Philip married Elizabeth de Valois in 1560, but she died in childbirth in 1568 aged only 22. In 1570 he made his fourth and last marriage, to his niece Anne of Austria, but she too died in childbirth ten years later, when she was only 31. Of his children, the eldest, Don Carlos, died insane in 1568, and his other sons all died young except for the future Philip III, born in 1578. Of his two daughters who survived childhood, Catalina left for Italy in 1585 and never saw her father again, leaving her sister Isabella (born in 1566) as the king's only family intimate.

Philip II seems to have filled the gap between these great expectations and his stunted family life with religion. There can be no doubt about his deep personal piety. A large section of his great library at the Escorial – which eventually numbered more than 14,000 volumes – was devoted to religious works, and the notes kept by his librarian show that these items were in frequent use (one evening in 1572, for example, he called for a Concordance to the Bible, because he wanted to check a reference before going to bed). Of the 42 books the king kept in a bedside bookcase, all but one (a serious historical tome) concerned theology. He attended Mass daily, heard a sermon at least once a week, and confessed and received Communion four times a year. He went into retreat each Lent, as well as at times of severe mental strain (for instance, after the death of his wife Elizabeth de Valois). The monks at the Escorial noticed that on occasion, when he was at prayer or in contemplation, tears would roll down the king's cheeks; and deeply religious people – including St Ignatius Loyola and St Teresa of Ávila – detected in the king a piety of profound and unusual intensity.

Some found it obsessive. From the 1560s onwards, Philip's correspondence with churchmen began to deal increasingly with relics, above all with the recovery of relics from Protestant countries and their safe dispatch to Spain. By the end of the reign the relic-keeper at the Escorial, Friar José de Sigüenza, could boast that 'We only know of three saints of whom we do not have some part or other here', and his inventory enumerated a grand total of 7,422 items, including 12 entire bodies, 144 heads and 306 complete limbs. Now for a Catholic, one relic is a sign of admirable devotion, and a few relics may pass as exemplary piety; but 7,422 suggests unbridled obsession. And, indeed, from 1587 onwards the king had 'his' relics brought out for adoration with meticulous regularity. Before long he was insisting that all of them, displayed on different altars in the Basilica at the Escorial, should be placed on view at the same time. 'The king went up there, sometimes alone and sometimes accompanied by his children' to see them, according to Sigüenza. 'When he arrived, the king asked me many times to show him this or that relic; and, when I took them in my hands, before I could cover them with a cloth or veil, the most pious king bent down and, having removed his hat or bonnet, kissed them in my hand'. And, 'because some of them were so small,' the friar added, with an understandable shudder, 'I too received a thousand kisses.'[1]

With such godliness in his heart and mind, it is not surprising to find that Philip II was unshakably convinced that he and his government enjoyed divine favour – in short, that God was on his side. In 1583, when news of the conquest of Terceira arrived, the king's personal secretary, Mateo Vázquez reflected that 'The care, zeal and resources with which Your Majesty attends to matters affecting the service of Our Lord ensures that He looks after those affecting Your Majesty. To have the sea under our control is most important . . . but more important still is the promise of more fortunate successes which we may expect from God's hand in return for the care with which Your Majesty has sought the honour of God and of His religion'.[2]

The king enthusiastically agreed. And accordingly, time and again his policies were pressed upon unwilling subordinates, or upon the taxpayers, on the grounds that the king's work was God's work. We have already seen spiritual blackmail of a high order being used against the duke of Alba in 1571 concerning the invasion of England; and we find the same formula in action frequently during the Armada campaign. When Parma objected to the king's plan for launching the invasion of England in the winter of 1587, Philip blandly replied (as he had already told Santa Cruz):

'We are quite aware of the risk that is incurred by sending a major fleet in winter through the Channel without a safe harbour, but . . . since it is all for His cause, God will send good weather'.[3]

When, somewhat later, Medina Sidonia tried to persuade the king that the contrary winds that had driven his fleet back to Corunna might be a divine warning, the king haughtily replied that, since the entire operation had been mounted for God's greater glory, such an interpretation simply could not be correct. And although the eventual destruction of his fleet, and of his hopes, temporarily shook the king's faith that God was on his side, his only public reaction was to order that the weekly prayers for the Armada's success be suspended, and to send a circular letter to his bishops asking for special services to be held in all churches to thank God that not everything had been destroyed,

'entrusting to Our Lord most sincerely all my deeds, so that His Divine Majesty may guide and direct them to whatever end may be to His greatest service'.

During the 1590s, finally, he justified his costly wars in France, in the Netherlands and on the high seas on precisely the same grounds: they were necessary, and they would succeed, because they were being fought in God's name. Thus in 1591, when his private secretary – the same man who had crowed over the Terceira victory eight years before – argued that 'If God had meant Your Majesty to remedy all the troubles of the world,

He would have given you the money and strengh to do it,' the king's reply was firm. 'I know you mean well,' he wrote to Mateo Vázquez, 'but these are not matters that can be abandoned.' The king's various crusades abroad could not be dropped 'because the cause of religion takes priority over everything'.[4]

That an early modern ruler should have found it necessary to write such things to a trusted adviser who was working, as it were, in the next room, may seem surprising. But that was how Philip II preferred to govern. Personal interviews were not his style. In 1576, for example, he scribbled the following refusal to the request of a senior military adviser for an interview: 'I would be glad to see him, but in all honesty I have very little time. And anyway,' he added for the benefit of his secretary, 'I forget so much of what is said to me at audiences . . . well, at most of them anyway, although you must not tell him that.' It was a strange but revealing admission. And two years later, when the duke of Medina Sidonia asked for an audience to discuss how he might best carry out the king's orders to invade southern Portugal, the king wrote back to him: 'If you happen to be close to court, it might be useful to hear the details from you in person; but since your letters will be delivered to me in complete secrecy, I think it would be best if you wrote.' Such a procedure may have saved the king time, and minimised his contact with other human beings, but it was a strange way to direct a war.[5]

So instead of face-to-face government, Philip II ruled from his desk by pen, usually working for eight or nine hours a day with his papers in a tiny office deep in the Escorial. He insisted that all orders should be issued over his personal signature, and the final decision in all major matters was taken by him alone. He arranged, of course, to receive papers of advice from experts, which were discussed and assessed either by formal councils or informal *ad hoc* committees; but, afterwards, the decisions were made by the king. The 'Diurnal' of the king's private secretary in the 1570s shows that 40 to 50 memoranda or reports requiring a decision came before the king every single day. It is a remarkable tribute to his stamina that many of the issues were resolved within a matter of hours. The system, however, was not perfect.

To be sure, maintaining a system of 'confuse and rule', in which no one knew as much as the king himself, offered Philip a number of advantages. First, it enabled him to retain the initiative in government and prevent any serious abuse of power by his subordinates, Second, it allowed him to avoid taking decisions on the spur of the moment, or under pressure from court factions: to a large extent, the king could take decisions at his own pace, and in his own way. But herein lay a catch, for this could lead to putting off, or overlooking, really difficult choices until it was too late. The weaknesses, as well as the strengths of Philip II's system of government were all to become apparent in the course of planning the 'enterprise of England'.

Throughout the reign, there had always been courtiers – many of them English Catholic exiles – who had urged a Spanish invasion to topple the Tudor state; and from 1559 onward (as we have seen) the king recognised that such action was both desirable and, ultimately, inevitable. But always he put off the fateful confrontation. Except for the Ridolfi conspirators in 1571, the plotters received no open support from Spain. Although the troops who left for Smerwick in 1579 and 1580 had admittedly departed from a Spanish port and in Spanish ships, the king was able to disavow them when things went wrong. He seems to have felt that, until the Netherlands were again pacified, it was better to leave England alone. There was, it is true, a flicker of interest following the conquest of the Azores. 'After the taking of the island of Terceira,' wrote a contemporary Spanish observer, 'the captains who accompanied the marquis of Santa Cruz . . . said openly that now we have Portugal, England is ours; and little by little we shall gain France also.' By August 1583 Santa Cruz himself was impressing upon Philip II the feasibility of a maritime expedition against England. A series of 'position papers' were drawn up, probably in the entourage of Santa Cruz, which discussed in detail the best way to invade England. There was a close study of past amphibious operations, from the successful landings of the Romans and Saxons in Kent to those of the Lancastrians in the fifteenth century on the periphery of the kingdom. The more recent attempts of the French (in 1545, against the Isle of Wight) and the Papal adventurers (at Smerwick) were also noted, along with the plan proposed in connection with the Ridolfi plot. All the available evidence suggested that the only sensible target for a Spanish invasion was London, since it was the seat of government and was easily accessible from the sea. It was considered a further advantage that, if the Armada landed in the estuary, reinforcements would readily be available from the duke of Parma's Army of Flanders.[6]

On receipt of this proposal, Philip II duly sought the advice of Parma: 'In order to terminate [the struggle in the Netherlands] once and for all,' he wrote to his nephew, 'it might be advisable to take steps to ensure that the war is not sustained from England.' Parma was asked bluntly whether it might be feasible to launch an invasion that would eliminate Elizabeth and replace her with Mary Stuart. The duke was not unsympathetic, although he preferred a surprise attack across the Channel by the Army of Flanders to a direct invasion from Spain; but, given his insecure military position in late 1583, he could not help feeling that it would be better to complete the conquest of the Netherlands before turning upon England.[7]

With this the plan was allowed to lapse. But in May 1585 a new pope was elected who burned with the desire to achieve some great triumph for the Catholic church: Sixtus V. Within the month he had mentioned twice to the Spanish ambassador in Rome, the count of Olivares, his zeal to commission 'some outstanding enterprise' for the Faith, specifying either the reconquest of the Moorish stronghold of Algiers or the invasion of England. The ambassador dutifully passed these details back to his master, but the king angrily scribbled on the back of the letter

Pope Sixtus V.

'Doesn't [the reconquest of] the Low Countries seem "outstanding" to them? Do they never think of how much it costs? There is little to be said about the English idea; one should keep away from such distant things'.[8]

For a time after this outburst it seemed as if the pope would settle for the recapture of Geneva, formerly a territory of the dukes of Savoy and now the citadel of Calvinism; however, Sixtus soon returned to his demand that Spain should invade England before moving against Holland and Zealand, whose powers of resistance had been so amply demonstrated in the 1570s. But again the king rejected the idea: the war in the Netherlands, he pointed out, was so expensive that no further commitments could be undertaken until all the rebellious provinces had been regained. He also called attention to the fact that the Low Countries' wars were 'fought so that there should be no concessions over religion' and 'to maintain obedience there to God and the Holy See'; and he invited the pope to contribute to the costs of maintaining his army and so facilitate a speedier victory there.[9]

Sixtus V, however, although an old man by sixteenth-century standards (he was born in the kingdom of Naples in 1521), was both tenacious and resourceful: he did not merely speak to the Spanish ambassador, but sent his own envoy to Spain. The agent was Luigi Dovara, a courtier of the grand duke of Tuscany, and he took with him a promise that, should

Spain attack England, both the papacy and Tuscany would contribute to the costs. The proposals were presented and discussed throughout the months of July and August, and Dovara was beginning to abandon hope when suddenly news arrived of Elizabeth's dramatic change of policy.[10]

Details of the Roanoke voyage, the attack on the Newfoundland fishermen and the treaty of Nonsuch arrived in September by courier from the Netherlands. And then information about Drake's increasingly impudent outrages reached the king more directly from Vigo and Bayona in Galicia, which the English had attacked and occupied from 7 to 17 October. The towns had not been treated with particular brutality, but a great deal of damage was done to church property – religious images and crucifixes were vandalised – and such acts of naked aggression and desecration, committed on Spanish soil, were highly provocative. They were intended to be. In the words of Drake's senior military officer, Christopher Carleill, the attack had been mounted 'to make our proceeding known to the king of Spain'.[11]

In this, the expedition was more successful than it can possibly have expected. The attack on Vigo seems to have been, for Philip II, the last straw – the final proof that the English problem could no longer be deferred. He became convinced that the time had come to carry out his threat of 1559 to make war on Elizabeth, now that Spain had enjoyed (for a while at least) some of the 'benefits of peace'. On 24 October 1585, scarcely a week after Drake sailed away from Galicia, simultaneous letters were sent to the pope and to the grand duke of Tuscany, accepting the suggestion conveyed by Luigi Dovara that Spain should invade England. But, the king warned, it would be expensive – at least 3 million ducats – and it would take time to prepare. He asked the pope for his blessing – and for some financial support.[12]

In the course of the next few weeks, while the answer from Italy was awaited, news poured in concerning both the build-up of English forces in Holland and the trail of desolation left by Drake in the Canaries and the Caribbean. If the king had entertained any doubts about the wisdom of the policy he had chosen they were now dispelled. On 29 December he returned to the rough plans put forward by Parma and Santa Cruz some two years before. Parma was now informed of the king's intention to launch a major assault on England, and was invited to send useful maps and information, together with his thoughts on the best strategy to adopt. Santa Cruz, who since 1584 had borne the title 'Captain-General of the

Ocean Sea' and had been charged with the task of building up a navy capable of defending the coasts of the Iberian peninsula against any attack, was ordered to do the same.

Replies from both commanders reached the court in March 1586. Santa Cruz presented a remarkable document which enumerated every detail of the resources which would be needed to put it into effect. Neither the tactics nor the strategy that were to be employed in its execution were spelled out, but the immense quantity and nature of the *matériel* specified, from capital ships down to the last pair of shoes, make Santa Cruz's intentions quite clear.

His scheme envisaged a vastly scaled-up version of the successful Terceira campaign. The task force would be built up at Lisbon and launched from there as a single amphibious operation under his direct command. His objective was simple: to land an army sufficiently strong, with all the supporting services it required, at a point on the enemy coast from which it could speedily achieve a decisive victory. There were four main elements in the strategic plan, of which the first was transport. A hundred and fifty ships totalling 77,250 tons would be needed to bring the projected 55,000 invasion troops together with equipment, munitions, and supplies to their destination. They would include 40 large merchant vessels from Ragusa, Venice, Sicily, Naples and the Mediterranean coast of Spain; 25 Spanish royal galleons and other vessels currently based at Lisbon and Cadiz; 20 ships, including fighting galleons, which had belonged to the Portuguese crown; 35 Basque merchantmen from Biscay and Guipúzcoa; and 30 German hulks which were already under contract to Spain for the transport of naval stores from the Baltic. An additional 400 support vessels of various sizes and types would be needed for the mustering and preparation of the great fleet.

The second element in Santa Cruz's plan concerned the defence of this massive force as it advanced towards the disembarkation point. The role of the Armada, while it was at sea, would be wholly defensive. São Miguel had demonstrated the futility, from the Spanish point of view, of a naval battle of attrition which achieved victory over an enemy fleet at the expense of the capacity to exploit that victory ashore. The fleet would be arranged – as it was to be in 1588 – so that rigid formation discipline coupled with vigorous self-defence would bring it to Elizabeth's shores, if not unscathed, then at least sufficiently intact to put the third phase of the operation into effect.

18. The Army of Flanders lays siege to Alkmaar in 1573. Supported by artillery, Spanish infantry advances along the narrow dykes, while engineers prepare a floating bridge (shown inset, at front) for the final assault.

19. An English spy's view of the Netherlands war-zone, enclosed with a coded letter to Walsingham on 31 March 1585. It shows the flooded countryside around Antwerp, the disposition of Parma's strongpoints, and the location of his great bridge over the Scheldt.

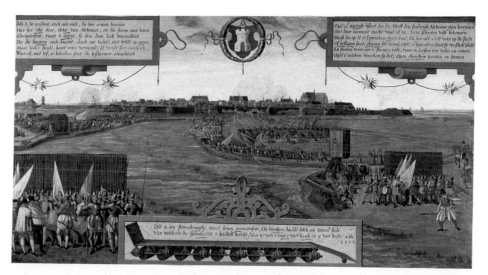

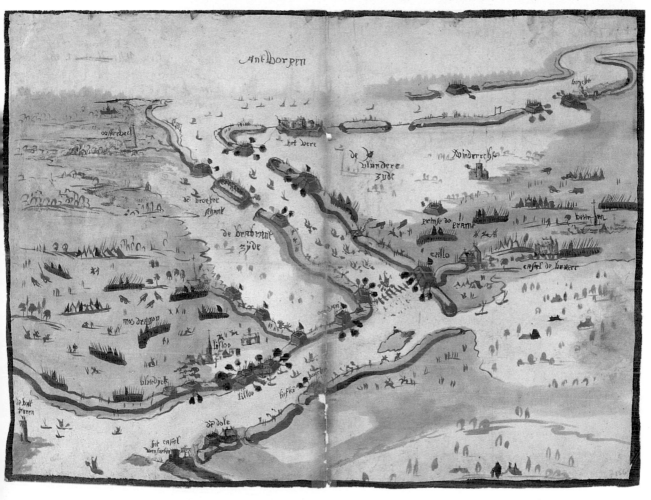

20. The 'Armada portrait' of Elizabeth I, attributed to George Gower.

21. The Queen's Ship *Jesus of Lübeck*, John Hawkins' flagship in the 'sorrowful voyage' of 1569, which was captured by the Spaniards at San Juan de Ulúa. This sketch was made by Anthony Anthony in his famous Roll of Henry VIII's navy of 1546.

22. Smerwick harbour in south-west Ireland during the action of 5 November 1580, probably drawn by an officer aboard the *Achates*. Other Queen's Ships present include the *Revenge*, the *Tiger*, the *Marlyon*, the *Swiftsure*, and the *Aid*. This detail shows the fleet attacking the isolated shore base of the Hispano-Papal force.

23. Artillery from the fleet is brought ashore to invest the landward side of the Hispano-Papal position – another detail from the Smerwick map. One gun is being hauled up the cliff by a team of seamen; 2 others are in position and firing from 'the maryners trenche'; and 2 others can just be discerned to the rear. All are mounted on naval pattern 4-truck carriages.

24. Alexander Farnese,
duke of Parma: portrait by
Vaenius.

25. The 'Terceira bowl', from the wreck of *La Trinidad Valencera*, which probably belonged to an officer who had taken part in the 1583 campaign. It depicts Santiago – St James – riding down the billowing waves of the Ocean Sea.

26. Drake's assault on Santiago in the Cape Verde Islands, prior to his descent on the Caribbean in 1585. Covered by the fleet anchored close inshore, a landing party of pikemen and calivermen (equivalent to Spanish arquebusiers) forms up in 3 groups to advance on the town, headed by drummers to beat out the step. The Spanish defenders flee.

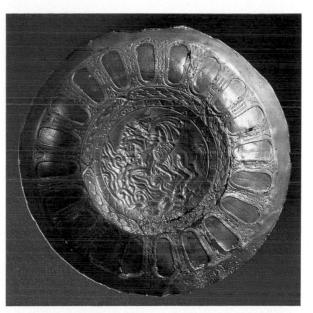

27. Philip II in 1583:
the portrait by Sanchez Coello.

28. A few items from Philip II's enormous collection of relics, each in a reliquary of appropriate shape (an arm for an arm and so on), still preserved at the Escorial.

29. The nearest thing to an 'Armada portrait' of Philip II: a miniature in a manuscript dated October 1588. Ironically, it comes from a petition for tax-exemption.

30. Don Alvaro de Bazán, marquis of Santa Cruz. He wears the enamelled gold cross of a Knight of Santiago.

31. A Santiago cross, from the wreck of the galleass *Girona*, which almost certainly belonged to Don Alonso de Leiva. Traces of the red enamelling can still be seen.

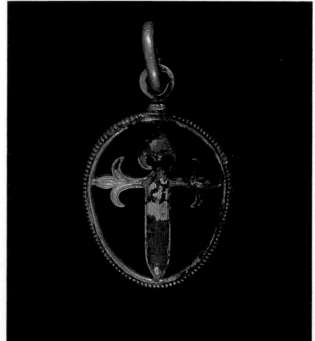

This was to land and secure a beach-head for the army and to this end 200 specially-designed landing-craft would be built. Such a feat would be, without doubt, the most difficult and crucial part of the whole enterprise; but it was one of which Santa Cruz and many of his subordinates had recent and successful experience. It would be little different from the Azores landings, though on a far larger scale, and Santa Cruz took care to specify those ingredients which had previously brought him victory at Lisbon and Terceira. In this part of the operation the forty galleys and six galleasses he had called for would come into their own. Unsuited they may have been to open-water combat with armed sailing ships; fragile they certainly were in heavy weather; but in sheltered waters close to land, screened from seaward by the main fleet, they would have been deadly. As swift and manoeuvrable destroyers they could operate right up to the beaches, bringing down fire on shore positions, while as support landing craft they could rapidly transfer heavy loads – particularly field and siege artillery – from the fleet to the beach-head.

Finally, once the initial landing had been consolidated, and the land campaign begun, the galley force would support the army's flank as it broke out from its beach-head, probing the rivers and harbours as required, just as Santa Cruz's galleys had done for Alba in the Tagus six years before.

When the troops and their equipment had been brought to the beaches the operation would move into its fourth and final phase. This was the conquest of a considerable part of Elizabeth's kingdom – Santa Cruz did not precisely define its limits – for which the army was to be provided with everything necessary to ensure quick success. Speed was of the essence: a swift blow at some vulnerable yet important part of the Tudor state would be the most certain solution to the English problem, and perhaps the cheapest one too. To put the issue beyond doubt, Santa Cruz reckoned he would need 55,000 front-line troops. Many would be veterans. They would be supported by a large siege-train, organised into four batteries of twelve 40-pounder *cañones de batir* and four 25-pounder heavy *culebrinas*. In addition there would be 16 heavy field guns, 24 lighter guns and 20 swivel pieces. An appropriate number of draught and pack animals, wheeled transport, and specialist craftsmen would be attached to the artillery train. There would also be a 3,000-strong corps of pioneers, equipped to construct field fortifications and siegeworks and to clear obstacles.

Santa Cruz's general staff would include administrative officers, a medical service, and a contingent of military police. And although no mention of it is made in the planning document (perhaps Santa Cruz felt that this was something the king would like to attend to himself), there would certainly have been a strong chaplaincy department to maintain the crusading zeal of the troops and add spiritual conversion to the temporal subjugation of the English heretics. This whole prodigious undertaking would cost, by Santa Cruz's meticulous reckoning (calculated down to the last earthenware platter), 1,526,425,798 *maravedis*, or about four million ducats (roughly £1 million).

It seems probable that Santa Cruz, like most commanders when they are asked by their political masters to draw up a plan of action, deliberately over-estimated his requirements so as to allow for the probability that they would later be scaled down. No doubt the marquis worked on the assumption that a smaller force might also be able to do the job, albeit with less certainty of outright success. Be that as it may, steps were taken almost immediately to prepare the task force called for by Santa Cruz. On 2 April 1586 authorisation was given for the naval preparations to begin in three places: Santa Cruz was sent to Lisbon with orders to create a fighting fleet to be called 'The navy for the defence of my realm, and for the destruction and punishment of the pirates who threaten its coasts'; shortly afterwards the duke of Medina Sidonia received orders to raise troops and concentrate supply vessels in the ports of Andalusia; and, in the north, eight large merchantmen and four pinnaces in the Cantabrican ports were embargoed and formed into a new squadron under the command of Spain's most experienced Atlantic seaman, Juan Martínez de Recalde.[13]

The crucial decisions were apparently taken in conference, and not committed to writing, so that the Armada's destination remained a closely guarded secret. In the absence of a written record one may speculate that, even at this early stage, the target was Kent, as it was to be in 1588. But there are other possibilities. It might perhaps have been the great natural harbour of Milford Haven, on the remote south-western tip of Wales, which was the objective of the abortive Armadas sent in 1596 and 1597. Much more probably, however, Santa Cruz suggested a descent on the south coast of Ireland – Cork, perhaps, or Wexford. At any event, this was the area designated for attack in many subsequent papers which discussed the Grand Design.

But if Santa Cruz favoured Ireland, he was at odds with another formidable strategist in the service of Philip II, the duke of Parma, whom the king had also asked for his views on a military solution to the problem of England.

The duke's appreciation of the situation was dispatched from Flanders just as the plans to create a fleet in Spain were finalised, on 20 April 1586. It consisted of a 28-page letter, examining each of the various possibilities open to Philip II, and further details were entrusted to an Italian confidant of the duke, the engineer Giovanni Battista Piatti. Parma began by regretting the lack of secrecy concerning the king's intentions. According to him, soldiers and civilians in Flanders were all openly discussing how England could be invaded. Nevertheless, the duke believed, the enterprise might still be feasible, provided certain basic precautions were taken. First, the king of Spain must be in sole charge 'without placing any reliance on either the English themselves, or the assistance of other allies'. Parma devoted a special paragraph to the danger of making the Papacy privy to the plan, because so many people would be involved that all the crucial details would inevitably leak out. Second, some assurance must be obtained that France would remain neutral, and do nothing to impede the invasion, either by sending assistance to Elizabeth or by intervening again in the Netherlands. Third, sufficient troops and resources must be available to defend the reconquered Netherlands against the Dutch even after the assault force had left.

If all this could be achieved, the duke considered that a force of 30,000 foot and 500 horse might safely be detached from the Army of Flanders and ferried across the Channel to the coast of England aboard a flotilla of sea-going barges. Provided his precise intentions remained a secret, 'given the number of troops we have to hand here, and the ease with which we can concentrate and embark them in the barges, and considering that we can ascertain, at any moment, the forces which Elizabeth has and can be expected to have, and that the crossing only takes 10 to 12 hours without a following wind (and 8 hours with one)', Parma felt sure the invasion could be undertaken with a fair chance of success. 'The most suitable, close and accessible point of disembarkation [he concluded], is the coast between Dover and Margate', which would permit a surprise march on London. The best time to undertake it would be the month of October, 'and if it cannot be done this year, it will be necessary to delay it until the same time next year'.

Parma only devoted two paragraphs of his letter to the possibility of naval support from Spain, and even then he considered only 'the worst possible scenario': that somehow details of his plan had become known in England. In that case, he suggested, since the king was being forced by Drake's exploits to mobilize a fleet to protect the Atlantic, perhaps this new navy could be used 'either to sail suddenly up here in order to assist and reinforce the troops who have already landed [in Kent] and keep open the seaway between the coasts of Flanders and England; or else – if your fleet is large, well-provided, well-armed and well-manned – it could create a diversion which will draw the English fleet away [from the straits of Dover].'

Philip II was thus confronted by two plausible plans. One was endorsed by his foremost naval commander; the other by his most experienced general. But which was the better?

To some extent, the appeal of Parma's strategy was reduced by the long delay which intervened before it arrived at court. The king had asked for it on 29 December 1585; despite a reminder on 7 February 1586 it was not sent until 20 April and was not received by the royal cypher clerks until 20 June. Four more days elapsed before the bearer, Giovanni Battista Piatti, was debriefed by the secretary of state for foreign affairs, Don Juan de Idiáquez. Questions were asked about exactly what shipping was currently available in the ports of Flanders to ferry a major army across the open sea, and about the possible advantage of seeking an alternative landing-place in the Thames estuary, closer to London. Then the whole dossier was turned over to the king's senior adviser, Don Juan de Zúñiga.

Zúñiga's opinion was based upon a lifetime's experience of political and military affairs. He had fought in the Netherlands in the 1550s, and then risen through the ranks of ambassador to the papal court and viceroy of Naples to become a councillor of war and state in Madrid. Since 1585 he had presided over the *Junta de Noche* (the 'night committee'), formed to coordinate central government policy and advise the king on major affairs of state. His reaction to Parma's proposal was extremely optimistic. Although he saw no advantage to Spain in the direct annexation of England ('because of the cost of defending it'), he strongly favoured placing the newly conquered realm under a friendly Catholic ruler. He suggested Mary Stuart – the obvious candidate – but recommended that she should marry a dependable Catholic prince. He mentioned the name of Parma himself.

More radical still was Zúñiga's proposed strategy. In effect, it combined the two plans already proposed. An Armada would sail from Lisbon, carrying as many troops as could be mustered together with most of the *matériel* needed for the land campaign, directly for Ireland. There it would put ashore its assault troops, and secure a beach-head. Its very existence would threaten and disrupt Elizabeth's naval forces, so neutralising their potential for resistance when, after some two months, the Armada would leave Ireland and make for the Channel. The main invasion force of 30,000 veterans would then be launched by Parma, who would transport his army from the ports of Flanders to Kent in his flotilla of flat-bottomed craft. The Armada, at this stage, would secure the local supremacy at sea necessary for Parma's crossing, and off-load the siege artillery and supplies necessary for his swift march on London.

Finally, once the two beach-heads had been established and the seas made secure, a fleet of supply ships concentrated by the duke of Medina Sidonia in the ports of Andalusia would bring up further reinforcements and replenishments.

With his foot thus on England's throat, Parma was either to create an interim administration pending the arrival of the new ruler; or, if he proved unable to defeat and capture Elizabeth, he was instructed to use his presence on English soil to secure three key concessions. Firstly, there was to be complete toleration and freedom of worship for Catholics throughout the kingdom. Secondly, all English troops were to be withdrawn from the Netherlands, and the places they garrisoned were to be surrendered directly to Spain. Finally, England was to be made to pay; a war-indemnity was to be exacted, and the invasion force was to remain in Kent until it was paid. With such high stakes, Zúñiga concluded, and with such a complex operation, it would be futile to attempt anything during the present campaigning season; so he suggested that the Enterprise of England should be launched in August or September 1587.[14]

One wonders whether Philip II realised the enormity of the proposed change of plan. There was, in retrospect, much to recommend Santa Cruz's proposal. The events of 1588 were to prove that, once they got their Armada to sea, the Spaniards experienced little difficulty in moving 60,000 tons of shipping from one end of the Channel to the other, despite repeated assaults upon it, and the Kinsale landing of 1601 showed how easily a beach-head in southern Ireland could be secured and fortified. Likewise, Parma's concept of a *Blitzkrieg* landing in Kent, without any warning, also had much to recommend it: time and again, his troops had proved their invincibility under his leadership, and it is hard to see how the largely untrained English forces, taken by surprise, could have successfully resisted the Army of Flanders as it marched on London.

The Armada's undoing was caused, ultimately, by the decision to unite the fleet from Spain with the army from the Netherlands as a prelude to launching the invasion. Nevertheless the individual strategies sent in by Santa Cruz and Parma were not beyond criticism. Martín de Bertendona, for example, in complete ignorance of Philip II's intentions, observed that the chief problem with the Santa Cruz plan lay in creating a task force in Spain powerful enough to win a battle at sea and then go on to win another on land. The Azores campaign had shown that artillery encounters could so damage even a victorious fleet that no further action was possible. So Bertendona pointed to the counter-examples of the Spanish relief of Malta in 1565, which had been achieved by a surprise landing in force on an undefended beach, and of the Terceira landing in 1583; might it not be possible, he queried, for the Army of Flanders to do the same on the coast of England, without any help from Spain? From Dunkirk to Dover was, after all, barely 40 miles.[15]

Other well-qualified observers, however, continued to believe that a fleet from Spain was essential for success against a country with as strong a navy as England. It was self-evident to the duke of Medina Sidonia, who had spent most of his adult life superintending the departure of the convoys sailing from Seville to America. In a ten-folio hand-written memorandum, covering such basic matters as the urgent need for improved defences around the Caribbean ports and better-gunned escort vessels for the trading fleets, Medina Sidonia argued strongly that a great fleet would have to be maintained in Spain, and if necessary even sail into the Channel, in order to reduce the English government to reason. The duke (who little thought that he would eventually lead the Armada himself) did not, in fact, favour invasion; but he believed the creation of a powerful navy to be indispensable for the nation's prosperity and security. Spain's commercial community evidently agreed with him: the correspondents of the prominent banker Simon Ruiz all welcomed the news that a major fleet was being prepared against England, for they saw it as the only way to restore security to Spanish overseas trade.[16]

What no one except Philip II and Zúñiga seems to have contemplated was the combination of these two strategies, separately conceived and elaborated, into a single Grand Design. No doubt they felt that two simultaneous attacks were more likely to succeed than one and that, since there seemed to be money enough for both, there was no need to choose between them. It is tempting to dismiss the whole plan as the crack brained theory of armchair strategists. But Zúñiga had played an outstanding role in coordinating the naval campaigns of the Mediterranean for almost twenty years; he might have been expected to know what he was doing. The real problem lay in Philip II's secretive system of government, which ensured that no one but he and his chosen confidant subjected the plan to critical scrutiny. There was no 'war cabinet' to demand how, precisely, two large and totally independent forces, with operational bases separated by more than a thousand miles of ocean, could achieve the precision of time and place necessary to effect their link-up; or how the vulnerable and lightly-armed troop transports to be collected in Flanders would be able to evade the Dutch and English warships stationed offshore to intercept and destroy them?

But the king's mind was made up, and nothing could change it. On 26 July Giovanni Battista Piatti was sent back to the Netherlands with details of a masterplan for the conquest of England that was, in all essentials, that put forward by Don Juan de Zúñiga. A parallel dossier was sent to Lisbon. But neither Parma nor Santa Cruz was invited to comment on the orders sent to them; they were merely instructed to carry them out. The king, for his part, sent instructions to all public authorities in Spain, Portugal, Naples and Sicily ordering the preparation of troops, munitions and other necessary equipment, and began a diplomatic offensive designed to ensure that, at the crucial moment, no foreign power would raise a finger to save Elizabeth Tudor from his combined assault.[17]

CHAPTER 7

Phoney war

In the event, Elizabeth herself removed a major diplomatic obstacle from Philip's path: on 18 February 1587 her officials executed Mary queen of Scots.

Perhaps there was no alternative. Since 1580 conspiracies against Elizabeth had become almost incessant, each aimed at placing Mary Stuart on the Tudors' throne. A vicious circle was established: with so many plots afoot, Mary was too dangerous for Elizabeth to set at liberty; and yet, in captivity, plots offered Mary her only chance of freedom. The exiled queen, detained by her cousin in a succession of draughty castles with little opportunity for exercise, entertainment or outside recreation, gradually allowed intrigue and conspiracy to become her principal pastime. In the summer of 1586, when a new plot was hatched by Anthony Babington, a young English Catholic who had once served in Mary's household, she rashly expressed her support in writing. Babington's plan involved the assassination of Elizabeth as a prelude to the invasion of a liberating Catholic army. But from the first Mary's correspondence had been intercepted and copied: Babington was unequivocally implicated and arrested in August. Soon after, Mary was herself placed under arrest, moved to the castle of Fotheringhay near Northampton, and there tried for treason. The verdict was inescapable.

In assessing the tangled sequence of events that followed, it is important to remember the fundamental insecurity of the Elizabethan regime. The queen, now over fifty, could not be expected to live for ever, and she had no heir except Mary. It is true that Parliamentary statutes existed which in theory barred a Stuart succession, but similar statutes had once been passed against both Mary Tudor and Elizabeth herself. In each case they had been overthrown without difficulty upon the death of the monarch who passed them. Most of those who influenced English politics in 1586

Hi mihi sunt Comites quos ipsa pericula ducunt

In quo quis peccat
In eo punitur.

B.H.f.

Babington with his Complices in S.ᵗ Giles fields.

The Babington conspirators and (*right*) the terrible fate that awaited them.

could still remember these earlier events. Many, indeed, had fled the country during the reign of Mary lest their Protestant sympathies led them to the scaffold. They cannot have expected to fare any better under a new Catholic regime.

Some took a more pessimistic and determinist view. A few of Elizabeth's advisers had always been convinced of the existence of an international Catholic conspiracy dedicated to the extirpation of Protestantism in England. After the Ridolfi plot their opinion was more generally shared – sometimes even by the queen – and every new setback suffered by the Protestant cause abroad and every new plot detected by Elizabeth's spies at home increased the fears of the alarmists that a concerted assault by the Catholic powers was imminent. In the summer and autumn of 1586 no one could be sure of how much (if any) foreign support Babington might have secured. In August, as a precaution, Sir John Hawkins was sent off with eighteen warships to patrol the Channel and reconnoitre the coasts of Spain and Portugal, where naval preparations were reported to be afoot. During his two month cruise Hawkins took prisoners who confirmed the worst: Spain was almost certainly on the point of launching a huge invasion.

Playing upon these fears, which were fanned by rumours (possibly invented) of a new plot against Elizabeth involving the French, the queen's ultra-Protestant councillors eventually persuaded her to sign a warrant condemning Mary Stuart to death. But she could not be persuaded actually to send it to Fotheringhay. At last her worried advisers boldly took the decision out of her hands, and dispatched one of their number, the militantly anti-Catholic William Davidson, to ride himself to Northamptonshire with the signed warrant and personally supervise the execution of his mistress's 'bosom-serpent'. Mary died with dignity on 18 February and the plots expired with her.

Some considered that Mr Davidson had done a good day's work for the Protestant cause, but it was not so apparent at the time. When she heard the news, Elizabeth's thoughts turned immediately to the potentially catastrophic repercussions of the deed. She had, after all, encompassed the death of a former queen of Scotland and France who was not her subject, an anointed ruler who was the mother of James VI of Scotland, the sister-in-law of Henry III of France, and the cousin of his most powerful subject Henry, duke of Guise, leader of the French Catholic League and the pensioner and ally of Philip II. The initial French reaction to news of Mary's death was alarming. In Rouen, English ships and goods were seized; in Paris, outraged clerics delivered inflammatory sermons that called for revenge, and exhibited pictures outside their churches luridly portraying the atrocities committed against English Catholics by the Elizabethan regime. In an attempt to appease these passions, William Davidson was tried, clapped in the Tower, fined heavily, and threatened with death (in the event he remained in prison for just 18 months and the fine was waived). Elizabeth's principal minister, Lord Burghley, was forbidden to come to Court for four weeks and was subjected to blistering abuse whenever his mistress caught sight of him for the next four months. Other councillors involved in Mary's execution had a difficult time.

It was not an atmosphere conducive to the rational formulation of foreign policy.

And yet never had diplomatic dexterity been more essential to England's survival. Philip II's agents were everywhere, capitalising to the utmost upon the 'illegal' execution of Mary Stuart, and using it to justify their master's maturing plans to extirpate the tyrannous 'English Jezebel.' In February 1587 the Venetian ambassador in Madrid noted in wonderment that 'the Spaniards are moving towards their great object in various ways and from many sides, no less by diplomacy than by preparations for war, and even by a union of the two.' But not everything went Philip II's way. To begin with, there was a risk that while Spain's army and fleet were tied down in northern Europe, her Mediterranean possessions might be exposed to attack from the forces of Islam. So Spanish envoys were duly sent to Istanbul, capital of the Ottoman empire, with orders to negotiate an extension of the armistice between the Turks and Spaniards.

But English diplomacy rose to the occasion. The queen's unofficial ambassador at Istanbul, William Harborne, persuaded the Sultan that nothing was to be gained from a deal with Spain and Philip's agents were sent away empty-handed. So, although the Turks did not launch another attack in 1587 or 1588, the government in Madrid remained fearful that they might.[1]

Elizabeth's statesmanship was also successful in Scotland. Matters here were severely complicated by the phantom Will of Mary queen of Scots, who in May 1586 had written to the Spanish ambassador in Paris, Don Bernadino de Mendoza, that she was about to 'cede and grant by Will my right to the succession of this crown to the king, your master'. In all probability the Will was never made (although Philip II ransacked the archives of Rome, Paris and Simancas to find some trace of it), but Mary's letter describing it was intercepted by Elizabeth's agents and a copy was sent to James VI. That young man, now aged 20, realised that his mother's action threatened to disinherit him both from his Scottish kingdom and from his expectation of succeeding eventually to the English crown. He therefore made clear his support for Elizabeth. Even the execution of his mother failed to alienate him: although he made a flurry of protests, he continued to pocket an annual English subsidy of £4,000. Later, James gave short shrift to a Spanish envoy sent in 1588 to persuade him to co-operate with the Armada plan: the unfortunate diplomat was immediately arrested as a spy. Finally, when the Catholic Lord Maxwell began a rebellion in south-west Scotland with the declared intention of providing the Spaniards with a base, the king rode out and put it down in person. Only the Armada's outright victory could have converted James VI into an ally of Spain.

English and Spanish diplomats also clashed in France. Following the treaty of Nemours the Catholic League had taken possession of several strategic towns with Henry III's permission. Their leaders, the dukes of Guise and Mayenne, also held numerous strongholds in the provinces of Champagne and Burgundy. But all of these places were in the east of France. So in April 1587 Guise's cousin, the duke of Aumâle, seized three towns in Picardy, near the frontier with the Netherlands, and replaced the royal garrisons with League troops. But they failed to capture their principal objective, the port of Boulogne. Earlier in the year a royalist spy in the household of the duke of Guise had overheard a conversation about the need 'for some way to take the town of Boulogne, which was said to be necessary for them to receive and shelter the reinforcements they were expecting from Spain'. The information was passed on, and the garrison of Boulogne was alerted: Aumâle and his men were refused entry. In June, to encourage this welcome spirit of independence, Lord Howard led part of the English navy to Boulogne and offered any necessary assistance.

Elizabeth also sent support by land. At the request of the French Huguenots, she provided money to raise troops in Germany to fight in France: all through the spring of 1587 rumours of their approach circulated, detaining both the duke of Guise and a detachment of the Army of Flanders in the east to resist them. When 11,000 German mercenaries finally crossed the Rhine in August, the Catholic army easily outmanoeuvred them; but their distracting presence kept Guise away from Picardy, and although he was able to keep control of the places seized in April his forces lacked the strength to take Boulogne. So in spite of spending over £50,000 in subsidies to the League in 1587, and sending a small army in its support, Philip II had failed to gain a safe port as a potential refuge for his fleet. It was a crucial defect: had the Spaniards possessed Boulogne in 1588, the Armada campaign might have taken a very different course.

The cost of this, and of all the other preparations required for the invasion of England, placed severe strains on Philip II's exchequer, and forced the king to introduce stringent economies elsewhere. Thus a plan by the council of the Indies in September 1586 to improve the defences of the Caribbean was turned down on the grounds that:

'As you can imagine, no one feels the damage [done by the English] more than I do, and no one desires more to repair it, if only there was a way to execute it as we wish; but your plans create a lot of problems, and the biggest one is the lack of money with which to pay for it all.'

The king concluded with the hope that future plans would be accompanied by concrete suggestions as to how they might be financed. The council of Portugal, for its part, called off a planned attack on the troublesome sultanate of Atjeh in Sumatra and a proposal to build a fortress at Mombasa in east Africa: the reason given for both was the need to concentrate all resources on the 'Enterprise of England'.[2] In March 1586 Santa Cruz had put the total cost of the 'Enterprise' at 4 million ducats (roughly £1 million), but the decision to involve Parma's army as well virtually doubled this figure. By the beginning of 1587 a group of the king's senior advisers estimated that '7 million ducats will be needed to implement plans made, and to be made, for this year.' And, in the event, all this money and more was spent: as the king observed with justifiable pride to his nephew Parma in October 1587: 'as for money, you will see that the 5 million that has been sent you this year exceeds anything that has been sent in living memory.'[3]

It was due to the cost of the enterprise that the king became increasingly obsessed with the promise made by Sixtus V to contribute financially to it. By the spring of 1586 the wily pontiff had already come to regret his earlier offer to pay one-third of the total, and he argued to the Spanish ambassador in Rome that the papal contribution was superfluous since the king would no doubt invade England anyway 'in order to avenge the insults done him; on account of the advantage this would provide in dealing with Holland; and because he cannot by any other means safeguard his trade with the Indies' (Ambassador Olivares later speculated that it was the pope's Neapolitan upbringing which made him always see 'vengeance and insults' as the mainspring of international affairs). Eventually, agreement was reached on a figure of one million ducats. But the Pope refused to pay anything in advance. He professed to fear that the king might use it for some other purpose, so he stipulated that the papal bounty would only become payable when confirmation reached Rome that the Armada had landed in England.[4]

This distrust seems to have aroused the king's own suspicions: on the back of the letter Philip ruminated on the possible financial consequences should the Pope die, since the promise was only a personal undertaking by Sixtus. On 19 November 1586 these doubts turned to demands: all the cardinals must forthwith be asked to swear that, in the event of Sixtus's death, each one of them, should he be elected Pope, would honour the promise to pay. The king was well aware of the risks this involved:

'Even though my desire to arrange this may lead to a breach of secrecy, because it may require a meeting of the college of cardinals, nonetheless it is a point of such importance that it should not be forgotten. Because if we are not protected, we may find ourselves deceived.'

Eventually the king was satisfied: all the cardinals were prevailed upon to agree, and the papal secretary of state signed an absolute undertaking to pay one million ducats to Ambassador Olivares once the Armada had landed. In due course, on 29 July 1587, two Roman bankers received a special deposit of the one million ducats in gold from the papal treasury, payable as soon as a public notary verified that the invasion had taken place. On the same day terms were agreed for the government of England after the conquest: Philip would nominate, subject to papal approval and investiture, a ruler pledged to restore and uphold the Catholic faith. In the meantime, the administration of England would be entrusted to Cardinal Allen, superior of the English College at Douai, assisted both by his Jesuit pupils and by local Catholics. They would superintend the restoration to the church of all lands and rights lost at the Reformation.

No doubt Sixtus V was unenthusiastic about the treaty, but he now had no choice. With Mary Stuart dead, and with France paralysed by civil war, a Catholic restoration in England depended utterly upon the good offices of Philip II. But for the king, too, the battle of wills with Sixtus involved losses as well as gains. He had wasted countless hours over these tortuous negotiations – his correspondence with Rome bears far more holograph annotations than his correspondence with Flanders – and yet, even so, the deposited money was only available for a limited time: if no news had been received by November 1587, all of it was to go back to the papal vaults.[5]

The limited credit thus obtained was far outweighed by a corresponding debit. Negotiations with the papacy had made the whole matter ever more public and, within a matter of weeks, all secrecy about the Armada evaporated when Oda Colonna, a nephew of one of the cardinals, was captured by the Dutch and interrogated by Count Maurice in person. Colonna offered little resistence, and speedily revealed everything he knew about the Armada: its detailed financing, its organisation, and above all its destination and timing. Suspicion and greed had blown Philip II's cover beyond recovery.

Elizabeth, of course, had already received intelligence from a large number of sources, including several spies in Lisbon and Madrid, who were able to provide relatively full reports on the preparation of the fleet. But these agents, many of them Jews, were unable to gain access to the circles where the precise objective of the Armada was discussed. There was always a possibility that it might be intended for the Caribbean, for

France, or (most plausibly) for Holland. Information provided from Florence, Venice and Rome by such spies as Sir Anthony Standen – alias Pompeo Pelligrini – was admittedly more detailed on policy, but even their data still lacked total reliability.[6] Yet Elizabeth could clearly see the growing threat, and she took basic measures to improve England's defensive capabilities. Four new warships were laid down in the royal yards, work on the fortifications of the south coast was resumed, and known Catholics in England were disarmed. At the same time, through the duke of Parma, she opened negotiations with Philip II.

Perhaps she hoped that, as in 1568-72, a retreat from the brink of war was still possible. No sooner had the queen signed the treaty of Nonsuch in August 1585 than she sent an envoy to Parma explaining her action and exploring the possibility of reaching some accommodation. To this end, in spite of her promises to the Dutch, she also ordered Leicester to delay his departure and refused to sign his commission to command in the Netherlands until 7 December. At the same time she authorised a new, secret peace initiative and from the summer of 1586 allowed informal talks to take place at Parma's headquarters.[7] Actions, however, spoke louder than words; and any progress that the negotiations might have made was lost when news arrived in the Netherlands of another daring raid by Sir Francis Drake on Spanish soil. In response to the reports of Philip's awesome naval preparations, the queen had ordered Drake to 'singe the king of Spain's beard' by preventing the junction of the Armada, by intercepting supplies travelling to Lisbon and, if necessary, by 'distressing the ships within the havens themselves'. Drake's fleet of 23 sail included only six vessels from the navy royal: the rest were provided either by himself and his privateering friends, or by a consortium of London merchants (four ships, for example, were supplied by the Levant Company). The warships and the armed merchantmen joined forces on 11 April 1587 – a mere two weeks after receipt of the queen's commission – and the following day Drake led his fleet hastily out of Plymouth Sound. As his sails filled with a welcome 'Protestant' wind, the admiral concluded a letter to one of his staunchest allies at court with evident relief that he had got away before his commission was revoked:

'The wind commands me away: our ship is under sail. God grant we may so live in His fear as the enemy may have cause to say that God doth fight for her Majesty as well abroad as at home.'

And Drake had indeed left in the nick of time. On 19 April, a week after he sailed, the queen rescinded her orders for the harrying of all Spanish shipping and stores and instead expressly forbade her fleet to 'enter forcibly into any of the King's ports or havens, or to offer violence to any of his towns or shipping within harbouring, or to do any act of hostility upon the land'. A pinnace sped after the fleet, but to no avail. On 29 April Drake's fleet, ignorant of the queen's new orders, appeared unexpectedly off Cadiz.

Preparations for the Armada had by now reached a critical stage. Long-term stockpiling of provisions for the fleet was in a particularly delicate state, for sixteenth-century Europe enjoyed few food surpluses, and supplies of the magnitude required might be difficult to obtain at any price if the notice given was too short. This consideration was balanced by the fact that, in an age without tin cans or freezers, the shelf-life of all types of food was short. Orders for biscuit and salt meat had been placed with contractors at Alicante, Cartagena and Málaga: to meet them 40 new biscuit ovens had to be built at Málaga alone. A contract was signed with Milan for a large consignment of rice, while grain purchases in Spain, where there was already a shortage, had an inflationary effect on the market price. Nearly half-a-million pounds of cheese were obtained from the Baltic, transported in 20 Hamburg hulks. Other hulks from northern Europe had been bringing in essential naval supplies – pitch, cordage, timber and sailcloth – via the 'north-about' route around the British Isles, to avoid interception by the queen's ships in the English Channel.

Meanwhile agents had been negotiating bulk contracts for the supply of military equipment. In Seville the duke of Medina Sidonia ordered a large number of campaign tents, and 12,000 sets of shoes, leather canteens, and knapsacks for the invasion troops. The same town later supplied picks, shovels and gabions for the pioneers. So many weapons were distributed to the new forces being raised that, according to the secretary of state for war, 'there is not a single arquebus, pike or musket in all Spain'. New supplies had to be ordered from Italy. Troops, too, were withdrawn from the trained garrisons of Naples and Sicily, and recruits to take over their duties were later sent by galley from Spain.

The preparation of the fleet also proceeded apace. To reinforce the royal fleets already assembled at Cadiz, the Basque ports, and Lisbon, private merchantmen were embargoed throughout the Iberian world for the king's service. The *Trinidad Valencera* from Venice, the *Rata Santa María*

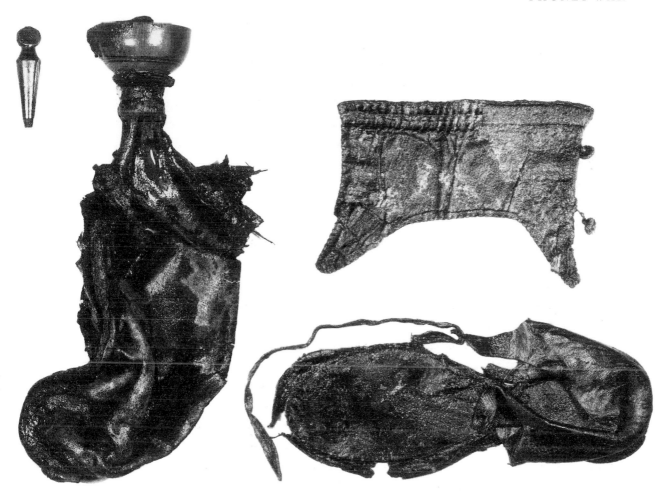

Leather wine bag with wooden stopper, a shoe and a cloth anklet from the wreck of *La Trinidad Valencera*.

Encoronada from Genoa, the *Anunciada* and *San Juan de Sicilia* from Ragusa, and the *Juliana* from Naples, were all commandeered by the viceroy of Sicily in December 1586. The *Gran Grifón* from Rostock, along with other Baltic hulks, was embargoed by the duke of Medina Sidonia at San Lúcar in March 1587. The *St Andrew* of Dundee, a Scottish trader suspected of carrying contraband, was confiscated at Málaga at the same time, as was the English *Charity* at Gibraltar. But the Armada was not yet a coherent force, and most of its scattered component parts were highly vulnerable to attack.[8]

No one knew this better than Drake when he brought his raiding force to Cadiz. Although Lisbon was to be the base from which the Armada would eventually sail, the main activity had at first centred on Spain's great southern port, which possessed extensive facilities for fitting out and victualling the Indies fleets. As the build-up continued ships began to crowd the anchorage between the seaward peninsula, upon which the town stood, and the mouth of the Guadalquivir, whence supplies could be brought down from Seville. The port of Cadiz, with its wide entrance, was less secure than Lisbon, but it was well defended with forts and artillery, and by a squadron of nine galleys. By the end of April nearly 60 vessels were in harbour: hulks and coasters loading for Lisbon, the tuna fishing fleet, and merchantmen of all types from small caravels to a 700-ton Genoese carrack about to depart for Italy with a cargo of cochineal, leather and wool. It was this motley and disorganised collection of ships and stores which, on 29 April, received the brunt of England's pre-emptive strike.

Drake's fleet, flying no colours so as to escape identification until the last moment, entered the outer haven and in less than 24 hours destroyed or captured 24 Spanish ships in the harbour, some of them large and powerful, together with considerable quantities of food and stores destined for the Armada. The English were only prevented from advancing into the inner harbour of Cadiz, and from capturing the town (as they were to do successfully in 1596) by the prompt arrival of the duke of Medina Sidonia with a strong body of militiamen. The duke swiftly reorganised the town's defences, and some of the shore batteries were able to damage the English vice-flagship *Lion* before the intruders sailed away on 1 May.

Their next destination was at first a mystery, and Medina Sidonia sent off fast caravels and dispatch riders to warn his compatriots elsewhere of possible danger: to the Canaries, to Lisbon, to the king. On 6 May he even sent one of his own ships to the Caribbean ordering the Treasure Fleet, which was assembling for the Atlantic crossing back to Seville, to remain where it was until further notice. But Drake had other plans. After an unsuccessful attempt to catch Recalde's Biscayan squadron on the high seas, he captured the castle and harbour of Sagres, near Cape St Vincent, on 9 May.

From this strategic location Drake's fleet could dominate and interdict the Armada's supply route between Andalusia and Lisbon. For the rest of the month, virtually all shipping which tried to run the gauntlet of the English blockade was either captured or sunk. Finally, on 31 May, the English abandoned their stronghold and, amid considerable publicity, set sail for the Azores in order (so they proclaimed) to intercept both the returning Portuguese fleet from India and the homeward-bound treasure fleet from America. In the event only the carrack *São Phelipe* was captured, with a cargo later valued at £140,000. Drake brought her triumphantly into Plymouth on 7 July.

News of this capture, coming so soon after the debacle at Cadiz, caused a sensation in Lisbon. There was an outbreak of anti-Spanish sentiment, with the Portuguese complaining that their new masters 'wanted to take away the cream of all that was good in Portugal', and muttering that no such disaster had occurred before the union with Spain. It was noted, sourly, that the Spaniards in Lisbon seemed completely unaffected, 'going to their bull-fights and playing their games as if nothing had happened'.[9] But, if this was indeed true, it was no more than an attempt to put on a brave face: the Spaniards were deeply concerned, and the government worked hard to assess and to limit the effects of the damage. Certainly the loss of 24 ships was a serious blow – many of the vessels that eventually sailed with the Armada were inferior in quality to those lost at Cadiz – and the destruction of stores (especially the food, sailcloth, cordage, barrel hoops and staves) was also tiresome. But there was already more than enough of everything to supply a formidable navy, and the build-up continued apace. In the summer of 1587 Recalde brought the twelve big vessels of his Biscayan squadron into Lisbon, and Santa Cruz led an impressive fleet of 37 fighting ships and 6,000 men to sea in July. But he was not yet able to lead it against England.

Drake's shrewdest move in the whole operation was his much-advertised departure for the Azores. Although the fleet from America had been warned of the danger awaiting it, the returning Portuguese Indiamen had not. The presence of a 'pirate fleet' of such strength in Iberian waters caused something close to panic throughout Spain and Portugal. The reports of the Venetian ambassador in Madrid abound with rumours about some new exploit plotted by 'el Draque', or some prize seized by him. All of them, apart from the capture of the *São Phelipe*, were unfounded, but at the time no one knew what had happened, or what might happen next.

Spain had to react. On 29 June, as soon as Drake's departure for the Azores was known for certain in Madrid, Santa Cruz was ordered to follow him and wait at the archipelago until all the treasure galleons had arrived, and then escort them home. The marquis sailed out of Lisbon on 12 July, and did not return for three full months.[10] During this period many of his ships suffered severe storm damage (not to mention routine wear and tear), most lost a substantial part of their crews, and all consumed an alarming quantity of the victuals accumulated for the descent on England. Recalde's squadron remained off the Azores for a little longer, and returned in even worse shape.

In effect, Drake had given his country another full year to prepare for the Spanish onslaught. But at last the 'phoney war' was over: neither England nor the Hispanic empire could now pull back from a fight to the finish.

CHAPTER 8

The Armada takes shape

There was one further, and momentous, consequence of Drake's raid. It caused Philip II to revise his entire strategy for the enterprise of England.

His plan, of course, had never been popular with Parma. As early as April 1586, even before the king first sent him detailed instructions, the duke had complained that everybody knew about Spain's intentions, so the enterprise lacked the vital element of surprise. The delivery of the papal sword in September – the same symbol of crusading virtue accorded to the duke of Alba fifteen years before – was also a symbol of the unwelcome publicity and lack of security which now surrounded the entire operation.

For three months – a measure, it would seem, of his disapproval – Parma held back his comments on the king's master-plan. Then, on 30 October, he enunciated all his doubts in a long letter. First he asked the king bluntly whether Spain could afford the operation. The cost of building up sufficient forces in Flanders to defend recent conquests, as well as to conquer Ireland and England, would be crippling: 'And I shall be bold to say,' wrote the duke, 'with the freedom your Majesty allows me, that if you find yourself without adequate resources to undertake such a great enterprise as this . . . I incline to the view that it would be better to defer or drop it.'

If the king was still determined to persist with his plan, Parma continued, he should consider a second point: 'It seems to me that it would be most useful if the Armada from Spain were to be ready for action at the same moment [as the invasion from Flanders], because I am afraid that the Irish dimension may do us some mischief.' On the one hand, argued the duke, Elizabeth might deduce that there would be a second attack and raise troops abroad for her defence; on the other, the Armada might well be unable, through adverse winds or other unforeseen circumstances, to move as precisely as the king's plan demanded.

Philip II's reply, dated 17 December 1586, oscillated between uncertainty and irritation. He pointed out that the invasion of Ireland was scheduled to take place only two months before Parma's assault, so that there would scarcely be time for Elizabeth to recruit foreign mercenaries. Troops would be drawn from south-east England for service in Ireland, he predicted, thus reducing opposition to Parma's cross-Channel attack.

But the king's confidence was evidently shaken by the reservations of his outspoken subordinate. At one point in his letter he asked his nephew to consider whether it might be better to land on the Isle of Wight instead of Ireland, and in a holograph comment he noted rather forlornly: '[you] must appreciate that . . . we cannot avoid building up the Armada we have here, because of the need to defend Portugal and for other things; and that, having thus created it, at so much cost, it would be best not to lose the chance of doing something with it . . .'[1]

This display of vacillation seems to have provoked Parma into making an even stronger criticism of the royal master-plan. Now he unequivocally condemned both the seizure of an Irish springboard and the idea of a prior landing on the Isle of Wight. The king (his nephew suggested boldly) should concentrate on one thing at a time: if there must be an Armada, then let it sail straight for the Flemish coast and make the narrow seas safe for the Army of Flanders to effect its crossing.[2]

But the king would give no more ground. Parma's many criticisms and complaints were considered, and demolished, one by one. Most specifically, the demand that the Armada should sail directly to Flanders was met with the very objection which, in the event, the king himself was to lose sight of:

'[There are problems in] sending an Armada like this one at the time we are contemplating (when the weather is usually foul) into the Channel between France and England without having a safe haven in either kingdom, or any port in Flanders except Dunkirk, which (apart from being the only one) is not suitable for ships as big as ours.'

So, in spite of Parma's arguments, the Grand Design remained unchanged; plans for the landing of the Armada in Ireland went ahead, and so did arrangements for the invasion of Kent from Flanders.[3]

And yet there were signs that the king, despite his strong words, was beginning to entertain doubts about the strategy he had chosen. In February he asked the duke of Medina Sidonia, who was in charge of the fleet which was to sail from Andalusia as a second supporting wave, whether the escort galleons of the Indian Guard, now at San Lúcar, might be spared to reinforce the Armada. The duke was appalled at the prospect of imperilling the annual rhythm of the American silver-fleet, pointing out that 'the link between the two continents is the foundation of the wealth and power we have here': the treasure from Philip's trans-Atlantic possessions was, indeed, Spain's life-blood. But that was before Drake's Cadiz raid demonstrated the vulnerability of this vital artery. In its aftermath, the cautious Medina Sidonia changed his views: he now favoured adding to the Armada several armed Indies merchantmen, as well as the galleasses from Naples and the ships which had been embargoed to carry troops and munitions from Sicily to Lisbon. At Lisbon, the duke suggested tentatively, all the separate units should be formed into a single Grand Fleet which would operate together at all times.[4]

That was at the beginning of June. Thereafter, for almost a month, there followed a silence which historians have found hard to explain. But the reason is simple: Philip II's health suddenly collapsed. Early in 1587, long before Drake's raid, a note of deep weariness crept into the king's orders to his secretaries: 'You can send me a memo about these matters,' he wrote on 6 February, 'so that I can look at it along with the rest; although, the way things are these days, I don't know when that will be.' The next day, the king felt worse: 'I cannot handle any further business just now, because I have a terrible cold – which I already had last night – and I certainly cannot read or write . . . So you can see from this how impossible life is just now.' But the king soldiered on. On 9 February, at 10 p.m., he complained that papers were still being brought for him to read and sign – 'Look what I get to cure my cold!' – and by the 14th he clearly felt overwhelmed: 'I have been here, working on my papers for a long time . . . but while I've been at it, 10 or 12 more dossiers have been brought. The rest will have to wait until tomorrow.' With increasing frequency papers were sent back unread because the king 'had no time', or 'could not face them'. Finally in mid-May, just after news reached him of Drake's destruction at Cadiz, he became seriously ill. [5]

By 26 May he could cope only with the most urgent papers, and by 14 June not even that – a pressing letter from Mateo Vázquez had to wait two weeks before it could be read out to the ailing king. On the 20th, Philip's valet regretted that the king was so restless 'that I can no longer take advantage of that hour after he wakes up, which is the best time to read him state papers, because then he is alone and has the leisure [to listen].' Ten days later, the same valet lamented that 'the king's eyes are running all the time, his legs are very weak and his hand still painful; and the world is waiting.'[6]

It was indeed. Part of the problem lay in Philip II's obsessive desire to supervise every decision for himself. Admittedly he had come to trust Don Juan de Zúñiga, who had drafted the Armada masterplan; but Zúñiga died in November 1586. This left a gap at the centre of power which, for some time, no one could fill. In May 1587, at the beginning of the King's illness, his secretary of state for war vented to a colleague his frustration at 'the considerable time wasted in consultation, for His Majesty is slow in replying and time is lost that cannot be regained'.[7] He expressed the hope that more responsibility might be laid upon the council of war, whose membership had increased to six by May and rose to nine by August.

The council's first major attempt to influence policy seems to have been made towards the end of the king's long illness, when news of Drake's outrages impressed upon the government the need to take action of some sort. On 23 June its members had insisted that Santa Cruz should put to sea with his entire fleet in order to protect the treasure ships; as we have seen, the king agreed. Then on 13 July they argued powerfully, following Medina Sidonia's earlier suggestion, that all the ships mustered in Andalusia should sail to Lisbon, so that when the marquis returned from the Azores he would have at his disposal a single fleet of irresistible force. The king agreed again, later the same day.[8]

Three weeks later 86 ships under Don Alonso de Leiva sailed into the Tagus, firing off their guns with such exuberance that (according to an eye-witness) one could not see the sea for smoke. They included the great-ships of the future Levant and Andalusian squadrons, together with 28 hulks and the four Neapolitan galleasses. For several weeks, crews and embarked troops on the fleet were required to sleep on board their ships, in order to be ready to sail as soon as a contingent of Guipúzcoan ships under Miguel de Oquendo came down from the north, and the Portuguese and Biscayan squadrons of Santa Cruz and his vice-admiral Juan Martínez de Recalde returned from the Azores with the treasure fleet.[9]

But the marquis did not return until 29 September, and Recalde not until early October. To set sail for England at such a time, even if the fleet had been in a seaworthy state, posed grave problems in view of the high risk of storms: the disaster which befell Charles V's expedition against

Algiers, which set out against all advice in October 1541 and ended with the loss of most of the fleet, was an oft-cited precedent. The council of war, which included men with long naval experience, noted even before Santa Cruz set sail for the Azores that 'in view of the uncertainty concerning the time at which the marquis and his fleet may return, bringing the treasure ships with them, and without knowing the strength in which they will return (whether because they have encountered and fought the enemy, which would cause some damage, or because of storm damage or sickness among the crew, which are all things that often occur), we cannot predict or plan what may happen after the ships get back.' One councillor went even further: 'It is already clear that we cannot undertake any other major enterprise this year beyond escorting home the fleets.'[10]

But this view was vigorously rejected by the king. On 14 September, perhaps in response to Don Alonso de Leiva's boast that his part of the Grand Fleet was fully prepared for action, Philip II issued a further detailed directive to the Armada. There was now no talk of invading Ireland – indeed two whole clauses of the instructions were devoted to explaining that, because of the delays caused by Drake's raid and the need to escort the treasure fleets, there was no longer time to secure a base in Ireland before going on to invade England. The purpose of the enterprise, the king emphasised, remained unchanged: to restore England to the Catholic Church and to end English attacks on Spain's interests. Only the strategy had been modified.

Santa Cruz, together with the fleet from Andalusia and Miguel de Oquendo's newly arrived squadron from Guipúzcoa, was now ordered to 'sail in the name of God straight to the English Channel and go along it until you have anchored off Margate head, having first warned the duke of Parma of your approach.'[11]

Then, however, came a crucial ambiguity in the king's instructions. 'The said duke,' Philip continued, 'according to the orders he has received, on seeing the narrow seas thus made safe by the Armada being either anchored off the said headland or else cruising in the mouth of the Thames, . . . will immediately send across the army that he has prepared in small boats, of which (for transit alone) he has plenty.' The king went on to insist that, until Parma and his men had made their crossing, the Armada 'was to do nothing except make safe the passage, and defeat any enemy ships that may come out to prevent this.' He also loftily asserted that 'from Margate, you can prevent any junction between the enemy

DOMESTIC LIFE

Most of the men who sailed with the Armada brought their own cooking and eating utensils, although cheap crockery and wooden vessels were provided (against stoppage of pay) for those who possessed none. The richest ate off silver or porcelain, those of lesser rank off pewter, the poorest off cheap earthenware or treen. Many examples of domestic utensils, together with other personal items, have been recovered from the wrecks.

(*Top*) A pair of pewter plates from the wreck of *La Trinidad Valencera*. Each bears the mark of a London maker and the initials I Z. These may be those of Juan Zapata whose son, Don Sebastián, sailed on the ship. (*Left*) A simple turned wooden bowl.

(*Top, left to right*) a brass candlestick; a wooden vessel, possibly a salt cellar; an oil or vinegar jug of green-glazed earthenware. (*Bottom, left to right*) The fingerboard of a cittern; wood and pewter spoons; a boxwood comb.

139

warships in the Thames and the eastern ports, with those in the south and west, so that the enemy will not be able to concentrate a fleet which would dare to come out and seek ours.'

But, for all this, certain important questions were left unanswered. To begin with, would the fleet go across to the ports of Flanders to meet the army embarked and ready to go, or were the invasion barges expected to put out to meet the fleet in open water? In the former event, how would the deep-draught ships of the Armada negotiate the shallows and sand-banks which fringed the Flemish coast; in the latter, how could a fleet cruising offshore protect the exposed barges from Nassau's Cromsters when they sallied out?

The parallel instructions sent to the duke of Parma shed scarcely more light on these vital questions. 'I have decided,' the king told his nephew, 'that as soon as the marquis of Santa Cruz gets the treasure fleet safely to Cape St Vincent, which we hope to hear about from one hour to the next, and surrenders them there to the care of the galleys of Spain, he will sail straight to Lisbon. There he will pick up the rest of the fleet which awaits him and they will all sail directly, in the name of God, to the English Channel, proceeding along it until they drop anchor off Margate head.' The king promised Parma that the fleet would send advance warning of its approach, and continued, 'you will therefore be so well prepared that, when you see the narrow seas thus secured, with the Armada riding off the said cape or else cruising off the mouth of the Thames, . . . you will immediately send the whole army over in the boats you have prepared.' There was, once again, the assurance that, until the army was safely across, the Armada would concentrate solely on maintaining a clear passage; and Parma, on his part, was commanded not to stir from the Flemish coast until the fleet arrived. But of precisely how the army and the fleet were to meet, there was not a word.[12] It was, to say the least, an unfortunate oversight.

But now that the king's mind was made up again, he would brook no further delays or objections. From the moment that Santa Cruz brought his storm-battered fleet back into Lisbon on 29 September, having delivered the treasure galleons safely to Seville, he was bombarded with royal instructions, first requesting and then requiring him to put to sea at once. One such missive (of 10 October) ended: 'and so there is no more time to waste in requests and replies; just get on with the job and see if you cannot advance the agreed departure date [25 October] by a few days.' On

21 October, the king moaned that 'so much time has been lost already that every further hour of delay causes me more grief than you can imagine. And so I charge and command you most strictly to leave before the end of the month.' After that, letters of exhortation, wheedling and hectoring by turn, were dispatched almost daily from the king's tiny desk in the Escorial to the marquis in Lisbon. When the marquis sent one excuse after another for the unpreparedness of his ships – from the perennial problems of logistics and maintenance to damage wreaked by a cyclone on 16 November – the king dismissed them out of hand. Instead he insisted that the Armada should sail in two waves. The first would consist of all the fighting ships, carrying some reinforcements for Parma, whose flotilla from Flanders they would escort to Kent. After this, the galleons would return and pick up the transports and auxiliaries at Lisbon, leading them either to Kent (if Parma had become bogged down) or to Ireland. And then, when Santa Cruz protested that he no longer commanded enough ships even for this task, the king pleaded with him to lead out those that *were* still seaworthy: even if there were only 48 (9 November); even if there were only 35 (10 December); even if . . .

Philip II's other principal commander, the duke of Parma, was also forbidden to argue with the royal plan. On 14 September the king plainly lost his temper as he replied to a long whining lament from his nephew concerning the difficulty of keeping his army together by the Flanders coast while it waited for a fleet that never came.

'I cannot refrain from reminding you [wrote the king] that, apart from the initial idea of this enterprise and the selection of yourself to command it (which were my decisions), everything else connected with your end of the plan, including the resources and plan prepared, were according to your own instructions of which you alone were the author. Moreover, for its preparation and execution, I have given you in great abundance everything you have asked me for . . .'

All further criticisms of the plan were commanded to cease. But then on 30 September, after regretting that he had heard nothing from Parma for six weeks, the king announced Santa Cruz's belated return from the Azores and advised his nephew that, if the English should move their fleet down to Plymouth, leaving the Thames estuary unguarded, he might slip across the Channel alone and launch a surprise attack. The same suggestion was made rather more forcefully in royal letters dated 11 and 24 December – indeed one of them actually enquired whether Parma was already in England, and, if not, why not?[13]

Now it was the duke's turn to lose his temper. 'Your letters seem to infer', he wrote back furiously to the king, 'that I may have done what Your Majesty emphatically ordered me not to do': to cross before the marquis of Santa Cruz arrives with his fleet to protect the operation. He warmed to his theme:

'Your Majesty is perfectly well aware that, without the support of this fleet, I could not cross over to England with the boats I have here, and you very prudently ordered me in your letter of 4 September not to attempt to do so until the marquis arrived . . . Your Majesty has the right to give absolute orders, which I receive as special favours and execute; but for you to write to me now with a proposal that runs so contrary to the previous express orders and command of Your Majesty, causes me great anguish. I beg you most humbly to do me the very great favour of telling me what to do next.'

Once again, the letter – perhaps the most disrespectful and critical that the king was ever to receive from one of his subordinates – remained uncharacteristically free of annotation from the royal pen.[14]

Parma's anger was justified: to suggest that he should 'go it alone' in the depths of winter, without any pre-arranged back-up from Spain, was lunacy. So was the king's demand that Santa Cruz must sail at once, however small his fleet. Such unreasonable intransigence raises questions about Philip II's sanity under extreme stress – for, as both Santa Cruz and Parma separately pointed out, should their forces be lost it would take years to replace them.

The king's reckless insistence on something being done at once, whatever the risks, went far beyond the bounds of common sense. Perhaps he suffered another nervous collapse; certainly his health was again a cause for concern, and over Christmas he took to his bed once more. He was unable to get up to eat until 17 January 1588, and not until the 20th did his valet pronounce him capable of governing his empire – and his Armada – once again.

But the four weeks' convalescence seems to have gone some way towards restoring the king's legendary prudence, and he now began to take more rational steps to save both the Armada and the enterprise for which it had been created. Although on 16 January Santa Cruz wrote from Lisbon to say that the Grand Fleet would be ready to sail by the end of the month, the king was beginning to lose his trust in the old marquis. To check the true state of affairs he dispatched to Lisbon the late duke of Alba's tough and resourceful nephew, the count of Fuentes, with orders to ascertain what was really happening. Fuentes carried with him the authority, if need be, to dismiss Santa Cruz from his command.[15] When Philip's hatchet-man arrived at Lisbon on 30 January he found a state of utter chaos. Santa Cruz was both seriously ill and in deep mental despair, feebly trying to direct the fleet's preparations from his sickbed. Even at the height of his powers, the marquis had been a fighting admiral rather than a staff officer; he got things done by a combination of bombast, ruthless energy, and a lifetime's experience of war. But the Armada was beyond such simple cures, and in any case Santa Cruz had lost the physical stamina and the will to apply them. Now, as he lay dying, the whole Enterprise was on the verge of collapse.

For months bad management, often compounded by bad luck, had inflated even simple problems out of all proportion. The preparation and embarkation of the task force's siege train is a case in point. It had turned out that the field carriages of the eight *cañones de batir* which were to be shipped aboard the Levant squadron were in bad repair, and of an outdated pattern, so it was decided in October 1587 to replace them before embarkation. Two full sets of new-pattern carriages were ordered for each gun. But seasoned timber could not be obtained, and so green wood was used in its place. Then the ship carrying the specially-made iron fittings for the carriages was wrecked. The work was not completed until January.

Further difficulties arose when the time came to embark the heavy guns and their awkward accoutrements. On 2 January 1588 the Captain-General of Artillery, Juan de Acuña Vela, wrote to Philip II from Lisbon urging that the guns should be put aboard the ships at once, despite Santa Cruz's assurances that the matter could wait: clearly the ailing marquis was losing both his grip and his energy. By the end of the month Acuna Vela was still struggling with the problem, and on 30 January he wrote again to the king explaining that in the course of the previous week he had only been able to stow five of the *cañones de batir* aboard the Levantine ships: he had hoped to get the remaining three aboard that day but the galleys, which were evidently capable of slinging heavy loads, were otherwise employed. The Levanters' big tenders, which were also required for the operation, were not available either: they were working flat out distributing biscuit among the fleet. Four days later Acuña Vela reported that two more *cañones* were aboard, and only one now remained ashore.[16]

SHIPBOARD CRAFTS AND ROUTINES

Life at sea involved a wide range of duties and skills. These finds from the wreck of La Trinidad Valencera *reflect some of them. The bellows probably belonged to a blacksmith from one of the field forges attached to the artillery train. Daily water rations would have been collected and distributed in the copper bucket. Foodstuffs were carefully weighed out with the steelyard. The facing page shows a rush broom, a wooden mallet, and (top right), a wooden heddle used to weave coarse cloth with which ropes were wrapped to prevent chafing.*

(*Above*) a brass steelyard; (*right*) its weight.

145

Similar difficulties had apparently beset almost every aspect of the fleet's preparations, from the maintenance of the ships down to the supply of cheap crockery for the troops. Over the winter months, as Fuentes found out for himself, the Armada had been reduced to a shambles of 104 unseaworthy ships and rotting supplies and – more critical because less easily cured – of dispirited and disillusioned men. And their numbers, too, were falling: a muster on 20 January showed 12,600 troops attached to the fleet. By 13 February there were barely 10,000.[17]

Among the dead was Santa Cruz himself, carried off by typhus like so many of his men. He was little mourned: according to a Lisbon chronicler the marquis had been proud, avaricious and cruel, so that although he was worth over half a million ducats, only four people were prepared to accompany his coffin to the tomb, 'and his death was regretted by no one'.[18] But it enabled the king to take what was probably the only wholly sensible decision he was to make in the course of the entire unhappy affair. What the Armada needed, if it were to sail at all, was not another fighting admiral but a determined and practical man with the kind of personal qualities and administrative skills needed to turn the muddle at Lisbon into a coherent fighting force. Such a man was Don Alonso Pérez de Guzmán, duke of Medina Sidonia.

Medina Sidonia's qualifications to succeed Santa Cruz were impeccable. He had taken part in the Armada's planning from the outset, overseeing with great efficiency the outfitting and dispatch of the units assembled in the ports of Andalusia. They had all arrived at Lisbon in good order, and on time. This was perhaps not surprising, for the duke's administrative talents had been proved year after year, whether in governing his own vast estates or in fitting out, arming, and manning the great trans-Atlantic *flotas* which sailed annually from Andalusia to America. Nor was Medina Sidonia lacking in naval knowledge, at least on a theoretical level: his father had been taught by Pedro de Medina, the leading Spanish expert on navigation, and the ducal library was strong in nautical items.[19]

And though he lacked combat experience, Medina Sidonia's military record was by no means insubstantial. He had led an army during the Portuguese campaign of 1580, and commanded the relief force whose expeditious arrival had saved the town of Cadiz from being sacked during Drake's 'beard-singeing' exploit in 1587. His effective response to the attemped English landings had earned the praise and gratitude of Philip II and his ministers: the Venetian ambassador at Madrid went further, and opined that the duke had been the only man who kept his head in the crisis.[20] Finally, and in some respects most important of all, he was the head of one of Spain's most ancient and aristocratic families. None of the senior officers already serving in the Armada – not even the fiery Moncada, nor even Recalde and Leiva, each of whom had proposed himself as the successor to Santa Cruz – could feel any resentment or injustice in serving under a duke of Medina Sidonia.

The duke, moreover, was already exceptionally well briefed. He was one of the few men outside the king's inner council who had been privy to decisions about the Armada, and for some time he had been involved in many of its administrative and technical aspects. In the autumn of 1587 he had spent some weeks at court, and had taken part in ministerial discussions on the conduct of the impending war with England.

In mid-January 1588, when it was resolved to send to Lisbon ten escort galleons and four large merchantmen of the Indian Guard, now repaired and renovated following their safe delivery to Seville the previous September, Medina Sidonia (now back at his ducal castle of San Lúcar) was instructed by the king to expedite the move. It was to be his last service to the Armada as a subordinate.

Not for one moment, it seems, had Medina Sidonia wished for or expected high military command. But to his surprise and shock, he received a letter dated 11 February announcing that, since Santa Cruz was clearly too ill to lead the Armada, the king wished him to take charge. Understandably, given the current state of the Armada – and no one knew better than the duke how chaotic that state was – Medina Sidonia was most reluctant to assume command, and the reasons he advanced for being excused the appointment have often been used to discredit him. 'I have not good enough health for the sea,' he wrote to the king's secretary, Don Juan de Idiáquez, on 16 February,

'for I know by the small experience I have had afloat that I soon become sea-sick, . . . furthermore the force is so great, and the undertaking so important, that it would not be right for a person like myself, possessing no experience of seafaring or war, to take charge of it. I have no doubt that his Majesty will do me the favour which I humbly beg, and will not entrust me to do a task of which, certainly, I shall not give a good account; for I do not understand it, know nothing about it, have no health for the sea, and have no money to spend upon it.'

But there was clearly more to Medina Sidonia's refusal than the reasons given in his uncharacteristically disorganised and rambling letter. The king, it is true, simply dismissed the duke's excuses as misplaced modesty, and refused to consider them further. What Philip did not see was a second letter written by the duke two days later, after he had had time to collect his thoughts and marshal his objections. This second letter was an uncompromising appreciation in which the duke argued that the whole Armada venture was ill-conceived and consequently doomed almost inevitably to failure.

But these cogent arguments never reached the king. His health was again failing; for most of February and March he complained of pains in his stomach, of tiredness, of over-work. Piles of urgent correspondence accumulated on his desk – some unopened, others unread, most unanswered. In any case, Medina Sidonia's vital letter of 18 February was not among them. It had been intercepted and retained by the two councillors of state who had inherited the mantle of Don Juan de Zúñiga: Don Juan de Idiáquez, a Basque whose family had long been prominent in the central government, and Don Crístobal de Moura, a Portuguese whose diplomacy and duplicity had played a key role in the annexation of his native land in 1580. Now they attended continuously upon the king and handled the day-to-day receipt, filing, and dispatch of the immense quantity of paperwork which the king's single-handed direction of the Enterprise of England generated. They resided at court thoughout 1588, and nothing of consequence concerning the Armada bypassed them.

When, in the course of these duties, they opened Medina Sidonia's frank letter of 18 February, they were appalled. 'We did not dare to show his Majesty what you have just written,' they chided the unfortunate duke, and went on to rebuke his pusillanimity – 'Do not depress us with fears for the fate of the Armada, because in such a cause God will make sure it succeeds' – and to warn him of the consequences of refusing such a signal honour from his king. Everyone knew, they reminded him, that the offer had been made; to refuse it now would lead to accusations of ingratitude, selfishness, even cowardice. 'Remember that the reputation and esteem you currently enjoy for courage and wisdom would entirely be forfeited if what you wrote to us became generally known (although we shall keep it secret)'. Here was a palpable threat, and it found its mark. Before the combined impact of moral pressure, special pleading, and naked black-mail, Medina Sidonia crumbled.

By the end of February 1588, the new Captain-General of the Ocean Sea was on his way to Lisbon.[21]

With the Armada now in safe hands again, the ailing king and his ministers turned their thoughts back to the diplomatic isolation of Elizabeth. The keystone of their policy, once again, was the paralysis of France. In spite of the defeat of the royal armies by the Huguenots at Coutras in October 1587, and the humiliation of Henry III by the duke of Guise, Spain still feared that the French government might offer support to Elizabeth. But at a meeting with the Spanish ambassador in late April, Guise agreed that he would engineer a general rebellion by the Catholic League the moment he heard of the Armada's departure. The deal was clinched by the immediate payment of 100,000 crowns in gold (£25,000) to the League's leaders.[22]

Guise, however, was no longer able to control the enthusiasm of his subordinates. Early in May the Paris Catholics began to agitate for a take-over of the city and when, on 12 May 1588, Henry III brought in his Swiss Guards to preserve order, the entire city erupted into violence, erecting barricades against the king's troops and forcing him to flee from his capital. The 'Day of the Barricades' made Guise the master of Paris and shortly afterwards he was named the king's 'lieutenant-general of the kingdom'.

Philip II's support for the French Catholic League following the treaty of Joinville had thus paid handsome dividends. It is true that he had intended Guise to capture Henry III, and force him to make concessions – including free access to ports like Boulogne and Calais – as the Armada entered the Channel. But, even without that crowning achievement, the towns of Picardy (as well as Paris) remained in League hands, and so rendered impracticable any attempt by Henry III to aid Elizabeth.[23]

Philip's diplomacy also ensured – rather more surprisingly – that the Dutch rendered precious little aid to England. In part it was an English 'own goal'. Leicester's government of the Netherlands had not been successful. The earl had proved unable to manage the prickly Dutch leaders as William of Orange had done: he was sworn in as Governor-General in January 1586, but his powers were left undefined. He tried to create a strong central executive, to levy higher taxes for defence, and to purge the provincial governments of those who opposed his policies. But his position was undermined. First, he failed to stop Parma, who in the 1586 campaign captured several towns along the great rivers that now separated the two sides. Second, early in 1587, two of Leicester's commanders betrayed his cause and delivered to Spain the strategic town of Deventer and a fort which dominated Zutphen. The earl was totally discredited and 'there grew a wonderful alteration in the hearts and affections of the people against the English. They uttered lewd and irreverent speeches of his Excellency and the whole nation.' But far more serious was Elizabeth's decision to resume the talks with Parma which had been broken off after Drake's raid on Cadiz.

On 12 June 1587 Parma laid siege to the deep-water port of Sluys on the Flemish side of the Scheldt. On the 24th bombardment began and, early the next month, the Spaniards managed to throw a bridge across the estuary below the town (as they had done at Antwerp), and cut it off from the sea. Elizabeth hurriedly sent reinforcements and money across to the Dutch, for not only was Sluys defended by English troops: it was a port from which England could be invaded. But the queen also re-opened talks with Parma about a cease-fire. Parma, however, continued with the siege and on 4 August, after 13 days of constant fighting around the walls (breached by some 14,000 rounds from Parma's guns), the English garrison ran out of powder and had to surrender. Elizabeth now began to regard the talks more seriously, and begged her Dutch allies to join her in negotiating with Parma. When they refused, Leicester made a half-hearted attempt to seize a number of strategic towns in the Republic, as Anjou had done three years before. Like Anjou he failed; and, again like Anjou, having failed he went home (December 1587).

The Dutch were now totally incapable of mobilising their own defence. They had 20,000 troops in garrison, with only 11,000 as a field army, plus the 6,000 of the English 'secours': without the latter, their defence by land would collapse. It was the same by sea. Although in 1584, a few months before his death, Orange had stated the urgent need for ten 'good ships' to patrol the coasts in case of Spanish attack, the States-General had refused to comply. Instead of warships of 300 and 400 tons, converted merchantmen of 200 were brought into service. As the Armada entered the Channel in 1588, the entire Dutch navy consisted of a mere 32 ships, all of them formerly merchantmen and most of them small.[24] When in May 1588 some further vessels were sent to Dover to join the English fleet they were ordered to return on the grounds that they were too small to be of service beside the queen's ships. If the Armada's target had been a port in Zealand, or even Amsterdam, there was virtually nothing that the Dutch could have done to resist. The reconquest of the Low Countries, and therefore the rebellion, might have been over in a matter of weeks.

But, as Parma was all too well aware, the Armada was aimed at England. Nevertheless, continuing the talks with Elizabeth served his purpose: on the one hand they cast some doubt upon his intentions; on the other they called into question England's commitment to Dutch defence. On Philip II's orders the talks were prolonged and concessions were hinted at; and each time the English accepted the bait – sending commissioners to Ostend (a town loyal to the States-General) in February; moving to Spanish territory at Bourbourg (near Dunkirk) in May. Parma's agents made much political capital out of it with the suspicious Dutch. It is true that Elizabeth also gained something from the talks (above all an observation post in Flanders from which to monitor Parma's military preparations); but she lost far more, by forfeiting the confidence and trust of the Dutch.

Most of Parma's energy after the capture of Sluys, however, was taken up with the concentration of sufficient troops for a successful invasion of England, and with obtaining transport vessels to convey them. The first proved easier than the second. 2,000 Spaniards were marched from Lombardy to Luxembourg along 'the Spanish Road' in September 1586, and a further 9,000 Italians and 4,500 Spaniards followed them during 1587. An assault force of 17,000 men could thus be dispatched to England, while still leaving behind enough troops to defend the Spanish Netherlands.

Finding sufficient vessels to transport this army was far more difficult. But Parma tried. 170 sailing barges and other flat-bottomed boats (several of them large enough to convey 30 horses at a time) were assembled in Antwerp and the coastal ports of Flanders; 16 larger ships were hired in Hamburg and brought to Dunkirk, where a further 13 French and 16 Flemish ships were embargoed. All were given new rigging, some small artillery and even a special campaign pennant. The royal standard was made of red damask, with the Spanish coat-of-arms picked out in gold on one side and a depiction of Christ crucified, flanked by the Virgin Mary and St John the Baptist, on the other. Lesser ensigns in yellow taffeta displayed the cross of Burgundy, the arms of the seventeen provinces of the Netherlands, and of Spain. The specially-commissioned flags were 'scattered with flames of fire' and the service of the Antwerp painter Hans Smit cost the government 2,400 florins (£240). They would, no doubt, have made a splendid show as they glided across the Channel; but of course none of these ships ever weighed anchor. Those at Antwerp, which included a flagship of 400 tons and three more of 300, were penned in by a strong Dutch squadron; while those in the coastal ports were small – the largest was only 130 tons – and, according to an English spy, most of them 'not to be adventured upon the seas, but in the shortest places of passage, and in fair weather'.[25]

Parma himself entirely agreed.

'My vessels here [he warned the king] are no good for anything except transportation, because for the most part they are barges and cobs, which in a fight would be so small and frail that four warships would be able to sink every boat they met'.

There were, admittedly, plans to strengthen the flotilla by hijacking 30 Scottish merchantmen with their 6 escort vessels as they sailed from Danzig to Aberdeen, and 10,000 ducats in gold was sent to Catholic leaders in the north-east of Scotland to arrange it; but neither the gold nor the ships were ever seen again. So Parma remained profoundly uneasy about his ability to get the army across.[26]

And yet the king seemed to be impervious to such doubts. Parma repeatedly drew attention, in his letters to both Philip II and his ministers, to the absence of any detailed procedure for uniting his troops from Flanders with the fleet from Spain, when he lacked both a deep-water port to shelter the fleet and a navy of his own capable of 'going it alone'.

It is curious that none of these communications bears any holograph comment from the royal pen, for Philip II normally festooned all that interested him with notes and observations. The absence of such apostils does not, of course, mean that the king did not read these letters, but it does suggest that he may have failed to grasp their full significance.

Nor did he heed the advice of those in command of the fleet who called the wisdom of the Grand Design into question. On 15 February 1588 Martín de Bertendona reported to the king a conversation he had had with Santa Cruz just before the marquis died. They had agreed, said Bertendona, that the key problem was the lack of any deep-water ports between the Isle of Wight and Flushing, and had reviewed the sort of difficulties that could arise in the Channel when storms blew. 'But,' Bertendona concluded serenely (and undoubtedly sarcastically), 'since it is your Majesty who has decided everything, we must believe that it is God's will.' Perhaps it was also Bertendona who informed a confidant of the papal nuncio, in May 1588, that

'Unless God helps us by a miracle the English, who have faster and handier ships than ours, and many more long-range guns, and who know their advantage just as well as we do, will never close with us at all, but stand aloof and knock us to pieces with their culverins, without our being able to do them any serious hurt. And so we are sailing against England in the confident hope of a miracle!'[27]

Between the death of Santa Cruz in February and this conversation in May, however, a minor miracle had indeed occurred. Under Medina Sidonia's firm but courteous direction, aided by his own prodigious capacity for hard work and a willingness to seek the opinions of his more experienced subordinates, the fleet was made seaworthy. The ships already at Lisbon were repaired and they were joined by several new ones: some additional great merchantmen, including the *Lavia* and the huge *Regazona* (which became Bertendona's flagship), by embargo in February; the galleons and armed merchantmen of the Indian Guard – which were named the 'squadron of Castile' – in April. One of the duke's less well-known achievements was to invent the printed military form: he took over a press in the city, and ran off multiple copies of his General Orders, with blank spaces left for non-standard items.

Printed ration receipt made out on behalf of Martín de Licarde, master of the Andalusian vice-flagship *San Francisco*, 6 May 1588.

But not all the problems could be solved by efficient paperwork. One outstanding worry was the lack of galleys. Both Santa Cruz and Bertendona had stressed that because of the amphibious nature of the operation these were even more essential than additional ships. At least twelve would be needed, they felt, for close support when Parma's army stormed the Kent beaches. Medina Sidonia clearly agreed. Within three days of his arrival at Lisbon he was writing to the king that the four galleys allocated to him were not enough, especially as three of them were so old. But this request, apparently, fell on deaf ears. Only four galleys eventually sailed, and none of them reached the English Channel.

The duke was more successful in his efforts to rationalise the bewildering and totally unstandardised hotch-potch of guns which had been gathered together from the length and breadth of Europe, and to match them with the available ammunition. On the question of ammunition Medina Sidonia backed his own judgement that artillery would play a major role in the battles to come. In this he was supported by the normally taciturn Don Francisco de Bobadilla, the fleet's senior military commander, who later wrote: 'There was great scarcity of cannon-ball . . . The count of Fuentes can bear witness how much I pleaded in this matter with Don Juan de Acuña, telling him that if the enemy did not allow us to board them and if the artillery fight lasted four days, he might tell me what we might do on the fifth.' Don Juan de Acuña Vela, the king's Captain General of Artillery, had estimated that 30 rounds per gun would be sufficient but, heeding Don Francisco's advice, the duke insisted that quotas should go up to the unprecedented minimum of 50. He petitioned the king, and they did.[28]

Right up to the end strenuous efforts were made to obtain more guns. Even trophies from former victories were pressed into service. A bronze gun bearing the royal arms of Francis I of France, perhaps captured at St Quentin in 1557 or even at Pavia in 1525 (when Francis himself was taken prisoner), was loaded aboard the Levanter *San Juan de Sicilia*. The *San Juan's* sister ship *Trinidad Valencera* was given a huge Turkish *cañón de batir*, possibly a relic of Lepanto seventeen years earlier. Meanwhile, the seven bronze foundries at Lisbon were working flat out, and when Medina Sidonia arrived to take command an initial batch of 40 new pieces had just been delivered. Another eleven were in the process of manufacture. Under Medina Sidonia's regime, steps were taken to speed up production still further. All royal guns were normally required to bear the king's arms (his full titles and escutcheon if the piece was of 20 quintals or above, just his name and a crown if they were lighter). But such embellishment took time, and so a special dispensation to omit it was obtained. This step was entirely sensible, but production pressures also took their toll on quality, and many corners were cut. There were horrifying accidents when inadequately baked moulds burst, or when guns failed their proofing tests. In one such incident a weak gun exploded, killing two gunners and taking off the arm of a third. Perhaps as a result, many pieces were not properly proofed, and on occasion sub-standard guns were evidently passed fit for service.[29]

Among the duke's other achievements in his first three months of office was to provide each ship with a printed set of pilotage instructions and a proper chart. Santa Cruz had obtained, on 25 September 1587, a 'careful relation of all the coasts of England with a note of the depth and size of the harbours' – almost certainly Waghenaer's *Mariner's Mirror* – and a chart of the coasts of England, Scotland and Ireland by the Lisbon cartographer Luis Teixeira. But these were single copies for his personal use. In January 1588 the king also provided a special itinerary for his fleet, which he had personally checked against his own maps; but once again only one copy was sent to the Armada. This was clearly of little use, so Medina Sidonia arranged for the itinerary to be printed and ordered Ciprián Sánchez of Lisbon to prepare 85 identical charts of the coasts of Spain, England and Flanders, for distribution among the fleet. They were all aboard by 12 May 1588, when the cartographer was paid. Individual captains now had a practical guide to the waters in which they were expected to sail.[30]

By then the fleet had been increased from the 104 ships of February to 130, and the troops from scarcely 10,000 to 18,973.[31] Many of those languishing in hospital were cured – even old Recalde, after being bled four times, came back aboard. Provisions and water were stowed according to a carefully planned turnover system, and the abysmal morale of the men had been replaced by a pious fervour to sail.

Such an achievement bespeaks leadership of a high order, and that leadership unquestionably came from Medina Sidonia. Even the duke himself, it seems, had become cautiously optimistic about the outcome of the campaign. After a series of parades in early April, and the consecration of the expedition's banner on the 25th, a general fleet muster was held at Lisbon on 9 May. Everything was now ready, or as ready as it would ever be.

In Paris, the wits had been giving odds of 6 to 1 against the Armada reaching the Channel. They lost. On 28 May 1588 the duke of Medina Sidonia led his great Armada down the Tagus towards the open sea, and the world held its breath.

PART III:

It Came, Went, and Was

CHAPTER 9

The advance to Calais

Great things were now expected of the Armada. 'All wars and affairs afoot today', wrote Don Juan de Idiáquez on the eve of its departure, 'are reduced to this one enterprise.' The king and his ministers saw the 1588 campaign as the simultaneous means of preserving the life-line between Spain and America, of protecting the Iberian peninsula from invasion, and of ending the war in the Netherlands – that 'voracious monster which gobbles up the troops and treasures of Spain.'[1]

The instructions issued to Medina Sidonia on 1 April 1588, however, did not entirely make clear how these momentous goals were to be achieved. In part, they merely repeated the orders issued to Santa Cruz the previous September, and commanded the Captain-General to lead his fleet directly to 'Margate head', there to 'join hands' with Parma and his army. At this point the instructions became bogged down in detail about the conduct of the fleet, and the behaviour of its human cargo on such a saintly enterprise. Theology and practical advice were inextricably muddled. There must be no blasphemy aboard the ships; the English fleet must be defeated if it tried to attack or halt the Armada; the two dukes must cooperate fully on terms of equality and respect. The king's only detailed comments on the fleet's strategic options related to what should be done if, by some mischance, the rendezvous between the Armada and Parma proved impossible. Then (and only then), the king conceded, the fleet might return through the Channel, capture the Isle of Wight, and wait there until a second attempt to join Parma could be made. If, on the other hand, everything went according to plan, and Parma was ensconced firmly in southern England, the fleet might sail back and accomplish the conquest of Ireland.

The two glaring omissions in Philip's instructions were the continuing absence of any detailed explanation of how, on the one hand, the rendezvous was to be effected, and how, on the other, the Armada could secure local command of the sea. There were indeed a few sentences on this point, but their implications were more alarming than illuminating:

'There is little to say with regard to the mode of fighting and the handling of the Armada on the day of battle . . . [but] it must be borne in mind that the enemy's object will be to fight at long distance, in consequence of his advantage in artillery, and the large number of artificial fires with which he will be furnished. The aim of our men, on the contrary, must be to bring him to close quarters and grapple with him, and you will have to be very careful to have this carried out . . . The enemy employs his artillery to deliver his fire low and sink his opponent's ships; and you will have to take such precautions as you consider necessary in this respect.'

We may admire the king's tactical insight on this problem; but we must censure him – as, no doubt, the Armada's officers were later to censure him – for his total failure to suggest a solution.[2]

For another two months, however, these difficulties remained academic, because the Armada was unable to leave Lisbon. On 14 May, at long last, it was pronounced ready to sail, but then, reported Medina Sidonia, weather conditions became as 'boisterous and bad as if it were December.' The ships were still at anchor a fortnight later, with a north-westerly gale howling up the estuary. At last, on 30 May, the Armada was at sea, but its progress northwards proved tortuously slow because of contrary winds and the abysmal sailing qualities of the hulks. Some of these squat bulk carriers, up to 36 years old, were notoriously clumsy. The big Levanters, designed for the Mediterranean grain trade, were not much better.[3]

Now that he could gauge the performance of his fleet at sea, Medina Sidonia's old doubts returned, and he expressed them in a dispatch to the king. Philip II's reply was sympathetic but uncompromising:

'I see plainly the truth of what you say, that the Levant ships are less free and staunch in heavy seas than the vessels built here, and the hulks cannot sail to windward; but it is still the fact that the Levant ships sail constantly to England, and the hulks hardly go anywhere else but up the Channel, and it is quite an exception for them to leave it to go to other seas. It is true that if we could have things exactly as we wished, we would rather have other vessels, but under the present circumstances the expedition must not be abandoned on account of this difficulty.'

But another, more serious, difficulty was now beginning to manifest itself. Despite the duke's careful preparations at Lisbon, the provisions had started to run out. Some of the food was putrid, and had probably been so from the start: considerable quantities had to be thrown into the sea in June. (In July the English who captured the *Rosario* noticed that the food aboard was unfit to eat: 'their fish unsavoury and their bread full of worms'). The shortage was made much worse by Medina Sidonia's outstanding success in boosting the size of his forces. The 10,000 or so fighting men of February had now swollen to almost 19,000, and they were consuming provisions faster than replacements could be assembled: on 9 July rations had to be cut to one pound of biscuit a day, with reduced quantities of meat ('on the days when it can be issued'). But, above all, rations were running out because the whole operation was taking far longer to execute than expected.[4]

The duke did what he could. Dispatches were sent to Galicia with orders for the provincial governor to collect supplies of fresh food and water, and ferry them to the fleet when it came level with Cape Finisterre. But in the event the Armada took two weeks to struggle the 250 miles to the Cape and, when it got there, the victualling tenders had departed. On 19 June, after waiting five days (during which the decks of each ship were cleared for action), a council of war was held at which it was decided to put in to Corunna for replenishment. By late evening the flagship *San Martín* and 35 other ships had reached harbour but the remainder, including the galleasses, the clumsy hulks, and the big Levanters, together with Recalde's squadron, stood off beyond the headland in the failing light intending to make their entrance the following morning at daybreak.

During the night, however, the ships lying outside Corunna were scattered by a sudden and violent south-westerly gale, and some were driven as far afield as the Scilly Isles.

The initial reaction of the duke seems to have been total despair. On 24 June he composed a long and detailed appeal to the king for the whole operation to be called off, marshalling his argument under two headings: logistical and theological. By now, it seems, the duke had got the measure his master.

He was moved to write, Medina Sidonia began, by the unusual severity of the storm the Armada had just experienced:

'At any time it would be remarkable; but since it is only the end of June and since this is the cause of Our Lord, to whose care it has been – and is being – so much entrusted, it would appear that what has just happened must be His doing, for some just reason.'

Perhaps, the duke speculated, the Almighty was issuing a warning that the Enterprise should be abandoned? Be that as it may, the Armada's situation was indeed perilous. Twenty-eight of the fleet's vessels, including some of the most powerful (along with the artillery train and around 6,000 men), were missing. Without them the forces remaining under his command were dangerously inferior to those of the enemy. Medina Sidonia could see two alternatives: either to press on regardless with the ships available, or to wait in Corunna for the missing vessels to return. Both proposals involved grave risks. Any attempt to carry out the Grand Design except in overwhelming strength, the duke pointed out, would prove counter-productive: the Armada would never be able to reach Parma's army, let alone shepherd it across the Channel. And yet further delays would mean sailing northwards during the season when navigation was most hazardous. Therefore, the duke humbly concluded, might it not be better to cancel the whole operation and make some honourable peace with Spain's enemies? At the very least, all these considerations seemed to him to 'make it essential that the enterprise we are engaged in should be given the closest scrutiny'.

The courier departed; the duke waited. He had risked his neck on two counts: first by suggesting that the king should make peace with his enemies, which came close to treason; second, and more seriously, by implying that perhaps Philip II no longer had God on his side – which, in the king's eyes, might verge on heresy.

On 27 June, perhaps for greater peace of mind, Medina Sidonia summoned a council of war to discuss the dilemma in which the Armada found itself. After a lengthy examination of the alternatives a vote was taken and, to the duke's profound relief, nine of his officers agreed that the Armada was too weak to carry out its task in its present condition.

Only one, the impetuous Don Pedro de Valdés, argued vehemently for an immediate surprise attack. Things would never get better, he thundered, and might well get worse: they must strike now, while they still could. His views were duly noted. All present then signed the minutes of the meeting, which were sent off to the king.

The great task of repairing and revictualling the ships then got under way, and gradually the stragglers returned to the main fleet (12 of them, in a body, on 5 July). 'The duke is working with great energy, as usual,' Recalde told the king; and indeed, once again, Medina Sidonia's tireless attention to detail and wide administrative experience brought the

32. Gold and silver coins, and a gold chain, from the *Girona*.

33. A Ming bowl from the wreck of *La Trinidad Valencera*. Officers and noblemen aboard the Armada took with them full dinner services and other fincry – not for the voyage or the campaign, but for use in England when they took up positions of state in a new Spanish regime.

coninginne   van schotlant

Den VIII february, werde onthalst Maria
Stuart Schots Coninginne's fervende Roomsch Catho-
lyck Hebbende gesocht veel onrusten aen te richten Haer schock-
nicesten te maecken van Engelant t dwelck haer vanden Raet
offte parlement Voleomelyck werde vertoont, Anno. 1587.
Metren XIII. fol. XIII. en XIIII. b.

34. The execution of
Mary Queen of Scots at
Fotheringhay Castle on
18 February 1587, from
a contemporary Dutch
watercolour.

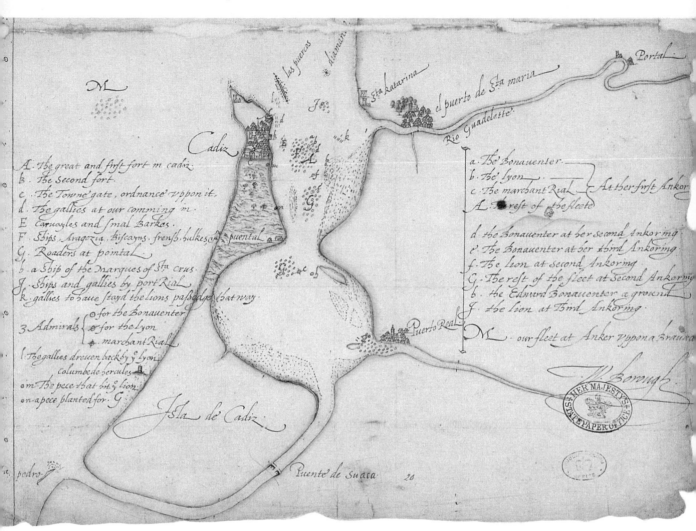

35. Cadiz harbour, showing Spanish and English dispositions during Drake's raid of 29 April 1587. This map was drawn by William Borough, Sir Francis's second-in-command.

36. View of Corunna harbour, from an early 17th century English report. The town lies at the neck of the bulbous peninsula towards the left, guarded by the fortified island of San Antón. Here the Armada sought shelter in June 1588. Although the bay is well sheltered from the weather, its wide entrance rendered it vulnerable to attack by sea. Towards the top right of the picture lies the land-locked harbour of Ferrol.

37. A cheap pewter medallion from the *Girona*, identical to several found on this and other Armada wrecks. They are almost certainly examples of the medallions issued when members of the fleet were shriven in batches on the island of San Antón, in Corunna harbour, before the final departure for England.

Signatures to the minutes of
the council of war held at
Corunna on 27 June 1588,
at which it was resolved – in
spite of Don Pedro de
Valdés's protestation that
the depleted Armada should
sail at once for England – to
wait until the missing ships
had returned. The signatories
include, from top left: Juan
Martínez de Recalde; Don
Francisco de Bobadilla;
Diego Flores de Valdés; Don
Pedro de Valdés; Miguel de
Oquendo; Don Hugo de
Moncada; Martín de Berten-
dona; Juan de Velasco;
Gaspar de Hermosilla; Don
Jorge Manrique.

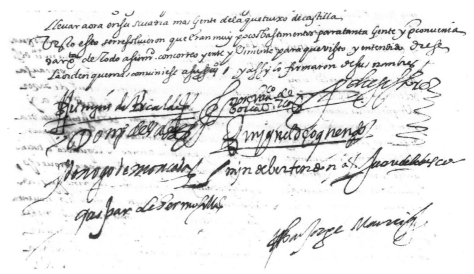

Signatures to the minutes of
the council of war held at
Corunna on 27 June 1588,
at which it was resolved – in
spite of Don Pedro de
Valdés's protestation that
the depleted Armada should
sail at once for England – to
wait until the missing ships
had returned. The signatories
include, from top left: Juan
Martínez de Recalde; Don
Francisco de Bobadilla;
Diego Flores de Valdés; Don
Pedro de Valdés; Miguel de
Oquendo; Don Hugo de
Moncada; Martín de Berten-
dona; Juan de Velasco;
Gaspar de Hermosilla; Don
Jorge Manrique.

Armada through another crisis. His style of command was not aloof or
remote: on 10 July, for instance, we find him personally supervising the
stepping of a new mainmast into the storm-damaged *Santa María de la
Rosa* – a task which took six hours, and caused much difficulty. 'When it
was finished,' he reported with genuine modesty to the king, 'I thought we
had not done badly.'

But by then, another courier had arrived from the Escorial. Medina
Sidonia's dispirited letter had caught the king at a bad moment. Shortly
before it arrived, there had been further royal lamentations about the
pressure of work and ill-health ('I have to spend so much time on
incoming papers that I believe it's making me walk badly . . . please tell
some of the ministers in Madrid to moderate the number of papers they
send'); but Philip roused himself to give careful consideration to the views
of the duke and his council. And in a letter of 1 July, he rejected them
outright. The first lines he read must have made Medina Sidonia blench:

'Duke and cousin [began the king's message]. I have received the letter written in
your own hand, dated 24 June. From what I know of you, I believe that your
bringing all these matters to my attention arises solely from your zeal to serve me
and a desire to succeed in your command. The certainty that this is so prompts me
to be franker with you than I should be with another . . .'

But after this terrifying start the rest of the missive, although firm, was
understanding and mild. Each of the original reasons for undertaking the
Grand Design was restated, and each of the duke's objections was
systematically demolished by Philip's perverse logic. First the theology:

'If this were an unjust war, one could indeed take this storm as a sign from Our Lord to cease offending Him; but being as just as it is, one cannot believe that He will disband it, but will rather grant it more favour than we could hope. . . .'

Then the logistics and strategy: the English had no allies and their forces, despite all Medina seemed to have heard, were inferior to Spain's; with a following wind, the fleet would be in the Channel within a week, whereas if it remained in Corunna the Armada could do nothing to compel the English to negotiate. Worst of all, now that Elizabeth had mobilised her warships, the disorganised and dispirited fleet in Corunna represented a sitting target, either to be destroyed at anchor or else blockaded in port while the English raided the Indies and captured the next treasure fleet. So the logic of the situation was clear, and the Captain-General of the Ocean Sea should need no further reminding of where his duty lay: 'I have dedicated this enterprise to God,' concluded the king '. . . Get on, then, and do your part!'[5]

This time, perhaps, the king's strategic argument was more soundly based. It made no sense to turn back before the Armada, collected with so much trouble and expense, had achieved any of its objectives; and the English fleet might indeed sail into Corunna harbour at any moment, with guns blazing, as it had done the previous year at Cadiz.

That was precisely what Drake and Howard intended. While the queen's commissioners continued to negotiate fitfully at Bourbourg, her admirals prepared for another pre-emptive strike against Spain. On 1 June Howard left the Downs, and two days later he was at Plymouth, where he and Drake now commanded 60 fighting ships. But the weather was against them. 'God send us wind' exclaimed Howard later; for 'if the wind had favoured us when we went out from hence . . . they [the Spaniards] should not have needed to come this far to have sought us.' On 4 July his prayer was answered, and the navy royal sailed for Spain. But it never got there. Storms off the Scillies, more storms off Ushant, and finally a flat calm when they were 60 miles off the coast of Spain kept the English away from Corunna. When at last the wind returned, their victuals were dangerously low, and in any case the wind was from the south and they were forced to return to the Channel.

And, as Howard later realised, 'The southerly wind that brought us back from Spain brought them out.' For on 21 July, with almost all the stragglers reunited, Medina Sidonia led his great fleet to sea again.

After the duke received the king's incisive letter of 1 July, a number of important steps had been taken by the Armada's high command. The holy nature of the campaign was once again emphasised, and the duke's orders to avoid swearing, gambling and blasphemy, and for prayers to be said twice daily, were repeated. In an attempt to improve motivation all the men of the fleet were landed in batches on the island of San Antón in Corunna harbour, where each was confessed, blessed, and issued with a pewter medallion showing the Virgin on one side and Christ on the other. Morale seems, understandably, to have been low: the island location was clearly chosen because the men might desert if taken ashore. Some of the more privileged gentleman-adventurers, whose shore leave was apparently less restricted, did indeed take their opportunity to cut and run: the medical officer aboard the *Nuestra Señora del Rosario* later reported that a number of these young men 'stayed in the Groyne [Corunna] and would not go forward.' These faint-hearts were probably no great loss. Old Recalde had already complained of command being given to men simply 'because they are gentlemen.' Very few of them, he went on, 'are soldiers, or know what to do.'

When the fleet eventually sailed from Corunna it was in much better heart. Fresh provisions had been embarked, the loads of some ships adjusted, and special efforts made to cure the sick. Some reinforcements arrived, but Medina Sidonia welcomed them with a critical eye. When a contingent of 400 fresh recruits arrived from Galicia the duke rejected them: he explained to the king on 19 July that they were so old, infirm and underfed, and so lacking in military experience ('not one of them knows what an arquebus is') that, rather than have them drop dead on board ship, he had succumbed to the 'lamentations of their wives' (who had come along too) and let them all go home.

On the same day there was a council of war to decide whether the Armada was ready to put to sea and, if so, what tactics to adopt when the English fleet was encountered. All of the commanders present voted to depart for England on the first favourable tide; all but one of them accepted the form of battle favoured at Lepanto and other naval battles, with an extended line of ships forming a crescent formation. The odd man out, once again, was Don Pedro de Valdés. He proposed that the fleet should be divided into three sections: the 'weak and slow vesssels in the centre 'so that with the fighting ships divided equally into a rearguard and vanguard around this, if the enemy should attack from behind the whole fleet can turn about. Thus the vanguard can support the rearguard or, should the attack come from the front, the rearguard can reinforce the van. . . .' Don Pedro was clearly a difficult man, but on this occasion he was undoubtedly correct, and after its first encounters with the English, the Armada did indeed adopt the more compact formation he advocated.[6]

Two days later the Grand Fleet was at last heading northwards again. On the 25th, Medina Sidonia felt confident enough to send a pinnace to Parma, announcing his approach, and four more days of brisk southerly breezes brought the Armada across the Bay of Biscay to the latitude of Ushant, beyond which lay the entrance to the English Channel. About this time they were spotted by a Cornish ship, bound for France to load salt: her captain noted with awe the great red crosses on the Armada's sails before fleeing homewards with his breathless story. But there were some unexpected casualties. Diego de Medrano's four galleys, which had belatedly joined the fleet off Finisterre, failed to weather the rolling Atlantic swells, and had to run for the nearest port; one, the *Bazana*, was wrecked at the entrance to Bayonne. The 768-ton Biscayan flagship *Santa Ana* also came to grief, losing one of her masts through a pilot's error; she sought shelter first at La Hogue, on the eastern side of the Cherbourg peninsula, and finally at Le Havre, where she was to remain throughout the campaign. Nevertheless early on 30 July the rest of the fleet began its stately advance up the English Channel.

They caught the English at a disadvantage. After the abortive raid on Corunna, the navy had only regained Plymouth Sound on 22 July, its victuals all consumed. But, of course, the Spaniards did not know this and so, instead of hastening to attack them in the uncertain waters beyond the Lizard, Medina Sidonia took in sail for the night, called a council of war, and waited for stragglers to catch up.

By the time the Armada was again under way, with a westerly wind behind it and had, amid squalls, caught its first sight of the English coast, Howard and his 105 ships had cleared harbour and were striving to gain a windward position. But the two fleets were still not in contact and, under cover of darkness on the night of 30/31 July, the Lord Admiral skilfully led most of his ships across the front of the Armada to gain the weather gauge on the right, while Drake's squadron, by tacking close inshore, reached a corresponding position on the left.

This was clearly a prelude to battle. 'Our Armada put itself in combat formation' runs the entry in the duke's diary, and his fleet spread out, as

Advance to Calais

agreed by the council of war, into its fighting formation: Leiva in command of the left wing (vanguard) with about twenty capital ships; Recalde in charge of the right (rearguard) with some twenty more; and Medina Sidonia in the centre (main battle) with the rest. The Armada's battle-array spanned at least two miles from flank to flank, and it was clearly an awe-inspiring sight. The English were certainly impressed. 'We never thought,' wrote an English observer, 'that they could ever have found, gathered and joined so great a force of puissant ships together and so well appointed them with their cannon, culverin, and other great pieces of brass ordnance.' There was no question in English minds, either, about the calibre of their crews. Only trained and disciplined seamen could have adopted and held so large and complex an arrangement of ships, especially ones whose sailing qualities were so varied. Whatever its failings – and, as yet, Howard and his officers knew few of them – it was clear that the Armada would be no soft touch.

War had never formally been declared between England and Spain and so, before battle commenced in earnest, Lord Admiral Howard thought it proper to perform an old-fashioned act of etiquette. He issued a challenge. From among the ranks of the English fleet emerged an 80-ton barque, appropriately named *Disdain*, which dashed to within hailing distance of the Armada's main battle and fired a derisory token shot into its towering midst. Then, his defiance of the Armada stated for all to see, Howard launched his first attack.

The Lord Admiral's tactics surprised and perturbed the Spaniards. Two of their officers described the English fleet as arrayed *en ala*, while Medina

Sidonia commented upon its good order, observing wryly that the enemy ships were 'extremely well armed, rigged, and handled'. *En ala* is a Spanish military term which means 'in file; in a line', and what the Spaniards witnessed was, in all probability, the first true line-astern attack in the history of European naval warfare.

This tactic exploited the mobility and firepower of the broadside-armed sailing ship, and presaged the end of rigid line-abreast fleet formations of which the Armada itself was one of the last examples. Its effectiveness lay in its simplicity. One ship, usually the flagship, led the attack, while the rest followed in a line with the vice-flagship at the rear, bringing each broadside to bear in succession. No rigid formation had to be kept, for the leader could move where he willed with the rest of his force snaking behind him. As long as each ship kept behind the stern of the vessel to its front, the line's cohesion could not be broken, however erratic the flagship's path might be. The whole line, moreover, could turn about on the flagship's command; and, led by the vice-flagship which had brought up the rear, it could then recross the enemy and present a second broadside while the disengaged side reloaded. These movements could be carried out as often as was necessary to keep the enemy, as Sir Walter Raleigh later put it, 'under a perpetual shot. This you must do,' he added, 'upon the windermost ship or ships . . .'

The windermost ships of the Armada were those which lay at the outer ends of its trailing horns. So Howard's galleons stormed across the Spanish rear, engaging first Leiva's vanguard and then, on the far wing, Recalde's rearguard. Some ships of the rearguard broke station in the face of this assault, and sought shelter among the main body, but Recalde himself in the *San Juan de Portugal*, supported by his Biscayan vice-flagship *Gran Grin*, stood firm, and for some time most of the English firepower was directed against these two ships.

In their subsequent reports, however, neither side made much of this action. Drake merely commented that 'we had them in chase, and so coming up unto them there passed some cannon shot between some of our fleet and some of them.' Hawkins described the same incident as 'some small fight'. Results confirmed his judgement. During the whole engagement Recalde's *San Juan* suffered only twenty casualties, two shots lodged in the foremast, and some stays parted; small enough penalty, it would seem, for two hours of sustained gunfire by the most powerful warships in Elizabeth's navy.

But it was long-range gunfire. Don Pedro de Valdés, aboard the *Nuestra Señora del Rosario*, later reported that little harm was done in this engagement 'because the fight was far off'. Clearly the disciplined formation of the Armada, and its evident strength, was having the effect for which it had been designed: the English were not prepared to close, even though, beyond point-blank range, their guns could do little harm. 'We durst not adventure to put in amongst them,' wrote the Lord Admiral of the first day's fighting, 'their fleet being so strong.' Henry White, captain of the 200-ton *Bark Talbot*, (later to be used as a fireship at Calais), put the matter more bluntly:

'The majesty of the enemy's fleet, the good order they held, and the private consideration of our own wants did cause, in mine opinion, our first onset to be more coldly done than became the value of our nation and the credit of the English navy . . .'

Recalde and his loyal supporter the *Gran Grin* were finally extricated by the *San Martín* and *San Mateo*, supported by Pedro de Valdés' great *Rosario*, which moved through the fleet to relieve the beleagured rearguard. But there were two major casualties that day, albeit neither directly caused by the English. First, the Guipúzcoan *San Salvador*, one of the most heavily armed ships in the fleet, and the headquarters of the Armada's Paymaster, was suddenly rent apart by a tremendous explosion. Mystery surrounds its cause. One explanation blames sabotage by a German gunner aboard the ship, who had allegedly been cuckolded by a Spanish officer. Others, more plausibly, had heard of 'the captain falling into a rage with the gunner and threatening to kill him if he shot no righter.' In a fit of professional pique, continued the story, 'the gunner cast fire into the powder barrels and threw himself overboard.' More probably it was a genuine accident. With so much gunpowder about, and so many lighted fuses and linstocks on the decks, it is surprising that such mishaps were not more frequent.

Whatever the cause, however, the damage to the *San Salvador* was serious: two decks and the sterncastle had been blown away, her steering-gear disabled, and half the 400 or so men on board either killed by the explosion or drowned after they jumped (or were thrown) into the water. The duke stopped the Armada in its tracks, went himself to the vessel's aid, and took energetic measures to limit the damage. The fire was extinguished before it could spread to the main magazines (which contained more than seven tons of gunpowder), and the vessel was brought into the safety of the fleet. Many of the wounded – most of them dreadfully burnt – were taken off. However the next day, after attempting to salvage and repair the burnt-out hull, Medina Sidonia decided that she would have to be abandoned. The 'principal persons' still aboard, and the royal treasure, were taken off in four small boats; but in the confusion and haste about 50 of the badly-wounded, together with the guns and the powder, were left aboard. They were still there when, later that same day, Sir John Hawkins and a prize crew came aboard. However, finding 'the stink in the ship was so unsavoury and the sight within board so ugly', they left abruptly and had her towed away to Weymouth.

The other casualty of the day was no less important. Don Pedro de Valdés in the *Nuestra Señora del Rosario*, one of the free-ranging 'troubleshooters' charged with the formation's defence, had gone to Recalde's aid when the English attack had threatened to disrupt the Armada's right wing. In the confusion he had collided with one of the Biscayans, damaging his bowsprit, and this minor accident had set in train a progressive series of mishaps. The temporary loss of her spritsail affected the *Rosario's* steering, and soon after she was involved in a more serious collision with her sister Andalusian *Santa Catalina*, which brought down the *Rosario's* foresail and yard and damaged the rigging of the foremast. Temporarily crippled, Don Pedro tried to repair the damage. But by now the sea was getting up, and suddenly the unstayed foremast broke at deck level to fall in a tangle of shrouds and sails against the mainmast. This was far more serious, for it rendered the ship unmanageable. Don Pedro sent a pinnace to ask the duke for aid and, according to one of the messengers (the Dominican friar Bernardo de Góngora, who wrote a lively account of the incident), 'the duke was willing to help and assist him, but Diego Flores de Valdés [Don Pedro's cousin, aboard the flagship] forbade him to do it, since it would put the entire fleet in jeopardy. In view of this,' Góngora continued, 'the duke continued on his way and left the good Don Pedro and his company . . . in the power of the enemy, who were never more than a league behind us . . . God knows what happened to them.'[7]

Don Pedro was furious: he had been, he felt, dishonourably deserted by his commander. But although the fleet's troubleshooters were duty-bound to support their comrades, the Armada was not itself bound to help them should they get into difficulties (though an attempt to do so had been made in the case of the *San Salvador*). Medina Sidonia's higher duty was to maintain the fleet's progress towards its objective, and so he sailed on, leaving behind several chests of his own luggage which had been shipped aboard the *Rosario*.

The first English vessel to probe the abandoned Andalusian flagship's defences was the 200-ton *Margaret and John*, a merchant ship from the squadron provided by the City of London, which came up at about 9 p.m. and discharged its muskets into the *Rosario's* towering bulk. Don Pedro responded with two rounds from his cannon, and after further skirmishing the *Margaret and John*, which was quite clearly unable to take the *Rosario* by force, left to rejoin the rest of the fleet. But the following morning Don Pedro found himself in the presence of a far more formidable foe: Sir Francis Drake in the *Revenge*.

How precisely the vice-admiral of the queen's navy happened to be there, all alone, was a subject of some dispute even at the time. Drake had been delegated to set watch for the whole fleet for the night by displaying a lantern on his stern for everyone else to follow. But, according to an irate Martin Frobisher, no lantern ever appeared – Drake's 'light we looked for, but there was no light to be seen'. Frobisher's explanation was simple, and deeply accusatory; Drake, he said, had spotted the stricken *Rosario* and 'kept by her all night, because he would have the spoil'. Sir Francis scarcely bothered to argue. He mentioned half-heartedly that he had glimpsed some strange sails in the darkness and (apparently forgetting about the lantern) had gone to investigate, 'not knowing what they were'. And then, as dawn broke, to his professed utter surprise he discovered 'we were within two or three cables' of the *Rosario*. 'Ay marry,' retorted Frobisher (who had been a privateer himself long enough to recognise a tall story when he heard one) 'you were within two or three cables length, [because] you were no further off all night.'

Be that as it may, the morning of 1 August found Drake and Valdés alone together. At first the Spaniard refused to surrender at all; then he refused to discuss surrender with anyone except Sir Francis Drake in person. When, at last, he came aboard the *Revenge* under flag of truce and Drake had pointed out to him the hopelessness of his position, Don Pedro's nerve broke. He asked to be left alone for a few moments to make up his mind and then emerged, with his face all flushed, to announce his surrender.

Pandemonium broke out aboard the *Rosario*. Four of the seven or eight Englishmen who had originally sailed with the ship had already prudently slipped away by boat: they could expect no mercy from their countrymen. But, curiously, no effort had been made by the Spaniards to save the king's 50,000 gold ducats. Many of the coins now disappeared: 'the soldiers merrily shared [the treasure] amongst themselves,' reported Richard Hakluyt, without specifying whether they were Englishmen or Spaniards. Some may have vanished during the transfer of the specie to the *Revenge*: it was brought across by boat in thin canvas bags and, according to another contemporary account, 'there is great likelihood . . . that some of the treasure was purloined away.' But it is unlikely that Drake was so naïve or unobservant as to let any such irregularity take place, at least on the part of others: Don Francisco de Zarate, whose ship was plundered by Sir Francis in 1579 off Acapulco, noted with grudging admiration that 'when our ship was sacked, no man dared take anything without his orders: he shows them great favour, but punishes the least fault . . .'

In the end, just over half the *Rosario's* treasure actually reached the queen's exchequer.[8] How much of the rest really fell into Drake's hands is anyone's guess, but suspicion naturally fell on him, expecially from Martin Frobisher, who later furiously exclaimed that Drake 'thinketh to cozen us of our shares of 15,000 ducats; but we will have our shares, or I will make him spend the best blood in his belly.' But that squabble lay in the future. On 1 August, no one was available to argue with Drake because the night before, without his lantern for guidance, the English fleet had become seriously disorganised. According to Howard, when dawn broke even the nearest of his ships 'might scarce be seen . . . and very many out of sight, which with a good sail recovered not his Lordship the next day before it was very late in the evening.'

Medina Sidonia made use of this respite to reorganise the Armada's formation in the light of the previous day's experiences. Don Pedro's Andalusian squadron was placed under the command of Don Diego Enríquez, son of the Mexican viceroy who had clashed with Hawkins and Drake twenty years before at San Juan de Ulúa. But further changes were clearly necessary. The duke's initial strategy had assumed that the English fleet would lie ahead of him, attempting to block the Straits with only a small detachment at Plymouth, but this had proved not to be the case. Moreover, the duke and his staff noted that against more nimble ships which held the weather gauge and did not intend to come within boarding range, the extended horns of the Armada's vanguard and rearguard had offered little tactical advantage, yet had proved vulnerable to isolation and attack. Accordingly he joined the two horns into a single body, which the English sources referred to (accurately enough) as a 'plump' or 'roundel'. He also introduced a new tactical element. To each of the heavily armed Levanters, *La Rata Encoronada* and *La Trinidad Valencera*, he allocated a pair of galleasses, establishing two very heavily-gunned battle groups which could be deployed, thanks to the towing capacity of the galleasses, irrespective of the wind. It was precisely the battle plan that the unfortunate Valdés had proposed at Corunna, and it would enable the fleet (in Medina Sidonia's own words) 'to withstand the enemy and prevent him from standing in the way of our junction with the duke of Parma. The whole fleet was split into two divisions: Don Alonso de Leiva having command of the rear, and the duke himself taking charge of the van.'

It was not that the extended formation had proved tactically defective. On the contrary, in spite of the two unexpected and serious accidents, and in the face of a strong English fleet to windward, Medina Sidonia had demonstrated during his first day of action both the tactical and strategic strengths of the Armada, and his own skill in commanding it. But some commanders had proved unequal to the strain of exposure to English gunfire: there had been a serious breach of formation discipline, when some of Recalde's right wing had deserted their posts in the face of the English assault. So following the reorganization six *pataches*, each with a sergeant-major, a provost-marshal, and a hangman aboard, now delivered to every ship in the fleet clear instructions which defined its exact station in the reorganised formation. Henceforward any captain who left his assigned position without authority would be hanged: only iron discipline could bring the fleet intact to Flanders.

This done, Medina Sidonia's thoughts turned once again to his over-riding worry: still no word had arrived from Parma confirming that his invasion force was ready, and explaining how he intended to bring it out to the fleet. So the duke took two decisions. On the one hand, he resolved to change the fleet's destination from 'Margate head' on the English side of the Channel, to Calais, far closer to the presumed position of the Army of Flanders; and on the other, on the afternoon of 1 August, he sent another pinnace to Parma, urgently requesting information about the proposed link-up.[9]

During the night of 1/2 August the wind fell, becalming both fleets some miles west of Portland Bill. But as dawn broke on the Tuesday a fresh breeze sprang up from the east to give the Spaniards, for the first time, the weather gauge. Responding to the danger, Lord Admiral Howard led his galleons, close-hauled, towards the north-north-east, attempting to place himself between the Armada and the land. But Medina Sidonia used his advantage of wind to counter this attempt, forcing the English ships to come about in a reach towards the south-south-west.

This gave the waiting troubleshooters of the strengthened Spanish rearguard a chance to intercept. For the first time since the fighting began some of the larger ships now came to close quarters, and an artillery fight began. Bertendona's *Regazona* bore down on a large English vessel, intent on boarding, but his adversary turned seawards and opened the range. This general mêlée continued for more than two hours, without definite tactics on either side beyond a strong Spanish desire to grapple and board and an equally strong English determination to stay clear and use their guns.

While this battle was taking place well to seaward of Portland Bill, a separate action had developed just to the west of it. When, at dawn, the English fleet abandoned its attempt to weather the Armada, the six leading ships had found themselves too far inshore to close-haul seawards. Five were medium-sized merchantmen of the London squadron; the sixth was Martin Frobisher's heavily-gunned *Triumph*, the largest ship in the English fleet. To the Spaniards she was an irresistible target. Medina Sidonia, who was fully engaged in the fight which was developing around his rearguard, therefore dispatched Don Hugo de Moncada with his four crimson-painted galleasses to deal with Frobisher's isolated force.

The attack was not a success. Earlier in the day Moncada had, according to some accounts, sought permission to engage Howard's *Ark Royal* but, it was alleged, Medina Sidonia had declined to give it on the grounds that no one but he could in honour challenge the English flagship. Whether or not this was so, it is clear that ill-feeling had developed between the two men. This may explain Medina Sidonia's reaction when he saw the galleasses struggling in evident difficulty some distance from Frobisher. An officer was dispatched to the flag galleass to 'say aloud to Don Hugo . . . certain words which were not to his honour.' But Moncada, though prickly, was certainly no coward: he had, in all probability, become trapped in the tide race which runs between Portland Bill and the Shambles reef, towards which, no doubt, the wily Frobisher had lured him. In any event the galleasses' attack, when it came, was disappointingly ineffectual. Their oar-given mobility, formidable enough in theory, was itself highly vulnerable. A well-directed concentration of English fire on the rowing banks – upon which even a light shot at long range could wreak dreadful carnage and still greater confusion – forced the galleasses to revert to sail power, under which they proved markedly inferior to Frobisher's small squadron.

At this point Howard and a number of his more powerful galleons disengaged from the Spanish rearguard, taking advantage of a change in the wind – first from the south-east, and later from the south-west – to move in support of Frobisher. The Lord Admiral now 'called unto certain of her Majesty's ships then near at hand and charged them straightly to follow him, and to set freshly upon the Spaniards, and to go within musket-shot of the enemy before they should discharge any one piece of ordnance.' And so they attacked in line ahead, firing their guns only when they came into close range. In Howard's estimation, 'the Spaniards were forced to give way and flock together like sheep.' According to Medina Sidonia, however, the Armada was able to put up a spirited response: although all the English fleet passed by, 'firing at him ship by ship . . . he, on his part, fired his guns very well and quickly, so that half the enemy's fleet did not come near, but fired at him from a distance.'

Yet for all that, it was an unequal fight. One of the Spanish officers aboard the flagship admitted that, in return for 80 shots discharged from the *San Martín*'s engaged side, the English fired 500 rounds at her, striking the hull and rigging, and carrying away the flagstaff and one of the mainmast stays. Another Spanish observer noted in wonderment that the flagship was so enveloped in gunsmoke that for 'more than an hour we could not see her'. Lord Admiral Howard confirmed that in this action a 'terrible value' of great shot was expended.

This being so, it is remarkable how little damage was actually inflicted by either side upon the other, even though at times the range appears to have been point-blank. The injury caused to the heavily engaged *San Martín* was, by any reckoning, minimal. Both commanders must have been surprised at the disappointing equation between the amount of precious roundshot expended and the damage it was able to cause.

For the English, the moment was one of acute crisis. The fight, as John Hawkins reported to Walsingham, had been 'sharp and long', and had cost 'a good part of our powder and shot'. It would not be wise, thought Hawkins, to engage the Spaniards further until ammunition stocks were replenished. It was one thing to have nimble ships which could take advantage of wind and tide, and thus always keep the Spaniards at arm's length; but to defeat the Armada it would be necessary to destroy its galleons, not run circles around them. On the one hand, Howard and his subordinates could see that their vaunted heavy artillery, despite the expenditure of so much shot at moderately short range, had not proved capable of inflicting serious damage on the Spanish ships. And yet, on the other hand, it was equally clear that if the English brought their ships much closer they would run the risk of being boarded by the Spanish troops, and that meant almost certain defeat.

Yet again, in tactical terms, the Spaniards had proved themselves to be the superior force. As soon as the battle was over, with the English fleet temporarily neutralised by its ammunition crisis, the Armada simply shook itself back into formation, its component parts virtually undamaged, and continued the eastward advance.

Spanish victory did not, however, depend solely on maintaining the Armada's continuing progress. In order to succeed, the link-up with Parma had to be achieved. The council of war aboard the *San Martín* on 30 July had recommended that until arrangements for the rendezvous were clear, and Parma's readiness assured, the Armada should proceed no further than the Isle of Wight. Once east of this point the fleet would be committed to the Flanders rendezvous: to beat back westwards in the teeth of the prevailing weather, with the English fleet to leeward, was unthinkable. And now the moment of decision had come. There can be little doubt that by the evening of 2 August, with the Isle of Wight looming on his port quarter, Medina Sidonia was seriously considering making his way into the anchorage off Portsmouth shown on his charts. Here, at least, he would have had the option of a safe and defensible haven until contact had been made with Parma.

The English were certainly aware of the danger. But what could they do to prevent it? The English strategy, insofar as there was one, was to cut out and overwhelm individual members of the Spanish fleet, to 'pluck their feathers by little and little', as Howard put it. And on the morning of 3 August, having obtained some meagre replenishment to his ammunition stocks (including some from the two captured Spanish galleons), an opportunity to do some more feather-plucking presented itself to the Lord Admiral. As dawn broke a large ship was observed trailing behind the seaward flank of the Armada, a few miles off the dangerous western

The document reproduced below records the delivery of 25 *alcancias* and 15 *bombas* to *La Trinidad Valencera* on 20 April 1588. *Alcancias* were earthenware pots filled with an inflammable mixture for use as fire-bombs; one, found on the wreck, is shown *near right*. A similar weapon, with fuses attached round its pinched waist, is shown (*far right*) from an illustration by Cyprián Lucar in 1588. One of the *bombas* was also found. This is a hollow wooden tube which was filled with a sequence of explosive and incendiary charges, and was used in boarding actions. A contemporary drawing of the weapon by Cyprián Lucar is shown below.

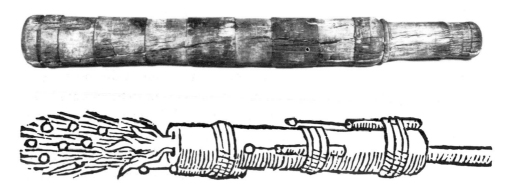

entrance to the Solent. The straggler was Gómez de Medina's wide-bellied Rostock hulk *El Gran Grifón*. Although the supply squadron of which she was flagship was regarded as non-combatant, the nobly-officered *Grifón* was herself a gallant if clumsy member of the Armada's troubleshooting elite. As the English ships closest to her crowded on sail to catch the light morning airs, a powerful galleon, almost certainly Drake's *Revenge*, glided abeam the wallowing *Grifón* and gave her a broadside at close range, swiftly coming about to discharge another, and then crossing her stern to rake it with gunfire. It was a devastating example of the mobile tactics which individual English captains had perfected. But the *Grifón* hung grimly on, struck by at least 40 roundshot, her decks still crowded with soldiers who remained firmly at their posts in spite of serious casualties, fully capable of boarding and carrying any English vessel rash enough to clap sides. The incident neatly encapsulated the strength of the Armada as a whole: it might be battered but it could not be destroyed; and yet, unless it were destroyed, its military potential remained as strong as ever.

As the fight developed more ships became involved, and Medina Sidonia sent in the galleasses to extricate the damaged *Grifón*. Having done so, he gave the signal for a general engagement, at which the English drew off, preferring to delay the Spaniards rather than to precipitate an all-out battle. The duke therefore turned his ships about, and the Armada continued relentlessly on its way.

The next few hours of the campaign were crucial, for the Armada had by now reached a dominant position close to the eastern entrance to the Solent. Now, if at all, Medina Sidonia had to put his alternative plan into effect. It was not an easy dilemma to resolve. The king's instructions on the matter had been explicit: alternatives to the main strategy could only be adopted if for some reason the rendezvous with Parma actually failed. But until he knew what practical arrangements Parma had made, the duke's best course was clearly to find a secure anchorage in which to husband and if necessary defend his fleet until the rendezvous could be accomplished. Entry to the Solent might therefore be seen as a wise precaution rather than a change of plan.

In the event, however, the English saved Medina Sidonia from having to make the choice. The previous evening, in response to his sustained lack of success, Lord Admiral Howard had ordered a major reorganisation of his forces. Until then his fleet had been little more than a loose agglomeration

Lead bullets of ¾″ and ½″ calibres showing the characteristics of high velocity impact, found on the wreck of *El Gran Grifón*. They are very probably relics of the ship's fierce engagements on 2 August, when much of the fighting, according to an eye witness, was conducted 'at half musket-shot'.

whose members, apart from a general obligation to support the flagship, acted as individual circumstances dictated. But now it was necessary to secure a wider strategic aim: somehow, the Spaniards had to be denied entry to the Solent. An urgent council of war was convened aboard the *Ark Royal*, and it was decided to organise the fleet into four quasi-independent squadrons under the commands of Howard, Drake, Hawkins and Frobisher. These squadrons were given tasks which, if performed in unison, would force the Armada inexorably onwards past Selsey Bill and towards the straits of Dover.

During the night of 3/4 August some units of the Grand Fleet again fell astern of the main body. They were the Portuguese galleon *San Luís* and the Andalusian hulk *Duquesa Santa Ana*: like *El Gran Grifón* the previous day, they presented the English with an obvious target. But this time there was no wind. Hawkins, whose squadron was closest to the Spanish stragglers, lowered his ship's boats and moved to the attack under tow. Medina Sidonia responded by sending in three of the galleasses, one of them towing Leiva's *Rata Encoronada*. As the ranges closed the guns began to thunder. The galleasses were now the main object of the English attack. One was seen to list, another lost her lantern, and a third received damage to her prow. But these modest claims, which came from the English side and are therefore likely to be over- rather than under-estimates, indicate that the damage inflicted by the English artillery was once again slight. In any case it failed to prevent the galleasses from completing their task, for they were able to take the *San Luís* and *Duquesa Santa Ana* in tow and withdraw them from the action. At this point a south-westerly wind sprang up, and the sailing ships on both sides were again able to manoeuvre.

Meanwhile, as the Spanish fleet concentrated on saving these stragglers from Hawkins and Howard, Frobisher, on the left wing, took his squadron into the seaway to the east of the Isle of Wight. Medina Sidonia led a small flotilla of powerful galleons towards them, and the English began to withdraw. Frobisher in the vast *Triumph* was apparently in difficulties: the ship's boats were lowered to tow him clear, but still the Spaniards closed the range. And then a breath of wind filled the *Triumph*'s great sails: her finely shaped hull took on way, and she escaped.

While the principal ships of the Armada were thus occupied on the left wing, where the crucial action was taking place, a furious and unexpected English attack suddenly developed on the unengaged right. This assault was delivered 'in such wise,' according to a Spanish officer who was there, 'that we who were there were cornered, so that, if the duke had not gone about with his flagship . . . we should have come out vanquished that day.' The surprise attack fatally unbalanced Medina Sidonia's dispositions, drawing him away from the eastern entrance to the Solent.

Who launched this sudden and decisive attack, which came at precisely the right time and from just the right direction to divert the Armada back into the Channel, pressing it towards Selsey Bill and the Ower Banks, from which the only escape was to make all sail towards the east? We can be almost sure that it was Drake.

No mention of Sir Francis is made in any account of the morning action, which suggests that he took no part in it. If so, the flagship which was seen leading the unexpected assault against the Armada's seaward wing in the afternoon can only have been the missing *Revenge*. The move was a brilliant one. While the Lord Admiral, Hawkins, and Frobisher had been engaged close inshore off the Isle of Wight, Drake had evidently worked his squadron unobtrusively seaward, anticipating the change of wind in the afternoon which would enable him to launch his surprise attack. Medina Sidonia's attempt to win a defensive anchorage by way of the eastern seaway, if that is what he had intended, had been foiled forever. He was now well east of Selsey Bill with both the wind and the English fleet at his rear.[10]

But at first this did not seem like a defeat. On the contrary it brought considerable short-term gains, for the Armada was left unmolested for three full days. 'Forasmuch as our powder and shot was well wasted,' runs Howard's journal, 'the Lord Admiral thought it was not good in policy to assail them any more until their coming near unto Dover.' For the moment, the Lord Admiral had time to spare, and he used it to confer knighthoods on Hawkins and Frobisher.

On Saturday 6 August, at 10 a.m., the Spaniards came into sight of Boulogne and, at 4 p.m., they dropped anchor off Calais. Medina Sidonia, with his great task force substantially intact, and the Army of Flanders only 25 miles distant, might have been forgiven for thinking that he had fulfilled his master's command, despite overwhelming odds, and 'done his part'.

CHAPTER 10

The Banks of Flanders

There can be few sets of military correspondence so one-sided as that which passed between the dukes of Medina Sidonia and Parma as the Armada made its way from Lisbon to Flanders. On 10 June, when Medina Sidonia had every reason to suppose that he would reach the rendezvous within a fortnight, he sent a *zabra* ahead to inform Parma of his progress, pointing out that because of the coastal sand-banks and the lack of a deepwater port there could be no question of his attempting a link-up close to shore. His next letter was dated 25 July, and was simply a

A copy of Medina Sidonia's final letter to Parma, written aboard the *San Martín* on 7 August 1588: 'Unless we can find a harbour we will perish without doubt.'

confirmation that, after the delay at Corunna, he was again on his way. No acknowledgement arrived to either dispatch, but Medina Sidonia persisted. On 31 July, as the Armada was approaching Plymouth, he put out a plea for more pilots who knew the coast of Flanders, while four days later, after the first bouts of fighting off the Isle of Wight, he was urgently demanding replenishments of powder and shot, and confirming his imminent arrival at the rendezvous.

Still there was no reply.

On 5 August, Medina Sidonia tried again: this time he sent a pilot to explain why the Armada was making such slow progress and how much it needed reinforcements. And yet, in spite of all this, when the fleet reached Calais there was still no word from the shore. Medina Sidonia came close to despair: 'I have constantly written to Your Excellency,' he protested, 'and not only have I received no reply to my letters, but no acknowledgement of their receipt. . . .'[1]

Here was an extraordinary situation: the joint commanders of the greatest amphibious operation in European history were not in effective contact with each other. Much has been made in the past of Parma's silence, some (including many Spaniards at the time) going so far as to accuse the duke of deliberately trying to sabotage the enterprise. But this is either malice or fantasy. It assumes that travel by land and sea, in early modern Europe, was easy, rapid and regular. Of course it was not. In the sixteenth century a journey between the same two points could take days, weeks or months, depending on the weather, the state of the roads and bridges, the availability and mode of transport, and the presence or absence of bandits.

A letter sent from Brussels or Paris to Madrid, for example, might reach its destination in as little as twelve days; but in the summer and autumn of 1588, a combination of atrocious weather and sustained activity by Huguenot partisans south of Bordeaux meant that some important missives took three weeks and more, while others apparently did not arrive at all. In normal times, it is true, communications by sea were often rather swifter and surer than those by land: but these were not normal times. In the first place, even if a messenger from the Armada might be expected to find his way in due course to a fixed destination on the shore, it was far more difficult for him to find his way back, because the fleet would by then have moved on to a different, unknown location. And, second, the English navy patrolled the waters in between. For Medina

Sidonia to have expected rapid and reliable communications between himself and Parma once he had put to sea reveals a profound misunderstanding of the logistical limitations of his position. It was one of his very few serious mistakes during the campaign, but it proved fatal.

For in the event not one of the couriers dispatched from the Armada reached Flanders in time to do any good. The officer sent to establish contact with Parma on 31 July, when the fleet was drawing level with Plymouth, could not make sail until the following morning, and he only reached Flanders early on 6 August. Later that same day the messenger dispatched by Medina Sidonia off the Isle of Wight on 4 August arrived at Parma's headquarters. Yet by this time the Armada had actually reached Calais, though it was another day before that fact became known in Flanders. Although the progress of the Grand Fleet up the Channel may have seemed slow to Medina Sidonia, it proved too fast for Parma.[2]

Eventually, however, late in the evening of Saturday 6 August, the long-awaited pinnace with a reply from Flanders – written three days earlier – came upon Medina Sidonia and his ships as they lay huddled before Calais. At first it was mistaken for an enemy vessel, and set upon by some of the Armada; but it swiftly identified itself and delivered its shattering message. The duke of Parma, it reported, would not be ready to bring his forces out until Friday at the earliest.[3]

On Friday? Another six days? Medina Sidonia was horrified, for the Grand Fleet had now been drawn into the situation he had dreaded all along. It had reached Calais, but it had done so without securing command of the sea – indeed the English fleet was now stronger than ever – and the army it was to pick up was not yet ready. What was to be done? As Medina Sidonia's last, despairing letter to Parma made clear, the Armada's situation was perilous in the extreme. Just out of artillery range to windward stood the English fleet, and to leeward lay the treacherous shallows off the Flemish coast known to mariners as 'the Banks of Flanders' – a natural hazard made even more treacherous by the Dutch, who had cunningly removed all the navigation marks and buoys from the coast and rivers prior to the Armada's arrival.[4] There was no way in which Medina Sidonia's cumbersome task force could get any closer to Parma's embarkation point, and so it could only wait outside Calais and hope for the best. But it was too much to expect that the English would allow the immobilised Grand Fleet to remain unmolested for a further six days.

The interrogation of Don Diego Pimentel, a senior infantry commander captured by the Dutch two days later, reveals that some (at least) of the Armada's High Command were still entirely in the dark about the state of affairs in Flanders. Pimentel made it clear to his captors that he had expected Parma to make a dash for it with whatever forces he happened to have ready. When asked if he did not realise that the Dutch had a powerful squadron of warships outside Dunkirk which would vigorously oppose any attempt by Parma and his men to sail out, Pimentel admitted that he and his peers had expected as much. But he also stated that, since Parma was known to have assembled 100 ships and an even larger number of barges (these, at least, were the figures given by Pimentel), 'it never occurred to them for a moment that the duke would not attempt a sortie'. Pimentel went on to wonder why Parma had not at least sent his small warships out, bristling with guns as he believed them to be, to drive off – or draw off – the Dutch fleet, even if they themselves perished in the attempt, and so allow the barges to slip out and join the Armada.[5]

Assuming that Pimentel's testimony reflects the thinking of Medina Sidonia at this point – and there is no reason why it should not, for he was, as the interrogators smugly noted, 'related to the principal families of all Spain' and had no reason to lie – then three distinct reasons for the failure to make the vital rendezvous envisaged by Philip II become apparent. First, the Captain General of the Ocean Sea assumed that news

Don Diego Pimentel, commander of the *tercio* of Sicily. He was captured when his ship, the Portuguese galleon *San Marcos*, was driven ashore near Ostend. A Dutch pamphlet in which his subsequent interrogation was published shows Don Diego in cuirass and colonel's sash, with the defeat of the Armada reflected in his polished shield.

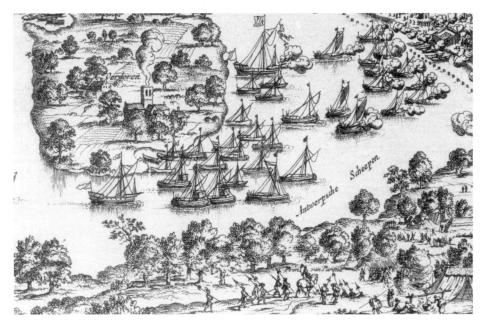

Coastal sailing barges of the kind gathered by Parma for the invasion of England, and dispersed among the inland waterways between Nieuwpoort and Sluys pending the arrival of the Armada.

of his approach had preceeded him. This, as we have seen, was entirely wrong. Not only did his own messengers fail to keep ahead of his fleet; so did everyone else. The first knowledge of the Channel battles to reach the Netherlands in fact came from the English: at 3 p.m. on 6 August, the English diplomats at Bourbourg received a letter from London announcing that the queen's ships had been attacked by the Armada off Plymouth. The delegation at once began to pack its bags, to the open amazement of the Spanish negotiators who suggested to Parma that this might only be 'some subterfuge or cover' intended to secure diplomatic concessions from Spain. They only discovered the real reason later. [6]

Medina Sidonia's second incorrect assumption, as revealed in the interrogation of Pimentel, stemmed from the first: he believed – wrongly – that Parma, being forewarned, would have his troops aboard the barges and small ships *before* the Armada reached the Narrow Seas, and would therefore be ready to put out the instant its sails were spotted. There was more to this misjudgement than poor communications; at its root was a fundamental failure of comprehension.

Here the duke must bear some of the blame, for the necessary information had been available to him before the Armada sailed. In the middle of May Captain Francisco Moresin, a staff officer from the Army of Flanders, had arrived in Lisbon to brief Medina Sidonia on the state of Parma's preparations. His news was not encouraging. First, Parma could muster only 17,000 infantry and 1,000 cavalry for embarkation; and, second, he had no escorts for the low-freeboard landing craft and barges in which they were to be transported. Perplexed, Medina Sidonia had referred the matter to the king, but he received little reassurance. As to the reduced size of the army, Philip replied, that would be more than compensated by the increased number of soldiers that were to be carried by the fleet: 10,000 of the Armada's men would land in England too. And the king simply glossed over the lack of escort vessels, passing the responsibility for clearing the seas squarely back to Medina Sidonia: Parma's vessels, stated Philip, were not of a kind 'that can put out and seek you at a distance, unless you have first cleared away all enemy ships from the straits first, because they are ships for transport and not for fighting.'

But Medina Sidonia seems to have forgotten, or failed to have grasped, this important fact. On 10 June, as the Armada approached Cape Finisterre, he revealed his misconception in a letter to Parma, confirming that he was 'coming towards your excellency, and will write to you again when I enter the Channel so your excellency will know where to come out and join us.' He dispatched the letter by fast packet, requesting Parma to send back news of 'how far your preparations are advanced, when you can put to sea, and where we can meet.' A copy of the letter reached Philip II, who noted ominously in the margin: 'This cannot be, if Medina does not first secure the seas with his fleet.' Too late, it seems, the king was beginning to recognise the deficiencies of his own plan.

Parma received Medina Sidonia's letter of 10 June, carried once more by Captain Moresin, eleven days later – an extremely fast delivery from Finisterre to Flanders – and at once dispatched a note of protest to the king:

'Medina seems to believe that I should set out to meet him with my small ships, which is simply impossible. These vessels cannot run the gauntlet of warships; they cannot even withstand large waves!'

Philip annotated this letter with uncharacteristic perception: 'Please God,' he scrawled, 'let there not be some slip-up [*embarazo*] here.'[7]

But neither he nor Parma managed to get a warning to Medina Sidonia on the high seas, for the messengers sent to convey it failed to find the fleet. At first Parma waited – he did not discover until 21 July that the Armada had been forced back to Corunna – but eventually he dispatched Captain Moresin on a second errand to Medina Sidonia, repeating his warnings about the need for the fleet to gain local command of the sea before he could bring his forces out. But Moresin was delayed by a bizarre combination of shipwreck, storms, and an encounter with the English fleet: his ship, dispatched on 14 July, only reached Spain on 2 August. So the Captain-General of the Ocean Sea remained in sublime ignorance of the facts, and right up to the moment he anchored before Calais he continued to bombard Flanders with fruitless letters asking where the rendezvous was to be, and when Parma was going to be there?[8]

These fatal misapprehensions were compounded by another. The Armada's commanders were clearly convinced that, after the arrival of Sir Henry Seymour and his squadron off Calais, only a handful of enemy ships remained to blockade the Flemish coast. But, once again, the officers aboard the Armada were seriously misinformed. Parma knew, as they did not, that the Dutch possessed (in addition to their small navy) a sizeable reserve of large but shallow-draught merchantmen capable of carrying

The governor of Calais, Giraud de Mauleon, Seigneur de Gourdan, 7 years after the Armada at the age of 83. He lost his leg during the recovery of Calais from the English in 1558.

and firing heavy artillery. His main concern, therefore, was to keep the Dutch fleet divided, for once it concentrated off Dunkirk or Nieuwpoort – from which it was possible to sail only at high tide – his own ships would be helplessly blockaded. To avoid this, Parma had employed two strategems. Firstly, he divided his fleet among several harbours. Some, including the 400 ton flagship, were at Antwerp; others (including the ships taken in the harbour when the town surrendered) were at Sluys; more still were at Nieuwpoort and Dunkirk. The barges, however, were kept hidden in various inland waterways, because the excellent canal system of Flanders – including some specially dug for the purpose – made it possible to concentrate them swiftly and secretly at the port of embarkation. Secondly, most of the troops were kept away from the Flanders ports, to give the impression that they might be about to invade Holland or Zealand. To camouflage his real intentions still further, Parma himself kept moving unpredictably between Antwerp, Ghent and Bruges.

And the deception worked. The records of the Dutch government show a complete failure to discern Philip II's intentions. Some, dismayed by the continuation of the talks at Bourbourg and the absence of a decisive battle in the Channel, supposed that the Armada was intended for either Flushing or Amsterdam; others feared that, even though the fleet might be directed against England, the Army of Flanders could take advantage of its presence in order to launch a surprise assault on the Republic. As the Dutch historian Pieter Bor wrote, early in the next century, his compatriots (unlike the English) feared Parma's small ships far more than Medina Sidonia's great galleons. The Amsterdam magistrates, for example, begged the Council of State not to send too many ships away to blockade Flanders and, in the end, only 32 warships were detached to patrol the Dunkirk roads. The rest hovered ineffectually off the Scheldt and Texel, waiting for an invasion which never came.

Thus, in spite of all the criticisms of 'unpreparedness', Parma's ruse achieved its vital objective. It even proved possible for one or two vessels to run the gauntlet of the blockade squadron and slip in and out of Dunkirk harbour. But to concentrate a whole army there and embark it – together with the store of livestock, weapons, provisions and equipment which had to go with it – would require (so Parma estimated) a lead time of six days. Therefore, since he had received confirmation of the fleet's approach on 6 August, he expected to be ready by the 12th. By the 13th he could be marching on London, if only the Armada would wait . . . .

At first it seemed as if this might prove possible, for while the Armada waited anxiously off Calais, the French Catholic governor of the port proved to be unexpectedly helpful. He sent presents to the duke, and welcomed ashore a number of Spanish dignitaries from the fleet – the duke of Ascoli (whom some thought, mistakenly, to be Philip II's bastard), the inspector-general Don Jorge Manrique, the paymaster-general Juan de Huerta, and many others. Better yet, he allowed the Spaniards to purchase water, fresh vegetables and other food; and throughout that Sunday a stream of small victualling craft plied to and fro between the Armada and the shore.

It may have been the warmth of this welcome that convinced the English commanders that they had to act without delay. With the arrival of further auxiliaries and, on the afternoon of 6 August, of Seymour's squadron from Dover, their fleet now numbered perhaps 140 sail. The situation was critical. For all the English knew, Parma might already be embarking his forces at Dunkirk, and the survival of the Tudor state thus depended entirely upon preventing him from reaching the fleet.

At a council of war on Lord Howard's flagship *Ark Royal*, early in the morning of 7 August, it was decided to launch a fireship attack on the Armada that night. Conditions for the stratagem were ideal. The Armada was crowded together at anchor, and its commander was uncertain (through no fault of his own) of his next move. To leeward lay the Flemish shoals, upon which the Spanish ships might be driven. Best of all, from the English point of view, the conjunction of spring tides with a freshening westerly breeze could be expected to carry the fireships swiftly into the Armada's heart.

Eight ships were prepared for the attack, at a total cost of £5,111 10s 0d – 'perhaps', as one naval historian has written, 'the cheapest national investment that this country has ever made'.[9] They were packed with combustibles, and their guns were loaded with double shot so that they would discharge spontaneously when the heat reached them, adding a psychological dimension to the stratagem. No Spaniard could forget Giambelli's terrible 'hellburners of Antwerp'; and it was known that Giambelli was now living in England. Howard was consciously playing on these fears: his objective was not so much to destroy ships as to create confusion and chaos throughout the Armada. If that could be done (he reasoned) then the forces of nature, aided by the English fleet, might be expected to do the rest.

And so it turned out. Medina Sidonia had been well aware that such an attack was likely, and had done what he could to counter it. Before night fell he set a screen of small craft to windward of the Armada, with orders to grapple and tow clear any fireships that approached. And when, at midnight, the attack came, two of the fireships were indeed intercepted and dragged into the shallows (an act of considerable heroism on the part of the pinnace crews). But the remaining six careered towards the midst of the anchored Armada. Medina Sidonia at once ordered all ships to cut or slip their cables and move from the path of the fireships, with instructions that as soon as the danger was past the fleet should re-anchor as close to its original position as possible.

But that was easier said than done. As the fireships came drifting closer, their pre-loaded guns discharging as the heat reached them, panic exacerbated an already tense situation. The strong tides which prevail in the narrowest part of the Channel made it hard to hold station in the open sea: every ship in the Spanish fleet had two or even three anchors out, and almost every one of them was lost. Most captains simply cut their cables and fled. Both of the clerical narratives of the campaign stressed the magnitude of this loss: although they harped upon the value of the anchors – 500 ducats per ship groaned Father La Torre; 100,000 ducats' worth in all, lamented Father Góngora – they both realised that the loss was not solely calculable in financial terms. It would now be extremely difficult for the fleet either to re-anchor while it waited for Parma, or to approach any coast with safety – and some of the world's most hazardous coastal waters would soon have to be negotiated. But that lay in the future: the immediate problem facing the Armada was the loss of its tight defensive formation and its battle discipline.

Panic, however, had not gripped the flagship or its loyal group of close supporters. The *San Martín* immediately anchored, as did Recalde's *San Juan*, Peñafiel's *San Marcos*, and two other Portuguese galleons. At dawn on 8 August these five ships found themselves facing the entire English fleet. For the first time in the campaign Medina Sidonia had no doubts as to where his duty lay. At last he could stand firm as honour demanded, shoulder to shoulder with his comrades, and defy the enemy to his last breath. Even so, he did not neglect his responsibilities as a commander; the ships' boats were sent scudding away to leeward to rally the scattered fleet. As they left, the first English ships came within range, and heavy firing began.

At this point Lord Admiral Howard's attention was diverted from the lion-hearted quintet of galleons which stood between him and the dispersed Armada. In the confusion which followed the fireship attack Don Hugo de Moncada's flag galleass, the *San Lorenzo*, had damaged her rudder and mainmast; and, in seeking to avoid capture, she had grounded at the entrance to Calais. Stuck fast on a falling tide, with her seaward broadside pointing impotently to the sky as she heeled over, she could offer little defence. Howard could not resist so important and vulnerable a prize, and he sent an assault party in ships' boats to take her. After a fierce hand-to-hand struggle, during which Moncada died with a bullet in his brain, the galleass was entered and sacked. The diversion ended when a French boarding party, of technically neutral status, was roughed-up by the rampaging English seamen: not unnaturally, the French shore batteries threatened to blow the galleass and everyone in her apart unless the English immediately withdrew.[10]

This prolonged sideshow brought little profit to Howard, however, for neither the galleass nor her guns could be shifted from beneath the alerted defences of Calais castle. But the delay greatly helped Medina Sidonia, who put the unexpected two-hour respite to good use by falling back, fighting all the way, to mobilise the defence of his now rapidly re-forming fleet.

The troubleshooters began to take station on either side of the flagship, and soon a ragged but determined protective line once again shielded the Armada's rear. Sir William Winter, a member of Lord Henry Seymour's eastern squadron which had reinforced the English fleet off Calais (and was therefore face-to-face with the Armada for the first time), observed this re-grouping with detached professional interest: 'They went into a proportion of a half-moon. Their admiral and vice-admiral, they went in the midst . . . and there went on each side, in the wings, their galleasses, armados of Portugal, and other good ships, in the whole to the number of sixteen in a wing, which did seem to be of their principal shipping.' It was the old trailing-horns defensive posture, this time composed exclusively of the troubleshooters, doggedly prepared to take whatever the English might yet throw at them.

The battle which followed lasted nine hours, and was fought along the fringes of the shoal waters between Gravelines and Ostend. It was fierce and very confused, but it may be summarised as a running fight in which the Spaniards strove to maintain their defence in a unified and compact

DOEVER

CALIS

The battle of Gravelines, after the Dutch artist Visscher. In this version Calais and Dover have been transposed, making it appear, incorrectly, that the Armada is fighting its way back through the Channel.

formation, and to keep as close as possible to Parma's ports of embarkation, while the English endeavoured to cut out the weathermost ships and force the rest leewards into the shallows. A vital factor was the wind, which veered steadily throughout the day from south-south-west to north-west, setting the Spanish fleet at an increasingly greater disadvantage as it did so. The weather too had deteriorated; the sea was now rough and the visibility poor.

Through the confusion, however, we can detect features which mark this battle as radically different from anything that had gone before. First, much of it was fought at very close range. 'Out of my ship,' wrote Sir William Winter of the *Vanguard* afterwards, 'there was shot 500 shot of demi-cannon, culverin, and demi-culverin: and when I was furthest off in discharging any of the pieces, I was not out of the shot of their harquebus, and most times within speech one of another.' The fact that the protagonists were within hailing distance (which, amid the noise and chaos of battle, must have been very close indeed), is graphically borne out by what purser Calderón of the hulk *San Salvador* saw from the Spanish side:

'The enemy inflicted such damage upon the galleons *San Mateo* and *San Felipe* that the latter had five guns on the starboard side and a big gun on the poop put out of action . . . In view of this, and seeing that his upper deck was destroyed, both his pumps broken, his rigging in shreds, and his ship almost a wreck, Don Francisco de Toledo [commanding officer of the *San Felipe*] ordered the grappling hooks to be got out, and shouted to the enemy to come to close quarters. They replied, summoning him to surrender in fair fight; and one Englishman, standing in the maintop with sword and buckler, called out "Good soldiers that you are, surrender to the fair terms we offer you." But the only answer he got was a musketball which brought him down in sight of everyone, and [Don Francisco] then ordered the muskets and arquebuses to be brought into action. The enemy thereupon retired, whilst our men shouted to them that they were cowards, and with opprobrious words reproached them for their want of spirit, calling them chicken . . . and daring them to return to the fight.'

Some time earlier the *San Felipe*'s sister, the *San Mateo*, had experienced an even closer encounter with one of the English ships. As the two vessels passed one another their sides scraped so close that a single foolhardy Englishman was able to leap onto the Spaniard's deck. No one followed him, and he was instantly cut down.

The English were now, for the first time, pressing their attacks home at a range close enough to inflict real damage on the Spanish hulls. We have already seen the shambles to which the *San Felipe* had been reduced, and she was one of many. The aggressive and persistent troubleshooters, now fighting to save the Armada from total annihilation, naturally suffered most. The *San Martín* herself received more than 200 hits, several of which penetrated her hull close to the waterline. Only the heroic efforts of two naked divers with oakum and lead patches kept the leakage under control. The *San Mateo*, singled out by a hard-hitting pack of English galleons, fought until 'she was a thing of pity to see, riddled with shot like a sieve'. And the damage she received from the enemy was exacerbated by the recoil of her own guns which, lashed directly to the hull frames, began to pull her whole structure apart.[11] She gaped open, and it was feared she would sink; but in the evening the flagship sent over a diver who managed to patch up the holes. Nevertheless the *San Mateo*, like the *San Felipe*, was mortally stricken, and the two Portuguese galleons began to fall behind the rest of the fleet. That night they ran aground between Nieuwpoort and

Ostend, and on the following morning they were captured, together with their exhausted crews, by Justin of Nassau's cromsters.

A group of English ships battered the Levanter *San Juan de Sicilia*

'so heavily with their guns that they completely shattered her . . . [we had to] repair the damage from the many shots which the ship had received alow and aloft and from the prow to the stern, and below the waterline in places difficult to repair. . . .'

Underwater damage was also sustained by the *Santa María de la Rosa* which, according to the sole survivor of her subsequent wrecking, 'had been shot through four times, and one of the shots was between the wind and the water, whereof they thought she would have sunk'. Both *La Trinidad Valencera* and *El Gran Grifón* sustained hull damage so severe that their crews were forced eventually to run them ashore. According to

Hull timbers from the Guipúzcoan vice-flagship *Santa María de la Rosa*, exposed on her wreck 120 feet down in Blasket Sound, County Kerry. 'This ship was shot through four times,' confirmed her only survivor, 'and one of the shots was between the wind and the water, whereof they thought she would have sunk.'

Father La Torre, in the thick of it aboard the *San Martín*, it 'rained bullets on all the leading galleons'.

For all this punishment, to be sure, only one Spanish ship actually sank during the battles. She was the Biscayan *María Juan*, which was surrounded by English ships and pounded to death: as she was 'in speech of yielding' to one of her assailants 'before they could agree on certain conditions, [she] sank presently before their eyes'. Only a single boatload of her people were saved.

Human casualties aboard many other ships were also high. No more than 127 men of the 457 who had embarked at Lisbon on the *San Felipe* ever came ashore again, and the death toll aboard the *San Mateo* was scarcely lower. The Armada's overall casualties that day were probably over 1,000 killed and 800 wounded. But the fighting spirit of the survivors remained strong. At one stage in the battle a great Italian ship, probably Bertendona's flagship *Regazona*, was observed to be 'running with blood', with her main guns dismounted, though she was still to be seen at her station in the defensive rearguard three hours later.

Action began to wane between four and five in the afternoon, when the English ammunition stocks started to run out. To escape, the Spaniards were now obliged to sail, without adequate pilots or charts, into the unknown waters off the Flemish coast. According to Father La Torre, 'There was scarcely a man who could sleep that night; we were all wondering when we would run aground'; so the men prayed, or cried to the Virgin to save them, while the chaplains confessed them until dawn broke to reveal that a fortuitous shift of wind had carried them to the open sea.

But the Armada was no longer together: yet again, the fleet was scattered and 'the duke's ship, which was usually in the van, seemed to be the last of all'. This was deliberate, for Medina Sidonia was still determined to wait for Parma as long as he could. He attempted once more to rally the fleet, as he had done the day before. But by now morale among the Spaniards was low. There was even speculation that the duke intended to surrender, and several sources stated that some members of his council of war advised this desperate expedient; but, reported La Torre, 'there was no pinnace available [to handle negotiations with the enemy], which was a particular favour from God and, in any case, the duke did not want to follow this course, preferring to die like a knight.'[12] Medina Sidonia and his officers confessed themselves, and prepared to

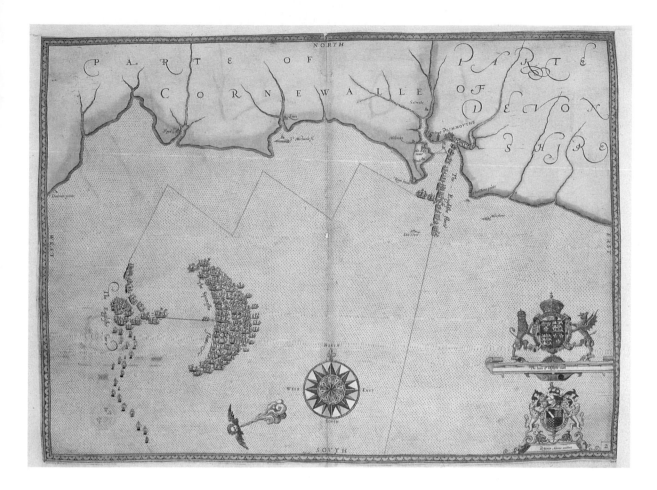

38. A chart by Robert Adams – the 2nd in a series showing the various phases of the Armada campaign, commissioned by Lord Admiral Howard shortly afterwards – shows how the English fleet gained the weather-gauge of the crescent-shaped Spanish formation. The main body, under Howard and Drake, had sailed boldly southwards from Plymouth, crossing the Armada's front to gain a position to windward of its right flank. Another group of English ships, which had cleared Plymouth rather later, tacked westward close inshore to reach the same position. Close to the centre of the Armada's rear can just be seen the tiny pinnace *Disdain*, firing the Lord Admiral's token 'defiance' into the heart of the Spanish fleet.

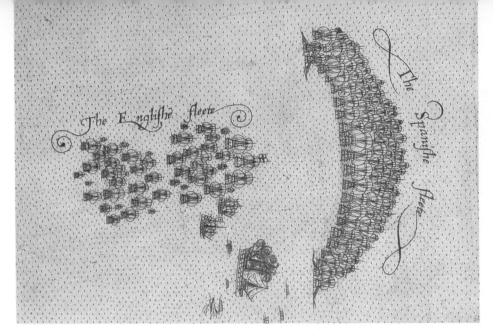

39. Detail of Adams chart 4, showing the *San Salvador* ablaze and abandoned after the explosion which crippled her.

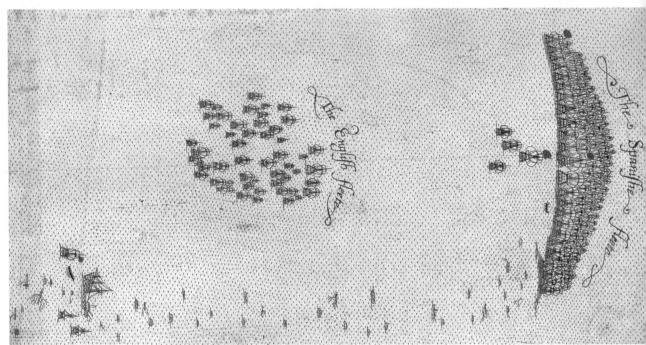

40. The *Nuestra Señora del Rosario* incident, as depicted in Adams chart 5. It is dawn on 1 August. The stricken *Rosario*, after the mishaps of the previous evening and now minus her foremast and far behind both fleets, is on the point of being captured by Drake's *Revenge*, which during the night had dropped back from its position at the head of the English fleet with the clear intention of capturing Don Pedro de Valdés, his ship, and his treasure. Meanwhile, Lord Admiral Howard in his flagship *Ark Royal*, confused by the absence of the stern lantern which the *Revenge*, as leading ship, had been ordered to show during the hours of darkness, finds himself as day breaks embarrassingly close to the Armada's rear. The remaining English ships, uncertain as to what is happening, mill about in a perplexed gaggle.

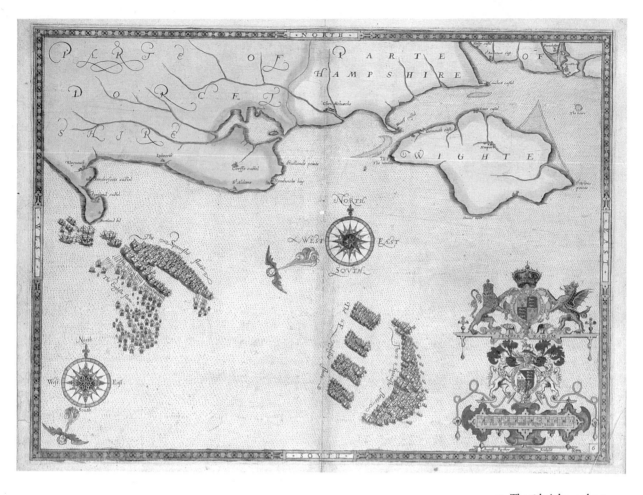

41. The 6th Adams chart depicts, on the left, the confused battle off Portland Bill on 1 August, during which the English 'feather-plucking' tactics were finally shown to be ineffectual. On the right of the chart, as the 2 fleets approach the Isle of Wight and the crucial eastern seaway by which the Armada might win the shelter of the Solent, the English fleet has been reorganised into the 4 squadrons which would counter this attempt.

42. Martin Frobisher in
1577, aged 39.

43. Chart of the Narrows
between Dover and Calais,
with the Banks of Flanders
shown towards the left.
Soundings are given in
fathoms. Off Kent, the
deepwater anchorage of the
Downs, between Deal and the
Goodwin sands, is clearly
marked. This large-scale
chart, which provides all the
information required by the
Armada for the crucial link-
up with the Army of Flanders
and the subsequent cross-
Channel jump, was
commissioned at Lisbon by
the duke of Medina Sidonia –
probably from the
cartographer Luis Teixeira –
for general issue to the fleet.
This copy, now in the
National Maritime Museum
at Greenwich, may well have
been taken from one of the
captured ships.

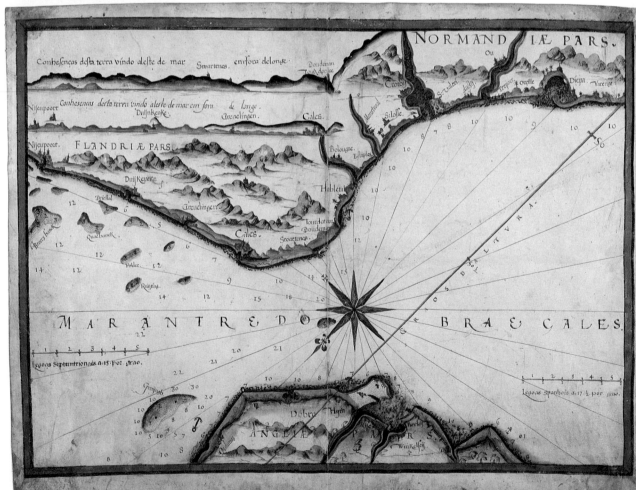

continue fighting, while the guns of the flagship fired three times to summon up the other ships. But nobody came, so the duke sent out his boats to the nearest ships to ask why they had not responded to his signal. Their captains were brought aboard, and La Torre has preserved the grim dialogue which followed:

'Didn't you hear the gun?' demanded Medina Sidonia furiously. They admitted that they had. 'Then why did you not rally?' 'We thought your flagship was sinking, and that we should all hasten away to safety' they replied. There was a short pause, and then the duke coldly delivered his verdict:

'Hang the traitors.'[13]

In the end only one captain was strung up from a yard arm and paraded round the fleet in a *patache* to re-establish shaken discipline. He was Don Crístobal de Ávila, the captain of a hulk and a neighbour of Medina Sidonia's at San Lúcar. But although the duke could still rally his fleet with this salutary example, there was no longer an objective for which to fight. The Spaniards could only allow the wind to carry them, albeit once more in a semblance of disciplined order, away from dangerous coast of Flanders and into the uncertain waters of the North Sea.

I ♣

The Admirall of Ld Sheffeild
Sr Tho: Howard and others
joyn with Drake and Fenez.
agt ye Spanish Fleet, & worst them.

II ♣

The Spaniards on sight of the
Fireships weighing Ancors
cutting Cables and betakeing
themselves to flight wth a hide-
ous noise & in great Confusion.

III ♣

8 Fireships Sent by ye English
Admirall towards ye Spanish
Fleet in ye Middle of ye night
Under the Conduct of Young
and Prowse.

IIII ♣

The Spaniards lying at Anchor
nere Cales and ye English Admir:
all riding with in a Shott of
Great Ordnance, the English
Navy consisting at this time of
140. Ships.

V ♣

The Earle of Oxford North:
umberland Cumberland, wth
many more of the Nobility
and Gentry going to visit the
English Fleet.

VI ♣

The Ld Admirall Howard
Knighting Thomas Howard
the Lord Sheffeild, Rog: Townsend
Iohn Hawkins, and Martin
Forbisher for their good service

II ♦

The 2d Fight betweene ye English
and Spanish Fleetes being the 23
of Iune 1588. wherein only Cock
an Englishman being wth his litle
Vessell in ye midst of ye Enimies died va:
liantly. but ye Spaniards much worsted.

III ♦

The Galleon of Don Pedro
taken Prisoner by Sr Francis
Drake, and sent to Dartmouth.

V ♦

The English Pinnace caled
ye Defiance sent from the
Admirall, and by a great Shot
Challinging the Spaniards
to Fight, the 23 of Iuly 1588.

VI ♦

Arthur Ld Grey, Sr Francis
Knolles, Sr Iohn Norris,
Sr Richard Bingham, Sr Rog:
Williams & others in a Councell
of War, consulting how ye land
Service should be Ordered

VII ♦

The Army of 20000 Soul-
diers laid along ye Southern
Coast of England.

VIII ♦

The Ld Hen: Seymor wth 40
English and Dutch Ships
keeping the Coast of the Netherlands to hinder ye Prince of
Parma's coming forth.

CHAPTER 11

Anatomy of failure

The Armada, wrote Emanuel van Meteren shortly afterwards, had 'vanished into smoke'. And it had also sailed into legend.

Practical men like Howard, Drake and Hawkins had known how close the call had been but, once the danger was past, their realistic appraisals had little popular appeal. Nor could Elizabeth's government, with eager support from Protestant factions throughout Europe, ignore this unique opportunity of mustering public opinion against Spain. The propagandists had a field day. The very enormity of the Armada, and its blatant appearance on the coast of England, demonstrated Philip II's greed, tyranny, and ambition for all to see: at the same time its dispersal and flight in the face of a gallant and (supposedly) tiny foe now added to Spain's catalogue of vices those of incompetence and cowardice. And to cap it all the Almighty had demonstrated, by sending His winds to destroy the proud and mighty Spanish fleet, exactly where His sympathies lay.

Thus was born the first and most persistent legend: the great size of the Spanish ships. They were so huge, reported the contemporary Englishman William Camden, that the winds grew tired of carrying them, and the ocean groaned under their weight. Some of the Armada ships were certainly large, and the fleet contained 55 vessels of 500 tons and upwards, but many of these were not fighting galleons. They were invasion transports, whose wide hulls and heavy cargoes made them clumsy and vulnerable. All of the thirteen English ships over 500 tons, however, were heavily armed royal galleons, and the largest of them – Martin Frobisher's 1,100-ton *Triumph* – was bigger than any comparable galleon in the Spanish fleet. Only four of the Armada's ships – all of them converted merchantmen rather than true warships – appear on paper to have been larger, but this may be illusory. The Spaniards and the English used quite different formulae for calculating tonnage, and it is probable that the Spanish method gave a rather higher figure.[1]

Once the size of the Spanish ships has been reduced to realistic proportions, another of the legends can be demolished. Their guns, it was claimed, were mounted so high on their towering sides that the balls flew harmlessly over the low English vessels – whose every shot, in return, told upon their huge adversaries.

This view, rejected by most serious historians since the late nineteenth century, now has few devotees. But, in the meantime, another erroneous and just as misleading hypothesis about the armament of the two fleets has emerged. Although Cesareo Fernández Duro in Spain and Sir John Laughton in England both correctly concluded that the Armada's total firepower was much lighter than that of the English fleet ranged against it, this conclusion was turned on its head by an English historian, Professor Michael Lewis, in the early 1940s. Lewis sought to establish the total armament of the Spanish fleet from the only sources then available to him – some very limited information published by Captain Duro in 1885, and the English inventories of the guns aboard the captured *San Salvador* and *Nuestra Señora del Rosario*.

In a most ingenious statistical exercise, Lewis used these figures to project a grand total for the entire fleet. But his argument is fatally flawed. Both the *San Salvador* and the *Rosario* were exceptionally heavily gunned, and were grossly unrepresentative of the fleet as a whole. Specific records of at least 75 per cent of the *actual* guns aboard the Armada are contained in the documents at Simancas, and Dr I.A.A Thompson has made a detailed and perceptive analysis of this information. He concluded that, in reality, the total effective firepower of the Armada was little more than half of Lewis's *minimum* estimate and, instead of its being nearly one third greater than that of the firepower mobilised by the English fleet, it was almost exactly one third less.

Nor can Lewis's other main contention now be supported. He sought to demonstrate that the Armada was greatly superior in heavy close-range 'ship-smashing' types of the short-barrelled 'cannon' variety, while the English had concentrated on the lighter shotted and much longer barrelled members of the 'culverin' family – which, it was thought, had a greater range. With the latter, ran Lewis's argument, the English ships could use their better sailing capabilities and higher speeds to dictate the distance at which they fought, keeping beyond the effective range of the ship-smashing cannons but within the distance at which they could ply their lighter culverins.

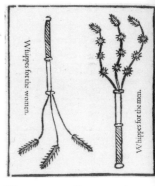

The propagandist at work: detail from Thomas Deloney's 'Ballet of the Whippes', published in 1588, in which it is averred that the Spaniards had designed one kind of whip for English men, and another (even more fiendishly brutal) for the women.

This erroneous view about the contrasting range capabilities of the two types of gun was widely held by artillery theorists in 1588 (and is followed today by most historians), although practising sea-gunners were coming to realise that excessively long pieces offered no obvious advantages in performance and were exceedingly difficult to handle aboard ship. In fact, it is now known that lengthening a smooth-bore gun barrel beyond a certain point, far from increasing the range, actually reduces it. A charge of black powder, when ignited, can only produce a set volume of gas, and when that is expended (or is not being produced quickly enough to maintain pressure behind the rapidly accelerating projectile), any further increase in barrel length will retard its velocity. The critical length is reached at a point roughly 24 times the diameter of the bore. In practice, however, quite wide variations of this length produce little noticeable effect, and a gun 15 or 20 times its calibre length – the proportions of a cannon – would have had about the same muzzle velocity, and hence range, as a culverin of 35 calibres. The important point to note is that, in spite of the difference in length, their effective ranges were much the same. And that range was very short: although a projectile might carry as far as 2,000 yards, its accuracy and hitting power beyond about 200 yards was minimal.

What mattered most was the weight of the projectile delivered. And here the Spaniards were at a definite disadvantage. Thompson has estimated that the Armada as a whole carried only 138 guns of 16-pounder calibre and upwards, and of these the 12 or so largest were siege pieces, unsuited to shipboard use. The corresponding English figure was 251, all of which were sea-service weapons. And although quite a high proportion of these were classed as 'culverins' the majority of them were, in fact, guns of culverin calibre – around 18-pounders – which had been cut down to a more manageable length. A Spaniard would have called the same guns *medios cañones*.

The misconceptions outlined above conditioned Lewis's subsequent interpretation of the battles, which has since become widely accepted. His scenario runs thus. During the initial engagements the English, wishing to keep clear of the heavy close-range batteries carried by the Spanish ships, kept the range open and pounded the Spaniards with their long-range culverins. They scored numerous hits, but the projectiles were not heavy enough, nor of sufficient velocity, to do the Armada serious damage. The Spaniards, however, were goaded into returning fire beyond the effective range of their heavy guns to such an extent that, by the time all-out battle was joined off Gravelines, they had run out of ammunition. This gave the English the chance, at last, to come really close to their adversaries without the fear of being crippled by short range 'ship-smashing' fire and subsequent boarding. And the English culverins proved, at these close ranges, to be capable of inflicting serious damage.

Certainly English gunnery achieved considerable success off Gravelines. Equally certainly the Spaniards meted out remarkably little damage in return. Apocryphal stories of the Spanish bombardment's supposed ferocity abound, the best known, predictably, coming from sources close to Drake. In one version a gentleman 'lying weary' in the *Revenge's* great cabin had the bed shot from under him by a saker ball; shortly afterwards (the bed having somehow been restored), a demi-culverin shot discommoded two more gentlemen, one of whom was the duke of Northumberland, in precisely the same place. But whatever superficial if spectacular damage of this kind may have been done to the upper works of Elizabeth's galleons, it is clear that they suffered little serious hurt, and few human casualties too (probably no more than 100 overall).

No doubt many minor repairs were carried out by the ships' carpenters without need for comment; but as to more substantial repairs, detailed and objective evidence exists in a full dockyard survey carried out on the queen's ships shortly after the emergency was over. In it a number of unserviceable components are noted for replacement, being variously described as 'worn', 'cracked', or 'decayed'. On occasion, perhaps, these were euphemisms for battle damage, although the frequency with which they occur is little greater than might be expected in any routine survey. Some damage, indeed, is directly attributed to enemy action: a smashed (or lost) ship's boat; the *Revenge's* mainmast 'decayed and perished with shot'. But it is almost all relatively minor, and the entries are few. Of substantial combat damage to the hulls – the kind of damage sustained by so many of the Armada's ships – there is not a single mention. It was to explain this apparent contradiction that Professor Lewis put forward the theory that, by the time the action off Gravelines was fought, the Spaniards had expended all their ammunition, and their heavy guns were therefore no longer a threat at close range.

But we now know for certain that they did *not* run out of shot. True, many of the participants remarked on the intensity of the artillery action on both sides. Spaniards who had also fought at Lepanto considered that, in comparison, the cannonading they experienced in the Channel was twenty times more furious. Lord Admiral Howard agreed: 'There was never seen a more terrible value of great shot,' he wrote, 'nor more hot fight than this was.' Petruccio Ubaldino, a Florentine resident in England who had close connections both with the Lord Admiral and with Drake, confirms this impression: 'The multiplied firing of the greater artillery . . . on both sides . . . [was] considered to be firing no less quickly than ordinary arquebuses in the hottest skirmish.' And even before Gravelines, Medina Sidonia was desperately concerned about his diminishing ammunition stocks, and urgently requested replenishment from Parma.

But a closer reading of his request reveals that he was not short of heavy calibre shot. What he wanted from Parma was 4-, 5-, and 10-pounder projectiles only. Since every gun in the fleet had (theoretically) been issued with 50 rounds, it would seem therefore that the bigger calibres were being less frequently used. But these were the very guns with which the duke might have hoped to cripple an adversary prior to boarding – the tactic which, above all else, the Spaniards sought to employ, for it exploited their great advantage of vastly superior manpower.

Nevertheless there can be no doubt that the big guns were not used to their full effect, or anything like it, because shot of all calibres, and especially the larger calibres, has been found in abundance on every

Sample of roundshot recovered from the wreck of the *Santa María de la Rosa*. When she sank off Ireland the ship still possessed plenty of ammunition for all her categories of armament, from 18-pounder *medios cañones* down to small swivel pieces and hand guns.

Armada wreck so far investigated. All of these ships had been heavily engaged: most, indeed, had been members of the 'troubleshooting' elite. Further evidence of unexpended shot lies within the mountains of administrative records which survive in the archives of Simancas for the Armada's hired ships. While the royal warships were issued with powder and shot which was used and replaced with a minimum of formality, the private ships which sailed with the fleet were each issued with specific quantities of munitions by crown officials before the campaign began, and were expected to record in detail each projectile and each pound of gunpowder thereafter expended.

These meticulous chronicles are extremely informative, for they give a day-to-day breakdown of the gunnery performance of individual ships throughout the fighting. The figures show, for example, that the 22-gun Levanter *Trinidad de Escala* fired 35 shots on 2 August (1.6 rounds per gun), 21 shots on 4 August (0.96 rounds per gun), and 38 shots during the Gravelines engagement on 8 August (1.7 rounds per gun). Similarly the Guipúzcoan *Santa Bárbara*, which appears to have had 20 guns instead of the 12 credited to her in the Lisbon Muster, fired 22 shots on 31 July (1.1 rounds per gun), 28 on 1 August (1.4 rounds per gun), 47 on 2 August (2.35 rounds per gun), and 167 − 56 of them stone shot − on 8 August (8.35 rounds per gun). Over the four days of actual fighting the Andalusian vice-flagship *San Francisco* (21 guns) discharged only 242 rounds, an average of less than three per gun per day, while her sister ship, the *Concepción Menor*, fired 156 balls from her 20 guns, an average of under two per gun per day. These figures come nowhere near to accounting for the 50 or more rounds with which, according to the Lisbon Muster and the ships' own records, each gun had been provided. Of the 1,421 shots which had been issued to the *Concepción Menor* at Lisbon, for instance, 1,256 were handed back on her return.[2]

So here at last is a full and sufficient explanation for the Armada's remarkable failure to inflict serious damage on the English fleet: the Spaniards simply did not fire their guns — especially their few heavy guns — often enough. But why was this so? The answer, it seems, lies in the highly specialised procedures and battle-drills for which the Spaniards were equipped and prepared, but which, in the event, they had been unable to use.

We know from Medina Sidonia's instructions to the fleet, and from actual examples of Armada artillery and its associated equipment

recovered from the wrecks, that the guns were kept loaded at all times. Whenever battle was joined one salvo was available for immediate use, and an operator holding a lighted linstock at the side of each gun was the only requirement for discharging the first round. This is exactly how a galley was expected to loose off its close-range cannonade immediately before ramming its foe; and since in such a situation there would be neither opportunity nor need for reloading, no procedure existed for disciplined reloading as a standard battle drill. Spanish sailing-ship tactics, in line with galley experience, also envisaged the broadside as a one-off device for crippling and confusing an adversary as an immediate prelude to boarding.

But the kind of warfare the English had developed, and applied so successfully at Gravelines, involved a continuous close-range bombardment intended to destroy an enemy by the attrition of gunfire alone. Given that their inferior sailing qualities prevented the Spaniards from closing and boarding as they would have liked, the Armada's only counter to such tactics was to attempt to reply in kind. To do this, however, they would have to reload and fire their guns time and again during the course of an engagement. Not only was this practice outside the tactical experience of the Spanish commanders and their crews, it was also one for which their equipment was fundamentally unsuited.

Partly through a close reading of Medina Sidonia's fighting instructions for his own flagship, and partly from the evidence provided by the wrecks, the Spanish battle drills can be reconstructed with some confidence. Before action was joined the guns were prepared, primed, run out, and lashed fast to the ship's side. Each was manned by a gun-captain, and two artillery officers were allocated to each side of the two main gun decks to control and direct the fire. The guns were actually handled by crews of six soldiers, who were withdrawn when required from their battle-stations on the ship's decks and in its fighting tops. These men, under the direction of the gun captains, carried out the tasks of scouring, sponging, and loading; and then heaved on the tackles and handspikes by which the guns were run out and adjusted. That done, the soldiers returned to their original positions – for during the battle itself their primary job was to act as marines, whose duty is was to bring down a hail of small-arms fire as the range closed, to wield the pre-boarding weapons of grapnel, shear hook, missile and incendiary device, and finally to enter and overwhelm the adversary. Once an initial artillery discharge had been made, therefore,

(*Opposite*) A gunner's linstock from *La Trinidad Valencera*, in the form of a clenched hand. This device was used to hold the length of slow-match with which the pieces of artillery were detonated. A metal spike, the concreted remains of which can be seen bent around the linstock's butt end, enabled it to be stuck in a bucket of sand to keep the burning match out of harm's way.

Roundshot and wadding in a loaded iron 4-pounder from *El Gran Grifón*, revealed by the partial erosion of its bore.

the guns could not be re-loaded until the crews had been called in again from the boarding stations to which they had dispersed.

No doubt, as it became apparent that the English ships could not be grappled and boarded as the Spaniards wished, efforts were made to continue working the guns after the first salvo had been fired. This was probably not too much of a problem with the smaller pieces – a conclusion reinforced by the fact that the *San Martín* did indeed run out of shot in the 4- to 10-pounder category. But it would not have been so easy to improvise effective reloading drills for the larger guns. There were two ways in which muzzle-loading artillery was worked at sea in the sixteenth century. The guns could either be brought inboard and the necessary operations carried out within the ship, or they could be left in the fully run-out position and loaded outboard. The much more efficient process of allowing a gun's own recoil to throw it inboard under the restraint of a breeching rope was not developed until well into the seventeenth century. Instead it was customary, after firing, to unhitch the piece and haul it back manually. This process was laborious but reasonably efficient, and during the course of it the crew would be covered from the view, and to some extent from the fire, of the enemy. Outboard loading, though it demanded a much smaller crew, was far more awkward and perilous, for it required the loader to straddle the gun outside the port and carry out all the clearing and charging operations from this exposed and difficult position.

Which of these procedures the Spanish gunners used in 1588 is not known for certain, but the inefficient design of the guncarriages, with their wide diameter wheels and long trails, suggests that it would have been impracticable, mainly because of the lack of working space on the gundecks, for the pieces to have been loaded inboard while a ship was closely engaged. On the other hand, it would have been little short of suicidal to have attempted outboard loading while a ship was within small-arms range of an enemy. The probability is that once close action was joined, most Spanish ships only managed to fire off their previously-prepared salvo, after which sustained heavy gunfire ceased. This does not of course mean that no further firing was possible. It seems likely that the galleasses, which carried their heaviest guns at bow and stern, had room to reload the larger pieces inboard. It would appear from their perform-ance in action that the galleons of the Portuguese squadron also managed, to some extent at any rate, to do the same. But on most other vessels, as we now know from the wrecks and from the records of shot expended, the

A graphic analysis of round-shot recovered from the wreck of the hulk flagship *El Gran Grifón* showing that this ship's guns, especially the larger calibre ones, had been grossly under-used during the fighting.

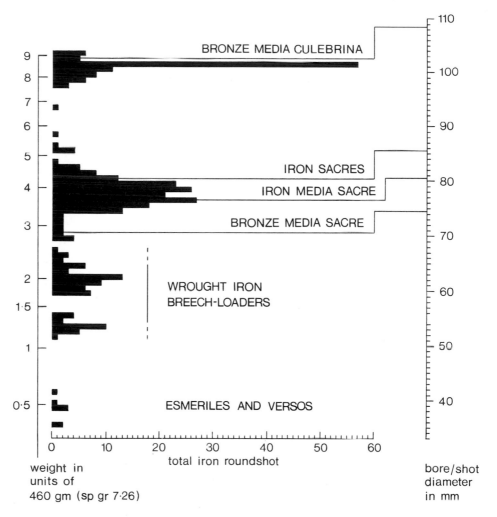

BRONZE MEDIA CULEBRINA

IRON SACRES

IRON MEDIA SACRE

BRONZE MEDIA SACRE

WROUGHT IRON
BREECH-LOADERS

ESMERILES AND VERSOS

total iron roundshot

weight in
units of
460 gm (sp gr 7·26)

bore/shot
diameter
in mm

guns that were fired most often were always the smallest – either light muzzle-loaders which could be hauled in and reloaded, or the breech-loading anti-personnel weapons. Of the 242 rounds discharged by the *San Francisco* during the campaign, for instance, only 22 were of heavy *cañón* calibre, while 188 were *sacre* or *media sacre* shot of 5- and 4-pounder calibre respectively.

Even aboard ships which did not carry particularly heavy guns the same trend is noticeable: proportionately, the lighter the ammunition the more likely it was to be used. Gómez de Medina's hulk flagship *El Gran Grifón*, wrecked on Fair Isle, had been issued with four *medias culebrinas* at Lisbon, and these 10-pounders were the heaviest pieces she carried. 97 of the 200 balls of this calibre issued to the ship have actually been recovered

One of the 4 bronze *medias culebrinas* issued to *El Gran Grifón* at Lisbon emerges from the sea off Fair Isle. The end of the barrel has broken off – probably during the shipwreck – to reveal that its bore is badly off-centre.

from her wreck, indicating that, at the very least, practically half of her heaviest available firepower was not discharged at the enemy. The figure is probably much higher, because there is almost certainly a considerable amount of shot on the wreck site still to be found. The picture for the *Grifón's* 34 lighter guns – 6-pounders and less – is very different. For these we have identified 273 rounds of ammunition, or only 16 per cent of the total allocation. On the basis of this very substantial sample, therefore, we can confidently say that the *Grifón's* lighter guns were on average fired three times more frequently than her *medias culebrinas*, even though the latter were the only pieces she had that were heavy enough to inflict serious damage on an enemy vessel.

The wreck of *El Gran Grifón* has revealed another crucial weakness in the Armada's artillery. The ship had been issued with eight bronze guns from the crash gunfounding programme at Lisbon just before the fleet sailed: four *medias culebrinas* and four *medios sacres*. An example of each of these types has been recovered and, in accordance with Juan de Acuña Vela's special instruction, they are plain and undecorated, without the normally mandatory royal arms. But the intensive production pressures evidently caused a dramatic drop in technical standards, for the *media culebrina* recovered from *El Gran Grifón* is bored so far off centre that in all probability it could never have been fired, and had certainly never been effectively proofed. Even a much reduced charge would have blown out its breech.

Nor was this an isolated case. An Italian *sacre* from the *Juliana*, recovered from her wreck off Streedagh Strand, suffered just such an accident at the muzzle, rendering it useless. The early seventeenth-century English gunner Robert Norton may not have been far wide of the mark when he wrote of Spanish and Italian gunfounding techniques that

'it is apparent that they commit great and absurd faults therein. Some of their pieces (and not a few) are bored awry . . . some are crooked in their chase, other of unequal bores some and a great many are come forth of the furnace spongy, or full of honeycombs and flaws . . . [Such guns] will either break, split, or blowingly spring their metals and (besides that mischief they do) they will be utterly unserviceable ever after . . . .'[3]

A final, insidious difficulty was heaped upon the unfortunate men who had to work the Armada's guns. The fleet was, it must be remembered, not a 'Spanish' Armada at all, but one drawn from the length and breadth of Europe, and the origins of its 2,431 guns encompassed most of the major foundries from the Baltic to the Adriatic and beyond. Not a few came from England. Even within the various foundries there was little enough standardisation of type and bore, while each country (and often individual regions within the same country) followed highly individual fashions of proportion and design, and employed its own, often widely differing, standards of weights and measurement. The confusion this engendered was immense, not least in the apparently simple business of allocating from a central supply source the calibres of shot appropriate to the guns aboard a particular ship. A further difficulty arose from the habit of expressing all calibres in terms of weight of shot rather than the actual diameters of the bores, for variations in the specific gravity of cast iron might easily determine whether or not a shot of a particular weight would actually fit its intended piece.

Gunners normally calculated the relationship between bore and shot-weight by means of simple instruments – a gunner's rule and a set of shot gauges. The former was a simple wooden scale, with graduations which determined the weight of shot appropriate to a given bore; the latter a set

This Italian *sacre* from the wreck of the Levanter *Juliana* off Streedagh Strand has suffered an explosive blow-out close to the muzzle.

Wooden gunner's rule and shot gauges from *La Trinidad Valencera*. The gunner first gauged the bore of his piece with the rule, reading off the weight of the shot required. He could then use the corresponding shot gauge to select the right size of ball. Unfortunately the graduations on the rule are inaccurate and inconsistent. They are, moreover, scaled to a light Italian pound entirely unrelated to the Castilian *libra* which was supposed to be the standard of measurement throughout the fleet.

of wooden rings which could be used to gauge a correctly proportioned ball. A gunner's rule and some of its corresponding gauges have been found on the wreck of the *Trinidad Valencera*, apparently scaled to one of the many contemporary Italian pounds. But the calibration of this scale is so inaccurate, and so full of inconsistencies, as to have rendered it virtually useless. If we multiply this one gunner and his error-laden instruments by the number of guns, gunners, and pieces of roundshot in the entire Armada, the scale of the inevitable muddle begins to emerge.

And muddle there certainly was on the Spanish gun-decks at Gravelines. Unfortunately no one has recorded it in so many words, but we may note the observations of the Dutch traveller Jan Huyghen van Linschoten, who in 1589 was involved in a minor action with English privateers while a passenger aboard a large Portuguese carrack. 'Whenever we shot off a piece,' he wrote, 'we had at least an hour's work to lade it in again, whereby we had so great a noise and cry aboard the ship as if we had all been cast away.'[4] It had doubtless been much the same aboard the Armada a year before. The conclusion is inescapable that, when it came to the test, Spanish sea-gunnery failed almost completely.

What then of the other side? There can be no doubt that the achievements of the English gunners, particularly at Gravelines, were better, but they were not without their critics. William Thomas, an English master-gunner stationed at Flushing at the time of the campaign, was one of them. On 30 September he wrote to Lord Burghley:

'. . . if it had pleased God that her Majesty's ships had been manned with a full supply of good gunners, according to the forces they carry . . . it would have been the woefullest time or enterprise that ever the Spaniard took in hand . . . What can be said but our sins was the cause that so much powder and shot spent, and so long time in fight, and, in comparison thereof, so little harm.'

There was some truth in all this. Throughout the campaign Howard and his captains had ceaselessly complained that they did not have enough ammunition. The English shot quota, initially, was probably no more than half the 50 rounds per gun carried by the Spaniards. A trickle of fresh supplies came out of local arsenals as the fleet sailed along the south coast, but without the powder and shot captured aboard the *Rosario* and *San Salvador* the situation would have been perilous. Between them the two prizes produced 229 barrels of powder – perhaps a quarter of the total English expenditure throughout the campaign. Even so, by dusk on 8 August, after only a few hours of combat, the English were almost entirely out of ammunition and, according to one source, 'were fain at last . . . to use plough chains instead of bullets'. Had full replenishment of powder and shot been possible at this point, it might indeed have been (as William Thomas speculated) the 'woefullest time' for the Spaniards.

And yet, as we have seen, it was woeful enough. The English seem to have surmounted those problems of working ship-killing artillery in a close engagement that had so debilitatingly baffled their adversaries. According to Sir Arthur Gorgas, who had been present, the queen's ships had been able to weave in and out among the Spanish fleet 'discharging our broadsides of ordnance double for their single' – and this was almost certainly an understatement. Several reasons may be adduced. First, the

English gunners were seamen, thoroughly familiar with the guns aboard their own vessels and conversant with the tasks of operating them at sea. Those detailed to work the guns were not expected, as were the Spaniards, to double as soldiers, and so they were unencumbered with military clothing and accoutrements. At least some of them, moreover, had undergone training with precious live ammunition, though apparently such prodigality met with official disapproval. But the familiarity thus engendered paid off. English gunners were, as William Bourne tells us, 'handy and without fear of their ordnance', and 'handsome about their ordnance in ships, on the sea'.

These considerable advantages of skill and familiarity were greatly increased by the design of the carriages upon which the guns were mounted. Although it had probably been in service with the navy for at least half a century, the sturdy four-wheeled truck carriage might well be regarded as England's decisive secret weapon in 1588. Sir Henry Mainwaring's *Seaman's Dictionary*, composed about 30 years later, entertained no doubt on the subject: 'The fashion of those carriages we use at sea are much better than those of the land', he wrote, 'yet the Venetians and Spaniards (and divers others) use the others in their shipping'. Archaeological evidence has confirmed his judgement: a massive Venetian sea-carriage of the type Mainwaring described has recently been identified on the wreck of *La Trinidad Valencera*, while iron fittings belonging to similar carriages have been found among the remains of the *Nuestra Señora de Atocha*, an Indian Guard galleon wrecked off the Florida Keys in 1623.

In contrast to the clumsy and inefficient gun mountings on the Spanish ships, which made reloading in action so difficult, the small wheels of the English truck carriages meant that the gun muzzles could protrude much further through the gun-ports, while there was no awkward trail with wide wheels to obstruct the sides and rear. Adequate working space was thus available for the crews to serve and fight their guns. Though the pieces were not allowed to recoil inboard for loading, as they were in Nelson's day (that practice probably started during the second quarter of the seventeenth century), it would not have been necessary to load them outboard, for there was ample room on the decks to haul them in manually after firing. Broadsides could therefore be delivered consecutively while a fight was in progress, the range being dictated by the superior sailing qualities of the English ships. All this surely explains the

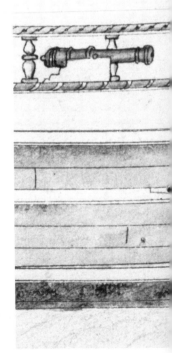

Detail from the late 16th century *Fragments of Ancient Shipwrightry* in the Pepys Library, Cambridge, showing the forward part of an Elizabethan galleon armed with a stepped truck guncarriage.

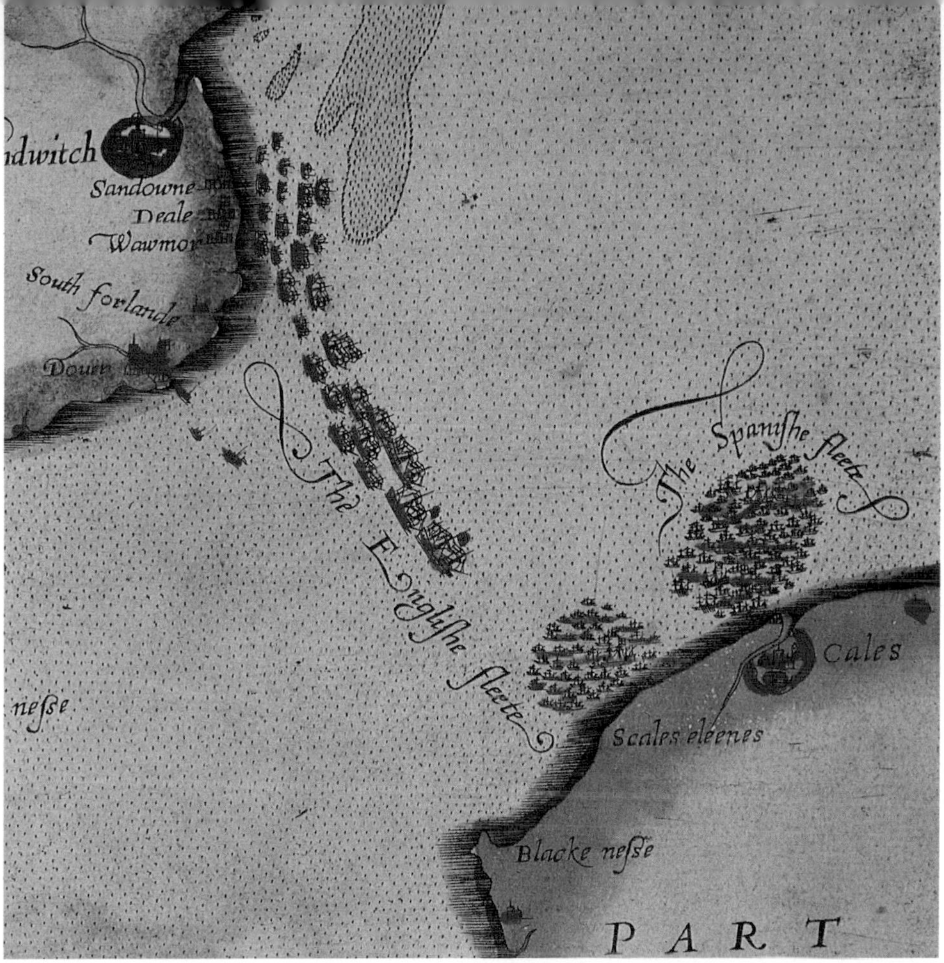

Sandowne
Deale
South forlande
The Englishe fleete
The Spanishe fleete
Cales
Scales eleenes
Blacke nesse
PART

44. Lord Henry Seymour's eastern squadron leaves its anchorage in the Downs to join the English fleet for its final assault on the Armada off Calais. A detail from Adams chart 8.

45. The fireship attack off Calais: detail from a painting by the Dutch artist Hendrik Corneliz Vroom.

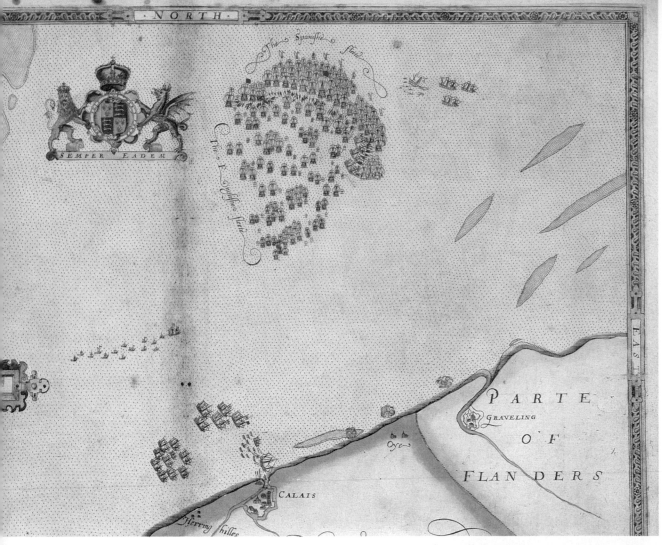

The Spanishe flete

The Englishe flete

SEMPER EADEM

P A R T E

GRAVELING

O F

F L A N D E R S

CALAIS

Herring billes

E A S T

46. The Armada's dispersal into the North Sea, with the English in hot pursuit. In this, the 10th of Robert Adams' series of charts, the events of 7 and 8 August are compressed. The Lord Admiral's assault on Moncada's grounded galleass off Calais can clearly be seen. Further along the coast 3 ships can be seen ashore and in flames: in fact only 2, the Portuguese galleons *San Mateo* and *San Felipe*, ran aground here, and neither was burnt. Towards the top right another casualty – the sinking *María Juan* – can be discerned.

47. A pair of navigator's dividers from *La Trinidad Valencera*.

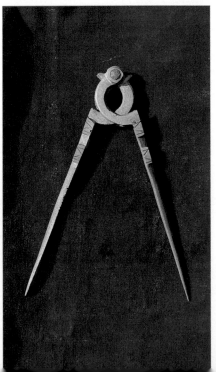

DRAVN AFTER THE QVICKE

48. 16th century Irish
warriors, drawn from life.

49. Detail of a manuscript
map endorsed by Burghley:
'The County of Sligo from Sir
Richard Bingham, 20 April
1589'. On it can clearly be
seen the 3 Levantine ships
breaking up in the surf off
Streedagh Strand.

50. Lacada Point, County Antrim, where the galleass *Girona* was wrecked with the loss of Don Alonso de Leiva and some 1,300 of his comrades.

51. Dunluce Castle, on the cliffs 5 miles to the south-west of the *Girona* wreck site. This was the stronghold of Sorley Boy Macdonnell, the Irish chief who helped many Armada survivors to cross over to Scotland.

After the Armada, an attempt was made to standardise ammunition sizes. This specification, signed by Acuña Vela at Málaga on 20 January 1590, orders the casting of 9,000 rounds for each of the 3-, 7-, 12-, and 16-pounder calibres. Though the different categories of shot will continue to be described by their nominal weights, from now on the diameters are to be *exactly* as indicated in the diagram, irrespective of variations in actual weight.

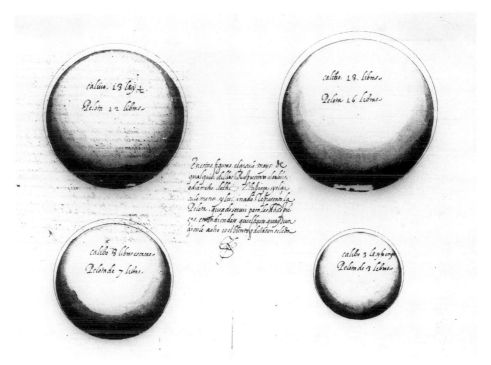

crippling hull damage meted out to the Spaniards, confirming Philip II's worst fears that the dastardly English would indeed fire low and hard.

And it was certainly their intention to hit low, and so inflict damage 'between the wind and water'. William Bourne, writing in 1587, stressed the importance of co-ordination between gunner and steersman, so that shots could be timed to hit an enemy's hull below the waterline as it heeled over. The English fleet's commanding position to windward of the Armada throughout almost all of the fighting gave it a considerable advantage in this respect, for it meant that their adversaries were normally heeled away from them, presenting their vulnerable lower hulls. But it was not until Gravelines that this advantage was fully exploited by the English galleons, and by then it was almost too late, for their ammunition stocks were all but exhausted.

Why had the English delayed so long? Their first encounters with the Armada had been cautious in the extreme: mere 'feather-plucking', according to the Lord Admiral; 'more coldly done than became the value of our nation' thought one of his more outspoken subordinates. The truth was that at the outset no Englishman knew for sure the strengths (or the weaknesses) of the Spanish fleet, but certainly it *looked* impregnable.

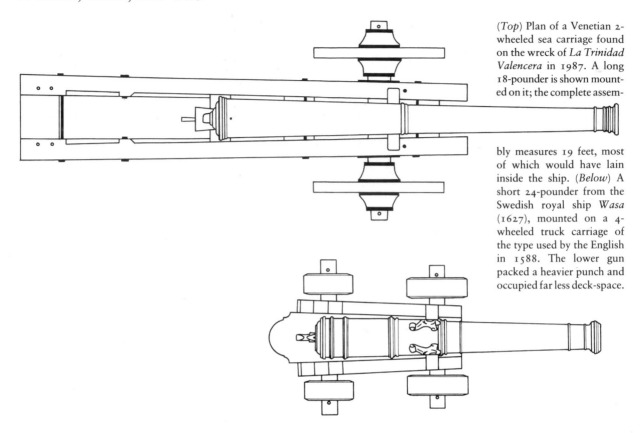

(*Top*) Plan of a Venetian 2-wheeled sea carriage found on the wreck of *La Trinidad Valencera* in 1987. A long 18-pounder is shown mounted on it; the complete assembly measures 19 feet, most of which would have lain inside the ship. (*Below*) A short 24-pounder from the Swedish royal ship *Wasa* (1627), mounted on a 4-wheeled truck carriage of the type used by the English in 1588. The lower gun packed a heavier punch and occupied far less deck-space.

So what were they to do? Go in close and risk disablement from those rows of gleaming bronze muzzles? Attempt to board the Spanish ships and be annihilated by their massed companies of troops? Howard's masters in the Privy Council had little grasp of his predicament: they wanted action; they wanted sunk or captured Spanish ships. When, on 31 July, the Lord Admiral begged desperately for more powder and roundshot, the Council responded by sending a contingent of musketeers to join in the hand-to-hand combat. Howard angrily sent them back. Even on 10 August, when thanks to Howard's tactics the Armada was at last in full retreat, the Council sent a messenger to demand of him 'what causes are there that the Spanish navy hath not been boarded by the queen's ships?' Perhaps fortunately, the Lord Admiral's reply has not been preserved.

But in spite of the Privy Council's unhelpful expectations, Howard and his fleet had, in the aftermath of Calais, radically improved their tactics. In the wake of the dislocation caused by the fireships to the Armada's hitherto tight and steadfastly maintained defensive formation, Howard's

(*Opposite*) Even before the Armada sailed, Spanish naval experts were coming to grips with the operational problems of working heavy guns at sea. This drawing of 3 different types of *medias culebrinas* was prepared at Lisbon by Don Juan de Acuña Vela, Captain-General of Artillery, and sent to Philip II on 25 July 1587.

The top gun, argues Acuña, is of the old pattern recommended by the marquis of Santa Cruz, but Don Juan considers that it is too slender for safety and too

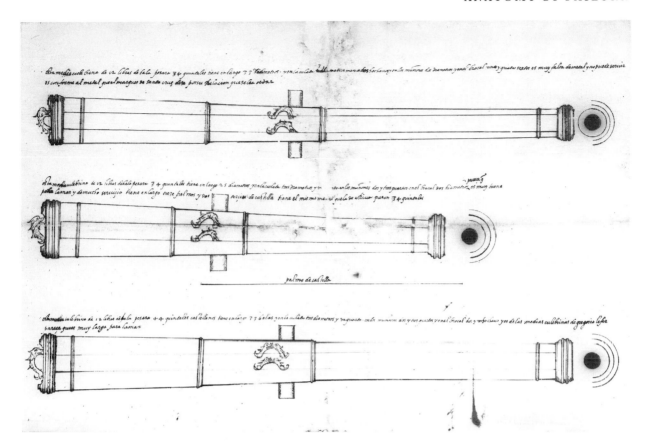

long for shipboard use. The bottom version has been strengthened but it is still too long, and now it is too heavy as well. Acuña's solution is the centre-piece, which has been reduced to a shorter length, and the metal thus saved used to make the barrel thicker and stronger. But these sound new ideas evidently took time to filter through the system: the *media culebrina* recovered from *El Gran Grifón*, cast at Lisbon in late 1587 or early 1588, was still made according to the outdated 'Santa Cruz' proportions.

galleons, now reinforced by Seymour's eastern squadron, launched an aggressive close-range gunnery assault on the retreating but fast reforming Spanish fleet. But should they not have done this from the beginning? Why did they at first hold back, and what precisely changed that caution to the vigorous and confident close action off Gravelines?

Somehow, it would seem, the bubble of the Armada's apparent invincibility had been pricked, and its shortcomings in gunnery clearly identified. This realisation must have dawned on the English at some point before Gravelines. We do not know how or why it dawned, but it seems certain that Howard and his captains had recognised the Spanish weaknesses before the Armada reached Calais. After the battles off the Isle of Wight on 3 and 4 August all fighting ceased for three days, while Medina Sidonia progressed towards his rendezvous with Parma. This suggests that on or before 4 August the English had made a firm decision to conserve their ammunition for an all-out attack on the Armada when it reached its vulnerable and uncertain station off Flanders. By this time, it would seem, they had discovered that they could come close enough to the Spaniards to deliver really effective ship-smashing broadsides without risking serious retaliation, so long as they used their decisive sailing advantage to avoid being grappled and boarded. From the Spanish guns, they now realised, they had little to fear.

Who first made this momentous discovery, and when, may never be known for sure. Perhaps it was a gradual realisation in the minds of many men. But a particularly likely candidate for the distinction is Sir Francis Drake, and a number of incidents which may have helped him towards this vital conclusion can be identified.

The first was Sir Francis's capture, on the morning of 1 August, of Don Pedro de Valdés's *Nuestra Señora del Rosario*. Here was the fourth largest and perhaps the best-gunned ship in the whole Armada, and yet she had put up a pathetic resistance. Drake and his officers must have wondered why. As they looked over their prize, they cannot have failed to notice the great gun-carriages, extending awkwardly beyong the centre-line of the deck, which had made it so difficult to fire frequently or accurately. Perhaps Sir Francis, with his ready wit and infectious charm, extracted a voluble explanation from the demoralised Don Pedro. In any event, he could have seen for himself the contrast between the purpose-built truck carriages of his own guns aboard *Revenge* and the clumsy two-wheelers of his adversary. And Drake, with his rigorous views on comradely team-work under a single captain, cannot have failed to notice the scratch crews of soldiers who tended the guns, the inefficient and divisive structure of command, and the huge reserves of unspent powder and shot. No one was better qualified than he to appreciate the full significance of all this, and it might be considered that Drake's capture of the *Rosario*, though bitterly criticised by some of his contemporaries, was in retrospect one of the most significant episodes in the campaign.

It is tempting to link the dawn attack on the straggling flagship of the hulks, *El Gran Grifón*, which took place off the Solent on 3 August, with the discoveries that Drake had made aboard the *Rosario* two days before. Here, for the first time, we hear of a really close ship-to-ship action in which the keynotes were mobility and firepower. Is it more than coincidence that the aggressor seems to have been the *Revenge*? Was Drake perhaps testing a developing theory about the Spaniards' inability to fight a mobile artillery action, and wisely choosing one of the less well-armed troubleshooters for his experiment? If so, he must have found the results deeply gratifying, for he struck his target 40 times and killed many soldiers on her decks, while the *Grifón's* four bronze *medias culebrinas* – the biggest guns she carried – remained virtually silent throughout.

A day later Drake repeated his experiment in full squadron strength, breaking the Armada's right wing off the Isle of Wight. The English now had all the information they needed to identify the Armada's fundamental weaknesses, and it was precisely at this point that a decision was apparently made to conserve ammunition – while there was still some left – for the final battle. Even if the Armada could not be defeated or broken at sea, it could be deflected irretrievably from its junction with Parma, and sent on its perilous homeward voyage. That was the measure of England's success at Calais and Gravelines.

But it was a close-run thing. The Armada, even at the last, still had a sting in its tail: some of its ships remained able to fire, reload, and fire again with their heavy artillery. Sir Francis Drake, according to his jaundiced critic, Martin Frobisher, made a serious tactical error when he 'came bragging up at the first indeed, and gave them his prow and his broadside', for his Spanish adversary was ready for him, and gave him a full broadside in return: Drake (added Frobisher with relish) was thereafter 'glad that he was gone again.' The *Revenge* was 'pierced with shot above forty times', and in the dockyard survey after the battle her mainmast was found to be 'perished with shot.' But this was the exception. Few Armada ships were able to mete out punishment of this severity, and most of the queen's ships stayed prudently clear of those that could.

At the last, Lord Admiral Howard was reduced to bluff. 'We put on a brag countenance and gave chase,' he noted, as the Armada disappeared into the northern seas, 'as if we wanted nothing.' In fact, they wanted everything, for by then the English galleons' shot-lockers were completely bare. Had the Armada at this point been entering the Thames estuary, with Parma's barges shepherded in its midst, the queen's navy could have done absolutely nothing to stop it.

But, of course, that horrifying scenario had been averted, and in the process a new form of naval warfare had been born. Within a year of the battles Petruccio Ubaldino, a Florentine artist, scholar, and historian who had come to England in 1545, wrote a manuscript account of the campaign for Sir Francis Drake. His account clearly reflects, in many ways, the experienced sea-dog's personal views. It also sums up, succinctly and accurately, the tactical doctrines which would, over the following two centuries, make England the world's most powerful maritime nation. The English fleet, wrote Ubaldino:

'. . . made good use of the most reliable quality of their excellent and speedy ships, not crowded out with useless soldiers, but with decks clear for the use of artillery, so that they could safely play it at any hour to harm the enemy, at any moment which suited them best to do so . . . It seems to us that next to be praised are the . . . gunners, [because] we must still recognise in that art not only manual practice, which is one of the most important parts of soldiering, but also the judgement of the eye and mind . . . among the artillery it had been absolutely decided by the English that all should be of one nationality, one language, and therefore one constant disposition to serve well, and we cannot consider that this was at all so among the enemy.'

And yet a thought should be spared for that enemy, now facing the perils of a hazardous return voyage. It had been a gallant effort, and it had certainly not failed because of the cowardice or incompetence of those who sailed in it. Among the delivered Protestants, perceptive men recognised in the Armada formidable strengths which, in different circumstances, might easily have prevailed. The Spanish fleet, to quote Emanuel van Meteren again, 'had many great vantages of the English, namely the extraordinary bigness of their ships, and also for that they were so nearly conjoined, and kept together in so good array, that they could by no means be fought withall one to one.'

So, in defiant if somewhat ragged array, the great Armada departed from England's shores. It had fought and failed, but it had not suffered outright defeat. Medinia Sidonia and his men had lost much, but they had not lost their honour.

ARTILLERY

Any attempt to classify sixteenth century artillery carries with it the danger of implying that precise specifications for each type were widely accepted. They were not. In spite of various attempts to impose standards – that by Charles V in 1549 is the best known – guns of the early modern period are in the main remarkable for their individuality and profusion of forms.

Even contemporaries were dismayed by the lack of ordered classification which resulted. 'Through an intolerable fault', wrote Cyprián Lucar in 1587, 'all our great pieces of one name are not of one weight, nor of one height in their mouths'. This difficulty was echoed in 1592 by the Spaniard Luis Collado, who noted that the guns in Milan Castle needed more than 200 different sizes of charging implements when 11 would have served had the guns been properly standardised. The problems created by unstandardised shot, he added, were just as serious. Gunners who sailed with the Armada would certainly have agreed with him.

Nevertheless, despite the almost limitless variety of forms sixteenth century ordnance might take, gunners usually applied quite specific names to particular types of gun. These names do not, however, imply any absolute precision of definition, for no such definition existed. The important factors are the weight and type of metal of which the gun was made; the charge it could bear; the weight and composition of the projectile fired; the proportion of projectile weight to gun weight; and the length of the barrel expressed as a multiple of its calibre. Beyond that, as one of the wisest of the sixteenth century technical authors put it: 'It does not matter what their names may be, except to know their sorts and kinds.'

An attempt must however be made, for descriptive convenience if nothing else, to group the various 'sorts and kinds' into named families. It is simplest to consider the Spanish side first. The Armada documents provide general parameters of classification for each named type and group of types as they were understood by contemporary Spaniards, and this classification is summarised below. The range of shot-weights for each group is taken from the maximum and minimum figures specified for the guns allocated to that group within the fleet. This summary is followed by a systematic sampling of actual guns, either recovered from Armada wrecks or redrawn from reliable contemporary sources.

Family	Type name	Shot-weight (in Castilian *libras*)
CAÑONES (heavy shotted guns 25 calibres or less in length)	Cañón de batir	40–50 iron
	Cañón	28–35
	Medio cañón	15–27
	Tercio cañón	10–14
	Quarto cañón	9–12
	Cañoncete	10
PEDREROS (short-barrelled stone-throwers with reduced powder chambers)	Cañón pedrero	12–20 stone
	Medio cañón pedrero	10–12
	other pedreros	4–12

CULEBRINAS	Culebrina	16–21 iron
(Light-shotted guns 30 or more	Media culebrina	7–14
calibres in length)	Sacre	5–8
	Medio sacre	3–4
	Falconete	2–4*
	Media falconete	1–1*
	Falcon	1–3*
		*often swivel mounted
MAN-KILLERS	Falcon pedrero	3–6 stone
	Esmeril doble	12ozs iron or lead
	Esmeril	6–8ozs iron or lead
OBSOLESCENT	Verso	1–3 iron
	Pasamuro	1–2 iron
	Lombarda	4–7 stone

EXAMPLES OF GUNS (*pages 218–22*)

The bronze muzzle-loading guns, numbered 1–12 (*pages 218–19*), are drawn to a common scale. A larger scale has been used for the smaller swivel pieces and iron guns, numbered 13–21 (*pages 220–22*). Wherever possible the guns shown come from one or other of the Armada wrecks, but where a particular type is not available the gap has been filled with an example drawn from a reliable contemporary source. Each gun is given the name which reflects, as closely as possible, late sixteenth century Spanish usage. Its origins, decoration, and any inscriptions are described, and its technical specifications summarised: weight and shot-weight (in Castilian *libras* of 460 grams: where necessary gun weights specified to other standards have been adjusted to conform); bore (in inches to facilitate comparison with English examples); length from muzzle to base ring (also in inches); bore/length ratio; and shot-weight/gun weight ratio. It should be noted that these calculations depend in part upon a number of factors which are variable and not always predictable, so in some respects the specifications presented here are arbitrary.

Shot diameters were normally one twentieth smaller than the gun bore to allow sufficient windage.

1. *Cañón de batir* by Gregorio Lefer of Augsburg, cast for Charles V in 1538. It carries the Emperor's full insignia. This drawing is based on a detailed diagram submitted to Philip II in 1587 (AGS *MPyD* V–18): the gun itself, identified by its weight mark, served in the Armada. It was originally shipped in the Levanter *Juliana*, but was later transferred to the squadron flagship *Regazona* (AGS CS 2a/280 fos 1504–6).
   Weight 5230lbs; shot-weight 38lbs (iron); bore c.7"; length 127.5"; bore/length 1:18.2; shot/gun weight 1:138.

2. *Cañón de batir* by Remigy de Halut of Mechelin, cast for Philip II in 1556. It carries the joint arms of Philip and Mary Tudor, and the name (latinised) of Don Juan Manrique de Lara, Captain-General of Artillery. This gun was recovered from the

wreck of *La Trinidad Valencera* in 1987, although its presence aboard had already been confirmed by the record of its weight mark in the ship's lading documents (AGS CS 2a/280 fo 1461). The same gun is illustrated in AGS *MPyD* V–18 (see above).
Weight 5186lbs; shot-weight 41lbs (iron); bore 7.2"; length 106"; bore/length 1:14.7; shot/gun weight 1:126.

3. 8" *pedrero*, based on Luis Collado's proportions of 1592. Note the narrow powder chamber and the thin-walled main barrel characteristic of these pieces: the combination permitted a large diameter projectile of low mass to be fired.
Weight c.2000lbs; shot-weight c.20lbs (stone); bore 8"; length 67"; bore/length 1:8.4; shot/gun weight 1:100.

4. *Medio cañón*, from a drawing in the 1587 discussion paper (AGS *MPyD* V–19).
Weight c.3500lbs (by Juan de Acuña Vela's calculation, which is certainly an under-estimate); shot-weight 20lbs (iron); bore c.5.5"; length 114"; bore/length 1:20.7; shot/gun weight 1:175.

5. Full *culebrina*, from an illustrated casting specification issued by Don Juan de Acuña Vela, Captain-General of Artillery, on 25 July 1587 (AGS *MPyd* V–16). The piece was to be decorated as shown. It was to be cast from a mixture of 92% Hungarian copper and 8% English tin.
Weight 6000lbs; shot-weight 18lbs (iron); bore c. 5.25"; length 158"; bore/length 1:30; shot/gun weight 1:333.

6. *Media culebrina* from *El Gran Grifón*, one of the four utility pieces issued to the ship at Lisbon just before the Armada sailed (see p 40). It carries no decoration or inscriptions. This gun's bore is grossly off-centre.
Weight c.2400lbs; shot weight 9lbs (iron), bore 4.25"; length 139"; bore/length 1:32.8; shot/gun weight 1:267.

7. *Medio sacre* from *El Gran Grifón*, evidently from the same utility batch as above.
Weight c.800lbs; shot-weight 2.8lbs (iron); bore 2.9"; length 90"; bore/length 1:31; shot/gun weight 1:286.

8. *Medio cañón* bearing the monogram and attributes of Francis I of France, recovered from the wreck of the *San Juan de Sicilia* in Tobermory Bay c.1740. It is now at Inveraray Castle.
Weight (by mark) 3253, (by estimation) 3154lbs; shot-weight 23lbs (iron); bore 5.8"; length 112.5"; bore/length 1:19.4; shot/gun weight 1:137.

9. Italian *media culebrina* from *La Trinidad Valencera*, perhaps by Nicolo di Conti of Venice.
Weight (by mark) 2950, (by estimation) 3025lbs; shot-weight 13.5lbs (iron); bore 4.9"; length 120"; bore/length 1:24.5; shot/gun weight 1:224.

10. Italian *sacre* from *La Trinidad Valencera*, by Zuanne Alberghetti of Venice.
Weight (by mark) 2529, (by weighbridge) 2596lbs; shot-weight 6lbs (iron); bore 3.75"; length 129"; bore/length 1:34.4; shot/gun weight 1:433.

11. Italian *sacre* from the *Juliana*, possibly Sicilian, dated 1570. On its breech is an ecclesiastical figure with crook and mitre, beneath which appears the name S[AN] SEVERO. A letter D, presumably the initial of the founder, surrounds the touch-hole. This gun has suffered an explosive blow-out close to the muzzle (see p 205).

Weight (by mark) 2082, (by estimation) 1800lbs; shot-weight 5lbs (iron); bore 3.5";
length 118"; bore/length 1:33.7; shot/gun weight 1:

12. Italian *pedrero* from the *Juliana*, possibly Sicilian. On its breech is a Virgin and Child,
   and its touch-hole carries a letter D similar to that on the *sacre* above.
   Weight (by estimation) 900lbs; shot-weight c.7lbs (stone); bore 5.8"; length 64.5";
   bore/length 1:11.1.

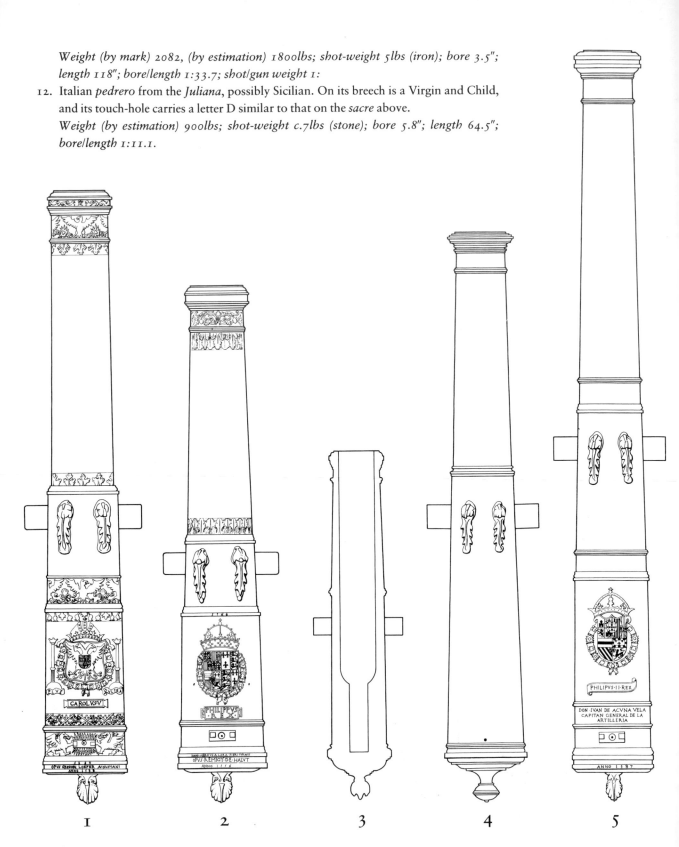

1   2   3   4   5

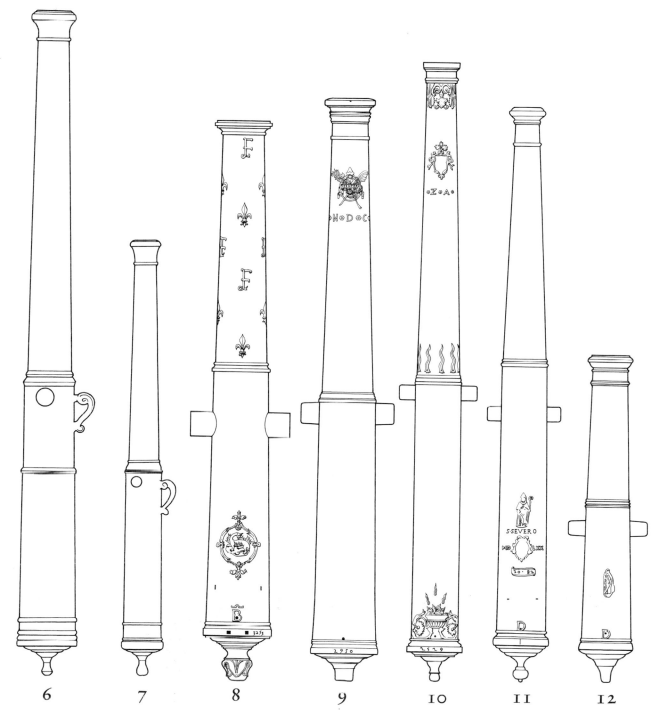

6   7   8   9   10   11   12

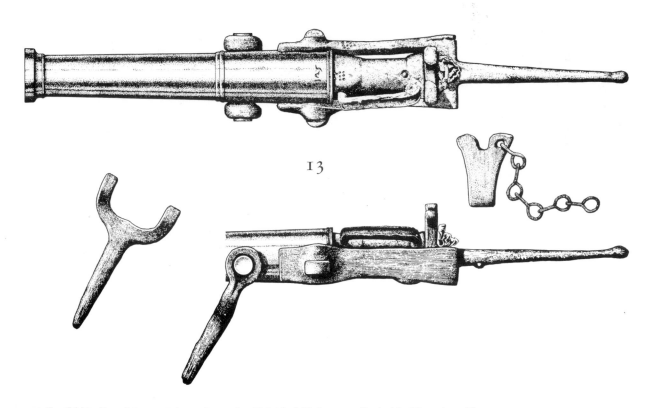

13

13. Breechloading *falcon pedrero* from *La Trinidad Valencera*. Probably Venetian. The barrel is cast in bronze, but the gun's other fittings – breech stirrup, removable breech-block, wedge with attachment chain, aiming tiller and mounting swivel – are made of wrought iron. The piece is as its gunner left it, ready for action, in 1588: it has a stone shot in the barrel, a charge (stoppered with a wooden plug) in the breech, and a twist of hemp in the touch-hole to keep the priming dry. A folded pad of leather has been inserted behind the wedge to ensure a tight fit. Guns of this kind could be reloaded much more quickly than the muzzle-loading types, but they were too small to be other than of anti-personnel use. There was also a considerable danger of blowback from the imperfectly sealed breech, and the associated clouds of smoke and gas restricted their use to open decks or the fighting tops.

Weight (by estimation) 300lbs (the 125 mark on the barrel refers to the bronze casting only); shot weight 1.7lbs (stone); bore 3.4"; overall length 68"; barrel length (excluding breech block) 35"; bore/barrel length 1:10.3; shot/gun weight 1:176.

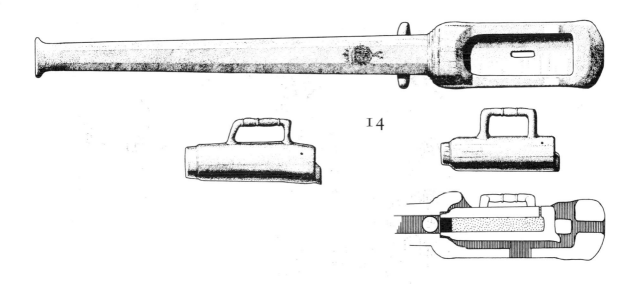

14

14. Bronze breechloading *esmeril* from the *Girona* with octagonal barrel bearing Philip II's arms. These guns were mounted along the side of the galleass, on walkways above the rowing benches. Each was equipped with two breech-blocks for rapid reloading. The *Girona* site also produced a number of breech-blocks for similar but larger weapons called *esmeriles dobles*.

Weight (by estimation) 200lbs; shot weight 1lb (iron); bore 2"; length (excluding tiller) 64"; bore/length 32; shot/gun weight 1:200.

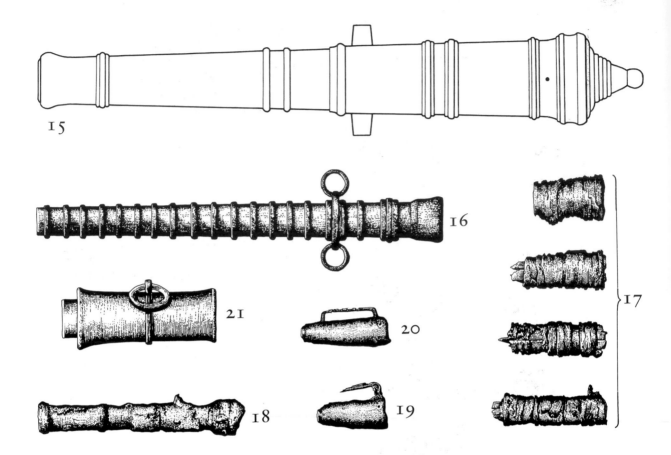

15. Cast iron gun from *El Gran Grifón*. This fits into no known Spanish category, but might loosly be referred to as a small *sacre*. It is one of the ship's original guns, and so almost certainly comes from Northern Europe – probably Sweden. It has efficient proportions (its bore/length ratio is close to the theoretical optimum) and is extremely well made.

    Weight (by estimation) 1560lbs; shot weight 4.5lbs (iron); bore 3.4″; length 87″; bore/length 1:25.5; shot/gun weight 1:346.

16. Breechloading wrought iron gun from *El Gran Grifón*. It has a 2.75″ bore appropriate to a 2-pound iron shot.

17. Breech-blocks for similar guns (*El Gran Grifón*).

18. Wrought iron barrel of a breechloading *falcon pedrero* from *El Gran Grifón*. Bore 3.4″; 1.7lb stone shot (cf. 13 above).

19. Breech-block for a similar gun (*El Gran Grifón*).

20. Wrought iron breech-block for a long iron-throwing swivel gun, perhaps a *verso*. *El Gran Grifón*.

21. Wrought iron breech-block for a 6″ bore breechloading *pedrero* from *La Trinidad Valencera*. The missing barrel was probably of bronze.

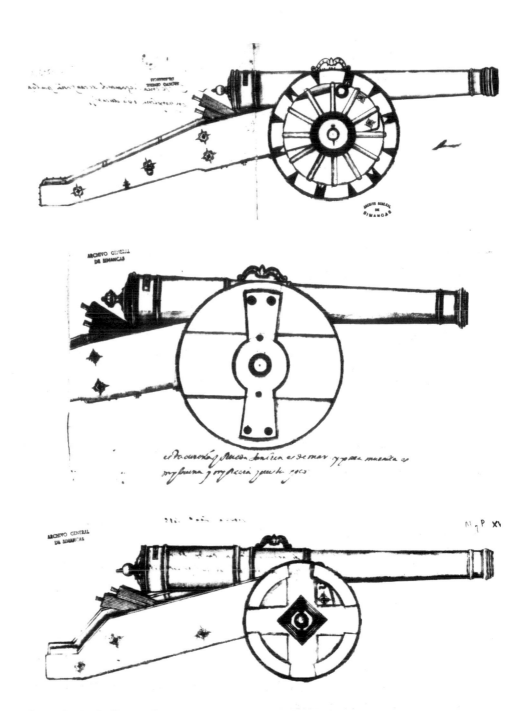

Late sixteenth century Spanish guncarriages, from a series of technical drawings, 1594. Top, a land carriage, similar to those on which the Armada's siege train was to be mounted; centre, a carriage 'for sea or fortress use' with large solid tripartite wheels; bottom, another type of ship carriage. All have the extended trails which made them awkward to handle aboard ship (AGS *MPyD* XVIII–47–9).

Unlike the Spaniards, the English kept no detailed records of the guns aboard their ships, and there are no wrecks to provide us with archaeological evidence. Not a single existing gun can unequivocally be said to have fought against the Armada in 1588. Several dozen Spanish guns, however, were obtained by the English when the *San Salvador* and *Nuestra Señora del Rosario* were captured during the early stages of the fighting. These were later subjected to careful descriptive inventories, in the course of which each gun was given the type name the English inventorist considered most appropriate to it. Since these same guns had also been inventoried by the Spaniards before the fleet sailed it is possible to compare the two sets of data and so obtain a 'translation' of Spanish-English gun names.

The result shows some unexpected divergencies in the comparative nomenclature of the two sides. When, for example, an Englishman spoke of a 'cannon' he meant the kind of gun a Spaniard would describe as a *'cañón de batir'* – that is, a battery piece seven or so inches in bore, throwing a shot of 40 to 50 pounds. But to a Spaniard the term *'cañón'* meant something altogether different: it was a relatively short-barrelled gun (25 calibres or less in length) firing shot of anything from 27 to 35 pounds. An Englishman would certainly have called the same gun a demi-cannon. But this was not at all the same as a Spanish *'medio cañón'*, which was a piece of 'cannon' proportions firing a ball of 15 to 27 pounds. To an Englishman in 1588, such guns would almost certainly be 'culverins' (with the heavier end of the scale encroaching on the demi-cannons), even though their length fell far short of the 30 or more calibres which classification into this family theoretically demanded. The Spaniards, in this respect, were more pedantic, reserving the term *'culebrina'* exclusively for 16–21 pounders of full 'long gun' proportions. In fact, there were very few full culverins on either side, for they were simply too cumbersome to handle aboard ship.

The long-held belief that the English went for 'culverin' types while the Spaniards concentrated on short-range *cañones* and *medios cañones* is substantially untrue: notwithstanding the widely held misconceptions about the relationship between barrel length and range (see p. 197 above), the majority of heavier guns on *both* sides were, broadly speaking, short battery pieces of the same general proportions; only the names were different. What *is* true – though only recently realised – is that the English, and not the Spanish, carried much the heaviest complement of artillery in 1588. Their advantage was compounded by a preponderence of shortened types, of all sizes, and by their manifest superiority in working them at sea. The Spaniards were correspondingly disadvantaged by the fact that a large number of their medium guns – particularly those in the 6- to 16-pounder category – seem to have been of 'culverin' proportions.

Although the full standardisation of gun types was still a long way in the future, the English probably came much closer to it than the Spaniards and their allies. At the very least, the adoption of a common language and a single standard of weights and measures must have made life on English gundecks a much more straightforward affair than the muddle which, as we have seen, obtained on the multi-lingual and arithmetically confused Spanish ones.

The following table of specifications is from a list drawn up by John Sheriffe in 1592 (or perhaps earlier). While it appears to be the work of a theorist rather than of a practical gunner, it is probably a reasonably accurate guide to English gun classification at the time of the Armada. Somewhat surprisingly, and possibly incorrectly, Sheriffe seems to regard the cannon-pedro as an iron-throwing piece.

Type name	Gun weight	Bore	Shot weight	Shot / gun weight
Cannon royal	7000lbs	8″	66lbs	1:117
Cannon	6000lbs	8″	60lbs	1:100
Cannon serpentine	5500lbs	7″	53lbs	1:103
Bastard cannon	4500lbs	7″	41lbs	1:109
Demi-cannon	4000lbs	6″	30lbs	1:132
Cannon pedro	3000lbs	6″	24lbs	1:123
Culverin	4500lbs	5″	17lbs	1:260
Basilico	4000lbs	5″	15lbs	1:262
Demi-culverin	3400lbs	4″	9lbs	1:364
Bastard culverin	3000lbs	4″	7lbs	1:428
Saker	1400lbs	3″	5lbs	1:263
Minion	1000lbs	3″	4lbs	1:250
Falcon	800lbs	2⅓″	3lbs	1:267
Falcon	660lbs	2¼″	2¼lbs	1:293
Falconet	500lbs	2″	1¼lbs	1:400
Serpentine	400lbs	1½″	⅔lb	1:601
Robinet	300lbs	1″	½lb	1:600

A gunner, holding his ceremonial halberd in his left hand, discharges his piece with a wooden linstock which terminates in a dragon's head (from a woodcut of 1590). Below, a dragon's-head linstock from *La Trinidad Valencera*, complete with its fuse.

1. Auguste 1588

Wee whose names are heerunder written have
determyned and agreede in counsaile to followe and
pursue the Spanishe fleete untill wee have
cleared owne owne coaste and brought the Fryse
coaste of us. And then to returne backe againe
as well to reuyctuall owre shipp (beinge in extreme
scarsitie) as allsoe to guarde and defend owre owne
coaste at home; nott further [pro]testinge that if
owre wante of vyctuallss and munition wore
supplied wee wold followe [pur]sue them to the further
that they durste have gonn.

Howard   George Cumbreland

[signature]   Edmunde Sheffeylde

Fra: Drake   Edw Hoby:

John Hawkyns

Thomas Fenner

CHAPTER 12

'God breathed'

The English commanders' signatures to the minutes of a council of war aboard the flagship *Ark Royal* on 12 August 1588, off the coast of Scotland: '. . . if our wants of victuals and munition were supplied, we would pursue them to the furthest that they durst have gone.'

On the evening of 9 August, with a south-westerly wind blowing the Armada clear of the Flemish shoals and into the North Sea, the duke of Medina Sidonia held a council of war to determine what strategy the fleet should now adopt. Should it, without hope of replenishment or reinforcement, in the face of the prevailing winds, and against an enemy who had already proved his superiority in battle and was operating close to his home bases, attempt the rendezvous with Parma once again? Should it perhaps mount some kind of offensive operation on its own initiative, like a landing on the Yorkshire coast? Or should it simply nurse itself back to Spain as best it could, via the north of Britain, and so keep losses to a minimum?

All the surviving general officers were present: Recalde and Diego Flores, Oquendo and Bertendona, Bobadilla and Leiva. For their benefit the duke gave a brief description of the extent of the damage to the fleet, and of the dwindling stock of food and munitions it carried. Then he asked for a vote on what should be done next. The council was unanimous: if at all possible, the Armada should turn about and go back to the Channel for a second attempt to pick up Parma's forces and invade England. Only if the wind proved contrary should the fleet attempt the long north-about return to Spain. For three days, while the south-west wind forced the Armada further northwards, the issue hung in the balance. On three occasions, according to Medina Sidonia's account, the English fleet appeared to mass for an attack; but as soon as the duke shortened sail and offered battle with his remaining fighting ships, the English had retired to a safe distance.

In fact, Howard's fleet was itself beginning to disperse. On the 10th Seymour's squadron departed to resume its station in the Channel, in case 'anything be attempted by the duke of Parma'. Two days later the rest of the English fleet, after a final bombastic flaunt in battle-array off the Firth of Forth, also broke off the chase, protesting that 'if our wants of victuals and munition were supplied, we would pursue them to the furthest that they durst have gone'. The crisis, though eased, had not passed: for all Howard and his captains knew the Armada might yet return, and they had precious little left with which to stop it.

But the winds had now pushed the Spaniards too far, and they did not turn back. Instead, on 13 August, the fleet's pathetic contingent of draught and pack animals was dumped overboard to preserve water, and, that same day, the *San Martín* issued sailing instructions for the homeward voyage. 'The course that is first to be held,' ran the orders, 'is to the north-north-east, until you be found under 61½ degrees; and to take great heed lest you fall upon the island of Ireland, for fear of the harm that may happen to you upon that coast.' After 'doubling the Cape' (that is, reaching a longitude beyond Ireland's most westerly point), the fleet was to head west-south-west to a latitude of 58 degrees (somewhere to the west of Rockall), and thence south-west to 53 degrees, from where a final south-easterly run might be made to the ports of northern Spain.[1]

There is nothing remarkable about this route; even in times of peace, ships making passage from the North Sea to the Atlantic frequently adopted it, particularly during autumn or winter. The prevailing south-westerlies made the run to the Northern Isles relatively easy, and the islands themselves could usually be rounded without difficulty, often with the help of the north-easterly Helm wind which springs up from the high pressure zone frequently found over Arctic Norway. Once the North Atlantic was reached progress could be made southwards, even against the prevailing wind, by employing a series of long tacks. This route would have been familiar to many of the Armada's seamen, particularly those aboard the Baltic hulks. What the ships did lack, however, were adequate charts and sufficient pilots. The former were simply not to be had, because no reliable ones existed. The west coast of Ireland remained *terra incognita* for mariners – except for those who had made a personal reconnaissance (as Recalde had done in 1580) – until the publication of a set of detailed maps by the Dutch in 1612. The *Derrotero* and charts supplied by Philip II's cartographers to every ship in the fleet stopped at the Moray Firth, and any officer who had the forethought to acquire a copy of the latest guide to navigation – Lucas Waghenaer's *Mariner's Mirror* (Latin edition, 1586) – would have found in it no charts of Ireland.[2]

In the 16th century latitude was usually measured, with varying accuracy, by recording the angle of the sun's zenith with an astrolabe. This instrument was found in the 19th century on Valencia Island, County Kerry, and may well have come from an Armada wreck – possibly the *Santa María de la Rosa*, which went down some 15 miles to the north in Blasket Sound.

Don Balthasar de Zúñiga, the staff officer aboard the *San Martín* who was sent by pinnace from Shetland to carry news of the Armada's failure to Philip II.

But Medina Sidonia was a resourceful commander. In the straits between Orkney and Shetland the Armada encountered Dutch and Scottish fishing boats from which the duke 'chose certain pilots, to carry them for the coast of Ireland , and so into Spain.' He also seized as much water and fish as he could, to augment the rapidly diminishing supplies on the fleet.[3] Food and drink were now the overriding problem. Immediately after the departure from Calais the daily ration had been cut – for the second time since leaving Lisbon – to one pint of water, half-a-pint of wine, and half-a-pound of biscuit per day. Even if all the food issued was edible – and much was clearly not – this represented a daily intake of less than 1,000 calories, scarcely enough to sustain life, let alone health, for any extended period.[4]

On 21 August, as the Armada sailed into the North Atlantic, Don Balthasar de Zúñiga, a staff officer aboard the flagship, was put ashore at Scalloway in Shetland with orders to sail swiftly for Spain, and prepare provisions and reinforcements in Galicia against the moment when the fleet returned. He also carried dispatches for the king, which reported moderate casualties (including about 3,000 sick and wounded) but confirmed that 112 vessels were still intact and under Medina Sidonia's command. The Armada had been a costly failure, but – as yet – it was by no means a disaster.

But, even as Zúñiga departed, disaster began to strike. Four ships, unable to keep up with the more weatherly members of the fleet, lost contact with the main body. They were the supply squadron's flagship, *El Gran Grifón*, two of her companions, the *Barca de Amburg* and the *Castillo Negro*, and the Levantine *Trinidad Valencera*. Together the four vessels struggled south-westward for twelve days, making little progress. Then, on 1 September, the *Barca de Amburg* signalled that she was about to founder. Her company of 250 was transferred to the *Valencera* and the *Grifón* just before she went down.

The *Trinidad Valencera* was a large Venetian grain ship, one of those especially capacious vessels embargoed to carry the Armada's heavy siege train. Under Don Alonso de Luzón, commander of the Neapolitan *tercio*, she had played a distinguished part in the fighting, but because of the damage she had sustained the pumps could no longer cope with her leaks. A decision was taken to run for the nearest land. The north coast of Donegal was sighted, and the ship ran eastward, probably with the intention of entering Lough Foyle. Before she got there, however, the

Valencera grounded on a reef at the western end of Kinnagoe Bay. Stuck firm, but with her upper decks well above water, the situation was perilous but not hopeless. Don Alonso with four companions set off for shore in the ship's only surviving boat, which was evidently a small one. As they approached they saw twenty or so 'savage people' standing on a rock, and when they landed on the adjacent shingle beach 'only with their rapiers in their hands', four or five of the natives came to help them out of the boat and 'courteously used' them. Soon a crowd of local men had gathered, and the atmosphere became less cordial. The Spaniards were roughly handled, and relieved of 'money, gold buttons, rapiers and apparel to the value of 7,300 ducats'.

Such treatment was typical of the response of the indigenous Irish population to the Armada survivors. They were considered fair game for plunder but were otherwise, with rare exceptions, left physically unharmed. On some occasions, as on this, they were given active

The point of land closest to the underwater reef upon which *La Trinidad Valencera* grounded on 14 September 1588. 'As they came near the land,' said Sergeant-Major Balthasar López del Arbol of the Sicilian *tercio* to his interrogators later, 'they saw some 20 of the savage people standing upon a rock, and in their landing about 4 or 5 of them came and did help them out of the boat, and used them courteously.' Later, however, the Spaniards were plundered of many of their valuables.

assistance. After the Spaniards' own boat was wrecked another was hired from the locals, and in due course most of the *Valencera's* complement was brought safely ashore. When this boat, too, was lost in the surf, attempts were made to hire another, but the Irish were now more intent on salvaging the ship than on rescuing its occupants. Two days later, when she suddenly split open and sank, a number of Irishmen and Spaniards still aboard her were drowned.[5]

On the beach, Don Alonso rallied the survivors and marched inland. His aim was to reach the west coast and the chance of ships to Spain, fighting his way through if necessary. They were still a formidable, if somewhat dispirited, military force. Sustained by local horsemeat and butter they covered the twenty miles to Illagh Castle, seat of Sir John O'Doherty, in whose territory they had landed. Negotiations with the Irish bishop who was apparently in charge of the castle drew an equivocal response. The Spaniards were requested to make a show of force, so that the bishop might then surrender to them, and give them assistance, without compromising himself. Though unfamiliar with the complexities of Irish politics, Don Alonso viewed the offer with some suspicion. His doubts were confirmed when a signal shot was fired from the castle to alert nearby English garrisons. The Spaniards withdrew, crossed a wide bog, and took up defensive positions in a ruined castle which stood nearby.

Don Alonso was unaware that an elaborate trap was being sprung. The peninsula of Inishowen, on whose northern shore he had landed, was bounded at its narrow southern neck by two parallel strips of boggy

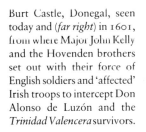

Burt Castle, Donegal, seen today and (*far right*) in 1601, from where Major John Kelly and the Hovenden brothers set out with their force of English soldiers and 'affected' Irish troops to intercept Don Alonso de Luzón and the *Trinidad Valencera* survivors.

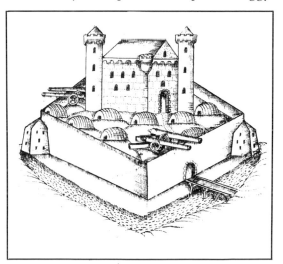

ground running between the sea-loughs of Foyle and Swilly. Illagh commanded the crossing of the northern bog; that to the south was guarded by the much stronger castle of Burt, garrisoned by English and 'affected' Irish troops under Major John Kelly and the brothers Richard and Henry Hovenden. Through their ignorance of local geography Don Alonso and his men had been lured into a killing ground from which there was no escape.

With drums beating the Burt garrison approached the Spanish position, and a parley was arranged. What business, asked the queen's officers, had the Spaniards in her majesty's dominions? Don Alonso replied that they had been shipwrecked and wished only to return to Spain. That, said Major Kelly, could not be; they must surrender as prisoners of war. The Spaniards refused, and returned to their trenches. A day later, however, after some skirmishing, negotiations were resumed and Don Alonso, seeing his position to be hopeless, agreed to surrender on fair terms. This he lived to regret; after plundering them all of their clothing and possessions, Kelly's men separated the common soldiers and seamen from those of ransomable status. The former were then taken into a field and slaughtered, though a number escaped in the confusion and of these a handful eventually reached Flanders via Scotland. The fate of those reserved for ransom was only marginally better. After a nightmare 100-mile march to Drogheda with little food and, for many of them, without adequate clothing or footwear, the survivors were incarcerated while haggling over their maintenance and ransom dragged on interminably. Many died in the process although some, including Don Alonso, were eventually repatriated.

El Gran Grifón, the hulk flagship which had become separated from *La Trinidad Valencera* on 4 September, had meanwhile been enduring her own tribulations. She had been badly shot-up during the battles and, as with the *San Mateo*, the recoil of her own guns had severely strained her hull structure. Aboard was the squadron commander, Juan Gómez de Medina, together with two companies of soldiers and a small group of priests and expatriate Irish volunteers. Alone, and in almost continually adverse weather, the ship had beaten south-westwards into the Atlantic, until on 7 September she was hit by a violent storm which caused her seams to gape further apart. An oncoming sea would certainly sink her, and so she ran northwards with the weather until she sighted St Kilda. Then the wind veered into the north-west, allowing her crew to turn once more 'towards our dear Spain'. For three days this wind held, but then it backed into the prevailing south-westerly quarter, driving the ship once more to the north. The exhausted Spaniards toiled ceaselessly at the pumps, and attempted to patch up the worst of the leaks with ox hides and planks. By 25 September they had sighted the Hebrides, at which point they decided to make for the nearest land, even if it meant running the ship ashore. Somehow they negotiated the Orkney archipelago by night, aided by the glow of the Northern Lights. On the morning of the 27th, with the hulk now wallowing with ten feet of water in her hold, Fair Isle was sighted. At dusk Gómez anchored on its sheltered eastern side, and at dawn the *Gran Grifón* was driven ashore. She fetched up against the overhanging cliff of Stroms Hellier, close to the south-eastern corner

The creek on Fair Isle in which *El Gran Grifón* was wrecked. The ship wedged between the extended rocky point and the central reef, allowing Juan Gómez de Medina and most of his men to escape by way of the overhanging cliff.

(*Below*) Extract from Lord Burghley's copy of the Lisbon Muster, showing the entry for *El Gran Grifón*. In it the ship's tonnage and munitions are recorded, together with the number of troops aboard and the names of their company officers – Patricio Antolinez and Esteban de Lagoretta. The annotations (after correcting 'Lopez' to 'Gómez') read: 'This man's ship was drowned 17 Sept [O.S.] in the Isle of Faire neare Scotland.' It is also noted that the ship came from Rostock, and that 'this was the general of the urks' (*urcas* = hulks). Finally someone has recorded, in Spanish, that 'Juan Gómez es vivo y reside en Cádiz.'

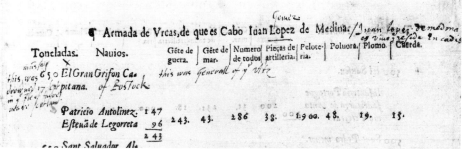

of the island, where she wedged fast. Most of those on board escaped by climbing the foremast, which lay against the overhang, but seven perished in the attempt and little could be saved from the ship.

Gómez de Medina's situation, though improved, was still fraught with danger. Fair Isle was small and storm-bound, and there seemed no immediate prospect of escape. With winter approaching the seventeen crofting families on the island had little to spare for the hungry castaways who, to their great credit, made no attempt to take over the islanders' provisions by force. Seabirds and fish were plentiful, but could not in themselves alleviate the illnesses brought on by four months of sustained malnutrition. Fifty of the Spaniards and German sailors, including the hulk's master, Burgat Querquerman, perished on the island.

After six weeks contact was made with Fair Isle's absentee landlord, Malcolm Sinclair of Quendale, and the survivors were brought over to the Shetland mainland. From there they were carried to Anstruther in Fife where, on the morning of 6 December, they dropped anchor. Their arrival caused something of a panic in the town, since fears of large-scale Spanish landings were still strong. Tensions eased, however, after Gómez de Medina explained their circumstances and friendly intentions to James Melville, the local minister; and, at the cost of enduring a lengthy sermon on the error of their ways, the Spaniards were given the charity of the burgh. The soldiers, wrote Melville in his diary, 'were suffered to come a land, and lie all together, to the number of thirteen score, for the most part young beardless men, silly, trauchled and hungered, to the which kail, porage, and fish was given'. Gómez de Medina was himself described by Melville as 'a very reverend man of big stature, and grave and stout countenance, grey haired, and very humble like.' After a few days of homely fare for the soldiers and local socialising for the officers, (during which they were shown, to their great distress, a pamphlet hot from the London presses which gloatingly reported the catastrophes which had befallen the Armada in Ireland) the contingent was shipped across the Forth to Leith, where negotiations for their repatriation were initiated. Technically, they were still free men, for Scotland had been neutral in the conflict.

It was not so in Ireland, where the scattered English garrisons could not overlook the possibility that Philip II's Grand Design might still include a direct assault on them. In August, rumours of the Armada's approach, according to an official in Dublin, 'doth work wonderful uncertain yet calm humours in the people of this country, who stand agape until the game be played, not daring to discover their real intentions'[6] And then in September numerous Spanish vessels appeared suddenly and unexpectedly, landing troops on Ireland's shores. A letter from Sir Richard Bingham, governor of Connaught, neatly caught the atmosphere of confusion and fear. There was, he wrote on 20 September:

'. . . further news of strange ships: whether they be of the dispersed fleet which are fled from the supposed overthrow in the Narrow Seas, or new forces come from Spain directly, no man is able to advertise otherwise than by guess, which doth rather show their coming from Spain, both by these falling from the west, and others which coasted along the north parts of Sligo . . . I expect very present news either from the one place or the other, for by all likelihoods they mind to land. I look this night for my horses to be here. . . . '

Sir Richard Bingham, Governor of Connaught, at the age of 36 in 1564.

Here was a frightening possibility: were these 'strange ships' indeed 'come from Spain directly', as part of that 'second Armada' of which several Spanish prisoners (such as Don Diego Pimentel) had spoken? Sir William Fitzwilliam, Elizabeth's Lord Deputy in Ireland, was not disposed to take chances in what he described as 'these dangerous and broken times.' His urgent dispatch to the Privy Council on 22 September pointed out that he had in all Ireland fewer than 750 soldiers at his disposal, and no cavalry mounts for want of horseshoes. Any serious Spanish landings, he felt, could not be contained. The chilling instruction therefore went out to his officers in the western provinces 'to apprehend and execute all Spaniards found, of what quality soever. Torture may be used in prosecuting this enquiry.'

His grim order had already been anticipated by some of his scattered agents in the west. On 19 September 24 men who came ashore from a pinnace wrecked in the Bay of Tralee had been rounded up and taken to the stronghold of Sir Edward Denny, an English plantation landlord with extensive properties in the district. Sir Edward was away, but his formidable wife took charge of the situation, and after a brief interrogation the prisoners were summarily executed. Three made efforts to save themselves by claiming that they had friends in Waterford who would redeem them, but when pressed would not – or could not – name them. And then, on 20 September, a large vessel came ashore at Doonbeg on the Clare coast. She was probably the 736-ton *San Esteban* of the Guipúzcoan squadron. Three hundred men were reported drowned, and some 60 captured. On the same day, a few miles to the north, another vessel was

235

wrecked on Mutton Island. Only four survivors reached the shore. The prisoners from both these ships were brought before Boetius Clancy, the sheriff of Clare, and after a brief incarceration they were publicly hanged on a hillock still called *Cnoc na Crocaire* (Hill of the Gallows). Even the nobly-born Don Felipe de Córdoba, whose safe return would have commanded a sizeable ransom, was not spared. Clancy's name, tradition asserts, was thereafter cursed in the church of Don Felipe's home town every seventh year, to ensure that his soul would never escape from purgatory.

A little to the south, on the same day as these two wrecks had taken place, another drama unfolded. The 703-ton Ragusan *Anunciada*, a member of Bertendona's Levant squadron, lay at anchor and close to sinking in Scattery Roads, off Kilrush at the mouth of the Shannon. She had arrived there a week before with five attendant pinnaces, leaking badly from damage sustained during the fireship attack off Calais. A day after her arrival she had been joined by the hulk *Barca de Danzig*, which was also in danger of foundering. The *Anunciada*'s carpenters successfully patched up the hulk, but were unable to save their own ship. At length, on the orders of her captain, she was fired and scuttled after the men, guns, and stores had been transferred to the other vessels, which then departed.

Up to this point the weather had been unsettled, though not particularly unseasonable. But on 18 September two Atlantic depressions, spawned of tropical storms far to the west, reached the coasts of Europe. By 21 September these had resolved themselves into a single deep depression centred off north-west Scotland, drawing in great frontal masses of cold Arctic air. The resultant gale was described by an English official in Ireland, who observed it from the safety of the shore, as 'a most extreme wind and cruel storm, the like whereof hath not been seen or heard a long time, which put us in very good hope that many of the ships should be beaten up and cast away upon the rocks'.

The same gale was experienced by Marcos de Aramburu aboard the Castilian vice-flagship *San Juan*, anchored precariously in Blasket Sound, off the exposed south-west tip of Ireland. 'On the 21st, in the morning,' he wrote, 'the west wind came with some terrible fury, but cloudless and with little rain.' Aramburu had come to the Sound during rough weather a week earlier, following on the heels of Juan Martínez de Recalde's great *San Juan de Portugal*, vice-flagship of the whole Armada. With superb seamanship Recalde, who had explored this coast after the landings at

Smerwick (only six sea-miles away) in 1580, won the shelter of Blasket Sound by driving through a gap in the outlying reefs barely wider than the beam of his lumbering galleon. There the two ships, together with a small pinnace, had made emergency repairs, exchanged anchors and cables, and taken on water from the spring on Great Blasket Island. Attempts to land on the mainland had been thwarted by English patrols, and a reconnaissance party of eight men was captured. One of them, a Portuguese seaman called Emanuel Fremoso, told his interrogators of conditions aboard Recalde's *San Juan*.

'He says that out of the ship there died 4 or 5 every day of hunger and thirst, and yet this ship was one of the best furnished for victuals... He says that there are 80 soldiers and 20 of the mariners sick, and do lie down and die daily, and the rest, he says, are very weak, and the Captain very sad and weak, There is left in this flagship but 25 pipes of wine, and very little bread, and no water but what they brought out of Spain, which stinketh marvellously, and the flesh meat they cannot eat, their drouth is so great. He says the Admiral's purpose is with the first wind to pass away for Spain. He says also that it is a common bruit among the soldiers that if they may get home again, they will not meddle with the English any more.'

And then, on 21 September, in deceptively cloudless conditions, the terrible eye of the storm struck the ships anchored in Blasket Sound. Aramburu, aboard the Castilian *San Juan*, describes the events that followed:

The flagship of Juan Martínez drifted down on ours, cast anchor and another cable, and having smashed our lantern and our mizzen tackle and rigging, the flagship secured herself. At mid-day the *Santa María de la Rosa*, of Martín de Villafranca, came in by another entrance nearer land on the north-west side. She fired a shot on entering, as if seeking help, and another further on. All her sails were in shreds except the foresail. She cast her single anchor, for she was not carrying more, and with the tide coming in from the south-east side and beating against her stern she stayed there until two o'clock. Then the tide waned, and as it turned the ships began dragging on our two cables, and we with her, and in an instant we could see that she was going down, trying to hoist the foresail. Then she sank with all on board, not a person being saved, a most extraordinary and terrifying thing.'

Pewter campaign plate recovered from the wreck of the *Santa María de la Rosa*, bearing the name 'Matute'. Captain Francisco Ruiz Matute commanded a company of 95 soldiers of the Sicilian *tercio* aboard the *Santa María*

The ill-fated *Santa María de la Rosa* was vice-flagship of Oquendo's Guipúzcoan squadron, a large Basque-built merchantman of 945 tons. There was, in fact, one survivor of the 250 or so men aboard her: he was Giovanni de Manona, son of the ship's pilot, who managed to cling to a plank and was washed ashore, where he was captured and interrogated by the local English garrison. His story was harrowing and dramatic. The ship's military officers, he said, had tried to save themselves in the ship's boat, but the *Santa María* had gone down so quickly that they had no time to untie it. One of them had accused Giovanni's father of wrecking the ship deliberately and, in a blind rage, had slain him where he stood.

The pilot's 'treason' was probably no more than a seamanlike attempt to get the stricken ship off the isolated reef upon which she had impaled herself, and run for the shore before she sank. To do this he would have had to cut the cable of the fouled anchor and, as Aramburu witnessed, set the ship's only surviving sail. Perhaps the landsmen aboard somehow misconstrued these sensible actions on the part of the pilot; at any event, the sequence of events was revealed in 1968 when the wreck of the *Santa María* was located in deep water at the eye of the tide-race which runs through the narrow neck of Blasket Sound. Then the true reason for the disaster became evident: the ship had struck amidships on a concealed pinnacle of rock which rears to within a few feet of the surface, ripping out her bottom so that she sank in a matter of seconds. Her great anchor, which she had dragged across the Sound under the combined influences of tide and wind, still remains hooked foul on the northern edge of the reef.

In the aftermath of the *Santa María*'s sinking, Recalde and Aramburu managed to re-anchor and ride out the storm. While they were doing so another ship – the merchantman *San Juan*, attached to the Castilian squadron – came into the Sound. She had lost her mainmast, and as she entered a squall blew her foresail to shreds. No assistance could be given that day, but on the following morning, when the storm had abated, her men were taken off and distributed among the other ships, since it was clear that she was about to sink. Nevertheless Recalde, in another impressive demonstration of fine seamanship and his high sense of duty, managed to save some of her guns before she went down.

The gale of 21 September had brought other notable victims to the Irish coast. *El Gran Grin*, the 1,160-ton vice-flagship of Recalde's Biscayans, was driven into Clew Bay, Mayo. Filling fast with water, she ran aground off Clare Island. Pedro de Mendoza, the senior officer on board, managed to bring 100 or so of his men ashore, though twice that number were drowned. For a time the Spaniards remained on the island, virtual prisoners of Dowdarra Roe O'Malley; but at length, when they made a spirited bid to steal boats and escape, the O'Malleys turned on them, killing 64 including Don Pedro.

About the same time three ships had become trapped in Donegal Bay. They were all big merchantmen of the Levant squadron: the Sicilian *Juliana* (860 tons); the Venetian *Lavia* (728 tons); and the Ragusan *Santa María de Visón* (666 tons). On board the *Lavia*, which was the squadron's vice-flagship, was Francisco de Cuellár, a staff officer who had originally shipped aboard the Castilian *San Pedro*, of which he subsequently became captain. But he had been relieved of his command after the breach of formation discipline for which Don Cristobal de Ávila was hanged, and had been lucky to escape with his own life. Only the personal intervention of the Judge Advocate, Martín de Aranda, had saved him from summary execution, and he had been transferred under open arrest to Aranda's ship, the *Lavia*. Of all the accounts given by Armada survivors, that of Cuellár, contained in a letter written to a friend when he reached Antwerp more than a year later, is the most detailed and dramatic.

In it he tells how the three ships were hit by the great storm of 21 September. They were able to gain some shelter by entering Donegal Bay, but at the cost of surrendering their chances of beating clear when the weather eased. From their anchorage half-a-league from the Sligo coast only a wind from the eastern quarter would allow them to weather Erris Head or the western tip of Tirconnell, and of such a wind there was little hope. The next storm came, predictably, from the west, and their few anchors, with only fluid sand to grip, failed to hold. Cuellár now takes up the story:

'. . . the cables could not hold nor the sails serve us, and we were driven ashore with all three ships upon a beach, covered with very fine sand, shut in on one side and the other by great rocks. Such a thing was never seen, for within the space of an hour all three ships were broken in pieces, so that there did not escape three hundred men, and more than one thousand were drowned, among them many persons of importance – captains, gentlemen, and other officials.'

The ships had come ashore on the long beach at Streedagh, a two-mile finger of sandhills fringing the lagoon at Milk Haven, ten miles north of Sligo. Grounded firm on the unyielding sand, the vessels had been pummelled and smashed by the breaking surf only a couple of hundred yards from the shore. There was enough time for those on board to appreciate the full horror of their predicament, and most of them made desperate efforts to escape. Aboard the *Lavia* Don Diego Enríquez had himself battened below the deck of the ship's boat, together with three companions and 16,000 ducats in jewels and coin. The boat was cast adrift, in the hope that it would reach the beach, but as it left it capsized under the weight of 70 survivors who hurled themselves in panic onto its deck. Eventually it was cast ashore, where it lay keel upwards for 36 hours. When at last it was righted and broken open by wreckers, three of its occupants were already dead. Don Diego, the only survivor, expired as his clothes and valuables were ripped from him.

Captain Cuellár was more fortunate. Certain as he was of his fate if he stayed with the breaking ship, the prospect if he reached land seemed no less dreadful. The beach, he observed, was

'full of enemies who went about jumping and dancing with delight at our misfortunes; and when any one of our people set foot on the shore, two hundred savages and other enemies fell upon him and stripped him of what he had on until he was left in his naked skin . . . all of this was plainly visible from the battered ships.'

But by now men were drowning on the ships, while others were throwing themselves into the sea or crying out to God in helpless resignation. In an instinctive bid for survival Cuellár and his erstwhile saviour, Judge Advocate Aranda, grasped a loose hatch-cover and launched themselves into the surf, but almost immediately a wave swept them from their makeshift raft. Cuellár went under, but somehow struggled to the surface and regained the hatch cover. The Judge Advocate, who was weighted down with coins sewn into his doublet and hose, sank, and – like many another – was never seen again.

At length Cuellár was thrown up on the beach. Almost naked, and covered in blood, he was spared the attentions of the ghouls who moved casually among the human flotsam which littered the strand, stripping them of whatever they possessed and clubbing them down if they offered the slightest resistance. Inch by inch, and in acute pain, Cuellár crawled towards the comparative shelter of the dunes behind the beach. Soon afterwards (he writes):

'. . . a gentleman came up to me, a very nice young fellow, quite naked, and he was so dazed that he could not speak, not even to tell me who he was; and at that time, which would be about nine o'clock at night, the wind was calm and the sea subsiding. I was wet through to the skin, dying with pain and hunger, when there came up two people – one of them armed and the other with a great iron axe in his hands. We remained silent, as if there was nothing amiss. They were grieved to see us, and without speaking a word they cut a quantity of rushes and grass, covered us well, and then betook themselves to the shore to plunder and break

Hollanders

Omnium dilecta Deo, tibi militat Æther
Et coniurati veniunt ad classica venti

52. Queen Elizabeth reviewing her troops and unfinished defences at Tilbury, after the danger had passed: a detail from the painted panel at St Faith's Church, Gaywood. 'I know I have the body of a weak and feeble woman, but I have the heart and stomach of a king, and of a king of England too . . .'

ARMÉE NAVALE DESPAIGN
SVRNOMMÉE INVINCIBLE VAI
PAR LES ANGLOIS LE 22. IVILLE

I R

53. An impression of the Armada campaign, painted early in the reign of James I. Several incidents and localities are conflated: though the setting is off the English coast, along which beacons, fortifications and militia units can be seen, the fireship attack off Calais is represented close by. On the far left, its distinctive two-masted rig and national flag identifies one of Justin of Nassau's cromsters which, though they never actually encountered the Armada at sea, played a vital role in bottling up Parma's invasion forces in the Flemish ports. That this particular cromster is shown attacking the Spanish flagship suggests that the painting may have been specially commissioned in recognition of the Dutch naval role in the campaign. The picture also clearly reveals the distinction between the race-built English galleons and the high-charged Spanish warships, packed with soldiers.

54. Members of the Hispano-Flemish delegation (*left*) face their English counterparts over the conference table at Somerset House in London, where after 18 meetings between 20 May and 16 July 1604 conditions for a 'peace of fine amity and friendship' were agreed upon. Queen Elizabeth had been dead for more than a year and her successor, James VI of Scotland (and I of the now united crowns), was anxious to terminate the expensive and inconclusive hostilities he had inherited. On 5 August the treaty was ratified, bringing to an end 20 years of war between England and Spain. The Spanish negotiators secured most of the concessions for which, in 1588, Philip II had sent the first Armada. English interference in the Netherlands would henceforward cease; the English Channel would be open to Spanish shipping; greater toleration would be given to Catholics in England; and trade restrictions between the two countries would be eased. Hardly a year was to pass, however, before Guy Fawkes's failed 'Gunpowder Plot' would blow most of these friendly aspirations to smithereens.

The commander of the anti-Armada fleet in 1588, Charles Lord Howard of Effingham (and now also Earl of Nottingham), sits 2nd from the window in the English delegation on the right hand side of the table.

open money-chests and whatever they might find, together with more than two thousand savages and Englishmen from garrisons nearby.'

Cuellár fell into a deep sleep, from which he woke during the night to find his companion dead, and English cavalry patrols scouring the dunes. But he lay undiscovered in his hide until the following morning, when he slipped away inland to start his momentous journey home.

Some weeks later Lord Deputy Fitzwilliam himself rode along the strand to view 'the bay where some of those ships wrecked, and where, as I heard, lay not long before 1,200 or 1,300 of the dead bodies.' Scattered the length of the beach, he observed, 'lay as great store of the timber . . . more than would have built five of the greatest ships that I ever saw, besides mighty great boats, cables, and other cordage answerable thereunto, and some such masts for bigness and length, as in mine own judgement I never saw any two could make the like.' Nor was the Lord Deputy exaggerating. The *Juliana*'s great rudder, recently discovered in the shifting sands off Streedagh, was no less than 36 feet long.

Another large Levantine ship lost on the coast of Ireland was the carrack *Rata Santa María Encoronada*. This vessel was the unofficial flagship of Don Alonso Martínez de Leiva, the commander of the Armada's vanguard who held a secret commission to take charge of the fleet should Medina Sidonia fall. Don Alonso's high birth and dashing military career had attracted many young noblemen to the *Rata Encoronada*, and during the Channel battles she had always been where the fighting was hottest. But like so many of her Levantine sisters, and the unwieldy hulks, she had been unable to keep up with the main body of the fleet during its north-about voyage, and she had been unable to maintain a safe offing from the Irish coast. Many of these big Mediterranean grain-ships, moreover, had been severely strained by the recoil of their own artillery, for their metal-fastened hulls were designed to accommodate the evenly-spread loads of a bulk cargo rather than the localised and violent stresses imposed by the firing of heavy guns.

On 17 September the *Rata* found herself off Blacksod Bay in County Mayo, and Don Alonso decided to enter this broad and well sheltered haven to make repairs and, if possible, take on fresh water. After sending a reconnaisance party ashore the ship eventually anchored off Fahy, a creek at the south-eastern end of the bay notorious for its dangerous tide-rips. Before long the *Rata* started to drag towards the sands of Tullaghan Bay, where she grounded immovably. Don Alonso brought his men ashore in good order, and then fired the ship.

The Spaniards dug themselves in at Doona Castle, not far from the wreck site, and took stock of their position. Then they received information that another Spanish ship, the 900-ton hulk *Duquesa Santa Ana*, attached to the Andalusian squadron, had anchored in Elly Bay, on the far side of Blacksod. Leiva gathered together his men and marched 25 miles overland to reach the *Duquesa*. With the joint complement of the two vessels crammed on board, the hulk set sail. A couple of days later, however, on 26 September, having been driven to the north, she ran aground in Loughros Mor Bay, Donegal. Once again Don Alonso brought his men safely ashore, but was himself injured by a capstan bar as he left the ship. As before, the Spaniards sought out a defensive position in case of English attack, and found a ruined castle on a small island in Kiltoorish Lake which they strengthened by mounting a light piece of ordnance salvaged from the wreck. Perhaps they had intended to hold out there until aid could be sent from Spain, but after about a week news reached them that the galleass *Girona* lay at Killibegs, some 19 miles to the south. A sedan-chair was rigged up for the wounded Don Alonso, and the party marched overland to Killibegs where they found the damaged galleass under repair.

For the next fortnight Killibegs bustled with activity. Another Spanish ship which had grounded at the harbour entrance was stripped of materials and gear to repair the *Girona*, and at length, in the early morning of 26 October, with 1,300 souls crowded aboard her, the galleass set sail, heading not for Spain but for Scotland. Don Alonso had wisely decided that the overloaded and crank vessel was unlikely to survive the perils of the open Atlantic, and that the short run to neutral Scotland was his best option. But off the north coast of Antrim the *Girona*'s jury rudder failed, and she was flung sideways onto the rocky fang of Lacada Point, close to the Giant's Causeway. Don Alonso and all save a handful of his comrades perished among the kelp-covered reefs.

Their fate was no worse than that of the majority of those who fell into English hands. The hulk *Falcon Blanco Mediano*, a 300-tonner with a complement of little more than 100 men, had been wrecked on a small island island off Galway on about 25 September. Her survivors included Don Luís de Córdoba and his nephew, Gonzalo, who were men of rank. For a time they were protected by the O'Flaherties of Connemara, but, in

Ireland and the Armada wrecks, Sept.–Oct. 1588

response to threats from Governor Richard Bingham (the aptly-named 'Flail of Connaught'), they were at length delivered under guard to Galway town. All except the two de Córdobas were hanged – even the ransomable officers, and six young Dutchmen forcibly pressed into the fleet, who had been spared by Bingham, were later executed on the personal orders of Lord Deputy Fitzwilliam. In all, Bingham claimed to have disposed of 1,100 survivors from the Connaught wrecks, though he regretted the wanton loss of ransom money brought about by the Lord

Deputy's draconian policy of extermination. But the hangings continued. On 18 November, commissioners were sent out from Dublin 'to make diligent search and enquiry for such of the Spaniards and Italians of the dispersed fleet as came with purpose to invade her Majesty's kingdom, and to apprehend and take them, and thereupon to execute them to the death by martial law without respect of person'.[7] Yet still Fitzwilliam complained that 'all the means the Council and I can work will not prevail to take these locusts and grasshoppers.'

The *Girona* was probably the last Armada ship to be wrecked on Ireland. A further drama, however, remained to be enacted not far away, in a sheltered harbour on the Isle of Mull among Scotland's Inner Hebrides. On 23 September a large ship had been sighted close to Isla, and a few days later she dropped anchor in Tobermory Bay. She was the 800-ton Ragusan *San Juan de Sicilia*, yet another member of the ill-fated Levant squadron. Apart from an acute shortage of water she was not in great distress, and arrangements were made for replenishment with Lauchlan MacLean of Duart, the local chieftain. He agreed to co-operate, for a modest if unconventional price: provisions would be supplied in exchange for the loan of a company of Spanish troops with which to settle the MacLeans' outstanding feuds. To this the ship's senior officer, Diego Tellez Enríquez, readily agreed, though he demanded five MacLean hostages as surety. For more than a month the ship lay at Tobermory, making repairs and taking on supplies, whilst a detachment of about 100 Spanish troops ravaged the MacLeans' enemies ashore, with notable success. But the long arm of Elizabeth's secret service eventually reached even this remote part of England's turbulent northern neighbour.

Among the merchants engaged in provisioning the *San Juan* was John Smollett of Dumbarton, who in the course of his services gained the confidence of the crew and free access to the ship. In reality he was an agent of Sir Francis Walsingham. What happened next is not entirely clear, for no immediate eye-witnesses survived. On 5 November, while the Spaniards were drying out some of their remaining powder on the forward deck, it seems that Smollett was able to drop a piece of smouldering lint nearby before departing ashore. Soon afterwards the ship was rent apart by a tremendous explosion which sank her and killed almost all of those still on board, including the five MacLean hostages. Of those ashore, Maclean of Duart retained the services of about 50 Spaniards in his local feuds for another year, and then shipped them home to Spain.[8]

So far as is known, the coast of England reaped only a single wreck. She was the hospital ship *San Pedro Mayor*, a 580-ton hulk which, after rounding the British Isles, fetched up on Bolt Tail in Devon on 6 November. Her bedraggled survivors were soon in custody; they included patients from the *San Salvador*, which had blown up in the Channel nearly three months before. Happily, the *San Pedro's* survivors fared better than their counterparts in Ireland; in sedate Devon they were not perceived as a threat to national security, though an unseemly argument arose between their captors and the State over who should pay for their meagre rations.[9]

A number of Spaniards did, however, escape from the horrors of Ireland. A handful of ransomable officers who had eluded Fitzwilliam's 'fury and heat of justice' were first imprisoned at Drogheda and then shipped to London, where negotiations for their release continued, in some cases for several years. Another group gained freedom more quickly, and much more dramatically. Thirty prisoners destined for England had been embarked on the pinnace *Swallow* in Dublin Bay for shipment to Chester. This vessel, which had a crew of eight and a gentleman-captain, belonged to Christopher Carleill, the Constable of Carrickfergus and Drake's deputy on the great West Indies raid. On the crossing the Spaniards rose and seized the vessel, which they sailed to Corunna. Understandably, but perhaps unfairly, the English crew was subsequently hanged, for although Carleill had been active against the Spaniards under Drake, he was the only Englishman in Ireland who behaved entirely honourably towards the Armada prisoners, having defied the Lord Deputy's express order to hang a batch of fifteen who had come into his custody. Instead, he shipped them to Scotland at his own expense.

It was in Scotland, too, that the humbler survivors — 'the rags that yet remain', as Fitzwilliam scathingly described them — sought sanctuary. Francisco de Cuellár, after an almost unbelievable catalogue of adventures and tribulations, at last reached Dunluce on the Antrim coast, where the colourful octogenarian Sorley Boy Macdonnell was operating an escape route in collusion with his Scottish kinsmen. Cuellár made the arduous crossing in an open boat, which almost sank in mid passage; but he lived to write the story of his escape, in the safety of Antwerp, in October 1589.

Thirty-two survivors of the Illagh massacre, where men from the *Trinidad Valencera* had been gunned down, and a handful from the wreck of the *Girona*, had earlier passed safely through Sorley Boy's hands to Scotland. Their reception there was not unfriendly. The townspeople of

Ayr gave them new shoes to help them on their way, and when they arrived in Edinburgh they were lodged in the town on the orders of King James VI. Within 30 days they were on their way to France in Scottish ships with letters of safe-conduct signed by John Arnot, provost of the town. Twice they had to put into English ports, and on both occasions their credentials were honoured. Finally, on 26 December, they reached Le Havre.

They were the lucky ones. Hard on their heels came the survivors from Fair Isle, to be followed by 300 more from two wrecks on Norway and a pathetic dribble of further refugees from Ireland. King James now adopted a more equivocal stance. Scotland was indeed neutral in the conflict, but her young king had well-founded hopes of succeeding to the English throne, and he had no wish to antagonise Queen Elizabeth. His small country, moreover, was far from stable: there was a strong pro-Spanish faction, mostly Catholic, though it included unprincipled Protestants like the earl of Bothwell who were playing for high political stakes. The supply-squadron's commander, Juan Gómez de Medina of *El Gran Grifón*, who was by far the most senior Spanish officer to reach Scotland, was a prime target for intrigue. By the beginning of January 1589 Thomas Fowler, an English agent in Edinburgh, was reporting to Walsingham that:

'Don John de Medina and divers captains of the Spaniards are going hence with great credit as they say from divers of the nobility here, as Huntley, Bothwell, Seton, and others . . . . On Sunday last I dined with Bothwell, where I found four Spanish captains whom he entertains.'

By then Medina was on the point of leaving in a 40-ton barque provided by Bothwell's agent, Colonel Stewart, with an exhortation to 'let the Spanish king know how many well-willers he hath in this country, and to procure but 4,000 Spaniards, good shot, and leaders, with a sum of money to be brought hither by his conduct with speed.'

Gómez de Medina, or for that matter Philip II, had no intention of getting embroiled in a Scottish revolt. But Colonel Stewart's barque, although it could carry only 30 passengers, gave him the opportunity he needed to get out of Scotland and so expedite the rescue of his stranded comrades. He departed in secret, taking with him the small but vulnerable band of priests and Irish expatriates who had come with him from Spain — men whose names, he knew, were high on the English death-list.

The voyage was an eventful one, and ended with their wrecking off Cape St Vincent. But Juan Gómez survived to reach Cadiz, where he showed himself to be a man of honour. An Anstruther ship had been impounded by the port authorities, and its crew imprisoned. Remembering the succour he and his men had found in this small Scottish seaport, he immediately secured their release, and sent them home with kindly messages to his Protestant benefactors. We need not doubt that he took similar steps to help his own comrades, still waiting at Leith for a safe-conduct and passage to Flanders. They, however, had not been taken into Medina's confidence before his escape, and had taken a less than charitable view of their commanding officer's motives. As soon as they learned of his stealthy departure, at the end of January, two of his officers, Captains Patricio Antolinez and Esteban de Lagoretta, had written to Philip II accusing Medina of 'an act unworthy of his obligations to your majesty's flag', and pleading urgently for ships to take them to Spain.[10]

They were not the only ones. Thirty-two surviving soldiers and their wives from the 'ship of the married men', which was wrecked off Norway, were stranded in Hamburg. Some 300 men from the galeass *Zúñiga*, which touched briefly on the Irish coast (where a boatload of her people was captured along with a copy of Medina Sidonia's sailing instructions for the return to Spain), were driven by storms to take refuge at Le Havre in October, where they waited restlessly for almost a year while their ship was entirely rebuilt.[11] At Morbihan (Brittany), the 168 survivors of the hulk *San Pedro Menor* sought rescue from Spain, as did the men aboard Recalde's original flagship, the *Santa Ana*, which had been abandoned to the English as it tried to return from its refuge in Le Havre to Spain.[12] By the end of 1588, however, almost all these isolated parties of survivors, including those from the flag galeass *San Lorenzo* (destroyed off Calais), had been rescued. This left about 200 prisoners in the Dutch Republic, and perhaps 700 in England itself – most of them off the *Rosario* and the *San Pedro Mayor* – as well as the 660 men in Scotland.

The rank-and-file prisoners were dealt with relatively simply and swiftly. Many had originally been treated roughly in England: 'The people's charity to them (coming with so wicked an intent) is very cold.' wrote one of their captors in August. And he added: 'We would have been very glad had they been made water-spaniels when they first were taken.' But, as the danger abated, their treatment improved; and in May 1589 the English government accepted a ransom of £10 a head for 500 of them

247

from the duke of Parma. Those captured by the Dutch were bought out of prison at the same time (and at the same price).[13] But this did not include the persons of rank, who were the subject of separate negotiations: Don Vasco de Mendoza and Don Alonso de Zayas (the nephew of one of Philip II's secretaries of state) were ransomed for £900; Don Alonso de Luzón and Don Diego Pimentel for £1,650; and so on. But Don Pedro de Valdés of the *Rosario*, to his mounting fury, remained in custody.

After the Armada's defeat, Drake took his distinguished captive to see the queen in St James' Park. Elizabeth refused to speak to Don Pedro, but looked at him meaningfully and said 'Drake, God give thee joy of this prisoner.' So the unfortunate Valdés was taken back to the house of one of Drake's relatives, and maintained there as a sort of trophy. Sir Francis visited frequently, and brought along other military and naval commanders to admire the captive (when music and dancing were laid on in the main hall the Spanish prisoners would emerge on the gallery to view it, and thus be on view themselves to 'the country people' who came from miles around for the purpose). Valdés spent some time helping to check the first Spanish-English dictionary, published in 1591, and managed to send reports on English affairs to his master in Spain. But not until 1593 was he ransomed – for £1,500, plus the exchange of a notable English prisoner in Spanish hands. As he left England for freedom, he discovered by chance that the master of the ship that had fouled the *Rosario* in the Channel battle was still in custody: observers noted that he laughed and seemed to sail away a happier man. His subsequent career in the king's service was a distinguished one, and from 1602 to 1608 he was Governor of Cuba. He died in 1614.

Many of the Armada survivors in Scotland were not so lucky. After the departure of Juan Gómez de Medina they waited in Edinburgh, Leith and Burntisland for arrangements for their return journey to be made, but two obstacles stood in the way: on the one hand the Scots shippers demanded payment of their costs (fixed at 10 shillings a head) in advance and a safe-conduct from Queen Elizabeth lest bad weather forced the ships into English ports; on the other, the queen was distinctly worried about Spanish activities in the unstable kingdom across her northern border.

In June two of her warships, *Vanguard* and *Tiger*, dropped anchor at Leith. A third galleon, *Achates*, patrolled the entrance to the Forth. Their mission was to pre-empt any Spanish plot in Scotland, and to encourage James VI to send the Armada survivors on their way. Though he might justifiably have objected to this high-handed infringement of his sovereign rights, the Scottish king's reaction was one of profound relief. The English officers were received with all honours at Holyrood Palace, and passes were given to some of the seamen to come ashore, unarmed, to sample the pleasures of the capital. Their arrival, however, created an explosive mix. After carousing fraternally with some Scots and Spaniards in a dockside tavern harsh words were evidently exchanged, and in the resulting fracas an English trumpeter was fatally stabbed by a Spanish soldier. For a time the incident threatened to disrupt the whole delicate process of negotiating the Spaniards' repatriation.

Early in August, however, Elizabeth unexpectedly granted a safe-conduct to the Spaniards in Scotland, promising that they would not be hindered or mistreated should they have to put into English ports on the way. Their safety apparently thus assured, 600 of them embarked on four Scottish ships. Among them was Francisco de Cuellár, whose escape out of Ireland we have already followed. The ships headed southwards for Dunkirk, putting in from time to time at English ports, where the safe-conduct was scrupulously observed. Then, within sight of its destination, the convoy was pounced upon by a waiting flotilla of Justin of Nassau's deadly cromsters. The safe-conduct had said nothing about the Dutch and, too late, the reason for Elizabeth's delaying tactics became clear. In concert with her allies, she had used the time to spring an elaborate ambush.

One ship was captured and everyone on board, Scotsman and Spaniard alike, was peremptorily thrown over the side. The three other vessels ran ashore in an effort to escape, and broke up in the surf under heavy fire from the Sea Beggars. Three hundred men were killed. But Cuellár's amazing luck still held. Wearing nothing but his shirt, and helped by a few other survivors, he managed to stagger to the safety of Dunkirk.

The full extent of the Armada's casualties can never be known. Survivors from the various wrecks continued to turn up in Madrid to claim their back-pay until at least 1597 when the last prisoners from the *San Pedro Mayor* were released from England. A large number of veterans from the fleet were incorporated into the Army of Flanders, and fought on there throughout the 1590s. A very few men may have settled close to the shores on which they had been cast away. Some, according to William Asheby in Edinburgh, preferred to remain in Scotland as servants than return to King Philip's service, since they were 'better entertained. . . [in]

noblemen's houses than they look to be, in following the wars'; others stayed on with those Irish chiefs who had sheltered them. Sorley Boy Macdonnell probably retained a few, along with guns and other spoils from the *Girona*, at his castles of Dunluce and Glenarm. Hugh O'Neill, earl of Tyrone, certainly welcomed all the Spanish soldiers he encountered, and used them to train his troops.

In 1596 there were still eight Armada survivors with Tyrone, helping him in his war against Elizabeth. One of them rose to be the earl's personal bodyguard. Pedro Blanco, who escaped from the *Juliana* at Streedagh, distinguished himself in several battles in the Irish wars and, when they were over, in 1607 fled with Tyrone to Flanders and thence to Rome. Just before the earl died, in 1616, he wrote a glowing testimonial for Blanco, who had 'fought so valiantly that I never wanted to be parted from him'. Now he was old, and Tyrone begged Philip III to bestow some reward on this faithful servant of the Habsburg cause.[14]

History does not relate whether this indefatigable survivor of the Armada campaign ever returned to his native land. But in the king of Spain's meticulous accounts there is no indication that he was paid a penny.

PART IV

The Armada in History and Legend

CHAPTER 13

Victors and vanquished

By 1616 the story of the Spanish Armada was already ancient history. Most of its leading actors had long since left the stage – many, indeed, in 1588 and 1589: Leicester and Walsingham in England; Santa Cruz, Oquendo and Recalde in Spain; Guise, Catherine de Medici and Henry III in France. Sixtus V followed suddenly in 1590, the 'Pretender' Dom António in 1595, Philip II after a long illness in 1598, Elizabeth in 1603. Parma died in 1592, in the shadow of royal disgrace; Ambassador Mendoza went blind and died in 1604; Hawkins and Drake perished on an ill-fated expedition to the Spanish Caribbean in 1595–6. Bobadilla, Valdés, Medina Sidonia and Idiáquez all died in their beds between 1610 and 1614, leaving only a handful of important survivors: Don Balthasar de Zúñiga, who, after a distinguished diplomatic career, became chief minister of Spain from 1618 until 1622; Don Diego Pimentel, who became a reforming viceroy of Mexico and provoked a rebellion there in 1624; Lord Howard of Effingham, who remained Admiral of England until 1619 and continued to exercise influence at court until his demise in 1624; and Justin of Nassau, who commanded Dutch forces by land and sea almost up to the hour of his death in 1631.

All of these men knew, within a few weeks of the battles in the Channel, almost as much as we do about the outcome of the Armada campaign. But they did not know it at once. When the queen's navy last saw it, the Spanish fleet was still over 100 strong and heading north in good formation. That was on 12 August: what was going to happen next? On the 18th, Howard confessed total ignorance: 'God knoweth whether they go either to the Naze of Norway or into Denmark or to the Isles of Orkney to refresh themselves, and so to return.' Drake was of the same opinion. The Armada, he warned, 'I think certainly to be put either with Norway or Denmark' because only there could it find 'great anchors, cables, masts, ropes and victuals; and what the king of Spain's hot crowns will do in cold countries for mariners and men, I leave to your good lordship.' If it could only refit, it would surely return to the Channel and try a second time to join up with Parma. But perhaps, Drake speculated, Parma would attempt an invasion on his own, while the English fleet was out of harm's way in the North Sea: 'I take him to be as a bear robbed of her whelps; and no doubt but, being so great a soldier as he is, that he will presently, if he may, undertake some great matter.' Two weeks later, Drake was still worried: 'We ought much more to have regard to the duke of Parma and his soldiers', he warned the Court, 'than the duke of Sidonia and his ships . . . The duke of Parma should be vigilantly looked upon for these twenty days, although the army [= armada] of Spain return not this way.'

These fears were by no means unfounded. We have already seen that the Armada's leaders fully intended to return to the Channel if they could; and Parma continued apace with embarking his army. By 8 August, the 10,000 men at Nieuwpoort were all aboard their barges, and the next day loading began at Dunkirk. The drills and rehearsals of the previous months soon proved their worth: by the end of the day a further 8,000 men had been embarked, along with their munitions and weapons. Although this process was necessarily reversed after a couple of days, the Army of Flanders was not stood down until 31 August, and neither were the hired barges and ships.

But there was still no certainty about the Armada's whereabouts. Parma had dispatched pinnaces in its pursuit, and on 15 August he even wrote a personal letter, urging Medina Sidonia to come back; but to no avail. The last confirmed sighting by any of Elizabeth's agents had been on 20 August, as the fleet rounded the Orkney islands, where Scottish fishermen saw 'monstrous great ships, being about 100 in number, running westwards before the wind'. But then there was silence and, as late as 18 September, William Asheby in Edinburgh could only speculate that this must mean that the fleet had either sunk, or had left Scottish waters; for otherwise 'we should have heard of them by fishermen'. But then, just as Asheby's letter reached London, an express courier came in from Dublin, with the first firm news of the Armada's doleful progress and of England's miraculous deliverance.[1]

But long before this it was clear that the immediate threat of invasion had passed. Queen Elizabeth was hunting in Epping forest when she heard of the Armada's retreat from Gravelines and, according to tradition, in a burst of joyful exultation she galloped her horse up the stairway of a nearby hunting lodge. But still she kept close to the capital and to her escort, for no one could be sure that some disaffected English Catholic or desperate Spanish hireling might not be waiting to dispatch the last Tudor, as four years before an assassin had laid low the prince of Orange. On 13 August, however, with the Armada reported to be off the Scottish coast, the Council decided it should halt the flow of militia units and new army recruits toward the south-east. But the 17,000 men mustered around the hastily fortified camp at Tilbury, under the earl of Leicester's command, were left intact; and on 18 August it was considered safe enough for the queen to sail down the Thames to join them. Soon after her arrival she delivered the short speech which has passed into legend.

'I am come amongst you as you see, at this time, not for my recreation and disport, but being resolved, in the midst and heat of battle, to live or die amongst you all, and to lay down for my God and for my kingdom and for my people, my honour and my blood, even in the dust. I know I have the body of a weak and feeble woman, but I have the heart and stomach of a king, and of a king of England too, and think foul scorn that Parma, or Spain, or any prince of Europe should dare to invade the borders of my realm . . .'

But the 'heat of the battle' (such as it was) did not last long, for two days after the speech orders went out to reduce the army in the south-east first to 6,000, and on 27 August to a mere 1,500 soldiers.

A little later there were moves to stand down the fleet. In a macabre sense the 16,000 men crowded about the English ships had already started the process themselves, for death and sickness were taking a heavy toll. Of the 500 men aboard the *Elizabeth Bonaventure* when she left Plymouth in July some 200 were dead of disease a month later and Admiral Howard feared that 'the like infection will grow throughout the most part of our fleet, for they have been so long at sea, and have so little shift of apparel and so [few] places to provide them of such wants, and no money wherewith to buy it, for some have been – yea, the most part – eight months at sea'. By early September, according to Howard, it 'would grieve any man's heart to see them that have served so valiantly die so miserably', and to see almost all the ships 'foul and unsavoury' with many 'so weakly manned that they have not mariners to weigh their anchors'. But the hearts of the men at court were evidently not grieved. Instead, Burghley callously expressed the hope that 'by death, by discharging of sick men, and such like . . . there may be spared something in the general pay'. It was his intention that such unfortunates should receive nothing for their part in defeating the Spanish Armada. Howard was appalled. 'It were too pitiful to have men starve after such a service', he remonstrated; and even if pity did not enter into it, there was still self-interest. At one point he reminded the Queen that 'if men should not be cared for better than to let them starve and die miserably, we should hardly get men to serve'.

But he was wasting his time. Elizabeth and her ministers were too busy celebrating to pay much attention. When William Borough went to Court to discuss arrangements for discharging the fleet, he found everyone at the windows of the palace, watching a victory parade, and could get no guidance or instruction. When the government later broke down the costs of the defensive effort against Spain, which had involved a total expenditure of nearly £400,000, it transpired that 'rewards to the injured' accounted for a mere £180.[2] And so, in the end, it was left to the commanders to look after their men. Hawkins, Drake and Howard set up a special fund in 1590 for 'poor sailors maimed in the navy'. It was run like an insurance scheme: a small deduction was made from the wages paid to each seaman, and the balance deposited in a large locked chest at Chatham dockyard. The 'Chatham Chest' then – as need arose – issued pensions to the old, burial money for the dead, and compensation payments for the injured or disabled. But these benefits only became available two years after the Armada's defeat. Those who had fallen ill or suffered wounds in the campaign of 1588 had to rely upon the individual charity of their officers – and here again Lord Admiral Howard set a noble example – or of the towns in which they were discharged. Perhaps only half of the men who fought for England in 1588 lived to celebrate the following Christmas. Even at the service of Thanksgiving held at St Paul's Cross on 24 November, 'a special day wherein all the realm might concur in giving public thanks unto God', at which numerous captured ensigns and other trophies were gleefully displayed, the humble architects of victory were scarcely mentioned. For them, to have preserved the Tudor state and the Protestant cause was to be its own reward.

Of those who sailed on the Armada, too, perhaps only one-half survived the year. But again, as in England, it was many weeks – even months – before the full scale of the disaster became clear. Indeed, the first reports of the Channel battles to reach Spain had been highly encouraging. A report from Dieppe dated 7 August, entitled 'A letter on the encounter of the English and Spanish fleets, and of the Spanish victory', seemed unequivocal enough; and it was forwarded to Spain, together with further confirmatory detail, by Ambassador Mendoza in Paris. It arrived towards the end of the month. As late as 5 September a printer in Seville could still issue a cheerful newsletter on 'What has happened to the most fortunate Armada so far': although the loss of the *Rosario*, the *San Salvador* and Moncada's galleass was noted, the rest of the news was all about the great victories won by the Spanish fleet. But, by then, the king (at least) knew it was false.[3]

Writing some forty years later, Philip II's biographer Balthasar Porreño played down the shock caused by the discovery that the Armada had failed, attributing instead stoic insouciance to his hero. 'I sent my fleet against men,' Philip is made to say, when he first heard the news, 'not against the wind and the waves.' But surviving correspondence of the king and his ministers from the autumn of 1588 tells a different – and far more revealing – story. On 31 August a letter arrived at court from the duke of Parma. Although it had been written three weeks before, on the 10th, it constituted the first full and reliable report that the king had received concerning the battles in the Narrow Seas. Parma, of course, had only known, when he wrote, that the Armada (having lost several ships) was running northwards under full sail; but that news was more than enough to disturb the king's tranquillity. At once he sat at his desk and sought to regain control of the situation with his pen. To Medina Sidonia, wherever he might be, he wrote: 'The news of your great reverse before Calais has caused me more anxiety than you can imagine'. But he urged the duke to try again. To Parma he permitted himself the hope 'that God will have allowed some improvement, and that the reputation of everyone (which is now so compromised) may be recovered'. But when the king re-read the letter, he hesitated and underlined this passage. 'It might be better,' he told his secretary, 'to delete what I have underlined, because in what God does, and in what we do for God, there is no gain or loss of reputation. It is better not to speak of such things.'[4]

The king's self-confidence had been dealt a shattering blow. Writing to Parma that same day, 31 August, Don Juan de Idiáquez admitted that:

'I cannot exaggerate the grief caused by seeing something that cost so much time, money and trouble – and is so important to the service of God and His Majesty – placed in jeopardy, just at the point when it was about to bear fruit. His Majesty has felt it more than you would believe possible, and if there were not some remaining hope in God that all this might have achieved something for His cause, . . . I do not know how he could bear such a great blow. Certainly this business leaves no time to think about anything else, nor to think of it without excessive grief.'

But time brought no relief. Instead, on 3 September, a courier from France brought more detailed news concerning the defeat and northward flight of the Grand Fleet. The cypher clerks and ministers blenched, and debated which of them should break the news to the king. The choice fell upon Mateo Vázquez, Philip's long-serving private secretary and chaplain; but even he did so by letter, and with great trepidation. Indeed, it took him some time to get to the point. 'If we consider,' he began cautiously, 'the case of King Louis IX of France, who was a saint and was engaged on a saintly enterprise [the Seventh Crusade in 1250], and yet saw his army die of plague, with himself defeated and captured, we certainly cannot fail to fear greatly for the success of our Armada'. Perhaps more prayers should be offered for its safety, ventured Vázquez. But this was too much for the king: 'I hope that God has not permitted so much evil', he scribbled angrily on the letter, 'for everything has been done for His service.'[5]

And then there was silence. For three more weeks no further reliable information about the Armada arrived in Spain. Parma had sent a pinnace to Scotland to try to locate the fleet, but when it got as far as Leith without finding any Spanish ships it turned back. Don Bernadino de Mendoza, in Paris, had been gathering an abundance of news, but since most of it came from England he dismissed it. The intelligence concerning Elizabeth's own fleet, however, he treated with greater respect; and this suggested that the queen's ships were regrouping, perhaps in preparation for a counter-attack on Spain. He dispatched an express courier to Madrid, who arrived on 20 September; the king's ministers promptly sent out orders to all major ports to ensure that, whenever the Armada got home, under no circumstances were the soldiers and sailors to be allowed to disembark. They were to be kept at their posts, come what may, ready to meet any emergency. The folly of all this became apparent a mere four days later, with the arrival at Court of a bedraggled Don Balthasar de Zúñiga.[6]

Zúñiga, it will be remembered, had left the fleet off Shetland on 21 August 'at 61 degrees north and 300 leagues from Spain', bearing a full report from Medina Sidonia, Don Francisco de Bobadilla and others on the Armada's proceedings in the Channel and its subsequent plight. He also brought a set of requests for supplies, medicines and provisions to be made ready for the fleet's imminent return. But Zúñiga's pinnace had been buffeted and driven back by the same storms that had so damaged the main fleet – a delay for which a high cost in human suffering was exacted, for, in the event, the remnants of the Armada struggled into various ports of northern Spain before the relief supplies arrived.

On 21 September, two months to the day since their joyful departure from Corunna and after an odyssey in which some ships may have encompassed as many as 5,000 miles, Medina Sidonia led eight battered galleons into Santander, Diego Flores took 22 into Laredo, and Miguel de Oquendo brought five more to the ports of Biscay. Two days later, with heavy heart and sick body, the duke dictated his first letter from Spanish soil to the king, his master:

'I am unable to describe to Your Majesty the misfortunes and miseries that have befallen us, because they are the worst that have been known on any voyage; and some of the ships that put into this port have spent the last fourteen days without a single drop of water'.

His flagship was letting in water so fast that she had to be cinched with three great hawsers wrapped round her to prevent the seams from opening. And thus, literally held together with string, she returned. Out of the 500 men who set out with the duke in July, '180 are dead already of sickness, as well as three of the four pilots' (an eventuality which perhaps explained why, having set course for Cape Finisterre, 'when we first espied land, we all believed it was Corunna . . . but in fact we were 100 leagues away from that harbour, without knowing where we were at all'). During the voyage Medina Sidonia had given the two warm cloaks he had taken with him to a frozen priest and a wounded boy; now he had only the thin short cloak he stood up in. Most of the survivors were ill with dysentery, typhus, or both. The duke himself, he reported, had 'arrived very close to death, and so I am in bed and cannot cope with everything, even though I want to . . . Even my own servants, who once numbered 60, have died and sickened so fast that I have only two left. God be praised for all His works.'⁷

The duke did what he could for his wretched men. He sent urgent appeals to the towns and churches of northern Spain, begging for the immediate dispatch of beds, clothes and (rather more surprisingly) of 'sugar, raisins and almond preserves' for the 4,000 sick survivors ashore. That total steadily increased as further ships limped home. Some were in a terrible state. On purser Calderón's hulk *San Salvador* there was no drinking water left at all on the last three days of the voyage, and the crew became too weak to pump fast enough to keep pace with the sea water flooding into the hold. Oquendo's flagship, having made a safe landing, was soon afterwards destroyed by fire when the powder magazine exploded, killing 100 of her crew. Other unfortunate vessels ran straight onto the Cantabrican coast, or else collided with each other, either for lack of anchors or because they had no men to work the sails.

At this stage there were still a large number of ships unaccounted for, but, as September turned to October, news of the losses in Ireland began to arrive. Yet the truth was hard to establish. Even survivors could not always shed much light on what had happened: one man from the *Trinidad Valencera* was still so traumatized by his experiences that 'it was difficult to understand what he was trying to say'. When asked where his ship sank, he could only 'show on the map that it was on the northern-most promontory of Ireland'. However, on 14 October there arrived witnesses who were in a better position to confirm all Spain's worst fears. Aramburu and Recalde, having escaped from Blasket Sound, brought their storm-tossed ships and emaciated crews back to port, and reluctantly stated that they believed there would be no more. Their report was sent to the king. 'I have read it all,' Philip wrote, 'although I would rather not have done, because it hurts so much.'[8]

It took another month for the full enormity of the disaster to sink in. On 10 November the king wrote to his chaplain and secretary, Mateo Vázquez, in total despair:

'I promise you that unless some remedy is found . . . very soon we shall find ourselves in such a state that we shall wish that we had never been born . . . And if God does not send us a miracle (which is what I hope from Him), I hope to die and go to Him before all this happens – which is what I pray for, so as not to see so much ill fortune and disgrace. All this is for your eyes alone. Please God, let me be mistaken: but I do not think it is so. Rather, we shall have to witness, quicker than anyone thinks, what we so much fear, if God does not return to fight for His cause. We have already seen all this in what has happened, which would not have been permitted except to punish us for our sins.'

The final tally of the Armada's losses was truly appalling. Of the 130 ships that had sailed against England, only 60 could now be accounted for – 44 at Santander, 9 at San Sebastián, 6 at Corunna, one (the *Zúñiga*) at Le Havre. Some of those missing – especially the hulks and small craft – may well have slipped off to their home ports unrecorded, but at the lowest estimate a third of the fleet had been sunk or wrecked. The highest losses were sustained by Bertendona's squadron of ten great Levanters, of which only two returned. Altogether only 34 major fighting ships survived the campaign, and many of these were so severely damaged that they were no longer seaworthy. They were, moreover, scattered in sundry ports along 500 miles of coast.

Equally serious was the loss of artillery – especially the costly and important siege-train cast for Charles V and Philip II by Gregorio Lefer and Remigy de Halut. But ships and guns could, in time, be replaced.[9] It was not so easy to replace so many trained and experienced men. Apart from those killed in action, drowned in the surf, or executed in Ireland, thousands more were claimed by exhaustion, dehydration and starvation. Rations on the fleet had been cut sharply when the decision to return by the north-about route was taken; but even that used up supplies too fast. In the 45 days which elapsed between then and the return to Spain, some of the survivors received only 30 days' rations; and others received even less. Given the remarkably cold weather encountered by the Armada in the north Atlantic – upon which every Spanish account dwells plaintively – it is scarcely surprising that on almost every ship four or five men died every day; or that, even after the longed-for return to Spain, many failed to recover from their privations. Don Agustín Mexía's *tercio*, which had numbered 2,659 men in May, could barely muster 1,000 at the year's end. Probably the exact total of those lost on the campaign will never be known. In January 1589, according to an eye-witness, the relations and friends of those who had served on the fleet were still going from port to port, trying to ascertain what had happened to them.

But at least the Spanish government did its best. In sharp contrast to the callous indifference of Elizabeth and her ministers, Philip II tried to ensure that his faithful soldiers and sailors were properly paid for their service. When, in December 1588, it was discovered that some Armada veterans were being discharged without a full settlement of their wages, the king immediately informed his commanders that:

'This is contrary to Christain charity and also very much alien to my will, which has been (and is) that those who have served – and are serving – me should not only be paid what they are owed, but rewarded as far as our resources permit.'

So before any veteran was dismissed from the king's army or navy, the council of war was to be notified of his service record, and his arrears, so that proper recompense could be arranged.

And yet, on a cynical calculation, even the loss of men (which may have totalled 15,000 in all) could be made good without too much trouble. In the event, by August 1589 there were once again 30,000 troops either attached to the Spanish fleet or guarding the northern and western coasts of the peninsula.[10] But they now served under different, less experienced commanders. Scarcely any of the Armada's senior officers were still in post by the end of the year. Santa Cruz, Oquendo, Leiva and Moncada were dead; Pedro de Valdés, Luzón and Pimentel were prisoners of war; Diego Flores was arrested and incarcerated in Spain; Medina Sidonia and Bobadilla, both with shattered health (and eventually writing each other 'sick notes'), left the fleet at the earliest opportunity in order to recover. Perhaps the saddest case was Juan Martínez de Recalde. Aged 62 in the Armada year, he was already a sick man when the fleet set sail, and spent many days in his bunk crippled with arthritis. But he was back on deck to pilot his ship into Blasket Sound, and out again; and he emerged again for the approach to Corunna. Of his ship's company of 500, 170 died on the journey; the rest, having been reduced in the end to only four ounces of biscuit per man per day, were sick and starving. On 14 October Recalde was carried ashore. He refused to see family or friends. Instead, having dictated a brief note of condolence to his king, he sought solace in a monastery where he died nine days later.

As Friar José de Sigüenza, one of the monks at the Escorial, wrote shortly afterwards, the defeat of the Armada was 'the greatest disaster to strike Spain in over six hundred years'. His colleague, Friar Jerónimo de Sepúlveda, agreed: for him, it was a misfortune

'worthy to be wept over for ever . . . because it lost us respect and the good reputation among warlike people which we used to have. The feeling it caused in all of Spain was extraordinary . . . Almost the entire country went into mourning. People talked about nothing else.'

The same was also true outside Spain, for the 'reputation' of Philip II had received a body blow. In Italy, those who feared or resented Spanish hegemony in the peninsula raised their heads; while in France, those who had supported Spain's grand design lost theirs – in December 1588 the duke of Guise was isolated by Henry III (and his supporters) and murdered. In the Netherlands, Parma at length abandoned his vigil by the coast of Flanders and, after some diversionary manoeuvres, laid siege to the Dutch town of Bergen-op-Zoom. But on 30 October, after six inconclusive weeks there, Philip II's forces were compelled to give up, having received (as Queen Elizabeth gleefully noted) 'no less blemish . . . by land than by sea'.

Needless to say, there was no lack of gloaters among the victorious English and Dutch. In Leiden, the great battle-pennant of the *San Mateo* was hung in the choir of St Peter's church (although it was so long that the end lay rolled up on the ground), and it inspired from the local bard, William Verheyden, a patriotic poem in Latin entitled *Oration on the Fleet of the Spanish Xerxes*. It was declaimed, for the first time, to the Leiden 'Chamber of Rhetoric' on 21 August. Latin verses by Theodore Beza, Philip Marnix and other Calvinist luminaries were read out at later meetings. In England, ballads were more favoured than odes, and no less than 24 contemporary popular songs about the Armada have survived. Even Elizabeth is supposed to have written one: like most of the rest, it can boast little artistic merit. And the Protestant creators of the anti-Hispanic 'Black Legend' had a field day, which perhaps reached the depths of lunacy in the (wisely) anonymous *Skeltonical Salutation or Condign Congratulation and just vexation of the Spanishe Nation*, which assured its readers that the fish which had feasted on Spanish blood could not pass on, through their own flesh, the venereal diseases thereby acquired!

But there was also more serious propaganda. Lord Burghley commissioned in September a pamphlet known (somewhat inelegantly) as *The copie of a letter sent out of England to Bernadino Mendoza*. It purported to be a letter from an English Jesuit to the Spanish ambassador in France, regretting that all his bold promises and boasts had come to nothing, and providing a detailed discussion of Spain's (unjust) reasons for attacking England, Elizabeth's (laudable) countermeasures, the course of the campaign, the names of the Spanish ships and personnel who perished, and the eventual safe return of the English fleet. It concluded with the ringing phrase: 'So ends this account of the misfortunes of the Spanish Armada which they used to call INVINCIBLE'. The word was capitalised — not unreasonably, since it was never used by the Spaniards themselves — and French, Italian, Dutch and German translations were swiftly issued, all referring with heavy irony to the 'Invincible Armada'. And so Lord Burghley's clever epithet passed into the vocabulary of all Europe.[11]

But England's reaction to the Armada's defeat did not stop at bluster. Elizabeth had tasted Spanish blood, and she wanted more. The only question was: how could it best be obtained? The negotiations for peace, which had reached an advanced stage at Bourbourg early in August, were shattered beyond repair; and, in any case, the Dutch had refused to become involved; because Philip offered them no guarantees for continuing religious toleration after hostilities ceased. For the Protestant United Provinces, at least, the Armada changed nothing: the war continued unabated. In June, indeed, they agreed to expand the theatre of operations by subsidising the French Protestant leader, Henry of Navarre. Although Elizabeth stopped short of following suit for another year, she did ask the Dutch to assist her in a direct attack upon Spain in 1589.

But neither England nor the Republic had enough money to spare for such a venture. The cost of fighting Spain had left the United Provinces bankrupt, while the cost of defeating the Armada had absorbed about £400,000 of Elizabeth's resources. So although in September 1588 the queen and her council decided to dispatch a fleet to destroy the Armada's surviving ships as they refitted in the ports of northern Spain, it was recognised that the expedition could not leave until the next spring. And even then, for lack of money, Elizabeth was forced to take her revenge by proxy: instead of sending her navy she allowed a consortium of adventurers – including Sir Francis Drake – to take some of her warships along with their own private fleet of some 80 vessels, with support from 60 Dutch transports, on the understanding that they would destroy what remained of the Armada before moving on to take the plunder and prizes that represented their principal objective.

This clear conflict of aims was serious, but Drake soon made it even worse: he agreed to take with him Dom António, the 'Portuguese Pretender', to make a further bid to regain his ancestors' throne. In the event, by trying to do too much, the expedition achieved virtually nothing. Admittedly there was a successful attack on Corunna, where three Armada vessels (including Recalde's *San Juan* and Bertendona's *Regazona*, the largest ship in the fleet) were destroyed. But then, instead of sailing east to Santander and San Sebastián where (according to an English spy) Spain's warships 'did ride all unrigged, and their ordnance on the shore', the English sailed to Lisbon.

It was a disaster. On the one hand it alienated the Dutch, who were deprived of their plunder; on the other, since Elizabeth's caution had denied the expedition the royal siege guns it needed for a successful land campaign, Lisbon could not be taken. Instead, the fleet sailed for the Azores in the hope of intercepting the returning treasure fleet and thus injuring Philip II by the 'method of Jason, by fetching away his golden fleece'. But here again the new argonauts were unlucky, for southerly gales drove them back to the coast of England. So £100,000 had been expended for nothing. There were no prizes, and only minimal losses were inflicted on the enemy: on the debit side, the queen's ships had suffered considerable damage from the elements, and some 10,000 of the men aboard were either dead or too sick to serve further. Drake was disgraced, and received no further naval command until his final voyage in 1595.

Worse still, with the failure of the 'Counter-Armada' died England's only chance of turning the deliverance of 1588 into a lasting victory. For Philip II was not about to abandon the war. Once he had overcome the spiritual crisis occasioned by the disaster, he convinced himself that Spain's destiny – and God's inscrutable design – could best be served by intensifying, rather than abating, the war against the heretics of northern Europe. Between 12 and 26 November 1588, in a remarkably frank (and hitherto virtually unknown) series of documents, the king invited his council of state to consider the possibility of negotiating rather than fighting. But he left them in no doubt of his own views: 'Right from the start,' he began, 'I was moved to undertake the Armada campaign for the service of Our Lord, the defence of His Cause, and the advantage of these realms. And I still feel the same now, and greatly desire that our efforts should achieve what has become all the more necessary because of what has happened.' The councillors immediately took the point: unanimously they recommended that the war should go on. The king was ecstatic, praising in extravagant terms their resolution and assuring them that 'I, for my part, shall never fail to strive for the cause of God and the good of these kingdoms, as much as I can.'[12]

A series of orders went out to improve the military and naval state of Spain: money was sent to refit the ships which had survived the Armada, and twelve new 1,000 ton galleons (predictably known as the 'Twelve Apostles') were laid down in the Cantabrican shipyards. They were to be designed along 'English' lines; shipboard guns were cut down to a more manageable length; and an attempt was made to rationalise calibres. Nor was this regarded simply as an academic exercise: before the year was out, the king had entered into a lively correspondence with Martín de Bertendona, one of the few surviving squadron commanders of 1588, concerning the best way to invade and land troops in England in the near future.[13]

It all came to nothing. Philip II's fleets sailed against England in 1596 and 1597, but they were driven back by storms. Instead, during the years 1589–91 alone, English privateers captured some 300 merchantmen, worth perhaps £400,000, belonging to Philip II's subjects; and the spoils flowed until the war ended in 1604. Meanwhile, English forces continued to strengthen Dutch resistance, to assist Henry of Navarre to become king of France (Henry III was assassinated in 1589), and to assault and sack Pernambuco in 1595, Cadiz in 1596, and Puerto Rico in 1598. At the same time, the Dutch took the offensive by sea, sending ever larger fleets into the Caribbean, the Indian Ocean and eventually the Pacific in order to usurp Iberian trade and destroy Iberian property. Even after a cease-fire was agreed in Europe in 1607, Dutch attacks on the Portuguese and Spanish seaborne empires continued unabated.

The Armada had thus clearly failed to attain any of the objectives set out by Santa Cruz, Parma and Medina Sidonia in their proposals of 1586, and by Philip II in his instructions of 1588. More seriously still, the spectacular failure of Philip II's fleet cleared away many illusions about the power of Spain. It encouraged English and Dutch attacks on Iberian shipping and on Iberian possessions overseas; it helped to silence those voices in the Dutch Republic which had favoured a compromise peace; and it confirmed Spain's inability to penetrate the North Sea in order to impose her will. Above all, it sapped Spain's self-confidence. The first work of Spanish literature generally seen to manifest a sense of *desengaño* – disillusion – with empire is a mock-epic poem *Farewell of the ladies of the court to the gallants sailing on the Armada*, which more or less ridiculed their mission and suggested that all they would gain from the venture was injury, discomfort and disease. After 1588 the *genre* became prolific.

Looking back, most observers – even Spaniards – saw the failure of the Armada as the point at which the decline of Spain as an imperial power began. But this was the wisdom of hindsight: at the time, and in the immediate aftermath, there were only two questions on men's lips. First, could the Enterprise of England have succeeded? And, if it could, who then was to blame for its failure?

CHAPTER 14

If the Armada had landed

Even as the Armada sailed away northwards from Calais, discussion of where it had gone wrong began. 'There is nobody aboard this fleet,' wrote Don Francisco de Bobadilla on 20 August, 'who is not now saying "I told you so" or "I knew this would happen". But it's just like trying to lock the stable door after the horse has bolted.' Bobadilla, nevertheless, went on to propound his own explanation of the debacle. On the one hand, he asserted, 'we found that many of the enemy's ships held great advantages over us in combat, both in their design and in their guns, gunners and crews, . . . so that they could do with us as they wished.' On the other hand, there was an acute shortage of ammunition on most ships. 'But in spite of all this,' he continued, 'the duke [Medina Sidonia] managed to bring his fleet to anchor in Calais roads, just seven leagues from Dunkirk . . . and if, on the day that we arrived there, Parma had come out [with his forces], we should have carried out the invasion.'[1]

This analysis – the earliest one of which we have notice – fully accords with the historical record. In spite of all the defects in supply, design, organisation and leadership, the Armada had managed to reach Calais with its order unimpaired. But for the fireships strategem, which broke the fleet's disciplined formation before the junction with Parma had been effected, Philip II's Grand Design might have succeeded. So who was responsible for its failure?

Many, like Don Diego Pimentel, blamed the duke of Parma. Why had he not been ready, in spite of repeated messages from the fleet, reporting its steady progress in late July? Why had he not at least attempted a sortie? According to the disillusioned Don Bernadino de Mendoza in Paris, many French observers believed that Parma had deliberately set out to sabotage the Armada and make himself the independent ruler of the Low Countries in alliance with England (his support of the peace talks at Bourbourg was seen as 'proof' of this). The following month, similar rumours circulated in Italy to such a degree that Parma felt obliged to send a special envoy to Rome to explain his own conduct and lay all blame for the fiasco at Medina Sidonia's door.[2]

The Spanish ambassador (who happened to be Medina Sidonia's cousin) was outraged, and wrote to chide Parma directly for his disloyalty and pettiness: 'It was God's will, not your fault – and not Medina's.' And in any case, the ambassador added tartly, 'explanations of how each commander behaved are due to His Majesty and nobody else'.[3] But Philip II never blamed his nephew, although some of the ministers in Madrid expressed shock that Parma did not have the invasion force already embarked, waiting for the moment at which the Armada came in sight. The king, however, seems to have accepted the duke's assurance that his boats and barges were as ready as they reasonably could have been:

'Those who came here off the fleet [Parma explained] and have tried to give the impression that we were not ready – because they could not see guns and munitions on my ships, nor the troops aboard – are mistaken. Everything was prepared as it should have been for the Channel crossing: . . . nothing would have been gained by embarking things in advance, because the ships are so small that there is not even room to turn round in. Undoubtedly, the men would have sickened, the food would have rotted, and everything would have perished.'[4]

In any case, there was plenty of evidence that as soon as Parma learned of the Armada's imminent approach he had actually commenced the process of embarkation. By the time the fleet had been forced towards its northward retreat, that process was well advanced. According to the Armada's Inspector-General, marooned at Dunkirk:

'The German, Italian, and Walloon troops, to the number of 18,000 were embarked, and the Spanish infantry together with the cavalry were at Dunkirk ready for embarkation. As they were boarding, the news arrived that the Armada had gone away; but everything remains in the same state, and the duke of Parma is present in person and will make no changes until there is certain news of our fleet.'[5]

The main problem arose from the crucial delay between the dispatch of each messenger by Medina Sidonia, and their arrival in Flanders. As soon as certain news was received of the fleet's approach, Parma's plan swung into action. Had that message arrived slightly sooner, or had the Armada taken slightly longer, the rendezvous might have become a reality.[6]

Parma's reputation, after a brief spell under a cloud, was thus vindi-cated: he could indeed have done no more. The same was true of Medina Sidonia. The duke, who had shown unquestioned courage in the face of the enemy, quit his command as soon as possible after leading the Armada back to Spain. After the *San Martín* reached Santander on 21 September Medina Sidonia stayed in port only long enough to ensure the recovery of himself and his personal entourage, and to collect his entire arrears of pay (no less than 7,810 ducats, in gold). He found the leisure to play cards twice (both times he lost), and early in the morning of 5 October, with his baggage loaded on 11 mules and 17 bearers, he set off for home.

Dispersing (according to the accounts of his household treasurer) generous benefactions to clerics and paupers along the way, he reached San Lúcar de Barrameda on the 24th. There was only one ugly moment: as Medina Sidonia tried to snatch a night's rest in Valladolid, his lodgings were surrounded by youths who chanted 'Drake, Drake, Drake is coming' until dawn, and taunted the unfortunate Captain General of the Ocean Sea with the offensive sobriquet 'duke of Gallina' (Chicken duke).[7] To what extent he considered himself responsible for the Armada's disgrace will never be known, but no criticism of his personal behaviour or his handling of the fleet was levelled at him by the king. Perhaps Philip recalled the duke's reluctance to accept the command, and how he had begged the king to call off the operation after the return to Corunna; or perhaps he was swayed by the praise bestowed by the expedition's survivors on Medina's courageous leadership. According to Don Franci-sco de Bobadilla, a stern judge, writing after the campaign was over, 'Even our enemies will admit, although it may grieve them, that no commander in the world has done more than this one.'[8]

Instead it was the duke's naval adviser, Diego Flores de Valdés, who was punished for the disaster. He had counselled the duke to abandon his cousin Don Pedro (and the king's 50,000 gold ducats) and he had panicked when the fireships came in, ordering all cables to be cut. Many of Diego Flores' brother officers had also been unimpressed by his perform-ance and by the excessive reliance placed by Medina Sidonia on his advice. According to a bitter rumour which went round the fleet, when the duke of Medina was facing the first furious attack of the English fleet on 8 August and found himself next to the flagship of the Guipuzcoan squadron, he called out to her commander 'Señor Oquendo, what should we do next?'. 'I don't know,' came the sarcastic reply. 'Why don't you ask

Diego Flores?' And then, finally, when the remnants of the fleet limped home to Spain, the fatal collision of two ships in Laredo harbour was blamed on the negligence of Diego Flores. So in the following months evidence was collected against him and just before Christmas, on the orders of Philip II, he was arrested and sent to prison in Burgos. Diego Flores was not solely responsible for the shortcomings for which he had been charged, but he remained the only scapegoat.[9]

In later years blame for the Armada's failure began to shift from the fleet's principal officers to its supreme commander in the Escorial. Perhaps the most intemperate attack was published in 1599, just after Philip II's death (which perhaps explains how it escaped the censor). According to Juan de Mariana's study of Monarchy:

'Great loss was suffered on the coasts of England [in 1588]. We sustained a blow, a disgrace, which many years will not be able to efface. That was the retribution exacted for grave delinquencies in our nation and, unless memory fails, it was the vile lusts of a certain prince which enraged the Divinity. This prince had forgotten the sacred personage he was, and the advanced age and even senility he had reached; and the rumour spread abroad that he had dissipated himself beyond reason in licentiousness.'

For the learned Spanish Jesuit, the king's failure was thus moral.[10] Don Francisco de Bobadilla, by contrast, shivering in the northern seas, took the more pragmatic view of a man on the spot:

'I don't know who had the idea [he began cautiously] that we could join forces [with Parma] in a place with such powerful currents, with a shore so open and liable to cross-winds, and with so many sandbanks ... But I believe it is impossible to control all the things that must be concerted at the same time, in order to bring together forces that are so separated, unless one has a different sort of ship from those we brought, in the place we were instructed to join.'

Once again, hindsight has amply confirmed Bobadilla's judgement.[11] In book V of his *History of the World*, written for the most part in 1613, Sir Walter Raleigh's verdict was remarkably similar:

'To invade by sea upon a perilous coast, being neither in possession of any port, nor succoured by any party, may better fit a prince presuming on his fortune than enriched with understanding.'

But perhaps this was too glib, too confident? The history of amphibious operations is as full of campaigns which failed in spite of the most confident predictions as it is of enterprises which succeeded in the face of all the odds. To Sir William Winter, even in December 1588, England's deliverance still seemed miraculous. 'When I consider that ships are subject to wind, weather and other haps,' he warned, 'it were not good, as I think, for to build our defence only upon them.' And yet that is precisely what Elizabeth had done. England lacked all the vital resources to resist an invasion: if ever the Armada had landed, there were neither fortifications, troops nor money enough to stop the Spaniards.

For Parma's orders were clear. His instructions from the king, issued on 1 April 1588, charged him to lead his troops from the beach-head near The Downs, through Kent and on to London, which he was to take by storm (preferably with Elizabeth and her ministers still in it) and hope that all Catholics, or at least those who were enemies of the Tudor regime, would rise in rebellion and aid the invaders to master the kingdom. But the plan did not hinge on such a rising: Philip was well aware that not all English Catholics would support a Spanish invasion, despite the propaganda directed towards them by the exiles at his court, by the pope's pamphleteers, and by the doctors at the English College in Douai. All that these polemics achieved, in fact, was to rouse the suspicion of the English government, which first disarmed the recusants and later interned some of their leaders. The English Catholics – like Cardinal Allen and his doctors from Douai – would be important props of the new regime *after* the conquest, but until then they could largely be ignored.[12]

Of much greater concern to the king was the possibility that Parma's invasion might become bogged down before gaining outright victory in the south-east. Here, his instructions were the same as those drafted by Don Juan de Zúñiga in October 1586. The duke was to use his presence on English soil to force Elizabeth to concede toleration of Roman Catholic worship; and to surrender to Spain all Dutch towns held by English troops (especially Flushing, which commanded the sea-approaches to Antwerp). On top of this, he could attempt to extract a war-indemnity from England, though this might be dropped in return for the main concessions.

But unconditional victory was by no means an impossibility. Not even Sir Walter Raleigh doubted that the Army of Flanders, once ashore in England, would have proved able to achieve it. Elizabeth's defences, he noted in his *History of the World*, were 'of no such force as to encounter an Army like unto that, wherewith it was intended that the prince of Parma should have landed in England'. Parma's only lack was a siege train; and that, of course, Philip II had thoughtfully provided aboard the Armada itself, ready for disembarkation and immediate use.

This was an advantage of critical importance, since there were very few towns and castles in south-east England which were capable of with-standing heavy bombardment. Indeed, the fortifications of most places in Elizabethan England were extremely poor. According to one disgruntled

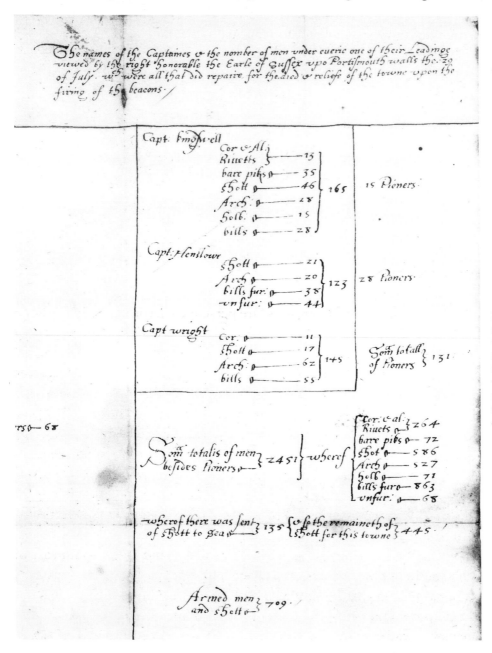

Part of the muster roll called at Portsmouth of the men who had repaired 'for the relief of the town upon the firing of 15 beacons'. They were reviewed on 29 July (O.S.) by the earl of Sussex, to reveal a motley assortment of weapons.

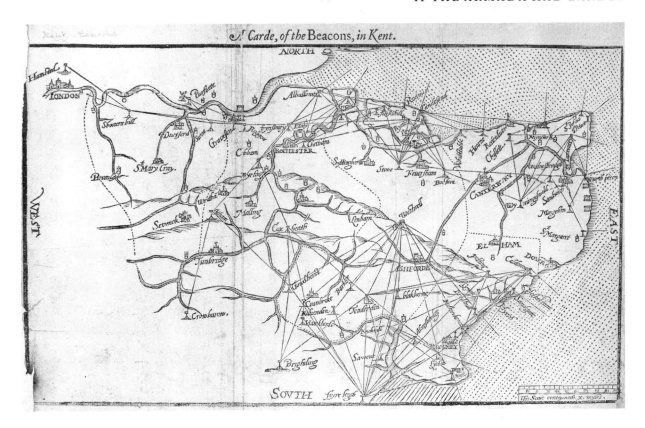

Map of beacon locations in Kent. Although the warning system seemed – in theory at least – comprehensive enough, it was not supported by effective troop dispositions on the ground.

old soldier, the Queen's ministers 'are persuaded according to the opinion of the Lacedacmonians, that fortifying of towns does more hurt than good.' Admittedly, Henry VIII had done a good deal to improve the defences of the Kent coast, with five new forts built between the Downs and Rye, and five more along the Thames estuary. But all these new defences (as a visit to the still extant castles of Camber and Walmer shows) were constructed with thin circular walls and curved, hollow bulwarks. They certainly maximised the potential for offensive firepower – Sandgate castle boasted 60 artillery and 65 handgun embrasures – but they possessed poor defensive capacity. Parma's assault squads would have made short work of them. Recent military experience had clearly demonstrated that only solid angular bastions, protected by wide moats, were capable of withstanding modern artillery; and in the south-east of England only the small castle of Upnor, built in the 1560s to defend the new naval dockyard at Chatham, had those. The larger towns of Kent – Canterbury and Rochester – were still defended only by antiquated medieval walls, while Rochester Castle, commanding the main crossing

271

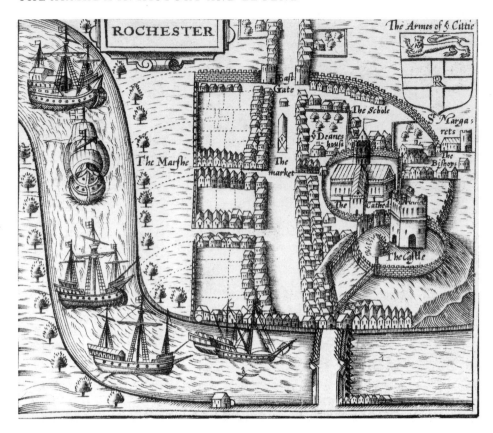

A 16th century view of Rochester, showing its out-dated medieval walls. Other important towns which might have stood in Parma's path, such as Canterbury, were similary ill-defended.

over the Medway, was thoroughly decayed. There seem to have been no defence works at all between Sandwich and the Medway. Unquestionably, Philip II had deftly selected his adversary's most vulnerable point.

With so few physical obstacles in their path, Parma and his veterans would have been able to move fast. When in 1592 he invaded Normandy with 22,000 men, the duke covered 65 miles in 6 days, despite tenacious opposition from numerically superior forces. Even in the face of stiff resistance the Spaniards might reasonably have covered the 80 miles from north-east Kent to London in a week. Such a rapid advance would have brought the advantage of surprise, and also the windfall of copious food supplies, since the harvest in Kent would have been in full swing. Even London did not represent a serious obstacle, because the city was defended only by its ramshackle mediaeval walls. These same walls had failed to deter an ill-equipped army of rebels which in 1554 had marched through Kent, crossed the Thames at Kingston and advanced with impunity through Westminster and down Fleet Street to Ludgate. In military terms, London presented far less of a challenge than Antwerp, a

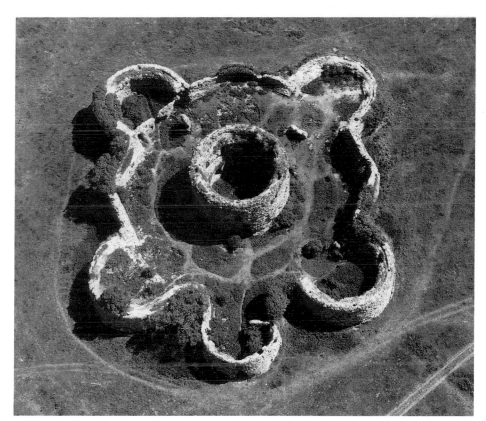

Camber Castle in Sussex, one of the coastal defence fortresses built by Henry VIII. Although it was capable of mounting powerful artillery, its thin walls and curved bastions were not themselves suited to withstand the kind of sustained bombardment that the Armada's siege train could have laid down.

city defended by a five-mile enceinte of walls built to the most sophisticated modern designs. Yet Antwerp's defences had not been proof against the Army of Flanders in 1585.

However, as Parma was well aware, the state of a town's physical defences was not always the decisive factor in wartime. Several places in the Netherlands with poor, outdated fortifications had, thanks to the determination of their besieged populations, managed to avoid capture; conversely, several towns protected by magnificent fortifications had fallen to the Spaniards with ease because their citizens, their garrisons, or their commanders succumbed to bribes. It is by no means certain that the defenders of the major English towns and castles would have resisted the Spaniards to the last man. After all, Queen Elizabeth's troops in the Netherlands had a distinctly uninspiring record in that respect: in September 1582 William Semple betrayed the stronghold of Lier to the Spaniards; in November 1584 the English garrison of Aalst sold their town to Parma for 45,000 ducats; in February 1587 Sir William Stanley and Captain Roland Yorke, together with over 700 men under their command, betrayed the places entrusted to their care to Parma and began to fight against their former comrades and allies.

Tudor apologists may protest that many of these men were either Irish or Anglo-Irish Catholics, and thus *ipso facto* unreliable; but it remains true that all had been recruited by, or with the consent of, the English government and had been sent abroad specifically to fight for the Protestant cause in the Low Countries. Elizabeth and her advisers, moreover, pinned many of their hopes in 1588 on the colleagues of these traitors, recalling 4,000 men from Holland to form the nucleus of the army which was intended to defend London. Its quartermaster-general was the brother of Roland Yorke, and its third-in-command was Sir Roger Williams, who had fought in the Spanish Army of Flanders for four years. One cannot exclude the possibility that some of these men might have been prepared to sell themselves to Parma in England, just as their fellows had sold themselves to him in the Low Countries.

Elizabeth, however, had no choice. She was forced to depend on the veterans from Holland because there were very few other experienced troops on hand in whom she could trust. A census carried out by her government in July 1588 to ascertain how many 'martial men' – i.e. veterans – resided in England, produced a list of only 100 (some of whom, with service going back to the 1540s, were considered too old to be of use). The 6,000 armed conscripts of the London trained-bands, who had been drilling twice weekly since March, were probably capable of putting up a good fight (although some doubted it); but little could be expected from the militias of the inland shires.

To begin with, they were poorly equipped. A survey of the 9,088 men mobilised in Hampshire revealed that many were 'very rawly furnished, some whereof lacketh a headpiece, some a sword, some with one thing or another that is evil, unfit or unbeseeming about him'. It is true that the militia of Kent was issued with muskets, for the first time, in July 1588; but they were far ahead of the field – most of the shire levies called up to resist the Armada included large contingents of archers. In any case, many units were not ordered to mobilise until 2 August and, worse still, were sent on their way without food or drink. When the Essex militiamen arrived at Tilbury – where the Spaniards were wrongly expected to land – they brought 'not so much as one meal's provision of victual with them, so that, at their arrival here, there was not a barrel of beer, nor loaf of bread for them.' That was on 5 August. The same day orders were sent to the officers of the levies coming from London to stop them where they stood 'except they had provisions with them.' England could scarcely be defended by starving men.

The fortifications at Tilbury itself were likewise unready and disorganised. Work had only begun on 3 August, and there were still no gun-platforms capable of mounting artillery. Giambelli's floating boom across the Thames was an improvised affair of masts, chains and cables which had broken on the first flood tide, while the pontoon bridge which would link Tilbury with the troops on the Kent side of the river was scarcely begun.

In Kent, the troops at Dover (most of them raw recruits) began to desert in considerable numbers when the Armada came into sight off Calais (perhaps through lack of wages, but more probably through fear) until in the end there were only 4,000 men left – a ludicrously inadequate force to throw into the path of the seasoned Spaniards.

In any case, they were in the wrong place. Until 2 August, the commander-in-chief (Leicester) had no powers to issue orders to troops outside the county of Essex, and in his absence a controversy over the appropriate strategy broke out between the general officer in charge of the south-east, Sir John Norris, and the local commander in Kent, Sir Thomas Scott. Even as the Armada approached, Scott was still arguing in favour of spreading out his forces along the coast in order to 'answer' the enemy 'at the sea side', while Norris wisely wished to withdraw all but a skeleton force inland in order to make a stand at Canterbury and there 'stay the enemy from speedy passage to London or the heart of the realm'.[13]

So it is reasonable to suppose that, had Parma and Medina Sidonia landed their 23,000 men in Kent early in August 1588, their march on London would have been opposed by inferior numbers of badly positioned and largely untrained troops, acting without clear orders, and backed up by only a handful of inadequately fortified towns. The invasion's success would therefore have hinged mainly upon the spirit of the ordinary citizens of south-east England. How determined would the defence of London and the Home Counties really have been?

Certainly there was considerable hatred of the Spaniards in these staunchly Protestant areas, a hatred stoked by evocative propaganda, expressed in such hair-raising accounts of their cruelty as George Gascoyne's *The Spoyle of Antwerp* (London, 1576) and the English version of Bartolomé de Las Casas's *Destruction of the Indies* (published in 1583). But the hate was conditioned by mortal fear — fear that the formidable power of Spain and her Catholic allies 'might swallow up little England, as the ravenous crocodile does the smallest fish'. In the last analysis everything would have depended upon the ordinary soldiers and citizens of England: would they have been able and willing to fight on the beaches and in the streets for Elizabeth Tudor, an ageing monarch with no acknowledged successor, and for her tottering church which (according to a contemporary) even in the 1590s 'the common people for the greater part' still called 'the new religion'? Or would they have stood sullenly by to await the outcome of the campaign? Even in 1588 there were men in Kent who were openly 'rejoicing when any report was of their [the Spaniards'] good success and sorrowing for the contrary'; while others declared that 'the Spaniards . . . were better than the people of this land'.

Of course, it was not necessary for the invaders to conquer the whole of England in order to achieve Philip II's aims: the occupation of Kent alone would have offered important advantages. Parma could have exploited his conquests, together with the threat of another Catholic rising in the north or in Ireland, to extract from Elizabeth the three key concessions: toleration for the Catholics in England, withdrawal from the Netherlands, and a war indemnity. And had England made a separate peace, it is unlikely that the Dutch would have fought on single-handed for long. When in December 1587, at Elizabeth's insistence, the States-General of the Republic debated at length whether they should send a delegation to the peace talks at Bourbourg, there were a number of voices raised in favour. Although most (though not all) of Holland and Zealand were opposed, the inland provinces which had to bear the brunt of the war against Spain (especially Gelderland, Overijssel, and Friesland) spoke out strongly in favour of a settlement. Queen Elizabeth's special envoy, appointed to convince the Dutch of the need to negotiate, informed the Queen that the 'The Common Wealth of these Provinces consisting of divers Parts and Professions as, namely, Protestants, Puritans, Anabaptists and Spanish Hearts, which are no small number; it is most certain that dividing these in five parts, the Protestants and the Puritans do hardly contain even one part of five'. And, the envoy continued, only the 'Protestants and Puritans' favoured a continuation of the war. The controversy over war or peace grew more and more acrimonious until the defeat of the Armada settled the matter; but had the Enterprise of England succeeded, pressure for a compromise would surely have become irresistable. In the context of the Dutch Wars also, Medina Sidonia would not have sailed in vain.[14]

It is always easy to be wise after the event. By emphasising the unrealistic aspects of the 'armchair' strategy devised by Philip II, or the perhaps excessive caution of Parma, or the naval inexperience of Medina Sidonia, it is easy to present the whole Armada project as a futile, crack-brained, overambitious adventure. But that is unjust. If an accurate and balanced assessment of the 1588 campaign is to be made, it must take into account the strengths as well as the weaknesses: the selection of an ideal invasion area; the formidable planning and immense resources which brought the fleet from Spain and the army from the Netherlands so close together; the patient and successful diplomatic efforts which secured both the paralysis of France and the complete isolation of England throughout 1587 and 1588; the carefully-fostered divisions within the Dutch Republic; the enormous benefits that the occupation of even a part of Kent – carefully exploited – could have brought to Spain. It must also leave room for luck – that, somehow, one of Medina Sidonia's messengers might have reached Parma before the fleet arrived at Calais; that the Armada might have been able to regroup after the fireship attack; that the wind might have swung round and allowed the reformed Grand Fleet to sail back into the straits, while Parma's forces remained embarked on the barges and the English shot-lockers were still empty.

Any or all of these contingencies might have occurred, and who can now tell what the consequences might then have been? Only one thing is certain. If, during the second week of August 1588, the Army of Flanders had been marching towards London, everyone today would regard the Invincible Armada, despite all its deficiencies, as Philip II's masterpiece.

Source notes and references

ABBREVIATIONS USED IN THE SOURCE NOTES AND REFERENCES

AGI   Archivo General de Indias (Seville)

AGRB *SEG*   Archives Générales du Royaume (Brussels), *Secrétairerie d'Etat et de Guerre* (with register and folio)

AGS *Estado*   Archivo General de Simancas (Spain), *Sección de Estado* (with legajo and folio)

AGS *CMC*   idem, *Contaduría Mayor de Cuentas* (with época and legajo)

AGS *CS*   idem, *Contaduría del Sueldo* (with época and legajo)

AGS *GA*   idem, *Guerra Antigua* (with legajo and folio)

AGS *MPyD* idem, *Mapas, Planas y Dibujos*

ASF   Archivio di Stato, Florence

ASP   Archivio di Stato, Parma

BL *Ms*   British Library (London), Department of Manuscripts (with collection, volume and folio)

BNP   Bibliothèque nationale, Paris (with manuscript collection, volume and folio)

Brugmans H. Brugmans, ed., *Correspondentie van Robert Dudley, graaf van Leycester en andere documenten . . . 1585–88*, vol. III (Utrecht, 1931)

CSPF   *Calendar of State Papers, Foreign series, of the reign of Elizabeth*, vols. XXI (in 4 parts) and XXII (London, 1927–36)

CSPI   *Calendar of State Papers relating to Ireland in the reign of Elizabeth, vol. IV: 1588–1592* (London, 1885)

CSPSp   *Calendar of State Papers relating to English affairs preserved . . . in the archives of Simancas. Elizabeth*, vols. I – IV (London, 1892–9)

CSPV   *Calendar of State Papers and manuscripts relating to English affairs existing in the archives and collections of Venice*, vol. VIII (London, 1894)

Co. Do. In. *Colección de documentos inéditos para la historia de España* (with volume number)

Duro   C. Fernández Duro, ed., *La Armada Invencible* (2 vols., Madrid 1884–5)

EHR   *English Historical Review* (with volume number)

HMC   Historical Manuscripts Commission: Reports (with volume number and description)

HS   Archivo de la Casa de Heredía Spínola, Madrid (with *caja* and folio number)

IVdeDJ   Instituto de Valencia de Don Juan, Madrid (with *envío* and folio number)

Japikse   N. Japikse, *Resolutiën der Staten Generaal van 1576 tot 1609*, vol. V (The Hague, 1921) and vol. VI (The Hague, 1922)

Laughton   J. K. Laughton, *State Papers relating to the defeat of the Spanish Armada, anno 1588* (2 vols., London, 1895: Navy Records Society I–II)

LCP   J. Lefèvre, ed., *Correspondance de Philippe II sur les affaires des Pays-Bas*, vol. III (Brussels, 1956)

Lyell   J. P. R. Lyell, 'A commentary on certain aspects of the Spanish Armada drawn from contemporary sources' (Oxford University B.Litt. thesis, 1932; and Houghton Library, Harvard, fMs Eng. 714. Harvard also owns the sources used.)

Maura   G. Maura Gamazo, duke of Maura, *El designo de Felipe II y el episodio de la Armada Invencible* (Madrid, 1957)

MM   *The Mariner's Mirror*

Oria   E. Herrera Oria, *La Armada Invencible* (Valladolid, 1929: Archivo Documental Español, II)

Pepys   Magdalene College Cambridge, Pepys Library

PRO   Public Record Office, London

Tenison   E. M. Tenison, *Elizabethan England* (14 vols., Leamington Spa, 1933–60)

Vázquez   A. Vázquez, 'Los sucesos de Flandes y Francia del tiempo de Alejandro Farnesio', 3 vols. (Madrid, 1879–80: Co. Do. In. LXXII–LXXIV)

MAJOR SOURCES

The principal printed collections are as follows. For Spain CSPSp, Duro and Oria, which print mainly documents from the state archives at Simancas; Maura, who prints documents from the Medina Sidonia archive; and LCP, which provides a précis of the correspondence between the government of Philip II and the Netherlands. And for England – Laughton and the relevant volumes of the four CSP series: Domestic, Foreign, Ireland, and Scotland, based on the corresponding series in PRO State Papers in London. The material printed in these various works has been cited so often in books and articles concerning the Armada that we have felt it unnecessary to provide detailed references. Our notes are therefore devoted to those sources, most of them manuscript, which we feel will be less familiar to readers. Their characteristics are discussed, as appropriate, in the sources for each chapter. There is a good review of other printed works on the English side in C. Read, *Bibliography of British History: Tudor period* (2nd. edn., Oxford, 1959), 300–3.

CHAPTER 1
'THE GREATEST AND STRONGEST COMBINATION'

It seems remarkable that so much has been written about so many relatively minor Elizabethan 'seadogs', and yet so little is known of even senior commanders aboard the Armada. There are a few details in Vázquez, III, 361–443, and in Duro, I, 209–16, but only one general officer (apart from Medina Sidonia) seems to have left a personal archive; Martín de Bertendona, whose papers are in the Lilly Library, Bloomington Indiana, *Bertendona Manuscripts*. For the Valdés cousins, and their relative Recalde, however, see E. Lyon, *The Enterprise of Florida: Pedro Menéndez de Avilés and the Spanish conquest of 1565–8* (Gainesville, 1976), appendix III.

Notes

1. Based on AGS *Estado* 455/492, Medina Sidonia to king, 31 July 1588; and Duro, II, 370–99: *Relación* of Alonso Vanegas, who was aboard the flagship. The version offered by Juan de Vitoria, who spent the summer of 1588 in the Escorial, is entirely unreliable on this episode (cfr. *Co.Do.In.*, LXXXI, 179ff). Although almost every previous account of the Armada states that Don Antonio Hurtado de Mendoza commanded the squadron of zabras and patches, in fact he died before the fleet left Corunna and was replaced by Captain Agustín de Ojeda (AGS CS 2a/286 fos. 480ff).

2. Hieronimo Lippomano, the Venetian ambassador at Madrid, reported on 12 July 1588 that Philip II had sent 'an order and plan' of the Armada's formation to Medina Sidonia, *CSPV* 367–8. The ambassador enclosed a copy of the plan 'from the original which lay on his Majesty's table'. Other clandestine copies survive (e.g. ASF *Mediceo* 4919/340, which is reproduced on p. 31). Filippo Pigafetta, evidently working from similar sources, gives further information about the formation in his *Discorso sopra l'ordinaza del' armata catolica* (Rome, 1588). Duro (II, 33) has published an undated and unprovenanced list of the ships allocated to the right and left 'horns' of the formation: internal evidence suggests a date early in 1588 and there is no reason to doubt its authenticity.

3. Details from Laughton, II, 209f, 'Note of certain plunder'; quotation from J. Deleito y Piñuela, *El declinar de la monarquia española* (2nd edn., Madrid, 1947), 177f, from a manuscript of 1610.

4. Details from the inventories of the 'Squadron of Castile' in AGI *Sección III* legajo 2934, and AGS *GA* 221/147–56, 'relaciones' of March 1588.

5. Reliable specifications for the galleasses are hard to find. The relevant archives in Naples (*Archivio militare* and *Giunta del Arsenale*) are fragmentary before 1600 and we have found no documents in Simancas which give their weight, and only one – GA 202/148 – which gives their age. However the 1589 'Addicioune' to John Mountgomerie's *Treatise Concerninge the Navie of England* (Pepys Ms. 1774) gave the weight as between 700 and 800 English tons. Since Mountgomerie's other facts about galleasses were correct, perhaps his estimate of their displacement is also accurate. The red colouring is recorded in BL *Sloane Ms* 262/66v, and the issue of matching red uniforms is recorded in AGS CS 2a/274, unfol., order of 18 February 1588 to B. de Navarette.

6. Guns on board the seven naves and four patches of Oquendo's squadron on 31 October 1587 are listed in AGS *GA* 221/41. See also Oquendo's indent for more guns, AGS *GA* 221/82, and the *Santa María*'s receipt of ordnance dated 14 May 1588, AGS *GA* 221/153.

7. Valdés to the king, March 1588, requesting more guns for his squadron, AGS *GA* 221/41; later that month he is reported as complaining that although he had enough guns they were too light, Duro, I, 436. For his success in obtaining 6 pedreros in exchange for 6 sacres see Colin Martin, 'The Equipment and Fighting Potential of the Spanish Armada' (St Andrews University Ph.D thesis, 1983), 437. Don Pedro also swapped a *medio sacre* for a *culebrina* from the *Duquesa Santa Ana*, AGS CMC 2a/1210, and a final issue of ten guns was made just before the fleet sailed.

8. See the inventory of arms and munitions loaded aboard Bertendona's squadron, 14 May 1588 in AGS *GA* 221/156; and the bundles of accounts concerning the ships' equipment on departure in AGS CS 2a/280.

9. See the list of arms and munitions issued to Gómez de Medina's squadron, 14 May 1587 in AGS *GA* 221/147; and the bundles of accounts concerning the *Grifón*'s equipment on departure in AGS CS 2a/280 fos. 1931ff.

10. The 'Lisbon Muster' of 9 May 1588 has been reprinted several times (e.g. Laughton, II, 376–87, with annotations, translating Duro, II, 60–82); but the best edition is Oria, 384–435. It may seem curious that this compendium of information, which would be today classified as top secret, was published and apparently disseminated by the Spanish government. But that was not Philip II's intention. When he first saw the document he was furious and complained that it would give advance warning to England of what to expect (see HS 143/77, the king to Mateo Vázquez, 3 June 1588). Publication was apparently Medina Sidonia's idea.

11. The proposed role of Cardinal Allen in the interim government of England is made clear by AGS *Estado* 165/176–7, the king to Parma, 5 April 1588. A task-force of 24 Jesuits were stationed in Flanders, in addition to those aboard the fleet, ready for the spiritual conquest of England (AGRB SEG 11/54v, order, 30 August 1588).

CHAPTER 2
'A FLEET TO IMPEACH IT'

The standard account of the Royal Navy under Henry VIII and his children remains M. Oppenheim, *A History of the Administration of the Royal Navy and of Merchant Shipping in Relation to the Navy from MDIX to MDCLX* (London, 1896), 45–183.

But see also T. Glasgow, 'List of ships in the Royal Navy from 1539 to 1588 – the navy from its infancy to the defeat of the Spanish Armada', *MM*, LVI (1970), 299–307 and LXI (1975), 351–3; and his series of articles (all with slightly different titles) on 'The navy in the French wars of Mary and Elizabeth I', *MM*, LIII (1967), 321–42; LIV (1968), 23–36 and 281–96; and LVI (1970), 3–26. Since these items were published, we have learnt much from a personal examination of the *Mary Rose*, now exhibited at Portsmouth dockyard; from Pepys Ms. 2991 (the 'Anthony Roll'); and from M. Rule, *The Mary Rose: the excavation and raising of Henry VIII's flagship* (Greenwich, 1982). On the English leaders, see R. W. Kenny, *Elizabeth's Admiral: the political career of Charles Howard earl of Nottingham, 1536–1624* (Baltimore, 1970); K. R. Andrews, *Drake's Voyages: a reassessment of their place in Elizabethan naval expansion* (London, 1967); and J. A. Williamson, *Hawkins of Plymouth: a new history of Sir John Hawkins and of other members of his family prominent in Tudor England* (London, 1949).

On the defence of Elizabeth's realm by land, see L. Boynton, *The Elizabethan Militia, 1558–1638* (London, 1967), 154ff, and HMC. *Fifteenth Report. Appendix, part V* (London, 1897) which publishes the 'Book of Musters, 1588' – an important collection of orders on the defence of the realm. Since the volume was unknown until 1897, it was not included in Laughton.

Notes

1. The map is reproduced in Tenison, VII, plate 21. See also the description of this, and three other contemporary maps of coasts liable to be invaded, in R. A. Skelton and J. N. Summerson, *A Description of Maps and Architectural Drawings in the Collection Made by William Cecil, First Baron Burghley, now at Hatfield House* (Oxford, 1971), 51f.

2. See J. S. Corbett, 'Fighting Instructions 1530–1816' in (London, 1905: Navy Records Society, XXIX, 42; and 'Addenda' in vol. XXXV (London, 1908), 364–71.

3. For the guns of the *Elizabeth Jonas* and the *Aid* see the indenture for the delivery of ordnance to Drake, 17 July 1585 OS, in J. S. Corbett, *The Spanish War, 1585–1587* (London, 1898), 27–32. The corresponding figure for the *Revenge* is based on a Spanish account of her last fight off the Azores in 1591 (Colección Sanz de Barutell (Madrid), Art 4, no. 121), which notes that she had '42 pieces of artillery of bronze without three which were given to another ship a few days before, the 20 on her lower deck of 40 to 60 quintals, and the remaining 22 of 20 to 30 quintals, all good'. On the Spanish side, the weight of ordnance aboard the *San Juan de Portugal* has been calculated from a list of the guns she had carried in 1588, drawn up in 1591 (two years after the ship's demise) as a guide to future policy, AGS *GA* 347, unfol. Figures for the *San Cristobal* are derived from AGS *GA* 221/147.

4. Quotation from M. Oppenheim, ed., *The Naval Tracts of Sir William Monson*, IV (London, 1913: Navy Records Society, XLV), 63–5. On the *camaradas* see G. Parker, *The Army of Flanders and the Spanish Road, 1567–1659. The logistics of Spanish victory and defeat in the Low Countries' Wars* (Cambridge, 1972), 177f and sources there quoted. On the stench, see Laughton, I, 9 and 301, and II, 156 and 186.

5. Details from M. F. Keeler, *Sir Francis Drake's West Indian Voyage 1585–86* (London, 1981; Hakluyt Society, 2nd series CXLVIII), 12–16; and K. R. Andrews, *Elizabethan Privateering: English privateering during the Spanish War, 1585–1603* (Cambridge, 1964), 89–94. The leading Spanish commanders (such as Oquendo and Bertendona) likewise owned their own ships, which they also hired out to the crown for the 1588 campaign.

CHAPTER 3
THE GREAT BOG OF EUROPE

Our account of the Low Countries' Wars is based on G. Parker, *The Dutch Revolt* (London, 1977); idem, *Spain and the Netherlands, 1559–1659: ten studies* (London, 1979); and L. van der Essen, *Alexandre Farnèse, prince de Parme, gouverneur-général des Pays-Bas, 1545–1592* (5 vols., Brussels, 1933–7). Details on Farnese's finances come from R. Romani, *Le corti farnesiane di Parma e Piacenza, 1545–1622*, I (Rome, 1978). On English policy towards the Netherlands, north and south, see R. B. Wernham, *The Making of Elizabethan Foreign Policy, 1558–1603* (Berkeley, 1980); idem, *Before the Armada: the growth of English foreign policy, 1485–1588* (London, 1966); and C. Wilson, *Queen Elizabeth and the Revolt of the Netherlands* (London, 1970). On the intervention of France, see M. P. Holt, *The Duke of Anjou and the Politique Struggle During the Wars of Religion* (Cambridge, 1986), chapter 5.

Details on the collapse of public authority in the Dutch Republic immediately after the death of Orange may be found in A. van der Woude, 'De crisis in de Opstand na de val van Antwerpen', *Bijdragen voor de Geschiedenis der Nederlanden*, XIV (1959–60), 38–57 and 81–104; and C. C. Hibben, *Gouda in Revolt: particularism and pacifism in the revolt of the Netherlands, 1572–1588* (Utrecht, 1983), chapter 7.

Notes

1. Quotations from O. Feltham, *A Brief Character of the Low Countries* (London, 1652), I, 5.

2. Two quotations from Don Luis de Requeséns in Parker, *Spain and the Netherlands*, 48f.

3. *CSPF*, XXI, part 4, 171: R. Spencer to Burghley, 15 March 1588.

4. Lincoln Record Office, *Ancaster Muniments*, vol. X, fo. 1, Lord Willoughby to (?) Cristobal de Mondragón, June 1586.

5. *CSPF 1581–2*, 346: Thomas Stokes to Walsingham, 22 October 1581; and 406: same to same, 28 January 1582.

6. Paolo Rinaldi, one of Parma's household officers, quoted by van der Essen, *Farnèse*, V, 295; Williams, from his *Art of Warre* (1590) by J. X. Evans, *The works of Sir Roger Williams* (Oxford, 1972), 14; Leicester by Brugmans, III, 284–6 (in a letter to Burghley, 15 November 1587 NS).

7. Bibliothèque nationale, Paris, *Ms. Espagnole* 182, fo. 212, Parma to Don Juan de Zúñiga, 16 September 1585; AGS *Secretarías Provinciales* 2534/212, Parma to the king, 30 September 1585; AGS *Estado* 589/120, same to same, 31 December 1585; and *Estado* 590/22–3, same to same, 28 February 1586.

CHAPTER 4
ARMED NEUTRALITY, 1558–80

The best account of the first decade of Elizabeth's reign is to be found in W. MacCaffrey, *The Shaping of the Elizabethan Regime: Elizabethan politics 1558–72* (Princeton, 1968). See also, however, the penetrating analysis of Simon Adams, 'Eliza enthroned? The Court and its politics' in C. Haigh, ed., *The Reign of Elizabeth* (London, 1984), 55–77. Among the many studies of Mary queen of Scots, the works of Gordon Donaldson stand supreme: see in particular *All the Queen's Men: power and politics in Mary Stewart's Scotland* (London, 1983).

Our account of the events of 1568–9, which led to the fateful breach between England and Spain, is based upon Williamson, *Hawkins*, chapters 8–9; K. R. Andrews, *Trade, Plunder and Settlement: maritime enterprise and the genesis of the British Empire, 1480–1630* (Cambridge, 1984), chapter 6; and C. Read, 'Queen Elizabeth's seizure of the duke of Alva's pay-ships', *Journal of Modern History*, V (1933), 443–64. On the delicate international situation of these years, see also the judicious remarks of E. Kouri, *England and the attempts to form a Protestant alliance in the late 1560s: a case study in Elizabethan diplomacy* (Helsinki, 1981: *Annales Academiae Scientiarum Fennicae*, Series B CXX).

Notes

1. See the calls for a Spanish invasion of England in the summer of 1559 by both of Philip II's ambassadors in London: *CSPSp*, I, 51 (Feria) and 84f (Quadra).

2. The letter offering marriage is relatively well-known: *CSPSp*, I, 22f, Philip II to Feria, 10 January 1559. Previously unknown, however, is the king's further holograph and secret letter of the same date. He felt, he told Feria, 'like a condemned man awaiting his fate' and he begged the ambassador to let him know as soon as possible what Elizabeth decided. On 28 January 1559 he again assured Feria that 'If it was not to serve God, believe me, I should not have got into this . . . Nothing would make me do this except the clear knowledge that it would gain the kingdom [of England] for His service and faith.' (Archivo de la Casa de Medinaceli, caja 7 legajo 249, nos. 11–12.)

3. *Loc. cit.*, Philip II to Feria, 21 March 1559. To the best of our knowledge this crucial document on the king's innermost thoughts about the 'English question' has never been used by historians.

4. There are many detailed accounts of the Ridolfi conspiracy from the English side, such as Wernham, *Before the Armada*, chapter 23, and MacCaffrey, *Shaping of the Elizabethan Regime*, chapter 15. But they rarely include material on the involvement of Philip II and Alba, although this is relatively abundant. See, for example, AGS *Estado* 823/150–8, minutes of the crucial debate of the Spanish council of state, 7 July 1571, which fully considered (and approved) Ridolfi's grand plan; Archivo de la Casa de Alba, Madrid, caja 7 fo. 58, the king to Alba, 14 July 1571 (that is, after the council meeting), ordering the duke to invade at once. The naval component is discussed in some detail in AGS *GA* 187/157, Martín de Bertendona to the king, 5 August 1586 (Bertendona had been designated to command the fleet sailing to the North Sea).

5. AGS *Estado* 547/3, the king to Alba, 14 September 1571.

6. The importance of this contemporary sketch (colour plate 22) was first brought to our attention by Dr Tom Glasgow. See also his article, 'Elizabethan ships pictured on Smerwick map, 1580', *MM*, LII (1966), 157–65. Much has been written about the Smerwick campaign, but the best study is the well-documented account of A. O'Rahilly, *The massacre at Smerwick (1580)* (Cork, 1938: Cork historical and archaeological papers I).

CHAPTER 5
COLD WAR, 1581–85

On Dom António see G. K. McBride, 'Elizabethan foreign policy in microcosm: the Portuguese pretender 1580–9', *Albion*, V (1973), 193–210, and P. Durand-Lapié, 'Un roi détrôné réfugié en France: Dom Antoine Ier de Portugal (1580–95), *Revue d'histoire diplomatique*, XVIII (1904), 133–45, 275–307, 612–40,

and XIX (1905), 113–28 and 243–60. The struggle for the Azores in 1581–3 is well covered by Tenison, IV, 175–213; R. B. Merriman, *The Rise of the Spanish Empire in the Old World and the New: vol. IV Philip the Prudent* (London, 1934), 390–7; and C. Fernández Duro, *La conquista de las Azores en 1583* (Madrid, 1866) – on the disastrous Valdés expedition of 1581 see pp. 11–17: Philip II had Valdés court-martialled and imprisoned for insubordination. Details on the much-disputed English participation may be found in Andrews, *Elizabethan Privateering*, 202f. The significance of the São Miguel battle for the evolution of naval tactics was first made clear by D. W. Waters, *The Elizabethan Navy and the Armada of Spain* (Greenwich, 1975: National Maritime Museum Monographs, XVII).

Notes

1. Quotations from J. F. Guilmartin, *Gunpowder and Galleys: changing technology and Mediterranean warfare in the sixteenth century* (Cambridge, 1974), 216f (Santa Cruz); and BNP *Fonds Français* 16,108 fos.365 and 425–7, Ambassador St Gouard to Catherine de Medici, 20 August, and to Henry III, 7 October 1582.

2. Quotations from C. Read, *Mr Secretary Walsingham and the Policy of Queen Elizabeth*, III (Oxford, 1925), 75. News of the treaty of Joinville reached Ambassador Stafford on 29 March 1585 NS (*CSPF*, XIX, 361f). The formation and early history of the *Ligue* has recently been retold by P. Chevallier, *Henri III: roi shakespearien* (Paris, 1985), 559ff; and J. M. Constant, *Les Guise* (Paris, 1984), chapter 7.

3. Quotations from W. T. MacCaffrey, *Queen Elizabeth and the Making of Policy, 1572–88* (Princeton, 1981), 338f, citing Camden's *Annals*. The memoranda of the Council meetings in October 1584 are worth consulting *in extenso*: see *CSPF* XIX, 95–8, and *HMC Salisbury*, III, 67–70. See also Burghley's formulation in a memorandum to the queen at this time: 'If he [Philip II] once reduce the Low Countries to absolute subjection, I know not what limits any man of judgement can set unto his greatness' (W. Scott, ed., *The Somers Collection of Tracts*, I [London, 1809], 164–70).

4. BL *Harleian Ms.*, 168/102–5, 'A consultacion . . . touchinge an aide to be sent in to Hollande againste the king of Spaine' (28 March 1585 NS).

5. Sir Walter Raleigh, quoted by H. P. Kraus, *Sir Francis Drake: a pictorial biography* (Amsterdam, 1970), 18. Burghley's doubts about the breach with Spain are in *CSPF*, XIX, 705, 'Certain things to be considered' (23 July 1585). See 'A declaration of the causes moving the queen of England to give aid to the defence of the Lowe Countries' (October 1585) in Scott, *Somers Tracts*, I, 410–19. Writing in 1593, Sir Richard Hawkins (son of John) argued that 'Spaine broke the peace with England, and not England with Spaine' through the embargo; but few were convinced: see C. R. Markham, ed., *The Hawkins Voyages* (London, 1878: Hakluyt Society, LVII), 318.

CHAPTER 6
THE GRAND DESIGN AND ITS ARCHITECT

The early part of this chapter is based upon G. Parker, *Philip II* (Boston, 1978), and J. M. Estal, 'Felipe II y su archivo hagiográfico de El Escorial', *Hispania sacra*, XXIII (1970), 193–333, based on the 'Libros de entrega' of relics donated to the monastery by Philip II and his son.

The genesis of the masterplan for the Enterprise of England is extremely difficult to pin-point. The king asked Parma for a strategic appraisal on 29 December 1585 (AGS *Estado* 589/15). It would seem that Santa Cruz was only asked for his opinion on 24 January 1586, and even then only in response to an unsolicited letter from the marquis to the king, dated 13 January, arguing that Drake's raid and Nonsuch amply justified an outright attack on England. See the documents in Oria, VII–IX. His reply was dated 22 March (Duro, I, 250ff) and no doubt arrived shortly afterwards. But Parma's reply only came in on 20 June (see note 14 below).

For Philip's system of government at this time see, for Portugal, F. Caeiro, *O archiduque Alberto de Austria, vice-rei e inquisidor-mor de Portugal* (Lisbon, 1961); and, for Castile, I. A. A. Thompson, 'The Armada and administrative reform: the Spanish Council of War in the reign of Philip II', *EHR*, LXXXII (1967), 698–725.

Notes

1. Details from Estal, 'Felipe II', 207–9.

2. IVdeDJ, 51/105, Vázquez to the king, and reply, 22 August 1583.

3. AGS *Estado* 594/5, the king to Parma, 4 September 1587; repeated in *Estado* 2218/152, the king to Parma, 14 September 1587; cfr. Oria, 37, royal Instruction of 14 September 1587.

4. Quotations from Maura, 278 f; IVde DJ 51/1, Vázquez to the king, and reply, 8 February 1591; and IVdeDJ 45/452, same to same, 5 February.

5. Quotations from IVdeDJ 53 carpeta 5 fo. 15, the king to Vázquez, 27 January 1576; and Maura, 38, the king to Medina Sidonia, 29 October 1578.

6. At least three documents associated with this early phase of the 'Enterprise of England' have survived, entitled 'Razones que tratan de algunas cosas tocante al gran negocio de Inglaterra'. They are discussed in Lyell, 14–25. We cannot, however, accept Lyell's argument that the documents date from 1586–7: (a) they must have been written before July 1584 because William of Orange is spoken of as still alive; and (b) Parma later mentioned having sent them in November 1583 (AGS *Estado* 590/125, to the king, 20 April 1586).

7. AGS *Estado* 2217/75 the king to Parma, 12 September 1583; and *Estado* 586/182, Parma's reply, 30 November 1583.

8. AGS *Estado* 946/43, Olivares to the king, 4 June 1585.

9. AGS *Estado* 946 fos. 85–8, Olivares to the king, 13 July 1585 (about the 'empresa de Ginebra'); 103f, same to same, 28 July; and 229, the king to Olivares, 22 August 1585.

10. The documentation is complex. ASF *Mediceo del Principato* 2636/123f, Instruction to Luigi Dovara, 28 February 1585, sent to secure support from Pope Gregory XIII for a Spanish invasion of England. The initiative was thus, in fact, Tuscan; but papal support was the critical element. The election of Sixtus, who was already keen on some 'outstanding enterprise', strengthened Dovara's hand immeasurably. Nevertheless, when in late June 1585 he reached Spain, he was rebuffed by the king and his ministers (cf. his letters to the Grand Duke in ASF *Mediceo* 5022/357–400 and AGS *Estado* 1452/20, the king to the Grand Duke, 27 July 1585).

11. See the report in AGS *GA* 179/87, Licenciado Antolinez to the king, 14 November 1585; one man's reaction in *GA* 176/160, Don Jorge Manrique to the Court, 25 March (1586); and the account of the English themselves of the damage they did in Keeler, *West Indian Voyage*, passim. Carleill's boast is recorded in Andrews, *Drake's Voyages*, 101.

12. AGS *Estado* 946/247–8, the king to the Pope, 24 October

1585; and *Estado* 1452/86, the king to the Grand Duke [24] October 1585.

13. Santa Cruz's patent and instruction as Capitán General del Mar Océano, both dated 23 June 1584, are in AGS *CS* 2a/286, fos. 8–15. His instruction to start preparations for an attack on England was sent with AGS *Estado* 2218/43, Don Juan de Idiáquez to Archduke Albert, 2 April 1586. The ships forming the squadron of Biscay were embargoed between 10 April and 7 May 1586 (AGS *CMC* 2a/1208) and Recalde was appointed to command them on 8 June (AGS *CS* 2a/286 fo. 759). Medina Sidonia's role in raising 6000 troops to sail with Santa Cruz's Armada can be followed in Maura, 145–59. These comings and goings were all noted – and correctly interpreted – by the Venetian ambassador, Gradinegro, in Madrid: *CSPV*, 159f, letter of 1 May 1586.

14. Our account of this complex but critical episode is based on AGS *Estado* 590/117, Parma to the king, 28 February 1586; *Estado* 590 fos. 125, same to same, 20 April 1586; 126, 'Lo que dixó Juan Bautista Piata de palabra a 24 de junio 1586'; and 127, holograph 'Parescer' of Don Juan de Zúñiga (undated, but shortly after 24 June); *Estado* 2218/52, the king to Parma, 18 July 1586; *Estado* 592/135, Parma to the king, 30 October 1586; and 592/32, same to same, 17 January 1587. See also explanation of the strategy to be followed by the Armada, including the preliminary attack on Ireland, given to Medina Sidonia on 28 February 1587 in Maura, 167f.

15. AGS *GA* 187/157, Bertendona to the king, 5 August 1586.

16. Medina Sidonia's memorandum of 25 October 1586 is analysed in Kraus, *Sir Francis Drake*, 129f and 189f; the merchants' views are given in H. Lapèyre, *Une Famille des marchands; les Ruiz* (Paris, 1955), 422–3.

17. On 7 August 1586 the king ordered his Governor of Milan to send Spanish troops to Flanders (*Estado* 1261/87). The towns of Spain were ordered to raise troops on 7 October 1586 (see list in AGS *GA* 189/119 and replies fos. 120–68). While the viceroys of Naples and Sicily were ordered to dispatch galleasses, artillery and troops 'to chase the pirates from the coasts of Portugal and make safe the seas around us' on 12 November (*Estado* 1088/210–12).

CHAPTER 7
PHONEY WAR

There is no satisfactory overview of Philip II's foreign policy during the 1580s. The story must therefore be pieced together from isolated fragments. For France, see Nicholas Poulain's report in M. L. Cimber and F. Danjou, eds., *Archives curieuses de l'histoire de la France*, 1ère série XI (Paris, 1836), 289–323; E. H. Dickerman, 'A neglected aspect of the Spanish Armada: the Catholic League's Picardy offensive of 1587', *Canadian Journal of History*, XI (1976), 19–23 and J. de Lamar Jensen, 'Franco-Spanish diplomacy and the Armada' in C. H. Carter, ed., *From the Renaissance to the Counter-Reformation: essays in honour of Garrett Mattingly* (London, 1965), 205–29. For the Spanish army diverted into Lorraine, see the report in AGS *Estado* 592/127, Havré to Parma, 10 September 1587; the subsidy payments to the League are given in AGS *CMC* 2a/23, 'Cuenta of Gabriel de Alegría'. For the diplomatic contest in Istanbul, see E. A. Pears, 'The Spanish Armada and the Ottoman Porte', *EHR*, VII (1893), 439–66; H. G. Rawlinson, 'The Embassy of William Harborne to Constantinople, 1583–88', *Transactions of the Royal Historical Society*, 4th series V (1922), 1–27; and S. A.

Skilliter, 'The Hispano-Ottoman armistice of 1581' in C. E. Bosworth, ed., *Iran and Islam* (Edinburgh, 1971), 491–515.

On the plots against the queen of England, Read, *Walsingham*, III, chapters 12–14, still stand as the definitive account. The foreign reaction to Mary's execution is described in P. Deyon, 'Sur certaines formes de la propagande religieuse au XVIe siècle', *Annales*, XXXVI (1981), 16–25, at p. 20; and *CSPF*, XXI part 1, 227, 229.

On Philip II and the Stuart claim, see J. de Lamar Jensen, 'The phantom Will of Mary Queen of Scots', *Scotia*, IV (1980), 1–15; which supersedes J. D. Mackie, 'Scotland and the Spanish Armada', *Scottish Historical Review*, XII (1914–15), 1–23. See also D. Masson, ed., *Register of the Privy Council of Scotland*, IV (Edinburgh, 1881), 227–316.

Notes

1. See the fears of the Knights of Malta, who had been on 'red alert' against a Turkish threat throughout the spring of 1588, in AGS *Estado* 1089/288, Grand Master to the king, 16 June 1588.

2. A. Heredía Herrera, ed., *Catálogo de las consultas del consejo de Indias*, I (Madrid, 1972), 597, the king's apostil to a consulta dated 3 September 1586; J. H. da Cunha Riva, ed., *Arquivo Português Oriental*, III (Nova Goa, 1861), 130f and 146, Philip II to viceroy of India, 23 February and 14 March 1588.

3. The Grand Duke of Tuscany, when he first raised the idea of an 'Enterprise' early in February 1585, estimated that the cost to the king (above his normal expenses) would be 3.25 million ducats (ASF, *Mediceo* 2636/124, Instruction to Dovara). The figure of seven million (2 million for the fleet and the rest for the Army of Flanders) was given two years later by a special committee (IVdeDJ 101/99–104, papers dated 31 January – 5 February 1587). In the end it was reckoned by the fleet's High Command that the Armada cost 60,000 ducats a day (see the interrogation of Don Diego Pimentel, discussed in note 5 to chapter 10 below).

4. AGS *Estado* 947 fos. 15, Olivares to the king, 24 February 1586; 111, same to same, 29 August 1586; and 113, same to same, 9 September 1586.

5. AGS *Estado* 947/115f, the king to Olivares, 18–19 November 1586; and *Estado* 949/86, declaration of G. A. Pinelli and G. Gentili, 29 July 1587. The treaty is printed in A. O. Meyer, *England and the Catholic Church under Queen Elizabeth* (London, 1916), 520–3, from the copy in the Vatican archives. The majority of the correspondence in *Estado* 946–949 concerns the 'Empresa', and many letters bear lengthy comments or corrections by the king.

6. *CSPF*, XXI, part 3, 448f: Count Maurice to Walsingham, 9 December 1587, with a transcript of the interrogation. There is some doubt about when the king's 'cover' was really blown. As early as 28 February 1586, Parma complained to the king that the 'Enterprise' was being openly talked about in Madrid, Rome and Venice (*Estado* 590/117); and there was some truth to this. The Venetian ambassador in Rome had certainly heard about the king's offer to invade England on 4 January 1586 (*CSPV*, 128); while the Venetian ambassador in Madrid was able to send his government details of Santa Cruz's plan on 22 March (*ibid.*, 147–9). But that does not mean that other states received a credible account; or that, receiving, they believed. As late as 15 November 1587, in a letter filled with details about Parma's preparations, the earl of Leicester still had no idea about their objective (Brugmans, 284–6); while on 6 May 1588, as the Armada prepared to weigh anchor, the French ambassador in

Madrid still thought it was bound for Zeeland (BNP *Fonds français* 16, 110/257, M. de Longlée to Henry III).

7. Details in *CSPF*, XIX, 671–3 (mission of Sir John Smyth to Parma); and XXI part 4, 145 ff ('Compendium' of Andrés de Loo).

8. Details from the records in AGS *CS* 2a/280 for each ship hired for the Armada. On the *Caridad Inglesa* and the *San Andrés Escocés*, see also *GA* 203/123–4. There has been much controversy surrounding the number of Ragusan vessels in the Armada: see J. de Courcy Ireland, 'Ragusa and the Spanish Armada of 1588', *MM*, LXIV (1978), 251–62, who argued for perhaps eight Ragusan argosies in the Grand Fleet; and V. Kostić, 'Ragusa and the Spanish Armada', in R. Filipović and M. Partridge, eds., *Ragusa's Relations with England: a symposium* (Zagreb, 1977), 47–61, who argued for three or four. Individual ship files in *CMC* 2a/1208 suggest that there were four: the *Anunciata*, *San Nicolás Prodaneli*, *San Juan de Sicilia*, and *Santa María de Montemayor*. Only the last survived the campaign.

9. For the costs of Drake's raid, see the list in AGS *GA* 197/182 – which gives the names of 16 ships burnt and 6 taken. See also H. and P. Chaunu, *Séville et l'Atlantique, 1504–1650*, III (Paris, 1955), 400f, for more details. The best account of Spain's counter-measures is given by Maura, chapter 10. The shore batteries and their damage to the *Lion* are shown in William Borough's chart of Cadiz bay; PRO MPF 318, our colour plate 35. For the impact of the raid on public opinion, see P. Roiz Soares, *Memorial* (ed. M. Lopes de Almeida, Coimbra, 1953), 238; and *CSPV*, 295, Lippomani on 16 July 1587.

10. See AGS *Estado* K 1566/86, *Avisos de Roan*, 7 April 1587, and *CSPV*, 273–300. The date of Santa Cruz's departure is given in Roiz Soares, *Memorial*, 239.

CHAPTER 8
THE ARMADA TAKES SHAPE

Ill luck has dogged the archives of the two Captains General of the Ocean Sea. Virtually no papers concerning Santa Cruz's tenure of the office seem to have survived: AGS *Secretarías provinciales* 1579, which is his Order Book for 1580–7, contains little of interest, and few copies of his correspondence with the fleet have been found. The duke of Medina Sidonia's papers for 1587–8 have also suffered grievous loss. A slim volume of his letters from the Armada campaign was separated from the Medina Sidonia archive in the 1840s, and was acquired (more than a century later) by the National Maritime Museum at Greenwich, England (see A. N. L. Munby, *Phillipps Studies*, V (Cambridge, 1960), 109; and a translation of the documents in Waters, *Elizabethan Navy*, 53–67). Then, some time this century, a much larger collection of Medina Sidonia correspondence was acquired by the New York collector H. P. Kraus. It includes most of the seventh duke's correspondence with the king for 1587–8, as well as his administrative papers as Captain General of the coast of Andalusia. In 1986 a small part of this collection, consisting mostly of patents and autograph letters by celebrities, was purchased by the Biblioteca Bartolomé March in Madrid. The rest remains in the hands of Mr Kraus, and is not available for scholarly research under any circumstances. Fortunately, however, the text of many of the royal letters owned by Mr Kraus may be read in Maura, *Designio*.

There are two excellent articles concerning the duke's appointment: P. O. Pierson, 'A commander for the Armada', *MM*, LV (1969), 383–400; and I. A. A. Thompson, 'The appointment of the duke of Medina Sidonia to the command of the Spanish Armada', *Historical Journal*, XII (1969), 197–216.

The papers concerning the duke of Parma's preparations have been rather better preserved. See van der Essen, *Farnèse*, V; and the series of articles published by H. O'Donnell y Duque de Estrada in *Revista de historia naval*, I (1983) – V (1987). On Parma's fleet of barges, see the material in W. F. Tilton, *Die Katastrophe der spanischen Armada* (Freiburg, 1894), 145ff; F. Riaño Lozano, 'Antecedentes sobre los medios navales de Farnesio', *Revista de historia naval*, II, no. 5 (1984), 115–43; and the documents cited in note 25 below.

On the condition of the Dutch, see J. L. Motley, *A History of the United Netherlands*, I and II (London, 1869); and R. J. Fruin, *Verspreide Geschriften*, III (The Hague, 1900), 118–224. However the best account by far remains the (unfortunately) unpublished dissertation of F. G. Oosterhoff, 'The earl of Leicester's governorship of the Netherlands, 1586–87' (University of London Ph.D. thesis, 1967).

There is no satisfactory account of the talks at Bourbourg. The English perspective is covered by C. Read, *Lord Burghley and Queen Elizabeth* (New York, 1960), 396–407, but see also the 'Diarie' of the English embassy in BL *Sloane Ms.* 262/41–86. For Parma's policy, see the correspondence of the Spanish commissioners in Haus- Hof- und Staatsarchiv, Vienna, *Belgien* P.C. 43/1–77, and the letters to the king calendared in *LCP*. For the Dutch reaction, see Japikse, V, 501f, 534f, 565–7, 571f, and VI, 56ff.

Notes

1. AGS *Estado* 590/125, Parma to the king, 20 April 1586; *Estado* 2218/70, the king to Parma, 18 September 1586, about the papal 'estoque y capelo'; *Estado* 592/135, Parma to the king, 30 October 1586; *Estado* 2218/80, the king to Parma, 17 December 1586 (draft and royal apostil). It should be remembered that Parma ceaselessly complained to the king that there was never enough money available for his army.

2. *Estado* 592/32 Parma to the king, 17 June 1587.

3. *Estado* 2218/92–3, the king to Parma, 28 February 1587. This was not the first time that the king had drawn attention to the lack of a deep-water port under Spanish control in the Netherlands. See *Estado* 589/15, the king to Parma, minute, 29 December 1585: 'And because of this [lack] it would be most useful to have some port there, something like Enkhuisen, facing Friesland, because nothing can be done without a port'. But his plan still included a pre-emptive strike on Ireland: see Maura, 167–8, Don Juan de Idiáquez to Medina Sidonia, 28 February 1587. The first paragraph makes clear that the secretary is commanded to reveal the king's secret intention, which is to get the English out of Holland and the Indies by 'putting the torch to their own house'. And 'since this cannot be achieved on the [English] mainland at the first stroke, we might start with Ireland, which we could use either as a pledge to exchange for the places they hold in the Low Countries . . . or as a springboard for a second strike against England'.

4. Maura, 163–74, Medina Sidonia to Idiáquez, 22 February 1587; Idiáquez's reply 28 February; Medina Sidonia again, 5 March; and Duro, I, document 26, the king to Medina Sidonia, 3 June 1587.

5. BL *Additional Ms.* 28,700 fos. 147, 151, 155 and 156, Vázquez to the king, 6, 7, 9 and 14 February 1587.

6. BL *Additional Ms.* 28,363 fos. 88, Juan Ruiz de Velasco to Vázquez, 26 May 1587; 112, Vázquez to Ruiz, 14 June and reply dated 30; and 116f, Ruiz to Vázquez, 20 June. The king began to

transact business again 1 July and got out of bed for the first time two days later (fo. 128).

7. BL *Additional Ms.* 28,376/336, Prada to Idiáquez, 17 May 1587. Some very similar observations about the king's tendency to run a one-man-ship were made at this time by the Venetian ambassador in Madrid: *CSPV*, 236f, Lippomani, 12 January 1587.

8. AGS *GA* 209 fos. 6–7 (consulta of 23 June 1587), 66 (same, 3 July) and 76 (same, 13 July). See also the notes of decisions taken: fos. 67 (29 June) and 78 (13 July). It seems to us that these consultas mark a new departure for the Council, for they deal with matters of military policy rather than (as previously) military administration. But it is nevertheless apparent that the councillors were not privy to the details of the Grand Design. They may, like several ambassadors, have heard vague rumours, but their opinions recorded in council show that they knew nothing for certain.

9. Details from Roiz Soares, *Memorial*, 240. On 5 September, Leiva told the king that 'his' fleet was all ready to leave Lisbon: *GA* 201/125.

10. *GA* 209/166, consulta of 3 July 1587. See also the pessimistic view of Prior Don Hernando de Toledo, reported by the Venetian ambassador on 5 August; *CSPV*, 302.

11. Confusion still surrounds the Armada's real destination. 'El cabo de Margat' appears in the king's instructions to both Parma and Santa Cruz in September 1587, and we would suggest that the choice of that precise location was made on the basis of Lucas Waghenaer's *Mariner's Mirror* (Latin edition 1586), which clearly showed Margate roads as the only safe anchorage at the mouth of the Thames. The fact that the map shown (colour plate 43) is a manuscript Portuguese copy of Waghenaer which almost certainly carried by an Armada ship strongly supports our interpretation. But in the event, the fleet made for Calais, not Margate Head. Why? The decision, which has attracted very little attention from historians, was apparently made on 30 July, when Medina Sidonia discovered that the bulk of the English fleet was at Plymouth and not (as he had anticipated) in the Narrow Seas. See the convincing reconstruction in Tilton, *Die Katastrophe*, 12–14.

12. AGS *Estado* 594/5, the king to Parma, 4 September 1587, draft. It is clear that this document was conceived and prepared at the same time as the parallel instruction for Santa Cruz dated 10 days later (printed in Oria, 33–7), because a particular phrase was recast by the king who added 'para lo de Portugal fue muy bien como está aquí'. [This phrasing would be fine for the one for Portugal.]

13. AGS *Estado* 2218 fos. 152, 157, 174, and 178, the king to Parma, 14 and 30 September, and 11 and 24 December 1587.

14. AGS *Estado* 594/6–7, Parma to the king, 31 January 1588. The king came close to an apology over this, however: see *Estado* 221/42, the king to Parma, 6 March 1588, claiming that he had only meant to authorise Parma to 'go it alone' should the opportunity present itself.

15. BL *Additional Ms.* 28,363 fos. 175–9v, Vázquez to Juan Ruiz de Velasco and reply, 16–20 January 1588; but fo. 188, dated 12 February 1588, reported that the king was still under doctor's orders. An instruction to Fuentes, which includes the possibility of dismissing Santa Cruz, is at AGS *Estado* 165/35.

16. Juan de Acuña Vela to the king, 17 and 24 October 1587, pointing out the need for new field carriages and the difficulties of constructing them, AGS *GA* 202/129 and 131. Problems of embarking the siege train are chronicled in AGS *GA* 219/32 (2 January 1588), 219/36 (30 January), and 220/7 (3 February).

17. The troop losses are noted in AGS *Estado* 431/fos. 124–6, Fuentes to the king, 13 February 1588; and 134, muster of 20 January.

18. Roiz Soares, *Memorial*, 245.

19. The duke's role in preparing the *flotas* is evident from the numerous letters he exchanged every year with the Casa de la Contratación at Seville; see, for example, AGI *Contratación* 5108 (for 1586–7) or *Indiferente General* 2661 (for 1586).

20. See the king's praise in Maura, 208, 214. Gabriel de Zayas, a veteran minister, suggested that the duke should be brought in to run the whole government ('si mi voto valiesse algo, mañana la dará la presidencia de Indias con el consejo de Estado') – BL *Additional Ms.* 28,363/50, Zayas to Vázquez, 10 May 1587. The praise of Ambassador Lippomano may be found in *CSPV*, 273ff. There was, however, one howl of rage: the Admiral of Castile thought Medina Sidonia was no better qualified than he was, and told the king so (AGS *Estado* 165/212, letter of 23 February 1588).

21. We have not located the letter of 18 February, but its contents may be deduced from the reply written by Idiáquez and Moura four days later: see Oria, 152. For the king's sickness see HS 143 fos. 12f (23 January 1588), 29 (27 February), 41 (8 March), and 46 (16 March).

22. AGS CMC 2a/23 'Cuenta de Gabriel de Alegría', entry for 29 April 1588, at Soissons.

23. The speculation that the king had intended the League to force Henry III to hand over a port like Boulogne for the Armada's use is taken from Constant, *Les Guise*, 164f. Certainly the duke of Aumâle and the Catholics laid siege to the town in the spring of 1588.

24. Dutch strength by land taken from *CSPF*, XXI part 3, 14f; and by sea from Algemeen Rijksarchief, The Hague, *Staten-General* 12561.3 fos. 1–2, and P. Bor, *Oorspronck, begin ende vervolgh der Nederlantsche Oorloghen*, III part 2 (Amsterdam, 1625), book 25 fos. 6f.

25. Details (including the quotation) assembled from the reports of English spies, most of them associated with the Bourbourg talks, in *CSPF*, XXI part 4, 14f, 208, 483f, 511 and 523; XXII, 228; Brugmans, III, 284–6, Leicester to Burghley, 15 November 1587 NS (noting that, *inter alia*, Parma had accumulated 7000 pairs of wading boots); and the accounts of the Paymaster of the 'Armada de los estados de Flandes', Thorivio Martínez, preserved in fragmentary form in AGS CMC 2a/1077, 3a/692 and 3a/713.

26. AGS *Estado* 592/147–9, Parma to the king, 21 December 1587, and 594/6–7, same to same, 31 January 1588, about the small boats. About the Scots see *Estado* 592 fos. 49, same to same, 22 March 1587, and 73, 28 April 1587, and *Estado* K 1566/100, Parma to Mendoza, 13 April; K 1566/128, Mendoza to the king, 20 May 1587; and K 1565/60, Robert Bruce to Don Bernardino de Mendoza, 2 October 1587.

27. Bertendona to the king, 15 February 1588; the nuncio quoted by G. Mattingly, *The Defeat of the Spanish Armada* (London, 1959), 202f. Mattingly thought it might have been Recalde; but we believe the parallel remarks of Bertendona make him a more likely source.

28. Bobadilla to Idiáquez, 20 August 1588, Lyell Papers, quoted by M. Lewis, *Armada guns* (London, 1961), 183. For the decision to raise the shot quota to 50 per gun see Medina Sidonia to the king, 15 March 1588, AGS GA 222/12 and 26.

29. AGS GA 223/24, Acuña Vela to the king, 10 April 1588, about the production of utility ordnance without the royal arms. For regulations regarding the application of arms to artillery see

AGS GA 206/295 same to same, 8 June 1587. Details of the Lisbon foundries, and the extreme production pressures of early 1588, are noted in AGS GA 220/15, Acuña Vela to the king, 25 February 1588; AGS GA 222/53, same to same 12 March 1588; AGS GA 222/22, Fuentes to the king, 12 March 1588.

30. The printed *Derrotero*, which contained excellent information on tides as well as coasts, was published by Oria, 155–180. The maps are noted in AGS CS 2a/283, payment to Ciprián Sánchez; *Estado* 2851, unfol., Idiáquez to Santa Cruz, 25 September 1587; and A. Cortesão and A. Teixeira de Mota, *Portugaliae monumenta cartographia*, III (Lisbon, 1960), plate 367 and pp. 81f. There were also excellent pilots aboard the Armada. The one on the *Rosario* was said by the English to be 'as perfect in our coasts as if he had been native born' (Laughton, II, 186). All the Armada lacked, in navigational terms, were charts of the west coast of Ireland.

31. AGS GA 204/160, *Relación* of 27 December 1587; *Estado* 431/134, *Relación* of 20 February 1588; and the 'Lisbon Muster'.

CHAPTER 9
THE ADVANCE TO CALAIS

The major official source for the voyage of the Armada is Medina Sidonia's *Diario* printed in Oria, 233–48 (which is a better transcription than Duro). There is an admirable English translation, juxtaposed with Howard's 'Relation of proceedings', in W. L. Clowes, *The Royal Navy: a history*, I (London, 1898), 564–82. Duro also included a large number of 'Relations' by others on the Spanish side, and Laughton did the same for the English. Nevertheless there are some gaps. Most accounts are either silent or superficial concerning the fighting on 3 August (or 24 July OS) 1588. Our details come from Duro, II, 384–6 – account of captain Vanegas. They are also almost silent about the fighting on the following day after the escape of the *Triumph*. The fortunate exception is the 'relation' of an anonymous officer from Seville aboard an Andalusian ship: Duro, II, 275–6.

There is also confusion concerning the inspiration for the Armada's famous crescent-shaped battle plan, described in Medina Sidonia's letter to the king dated 28 May 1588 (Duro, II, 101–5). Where did he get this idea? There are two obvious precedents. On the one hand, this was the traditional formation for galleys in battle, from the battle of Salamis in 480 BC (where Herodotus describes the Athenian fleet as attacking in a semi-circle) to Lepanto in AD 1571 (page 31). On the other, the Indies *flotas* also normally sailed with a centre of transports and two 'wings' of warships. Most historians, starting with Pigafetta in 1588, have considered only the Mediterranean parallel but, given Medina Sidonia's earlier experience with the *flotas*, and the acknowledged purpose of the Armada, it seems just as likely that he adopted the tactical formation whose worth had already been amply proved by the armed convoys on the Americas run. We are grateful to Professors Richard E. Mitchell and Peter O. Pierson for shedding much light on this problem.

Finally, there is also considerable uncertainty about the actual size of the fleet which Medina Sidonia led against England. The Lisbon muster of 9 May listed 130 ships, but there had been several changes since then. A list of ships dated 13 July 1588 noted that the hulk *David* was too badly damaged to sail further, and that the zabra *Concepción* had already sailed to Flanders (with Captain Moresin) and another hulk, the hospital ship *Casa de Paz Grande* also stayed at Corunna. That brought the total down to 127, but this was compensated by the addition of 9 caravels to reinforce the communications squadron, and 6 oared *faluas* which had been hired at Lisbon as ship's tenders (details in AGS CS 2a/280 fos. 3082–3129). If all the caravels sailed with the rest of the fleet on 21 July, the duke would have commanded 136 vessels. Ten days later, without the galleys and the *Santa Ana* of Recalde, there would therefore have been 131. But since few of the caravels are mentioned by later sources, it may well be that some (or all) of them stayed behind. Perhaps it is best to retain the traditional figure of 125 ships for the strength of the Armada when it entered the Channel. The size of the English fleet that opposed them was reliably established by Laughton, II, 323–42.

Notes

1. See AGS *Estado* 2855, unfoliated, 'Lo que resolvió el Consejo en materia de Inglaterra', 20 January 1588; Oria, 148f, Idiáquez to Medina Sidonia, 20 February 1588; and Maura, 167, same to same, 28 February 1587 ('aquella gomia que consume el dinero y gente de Espana').

2. Quotations from *CSPSp*, IV, 245–50, which is an almost integral translation of AGS *Estado* 165/104–14 (but note that, on p. 245, 'my nephew' is the Archduke Albert, not Parma). The Instructions for Medina Sidonia were in fact a slightly amended version of those prepared for Santa Cruz in late January, but never sent; AGS *Estado* 165/29, *Instrucción*, and *Estado* 594/4, 'Lo que su magestad es servido que el Señor Cardenal Archiduque diga' (there is an English translation of some of these documents in Waters, *Elizabethan Navy*, 55ff).

3. The king to Medina Sidonia, 5 July 1588, replying to the latter's complaints about the laggardly sailing qualities of the Mediterranean merchantmen and the hulks, Duro, II, 150–4. For a discussion on the construction of the Mediterranean grain ships, which made them excellent bulk carriers but poor warships, see Colin Martin, '*La Trinidad Valencera*: an Armada invasion transport lost off Donegal', *International Journal of Nautical Archaeology* VIII. 1 (1979), 8.1:13–38.

4. AGS CS 2a/278 fo. 617 'Relación de los bastimientos podridos' thrown into the sea, 30 June 1588; CMC 2a/772, unfoliated, printed ration orders of the duke, 9 July 1588.

5. The king's further bout of ill-health is recorded in HS 143 fos. 97 (the king to Mateo Vázquez, 18 June 1588), and 111 (28 June). On re-stepping the Santa María's mast, see Duro, II, 169f, Recalde to the king, 11 July 1588. See also the praise of Oquendo to the king, 15 July, in Oria, 248; and Duro, II, 175, Medina Sidonia to the king, 11 July.

6. AGS GA 225/55–6, Valdés to the king, 15 and 19 July 1588.

7. Houghton Library, Harvard, *fMs. Span* 54; letter from Fray Bernardo de Góngora to Fray Martín de Los Angeles, 15 August 1588. Medina Sidonia's *Diario* gives broadly the same story. Nevertheless several observers, both at the time and afterwards, felt that it was a mistake to abandon the Rosario. Don Juan de Cardona, for example, writing to the king on 20 November 1588, saw this as 'the origin and cause' of all later disasters because, afterwards, the 'rumour went round the fleet that no ship should take any risks; for if a flagship had not received any relief, who would rescue the rest from any danger in which they might place themselves' (Oria, 352f). See similar sentiments in Duro, II, documents 171 and 185.

8. PRO *Exchequer* 133/47/3, 'Drake versus Drake, 1605': depositions of George Hughes, Simon Wood and Evan Owen. Paula Martin is currently preparing a study of the *Rosario*'s fascinating story.

9. All from the *Diario*: see Oria, 236f. On the reorganisation of the fleet's formation, see Medina Sidonia's order to Moncada, dated 2 August 1588: *CSPSp*, IV, 359

10. Mystery surrounds 'the Isle of Wight alternative'. On 30 July Medina Sidonia and his council of war definitely resolved to wait in the eastern Solent, if by the time they arrived there was still no word from Parma; AGS *Estado* 455/492, Medina Sidonia to the king, 30 July 1588 – see the decoded postscript. The king was furious at this departure from his plan, and fired off an immediate (if vain) protest (*Estado* 165/146, the king to Medina, 14 August 1588). But this is the last we hear of the plan. Neither the *Diario* nor any other Spanish account mentions any desire or attempt to force an entrance to the Solent. Although we have inclined to the view that the English attacks forced the Armada to continue on its way – which is undoubtedly what the English intended – it is perfectly possible that Medina Sidonia had already decided not to linger in the area. After all, he had formulated the 'Isle of Wight alternative' before he saw the English fleet in action. It might well be that, once he had experienced the superiority in speed and guns of the queen's ships, Medina realised that nowhere was now safe. If he anchored off Portsmouth, his fleet might be bottled up, and attacked by land as well as by sea (just as the French invasion fleet had been in 1545). But this is pure speculation. We are on firmer ground, however, when we rule out a third possibility: that the Armada was swept involuntarily past Selsey Bill by natural forces. The tides off the Isle of Wight are complex – there is, for example, a double high tide in the Solent – but relatively weak. It is therefore highly unlikely that the tide swept the Armada past its eastern entrance against its will, as many authorities have claimed. The winds over the crucial period, too, were (by general admission) at first absent and then light and from the south. They, too, would hardly have driven the slow-moving fleet irresistibly eastwards. We therefore conclude that the Armada sailed on past Selsey Bill through human, not natural causes: either because the Spaniards took a positive decision to do so, or because English pressure forced them to, or both. We are most grateful to Alan Ereira for an illuminating discussion of these points.

CHAPTER 10
THE BANKS OF FLANDERS

On the problems of distance in the sixteenth century, see the masterly pages of F. Braudel, *The Mediterranean and the Mediterranean World in the age of Philip II*, I (London, 1973), 354–94. The king had foreseen the importance of secure communications between Medina Sidonia and Parma, and had devoted a paragraph to the subject in the Instructions of April 1588. But it blandly stated that it would be possible either for a zabra to sail to Dunkirk, or a pinnace to row to 'some beach in Normandy'. What the king failed to anticipate was both the time that this might take, and the total disruption of the postal system in 1588. On the former, the detailed fate of Medina Sidonia's letters and Parma's replies is given on pages 179–84 above. On the latter, see *CSPV*, 381; AGS *Estado* K 1567/110, Don Bernardino de Mendoza to the king, 20 August 1588; and many others. We are very grateful to Professor W. L. Warren for several insights into this problem.

The principal sources for the events of 6–9 August remain. Duro and Laughton, for the Spanish and English respectively. For Parma and the Army of Flanders, there is an eye-witness account in Vázquez, III, 347–52; for the Dutch, see Bor, *Vervolch*, book 25 fo. 5f; Japikse, VI, 70ff; Brugmans, III, 424–6; and J. B.

van Overeem, 'Justinus van Nassau en de Armada (1588)', *Marineblad*, LIII (1938), 821–31.

Notes

1. Copies of all Medina Sidonia's letters to Parma were sent to the king and are preserved in AGS *Estado* 594/114–22 (eight letters 25 July – 7 August) and *GA* 226/6 (7 August 1588). There is one original – also 7 August – in ASP *Carteggio Farnesiano: Spagna 6*.

2. See details in AGS *Estado* 594/113, Parma to the king, 7 August 1588; and *CSPV*, 382f, Parma letter of 12 August 1588.

3. Considerable confusion surrounds the exact date given by Parma for his estimated departure time. No copy of his letter to Medina Sidonia seems to have survived, but according to Medina's reply of the 7th, it was written on the 3 August (AGS *Estado* 594/122). The account of Fray Gerónimo de la Torre (Duro, II, 402f), notes the attack on Parma's pinnace but merely says its message was that the duke was not yet ready, being at Dunkirk 'seven leagues away, to which we could not go for fear of the sandbanks, and from which he could not come because he was not ready'. Medina Sidonia's *Diario* records the arrival of another messenger, sent by his own secretary at Dunkirk, who asserted that neither Parma's men nor their munitions were yet embarked, 'and that it seemed to him impossible that everything could be done in less than 15 days' (Oria, 242). Exactly the same information was also recorded in an Aviso from Rouen dated 11 August – AGS *Estado K* 1567/102. But both sources were mistaken for, in the event, Parma's entire army was embarked by Tuesday, 10 August. The most ingenious account of Parma's message to Medina was recorded by the Dutch historian, Pieter Bor, writing some 30 years later: Parma said he 'could not come out before Friday', but no one could be sure which Friday he meant! (Bor, *Oorspronck*, book 25 fo. 9v.)

4. AGS *Estado* 693/30, Don Guillén de San Clemente (Spanish ambassador in Vienna) to the king, 13 September 1588, referring to a complaint lodged by the town of Emden.

5. From the pamphlet *Breeder verclaringhe van de vloote van Spaengnien: de bekentnisse van Don Diego Pimentel . . .* (The Hague, 1588: Knuttel pamphlet no. 847. Most of this, which was a transcript of Pimentel's interrogation, was later published in Bor, *Oorspronck*, book 25 fos. 11–11v). There is an important contradiction here. Both Pimentel and Medina Sidonia seemed to be totally convinced that Parma and his army were supposed to attempt a sortie towards them; and yet, in a letter of 21 June 1588, the king clearly warned Medina Sidonia that Parma could not leave port until the Armada had gained local command of the sea (Oria, 202). But the letter was not sent to Corunna where, unknown to the king, Medina had just taken refuge. One wonders if he ever received it?

6. BL *Sloane Ms* 262/62 ('Diarie' of the English commissioners); and Haus-, Hof-, und Staatsarchiv, Vienna, *Belgien PC* 43/1, Spanish delegates to Parma, 6 August 1588. Even the letters written from the fleet on 25 July, announcing its departure from Corunna, only arrived in Flanders on 2 August: see AGS *Estado* 594/113, Parma to the king, 7 August 1588, and ASP *Carteggio Farnesiano 129: Spagna 6*, Don Francisco de Bobadilla to Parma, 25 July 1588, endorsement.

7. AGS *Estado* 455/320–1, Medina to the king, 10 June 1588, copy with royal annotations. The 21 June letter in Oria, 202, was in response to this. Parma's reply to the king is in *Estado* 594/79, dated 22 June 1588.

8. AGS *Estado* 594/107, Parma to the king, 21 July 1588 rehearses what Moresin had been instructed to say to correct Medina's misconceptions; but he never arrived. See AGS *Estado* 165/271, 'Lo que refiere Don Rodrigo de Avilés', and *Estado* 594/105, Parma to the king, 18 July 1588. Parma's letter to the king of 22 June finally got through, but only on 7 August – too late to be of much use (see endorsement on *Estado* 594/79, and also *Estado* 2219/78, the king to Parma, 7 August 1588).

9. Oppenheim, *History*, 163. On the other hand, the accounts were undoubtedly 'padded' – Drake charged £1000 for his 200-ton bark *Thomas* (Devon Record Office, Deposit 346/F588, 'Accompte of sondrye charges'). Four of the eight (the *Barks Talbot*, *Bond* and *Thomas*, and the *Hope*) had been with Drake to the Caribbean in 1585: Keeler, *Drake's West Indian Voyage*, 45f.

10. Apart from Richard Tomson's lively account in Laughton. I, 344–50, there is a fine (though anonymous) description of the stranded galleass and her capture in BL *Sloane Ms.* 262/66v–67v. Also see BNP *Fonds français* 5045/152–6, and AGS *Estado* 693/31, M. de Gourdan's reports to the French government, 10 August 1588. In the end, all the *San Lorenzo*'s guns and stores, along with many of the abandoned anchors, were salvaged and sent to Parma (see AGS *Estado* 594/152; and *CSPF*, XXII, 228). According to the Spanish Ambassador in France, 'The sailors and pilots blame Don Hugo de Moncada for the loss of his galleass, because he did not wish to remove the rudder when they told him to' (AGS *Estado K* 1567/105, Don Bernardino de Mendoza to Don Martín de Idiáquez, 12 August 1588).

11. Duro, II, 405, account of La Torre: AGS *GA* 226/8, Don Jorge Manrique to the king, 19 August 1588. It was claimed that *El Gran Grifón* was also severely damaged by the recoil of her own guns: AGS *CS* 2a/280 fo. 941, Philip II cédula of 5 June 1591 ('maltratada de la mucha artillería con que . . . la armada inglesa la batió, y de la que ella asímismo jugó contra ellas en 7 de agosto').

12. The possibility of surrender is mentioned by La Torre (Duro, II, 407); corroborated by Vanegas (Duro, II, 393) and Don Orduño de Zamuzio (Oria, 325).

13. Duro, II, 407f. According to the other captain, Francisco de Cuellár, it was Bobadilla who condemned them and the duke who pardoned him: see H. Allingham, ed., *Captain Cuellár's Adventures in Connacht and Ulster AD 1588* (London, 1897), 47.

CHAPTER II
ANATOMY OF FAILURE

Our account rests upon two separate bodies of evidence. On the one hand, there are the volumes of accounts for most of the hired ships: AGS *CMS* 2a/942 ('Libro segundo de quentas fenecidas de las naos que sirvieron en la Armada que fue a Inglaterra'); 2a/773 ('Libro tercio'); 2a/460 ('Libro quarto'); 2a/963 ('Libro quinto'); and 2a/905 ('Libro sexto'). Most of the ships hired or embargoed by the crown are represented in these volumes, but there are also further papers in other legajos of the series, as well as in the massive volume (3164 folios) AGS *CS* 2a/280, which includes material on almost every ship in the fleet except for those from the squadrons of Castile and Portugal. Those concerning the former are in AGI *Sección* III legajo 2934; those concerning the latter have not so far been found. A few isolated documents may be found in the 'Proveedor's Book': Pepys Ms. 2269. And then, on the other hand, there is the evidence of the excavated Armada wrecks. See R. Sténuit, *Treasures of the Armada* (Newton Abbot, 1972); C. Martin, *Full Fathom Five: wrecks of the Spanish Armada* (London, 1978); Martin, 'The equipment and fighting potential of the Spanish Armada' (St Andrews University Ph.D. thesis, 1983); and various excavation reports published in the *International Journal of Nautical Archaeology*.

The vexed question of the Armada's guns is also discussed by I. A. A. Thompson, 'Spanish Armada guns', MM LXI (1975), 355–71, which entirely supersedes Lewis, *Armada Guns* and, in consequence, the conclusions of the same author regarding Spanish and English tactics in his *The Spanish Armada* (London, 1960). For technical data on the external and internal ballistics of smooth-bore artillery we have drawn extensively on J. F. Guilmartin, *Gunpowder and Galleys* (Cambridge, 1974). On the construction of Master Remigy's guns, see the comprehensive account of B. Roosens, 'Het Arsenaal van Mechelen en de wapenhandel 1551–1567', *Bijdragen tot de geschiedenis*, LX (1977), 175–247. On the lack of impact of these and other Spanish guns, see the Dockyard Survey of the queen's ships summarised in Laughton, II, 241–54.

Notes

1. The Spaniards and English used quite different formulae for calculating ship tonnages, and neither was intended to give a mathematically exact figure for the displacement or burden of the ship. Such calculations were for administrative purposes only; upon them hire charges or port dues would be assessed: see Colin Martin, 'Spanish Armada tonnages', *MM*, LXIII, 365–7, for a recent discussion. The Armada campaign does, however, provide directly comparable data for one particular ship: an English assessment of the captured *San Salvador*, rated by the Spaniards as 958 tons, puts her at only 600 tons. The latter figure may not, however, take into account a 'war rating' increment – one fifth by the Spanish system, one third by the English. The question must remain open, though it seems likely that the Spanish method tended to give somewhat higher tonnage figures.

2. The details in our text came from AGS CMC 2a/773 (San Francisco and Concepción Menor), and 2a/460 (Santa Bárbara) and 2a/942 (Trinidad Escala).

3. Robert Norton, *The Gunner* (London, 1628), 67–8.

4. A. C. Burnell (ed.), *The Voyage of John Huyghen van Linschoten to the East Indies* (from the English translation of 1598), (London, 1885), II, 268–9. On the question of shipboard gun drills there is almost no explicit contemporary written evidence. Some oblique information may be gleaned from William Bourne, *The arte of shooting in great ordnaunce* (London, 1587) and, on the Spanish side, from Diego García de Palacio's *Instrucción nautica* (Mexico City, 1587; see also the modern translation by J. Bankston, privately published, Bisbee (Arizona), 1986).

CHAPTER 12
'GOD BREATHED'

As in the preceding chapter, material on the wrecks has been freely taken from the work of Robert Sténuit and Colin Martin. The saga of the *San Juan de Sicilia* is narrated by A. McLeay, *The Tobermory Treasure. The true story of a fabulous Armada galleon* (London, 1986). Cuéllar's story is in Duro, II, 45–70, and in English translation by Allingham, *Captain Cuéllar*. The story of Captain Carleill's prisoners is told by D. B. Quinn, 'Spanish Armada prisoners' escape from Ireland', *MM*, LXX (1984), 117f.

The papers of the Spanish government on most of the ships are in AGS *CS* 2a/280 and in the 'libros de quentas fenescidas' of

CMC 2a época. One absentee is the *Santa Ana* of Recalde. Her story, however, can be reconstituted from the correspondence between Parma and the senior officers aboard the ship: see AGS *Estado* 594/130–2 (*Relaciones* of events which include transcripts of key letters) and AGRB *SEG* 11/19v, 29v. On the galleys, which dropped out first, see M. Grácia Rivas, 'El motín de la *Diana*', *Revista de historia naval*, II, no. 4 (1984), 33–45.

There has been an attempt to reconstruct the unusual weather conditions which afflicted the Armada: K. S. Douglas, H. H. Lamb, and C. Loader, *A Meteorological Study of July to October 1588: the Spanish Armada storms* (Norwich, 1978: University of East Anglia Climatic Research Unit publications, VI).

Notes

1. *CSPI*, 49f, prints the only known example of Medina's sailing orders, taken from a wrecked Armada vessel, translated (perhaps inaccurately in parts) and sent on to London. Although it is undated, Calderón states that the orders were issued on 13 August (*CSPSp*, IV, 447). There were probably only 200 horses and mules aboard the fleet – in the *San Gabriel, El Gato* and *Santiago*. More had been on the *David*, which never sailed: AGS *GA* 221/64, *Relación* of 16 February 1588.

2. See W. Voorbeijtel Cannenburg, 'An unknown "pilot" by Hessel Gerritsz, dating from 1612', *Imago mundi*, I (1935), 49–51 – describing three maps specially prepared for the Dutch fleet sent in 1612 to clear the west coast of Ireland of pirates. The Armada needed nothing less.

3. BL *Cotton Ms*. Caligula D.I fos. 292 and 305f, William Asheby to Walsingham, 1 and 18 September 1588 NS (from Edinburgh). Medina also confiscated some of the boats and crews, to replace the patches and sailors he had lost: see AGS *CMC* 2a/1210, unnumbered folio concerning 'Robert Ler, escocés'.

4. The reduced rations are noted in CMC 2a/772, file concerning the *San Francisco*.

5. PRO *State Papers* 63/137/16: examination of B. López del Arbol, Drogheda 23 October 1588 NS.

6. J. S. Brewer and W. Bullen, *Calendar of the Carew manuscripts*, II (London, 1868), 469, Carew to Vice-Chamberlain, 4 August 1588.

7. C. McNeill, 'Report on the Rawlinson collection of manuscripts' in *Analecta hibernica*, I (1930), 95, order to Mr Matthew Smythe, 18 November 1588.

8. See McLeay, *Tobermory Treasure*. The hostages are noted in *CSPI*, 121, Lord Deputy to Council, 21 February 1589 NS.

9. For a complete list of the 158 survivors from the *San Pedro* see PRO SP12/218/14.I. At first the Privy Council ordered all the 123 Spanish nationals to be executed, though they were reprieved almost immediately. The non-Spaniards were then released – 10 French, 10 Dutch, and 2 Italians unconditionally; 13 Portuguese on condition that they enlisted with the forces of Dom António, the Pretender. As far as the Spaniards were concerned, it was decreed that since the ship was wrecked on its way home, and not on its way to invade England, the men were shipwrecked mariners rather than prisoners of war and that responsibility (including payment) for their keep should therefore fall on the local authorities and not on the crown (*Acts of the Privy Council of England* xvi, (London, 1897), 328–9; 347; and 373–4).

10. AGS *GA* 244/257, Patricio Antolinez and Esteban de Lagoretta to the king from Edinburgh, 22 January 1589. See also Gómez de Medina to same, 4 March 1589, AGS *GA* 246/159.

11. AGS *Estado* 596/77, Diego de la Barra to Parma, 2 April 1589, on the 'nave de los casados'; and *CSPI*, xxvii, AGS *Estado* K 1568/119, *Relación*, and AGS *CS* 2a/273, on the Zúñiga.

12. AGS *GA* 228/117, 236/138 and 236/153 on the *San Pedro*; AGS *Estado* 594/130–2, *Relaciones*, and AGRB *SEG* 11/29v, Parma order of 3 September 1588, on the *Santa Ana*.

13. *CSPF*, XXII, 214, Elizabeth agreed to accept a ransom for ordinary prisoners of war on 2 October 1588. Arrangements for their release can be followed in AGS *Estado* 596 fos. 9 and 72, Parma to the king, 13 January and 6 May 1589; and AGRB *SEG* 11/150 and 163v, orders to pay ransoms, 2 and 17 March 1589.

14. Details from M. K. Walsh, '*Destruction by Peace*'. *Hugh O'Neill after Kinsale* (Monaghan, 1986), 140, 370; and idem, 'The anonymous Spaniard of the flight of the earls', *Irish Sword*, III (1957–8), 88f.

CHAPTER 13
VICTORS AND VANQUISHED

The English response to the Armada campaign may be followed in more detail in L. B. Wright, *Middle Class Culture in Elizabethan England* (Chapel Hill, 1935), 422f; the early chapters of R. B. Wernham, *After the Armada: Elizabethan England and the struggle for western Europe, 1588–1595* (Oxford, 1984); Laughton, II; and, above all, Lyell, 168–387. The queen's famous Tilbury speech is given in Tenison, VII, 292, who argued for its authenticity because it was copied down, at Leicester's order, so that soldiers further away from the queen could also enjoy the speech. See also M. Christy, 'Queen Elizabeth's visit to Tilbury in 1588', *EHR*, XXXIV (1919), 43–61. On the Portugal expedition see Andrews, *Drake's Voyages*, chapter 9; Wernham, *Making of Elizabethan Foreign Policy*, 64–9; and idem, 'Queen Elizabeth and the Portugal expedition of 1589', *EHR*, LXVI (1951), 1–26 and 194–218. The Dutch jubilation is described in J. Scheltema, *De uitrusting en ondergang van de onoverwinnelijk vloot van Philips II in 1588* (Haarlem, 1825), 220ff.

The numbing impact upon Spain clearly emerges from T. López Mata, *La ciudad y el castillo de Burgos* (Burgos, n.d.), 198ff; J. de Sigüenza, *Historia de la Orden de San Gerónimo*, III (Madrid, 1605), xvi; and J. de Sepúlveda, 'Historia' in *Documentos para la historia . . . de El Escorial*, IV, 59.

The later history of Don Diego Pimentel was bizarre: on his way back to Spain in 1628 after his tempestuous spell as viceroy of Mexico, he again met the Dutch when Piet Heyn defeated and plundered the fleet on which he sailed. (See J. I. Israel, *Race, Class and Politics in Colonial Mexico, 1610–1670* (Oxford, 1975), 176.) On the later career of Don Balthasar de Zúñiga, see J. H. Elliott, *The Count-Duke of Olivares: the statesman in an age of decline* (New Haven, 1986), chapter 2; and of Howard, see Kenny, *Elizabeth's Admiral*.

Notes

1. BL *Cotton Ms*. Caligula D.I fo. 292, Asheby to Walsingham, 18 September 1588; Laughton, II, 218; and *Calendar of Carew Manuscripts*, II, 470–2, Carew to Walsingham, 28 September 1588 NS, with lists of ships lost. Parma interpreted the total silence concerning the Armada to mean it was in Danish waters, preparing to return: see ASP *Carteggio Farnesiano 129: Spagna 6*, Parma to Medina Sidonia, 15 August 1588; and AGS *Estado* 594/130–2, *Relaciones*. Evidence that the Flanders flotilla was only paid off at the end of August is in AGS *CMC* 2a/1077, accounts of Thorivio Martínez. Parma started to issue exeats for individuals who had arrived for the invasion 'attento a haverse, segun paresce, alargado la occasión de la Jornada', on 12 September (AGRB *SEG* 11 fos. 40, passport for Juan de Anaya Solís, and 46v, to marquis of Favara).

2. BL *Harleian Ms*, 168/180–5, Accounts.

3. [P. le Goux], *Copie d'une lettre envoyé de Dieppe* (Paris, 1588: see Lyell, nos. 95–97); and *Relació de lo que hasta oy a los 5 de septiembre . . . se ha sabido* (Seville, 1588: Lyell, no. 80).

4. AGS *Estado* 2219 fos. 84 and 87, the king to Parma and Medina Sidonia, 31 August 1588.

5. AGS *Estado* 2219/82, Idiáquez to Parma, 31 August 1588; IVdeDJ 51/190, Vázquez to the king, 4 September 1588. The news received was *Estado* K 1567/102, 'Avisos de Roan'. It is interesting to find an extremely cautious tone concerning the Armada adopted in Philip's next letter to Rome; AGS *Estado* 951/97, the king to Olivares, 5 September 1588.

6. AGS *Estado* 594/131–2, *Relaciones*, on Parma's pinnace; BL *Additional Ms*. 28,376/66f, Idiáquez to Prada, 20 September 1588, on emergency measures. There can be no doubt about Zúñiga's late arrival, even though historians have always assumed that he reached Spain long before: see *CSPV*, 394, Lippomano to Doge, 29 September 1588, and AGS *Estado* 165/149, the king to Medina Sidonia, 27 September 1588.

7. AGS *Estado* 455/518ff, Medina to the king, 23 and 27 September 1588; and Oria, 293, same to same, 25 September. The estimate of 5000 miles is in *CSPV*, 396; the cinching of the *San Martín* comes from the *Relación* of La Torre.

8. AGS *GA* 244/47, Francisco Duarte to the king, 11 January 1589; *Estado* 2851, unfol., undated *billete* from Idiáquez and Moura to the king accompanying Recalde's letter, October 1588. The king's anguished – and hitherto unnoticed – plea for an early death is in HS 145/76, to Mateo Vázquez, 10 November 1588. The king added (understandably) 'This is for your eyes alone.'

9. See AGS *Estado* 1089/339 and 1155/223, the king to the viceroys of Naples and Sicily, 23 October 1588, ordering them to send to Spain immediately as much artillery, powder and other munitions, as they could spare.

10. The king's autograph order is at HS 122/120, to the Captain General of Guipúzcoa, 26 December 1588. See also *CSPI*, 121, Report of John Brown of Clontarf, recently escaped from Ribadeo. Mexía's losses are recorded in AGS *GA* 227/113. Likewise, of 4638 soldiers in 40 companies mustered at Lisbon in May 1588, only 3217 were present in November – a loss of almost one-third; and several other companies were lost altogether (calculated from AGS *CS* 2a/276). The rations actually consumed are recorded in AGS *CMC* 2a/29 and 31, Accounts with mutineers of La Chapelle (1596), company of Francisco de Frías.

11. Lyell, chapter 8, gives an excellent account of where the term 'Invincible' originated. *The Copie of a letter* was clearly written by Burghley himself (see the manuscript draft, with corrections in his own hand, in BL *Lansdowne Ms* 103, no. 55, fos. 134–64), and completed before 9 September. The Italian translation was registered with the Stationers' Company on 28 October, and was printed together with a translation of *Certain advertisements out of Ireland* (strictly speaking 'Invincible' appears at the end of the latter). The word was also used in a polemic published by Philip Marnix of Ste Aldegonde, called *The Holy Bull and Crusado of Rome* (London, 1588), whose title-page includes the phrase 'the setting forth of the "invincible army" as they terme it' (though there is absolutely no evidence that 'they' did). (We are grateful to Mr Bertrand T. Whitehead for bibliographical assistance on this point.)

12. AGS *Estado* 2851, unfol., 'Lo que se platicó en el consejo de Estado a 12 de noviembre 1588', and following documents.

13. Lilly Library (Indiana), *Bertendona Ms*. 14 and 21 on a new invasion strategy. It was, of course, Bertendona who eventually sank the *Revenge*.

CHAPTER 14
IF THE ARMADA HAD LANDED

This chapter is based upon G. Parker, 'If the Armada had landed', *History*, LX (1976), 358–68; H. Colvin, *The History of the King's Works*, IV (London, 1982), 415–65 and 602–6; and J. Bruce, *Report on the Arrangements Which Were Made for the Internal Defence of These Kingdoms When Spain, by its Armada, Projected the Invasion and Conquest of England* (London, 1798). Examples of the equipment of the trained bands are taken from HMC. *Fifteenth Report. Appendix, Part V* (London, 1897), 40–2; *CSPD 1580–9*, 485 (order of 30 May 1588); and BL *Harleian Ms* 168/166–74 (Kent had 567 archers and 1172 'shot', but they were said to lack 'powder, match, lead, nagges and carters').

On the English Catholics and their possible support for Parma, see G. Mattingly, 'William Allen and Catholic propaganda in England', *Travaux d'humanisme et renaissance*, XXVIII (1957), 325–39; S. Adams, 'Stanley, York and Elizabeth's Catholics', *History Today*, XXXVII (July, 1987), 46–50; A. J. Loomie, 'The Armadas and the Catholics of England', *Catholic Historical Review*, LIX (1973), 385–403; and C. Z. Wiener, 'The beleaguered isle: a study of Elizabethan and early Jacobean anti-Catholicism', *Past and Present*, LI (1971), 27–62. On the survival of Catholic practices, in the hope that they might again come into fashion, see Haigh, *Reign of Elizabeth*, 197f.

Notes

1. AGS *Estado* 455/602f, Bobadilla to Don Juan de Idiáquez, 20 August 1588. This fascinating document was printed, while it was in the Cabra archive, by F. Belda y Pérez de Nueros, marques de Cabra, *Felipe II. Cuarto centenario de su nacimiento* (Madrid, 1927), 64–6.

2. AGS *Estado K* 1568/113, Mendoza to the king, 24 September 1588; *Estado* 1261/115, Josepe de Acuña to the king, 6 September 1588 (reporting the duke of Savoy's criticisms of Parma). Parma was still defending himself three months later: see *Estado* 594/163, to Idiáquez, 30 December 1588.

3. AGS *Estado* 950 fos. 227, Olivares to the king, 29 October 1588, and 229, to Parma, 15 October 1588. See also *CSPV*, 402 and 407, reports of the Venetian ambassador in Rome, 15 and 22 October 1588. *Estado* 2219/82, Idiáquez to Parma, 31 August 1588, informed the duke that the king 'has felt more than you could believe' the news of the Armada's defeat off Gravelines, and wondered rather pointedly why Parma was at Bruges rather than Dunkirk at the time.

4. AGS *Estado* 594/124, Parma to the king, 8 August 1588. It was not only 'those who came here off the fleet', however. Alonso Vázquez, who normally had nothing but praise for Parma, noted that the few warships in the Flanders flotilla had neither all their guns in place nor their castle-works complete when the Armada arrived. He wondered why. (Vázquez, II, 349.)

5. Oria, 266, Don Jorge Manrique to the king, 12 August 1588.

6. See the discussion of the dates on pages 179/84 above.

7. Details from marquis of Saltillo, 'El duque de Medina Sidonia y la jornada a Inglaterra en 1588', *Boletín de la Biblioteca de Menéndez Pelayo*, XVI (1934), 167–77, at pp. 174ff; AGS *CS* 2a/286 fo. 27f (salary paid); and J. de Vitoria, 'Noticias de la Invencible', *Co.Do.In.*, LXXXI (Madrid, 1881), 219, written in November 1588 (and therefore probably more accurate than the rest of the Court gossip purveyed by Vitoria).

8. AGS *Estado*, 455, unfol., Bobadilla to the king, 27 September 1588; see also the praise of Recalde, in his last letter, in Oria, 307; and the sensible advice of Don Juan de Cardona, sent to Galicia to reorganise the fleet, that no attempt should be made to find a scapegoat (Oria, 354).

9. Oria, 325, Orduño de Zamudio to the king, 5 October 1588; AGS *GA* 244/46, Pedro Coco Calderón to the king, 24 January 1589; and Lilly Library, *Bertendona Ms*, no. 21, Bertendona to the king, 23 June 1589, all blame Flores for the Armada's failure. His imprisonment is reported in AGS *GA* 228/131, Licenciado Santillán to the king, 23 December 1588. He remained there for over a year.

10. J. de Mariana, *De rege et regis institutionis* (Toledo, 1599), book III, chapter 10. We have used the translation in A. Soons, *Juan de Mariana* (Boston, MA, 1982), 124, n19.

11. AGS *Estado*, 455/602f, Bobadilla to Idiáquez, 20 August 1588 (see note 1 above).

12. See Parma's instructions, sent with Medina Sidonia (and therefore never seen by Parma himself) in AGS *Estado* 165/174–6, dated 1 April 1588 (précis in *CSPSp*, IV, 250–2).

13. PRO *State Papers* 12/213/45, Sir Thomas Scott to Burghley, 6 August 1588 NS; J. R. Scott, 'Pay-list of the Kentish forces raised to resist the Spanish Armada'. *Archaeologica Cantiana*, XI (1877), 388–91; and G. Scott Thomson, ed., *The Twysden Lieutenancy Papers* (Maidstone, 1926: Kent Records Society, X), 70–1.

14. Quotations from Kent in P. Clark, *English Provincial Society from the Reformation to the Revolution: religion, politics and society in Kent, 1500–1640* (Hassocks, 1977), 249; and from Holland in *Cabala sive scrinia sacra* (3rd edn., London, 1691), II, 37: Lord Buckhurst to Queen Elizabeth, 27 May 1587 OS.

Index

Entries in **bold** refer to pages with illustrations; entries in *italics* refer to ships.

Picture credits

The authors and the publishers give their warm thanks to all those who have supplied pictures for this book. All sources are listed below. Figures in ordinary type refer to page numbers on which black and white illustrations appear. Figures in **bold** refer to colour plate numbers.

Stedelijk Museum, Alkmaar: 69, **18**.
Rijksmuseum, Amsterdam: 67.
By kind permission of the Marquess of Tavistock and the Trustees of the Bedford Estates: **20**.
Ulster Museum, Belfast: **4, 5, 6, 7, 8, 10, 11, 31, 32**.
Musée des Beaux-Arts, Brussels: **24** (1327).
By permission of the Master and Fellows, Magdalene College, Cambridge: 208, **12, 13, 21**.
Cambridge University Collection: 273.
University Library, Cambridge: 272.
Scottish National Portrait Gallery, Edinburgh: **34**.
Archivio di Stato, Florence: 31 *below* (Mediceo 4919/340).
Konijklijke Bibliotheek, The Hague: 182.
By courtesy of the Marquess of Salisbury, Hatfield House: 104 (CPM 1/13).
Tiroler Landesmuseum Ferdinandeum, Innsbruck: front cover and 3 and **45** (Gem 1668).
St Faith's Church, Gaywood, King's Lynn: 52.
Stedelijk Museum de Lakenhal, Leiden: **45**.
British Library, London, Department of Manuscripts: 80 *right* (D.C., H.77), 226 (Add.Mss.33740, f.6), **1** (Cotton Aug. 1.1.33), **2** (Cotton Aug. 1.1.38), **26** (Eg.Mss.2579).

British Library, London, Department of Maps: 92 (C.7.e.2(39)).
British Library, London, Department of Printed Books: 25 *right* (G.6067), 52 (Lant, *The Funeral of Sir Philip Sidney*, 1588; C.20.f.12), 61 and 233 *below* (192.f.17 (i)), 121 (G. Carleton, *A Thankful Remembrance*, 1609; G.5117), 196 (Deloney; C.18.e.2, f.63), 271 (Lambarde, *Perambulation of Kent*, 1596; C.32.e.34).
Reproduced by courtesy of the Trustees of the British Museum, London: 82 *right*.
National Maritime Museum, London: 3 and 189 (A3683), 14 (A2251), 15 (A2338), 39 (1406), 44 (1737), 75 (X1869), 182 *below* (X1872), 194 (A8121), 228 (C9149), **9** (A6715), **15** (A87), **17** (A1730), **38** (8818), **39** (A7297), **40** (B1595), **41** (8819), **43** (C4578), **44** (A89), **46** (9884), **53** (C7802).
National Portrait Gallery, London: 48 *below* (4197), 80 *left* (429), 99 (1704), 100 (362), 235 (3793), **16** (4032), **54** (665).
Public Record Office, London: 64 (SP12/213/91), 83 (SP69/6/380), 231 *right* (MPF 335(2), 270 (SP12/213/214), **19** (MPF 156), **22** and **23** (MPF 75), **35** (MPF 318), **36** (MPF 217), **49** (MPF 91).
Archivo de la Casa de Heredia Spinola, Madrid: 29.

Museo Naval, Madrid: 30.
Museo del Prado, Madrid: **27**.
Patrimonio Nacional, Madrid: **28**.
Colin Martin: 17, 19, 34, 41 *below*, 42, 43, 56, 57, 71, 82 *left*, 129, 138–9, 144–5, 175 *top*, 175 *bottom*, 177, 191, 199, 200, 201, 203, 204, 205, 206, 210, 218–9, 220–21, 222, 225 *left*, 230, 231 *left*, 233 *above*, 237, **14** (courtesy of the Mary Rose Trust), **25, 33, 37, 47, 50, 51**.
The Montreal Museum of Fine Arts: 25 *left*.
Castle of Nelahozenes, Czechoslovakia: 229.
Ashmolean Museum, Oxford: **48**.
Bodleian Library, Oxford: **42**.
Bibliotheque Nationale, Paris: 31 *top* (C.6669), 184 (Clair.1231, f.173).
Plymouth City Museum and Art Gallery: 12.
University of St Andrews Library: 48 *above*.
Archivo General de Simancas: 153 (CMC 2a 772), 161 (Estado 455, f.598v), 175 *centre* (CS 2a 280/1476v), 179, 209 (MPyD V–20), 211 (MPyD V–17), 223 (MPyD XVIII–47,48,49).
Monumenti Musei e Gallerie Pontificie, Vatican City: 110.

Thanks also to Geoff Green for help during the early stages of the development of this project.